From Soap Stars
to Superstars

From Soap Stars to Superstars

to Superstars

Annette M. D'Agostino

RENAISSANCE BOOKS
Los Angeles

Library of Congress Cataloging-in-Publication Data
    D'Agostino, Annette M.
        From soap stars to superstars / Annette M. D'Agostino.
            p. cm.
        Includes bibliographical references, filmographies, and index.
        ISBN 1-58063-075-8 (pbk. : alk. paper)
        1. Soap Operas—United States. 2. Actors—United States Biography
    Dictionaries. I. Title.
    PN1992.8.S4D34   1999
    791.43'028'092273—dc21
    [B]   99-21726
                                                             CIP

10 9 8 7 6 5 4 3 2 1

Design by Tanya Maiboroda

Distributed by St. Martin's Press
Manufactured in the United States of America
First Edition

Dedicated to my grandmother,
Josephine Pepe Schiraldi (1902–1989),
and my great aunt,
Rose Pepe Contrino (1906–1984),
who introduced me to the wonderful world of soap operas
when I was a mere tot.

Grazie, Belle Donne!

Contents

acknowledgments   viii

key to book features   x

introduction
History of Soaps   12

chapter 1
Biographies of Sixty of Daytime Television's Hottest Graduates   25

chapter 2
Look Who Else Began on Daytime!   231

chapter 3
They Were on Soaps, Too?   237

chapter 4
Your Guest Guess...   241

appendix a
Alphabetical List of Daytime Network Television Soaps   248

appendix b
Chronological List of Daytime Network Television Soaps   251

appendix c
Chronological List of Daytime Emmy Acting Awards   254

bibliography   275

index   279

Acknowledgments

I have long been attuned to the great wealth of talent that has emanated out from the genre of daytime drama; thus, the realization of this book is a tremendous thrill for me, not only as an author, but also as a long-time soap fan. There are a number of individuals I wish to thank who have helped me, either through encouragement or their gifts of insights and information. For sharing their unique expertise, I thank Jim Armstrong, Mike Danahy, Robert Lambright, and David Sperber. The king of soap research, Gerard Waggett, has grown to be both a friend and a model of excellence, and I thank him for his help. I am grateful for the assistance of the staffs of the Frances Howard Goldwyn Public Library, the Los Angeles Public Library, the Margaret Herrick Library, the Museum of Television and Radio (Jonathan Rosenthal—Research), and the New York Public Library. For their unending encouragement, I thank all of my friends, especially Richard Braff, Kelly Brown, Jerome P. Chamberlain, Sally Dumaux, H.E.L.L.O.! members worldwide, Bernice LaPorta, my future stepdaughters Jessica and Sarah Lloyd, Joan Moran, Ed and Barbara Organ, and each student that ever graced my twelve years' worth of classrooms: you *all* inspire me.

In remembrance of Harold Lloyd: "I know it's good. I wrote it myself" (from *Bumping into Broadway*, 1919). To my big Italian family of aunts, uncles, and cousins, I chant a rousing, "*A la famiglia*!" As in all things, I will forever thank my parents, Michael and Annette D'Agostino, for their guidance, example, and for three dozen years of love: you two are *the best*. To my fiancé, Scott Lloyd: sweetie, you'll always be my *guiding light*, and I'll be *young and restless* until I become your bride, and we *search for tomorrow* together. I wish to thank my incredible editor and friend, James Robert Parish, whose enduring support and belief in me helped make this project infinitely easier.

Lastly, to soap fans everywhere, be proud, because a lot of good has grown out of daytime television. *Let's Go!*

....

Key to Book Features

Introduction

This section begins with a brief history of the soap opera, from its roots in radio through its graduation to television and beyond. Numerous programs are cited, with running years. A subsection, "A Typical Week on Soaps," brings to light the challenging nature of the work in daytime TV and introduces the book's focus: the shining talents that have emanated from soap operas.

Biographies

The main section of the book, chapter 1, is dedicated to a biography and filmography of the sixty hottest graduates of daytime television. These are listed in alphabetical order by the last name of the performer. If you are looking for a particular name or program, check the index.

Each of the chapter's sixty biographies include the following sections:

- A quote by the star and the date it was spoken.
- A "fast facts" box listing date and place of birth, education, career highlights, debuts by genre (with roles on daytime soap operas indicated), awards, honors, marital status, work with current spouse, books by/about, albums, and any other fun data available.
- A brief biography of the star. Cross-references in **bold** refer only to the other stars who are fully chronicled herein.

- A complete filmography of the star, including (where applicable) work in movies, television (films, miniseries, and series), interactive, and video. These are listed in ascending chronological order.
- A chronicle of the soap opera character(s) each of the stars portrayed. Other actors who played the role are also listed, with dates.

Sidebars

Fun facts about soaps, characters, and genre performers are sprinkled throughout the book.

Other Lists

Other famed graduates of daytime television are listed alphabetically in chapter 2, with birth/death dates (where applicable/available), and their soap(s) and character(s).

Established stars who later in their careers joined casts of soaps are listed in alphabetical order in chapter 3, with birth/death dates (where applicable/available), and their soap(s) and character(s).

Prominent guest stars on daytime serials are enumerated in chapter 4. The soaps are listed alphabetically, and the guest stars follow, in alphabetical order within the program. If they could be located, the character played, and the year, accompanies the star's name.

Appendices

Appendix A is an alphabetical list of all American network television daytime soap operas, with complete running dates and network(s).

Appendix B is an ascending chronological list of the soaps listed in appendix A, with complete running dates and network(s).

Appendix C is a listing of all Daytime Emmy acting awards, chronologically listed in ascending order. Nominees and winners are included, with a star (★) accompanying the victors' names.

Bibliography

All works consulted in the research and building of this book are shared. Included are magazines, newspapers, and journals, followed by books, major World Wide Web sites, and Usenet news groups. Given the ever-changing nature of the Internet, only major Web sites (especially TV network-generated pages) are referenced. However, two of the premier search engine addresses are also given to assist in locating numerous other soap and star Web sites.

History of Soaps

If you are anything like me, the TV soap opera is a part of your personal history. I have very fond recollections of my childhood on Staten Island, New York, spending time with my mother, my grandmother, and my aunt watching the soaps. Looking back, I realize they probably understood little of what was going on, but enjoyed "looking at" the action. For us, it was an integral part of the day, not just a way to while away the hours: Joanne Barron, Bert Bauer, and Alice Horton were friends of ours, people in our lives. These characters' shows, respectively, *Search for Tomorrow* (1951–86), *The Guiding Light* (1952–present), and *Days of Our Lives* (1965–present), among many others, were institutions, offering us ways to see extensions of ourselves on our small, black and white screen.

My Italian grandmother and aunt spoke very little English, yet watched faithfully. I grew up watching the soaps, and consider them an important part of my history.

- At the age of six, I taperecorded the opening theme to *As the World Turns* (1956–present), as I thought it was one of the most beautifully orchestrated soap themes I had ever heard—listen, ma, no organ!

- I was very shaken when *Search for Tomorrow*'s Marge Bergman died, after her portrayer, Melba Rae, succumbed to a cerebral hemorrhage on New Year's Eve, 1971. For the first time, I was directly affected by the soap character, as if someone I knew personally had died.

- In 1972, at the age of ten, I cried when Bruce and Vanessa Sterling remarried on *Love of Life* (1951–80).
- On the day *The Young and the Restless* (1973–present) debuted, I went home for lunch to watch. Just the name of the show thrilled me and, when I heard the haunting title-credit tune, "Nadia's Theme," I was hooked.

For those of us who feel so attuned to the daytime dramas, the soap-opera milestones take on a similar pertinence to such real-life memories as where we were when FDR, JFK, Elvis, or Princess Diana died. Yet, we can see that soaps essentially grew up with the media of radio and television, and the future holds continued growth for the genre.

"Yes, there's the clock in Glen Falls' town hall telling us it's time for Rinso's story of *Big Sister*."

The usual first question is an obvious one: Why are they called "soap operas"? Chiefly, the evolution of that term began with the sponsors of these daily daytime dramas—soap companies (Consider, for instance, "Oxydol's own *Ma Perkins*" [1933–56] and the above introduction to the Rinso-sponsored soap, *Big Sister* [1936–52])—coupled with the grand scale in which the lives of the players were portrayed, "operatic" in scope.

For those of us who have shared in the complex lives of these beloved characters, we not only feel for them, but see ourselves in them. These characters live out our fantasies, our desires, our hopes, and our worst nightmares. For us, the escape and the heightened drama are a way to experience the virtually impossible. (Truly now, how many of us will marry nine or ten times, choosing whatever attractive new individual crosses our path? How many of us will kill our enemy, and endure trial and jail? How many of us—hopefully, few—will suffer dread illness, natural disaster, and immeasurable heartache, daily?) The daytime drama is, in many ways, a grand opera—larger than life, wackier than reality, and virtually irresistible for those with the imagination and inclination to enjoy it.

Soapy Music

Here is a sampling of CDs that feature music from the soaps. Each is available in music stores, or on the various Internet music retailer sites. Listed with the title is the CD label.

Dark Shadows: 30th Anniversary Collection (UNI/Varese Sarabande)
House of Dark Shadows/Night of Dark Shadows (WEA/Atlantic/Rhino)
Love on the Air: Soap Opera's Greatest Love Themes (Polygram Special Markets)
Soap Opera's Favorite Wedding Music by Various Artists (BMG/Scotti Brothers/Streetlife)

Soap Opera's Greatest Love Themes Vol. 1 by Various Artists (BMG/Scotti Brothers/Streetlife)

Soap Opera's Greatest Love Themes Vol. 2 by Various Artists (WEA/Scotti Brothers)

With Love from the Soaps by Various Artists (Quality Records)

The Young and the Restless (MCA)

The Young and the Restless (Paradigm)

• •

We Couldn't See the Suds Then

Daytime dramas began on radio, then television came along. In one way this technological development is a shame: listening to the radio stirs our imagination more than the television, where we hear it and see it. In the days of radio, the faces of the players were unseen—only their voices could tell the story—and the listener, who sat by the radio, sometimes staring at it, had to imagine the visuals. More often than not it was perhaps the face of the listener that was the imagined on the face of the character. This was, thus, a form of entertainment that could not fail, and has not yet.

Historically, the first radio program that can be called a "soap opera" was *The Smith Family*, a 1929–32 drama starring Jim and Marion Jordan (who would later rise to fame as *Fibber McGee and Molly* on their own 1935–59 series). This program established two important traditions: dramatic and daring plot lines, and the "continuing story," which compelled the listener to "tune in tomorrow." Another groundbreaker was *Clara, Lu 'n' Em* (1931–42), an NBC nighttime drama. This was the first entry to be true to the label, as this program was sponsored by Colgate, a soap company, and, in addition, the now-common story line of the less-than-faithful husband was portrayed for the first time. The popularity of the drama was enormous, particularly with women (who, at that time, were customarily in the home). As a result, network executives quickly shifted the time slot of this, and other popular dramas, to daytime hours. By the mid-to-late 1930s, listeners had a bounty of choices of radio serials to enjoy during the daily dishwashing and laundry-duty hours.

What Was It All About?

The appeal of these early soap operas was escapism, imagination, and realization of fantasy. The stories concerned real people with unreal problems. Combine this plot line with the element of, "What will happen next?" and you have a dynamite premise. They knew it then, and still do. But, in the early days, it seemed that the "escape into another life" sometimes went too far.

- Take, for example, the saga of *Our Gal Sunday*, (1937–59) a Depression-era soap: "The story of an orphan girl named Sunday from the little mining town of Silver Creek, Colorado, who in young womanhood married England's richest, most handsome lord, Lord Henry Brinthrope. The story asks the question: Can this girl from a mining town in the West find happiness as the wife of a wealthy and titled Englishman?"

- Consider also, the Mutual network's serial *Mary Noble, Backstage Wife* (1935–59), which told "The story of Mary Noble, a little Iowa girl, who married Larry Noble, handsome matinee idol, dream sweetheart of a million other women, and her struggle to keep his love in the complicated atmosphere of backstage life."

- Witness, finally, *Betty and Bob* (1932–40), who "surmounted everything: divorce, misunderstandings, the interference of other people and, sometimes the worst of all foes, the passage of time."

Indeed, the tradition of the soaps we know today grew out of these, and numerous other, radio programs which revolved around less-than-perfect families with problems you would never, ever, dream of.

Today, the TV networks run their soap operas in a set block of time, interrupted perhaps by the noon local news, or a talk show. That pattern started in radio days when, in 1933, the CBS radio network scrambled their schedule and placed most of their chiefly-fifteen-minutes-long daytime serials one after another. In that way, the busy housewife could arrange her chores and cooking duties around her favorite shows.

The center of most radio soap operas was the family, and from it all action emanated. Yet, within two weeks in 1933, two CBS soaps debuted that veered away from the family drama orientation and had new themes for the story focus.

- October 16, 1933, welcomed *Just Plain Bill* (1933–55), the "Story of people we all know…"

- October 30, 1933, introduced *The Romance of Helen Trent* (1933–60), a thirty-five-year-old widow whose mysterious past (she was a seamstress-turned-Hollywood fashion designer) thrust her into any number of exciting and fantastic adventures in the present.

Both premises worked well: the narrative of the known and the chronicle of the unknown; the story of the commonplace and the tale of the fantastic. As the soap opera matured, both concepts would provide the bases for the serials to come.

In contrast to the common, stereotypical line of thinking, all action did not emanate from the kitchen (although radio audiences heard a lot more sipping of coffee than we see today). True, *Ma Perkins* (first of the now-legendary Proctor and Gamble-owned soaps) did dish out plenty of advice near her oven, but there were other means as well.

- The Camay-sponsored *Dreams Come True* (1934–35) featured a singer and his friend, a female novelist who traveled around in search of stories.
- *Song of the City* (1934–35) introduced the bedside manner of a doctor who did make house calls.
- The CBS soap, *Mrs. Wiggs of the Cabbage Patch* (1935–38) did what its 1919 silent film predecessor of the same name did: bring to the forefront the horror of poverty coupled with the ultimately successful potential of child rearing under adverse conditions.
- In the mid-1930s came *John's Other Wife* (1936–42). No, he wasn't a bigamist, but he had a secretary, his "wife at the office," where the action took place.
- The heart of *The Guiding Light* (the only radio soap, 1937–56, that is still airing, after its transition to television) was Reverend Rutledge, the guiding light for those who sought his advice in their daily struggles. Early on, the serial was introduced daily as follows: "There is a destiny that makes us brothers—none goes his way alone. All that we send into the lives of others, comes back into our own."

Soaps, as should now be evident, were not all domestic dramas, and were, in their infancy, diverse and exciting in setting and story. For us, nowadays, soaps are a staple; for those who saw them take form, the thrill must have been tremendous.

The Television Revolution

Radio soaps had been thriving for nearly twenty years when, in 1944, the fledgling DuMont TV network's New York affiliate, WABD, began an experiment: three weeks of daily television versions of the radio soaps *Big Sister* and *Aunt Jenny's True Life Stories*. These telecasts were sponsored by soap company Lever Brothers. The trade journal *Sponsor* reported that the "results were good to excellent, but [the TV productions] were primarily the result of an advertiser's desire to 'feel the way' into TV, and to give his staff a workout with visual technique." Less than a rave, but enough of a boost to promote more experimentation with television soap operas. The one-day airing of *Big Sister* on a local Chicago station, and the airing of the thirteen-part *War Bride* on a local Schenectady, New York, station, paved the way for the launch of the first network television-only soap opera, *Faraway Hill*, which ran evenings on the DuMont network beginning October, 1946.

Why, then, did television come in and, in the relatively short time span of 1946–60, essentially supplant the radio soap format? The answer ultimately lies in our generational preferences: most post–World War II viewers seemed to want to see *and* hear, and by the late 1940s TV was much more available to the average household. Perhaps, too, what kept the radio serial going for as long as it did was the fact that televisions were not readily available to all homes right away: if homes had televisions (and, year-by-year, the percentage of households that owned TV sets grew), most were only watching at prime time, after dinner. As the technology became available, and as it made its way into more homes, the eventual death knell for the radio soap grew louder and louder.

NBC began the television soap opera tradition with the first continuing daytime drama on a major network, the 1949 serial *These Are My Children* (which aired for only one month), based on Irna Phillips' first radio shows, *Painted Dreams* (1935–40) and *Today's Children* (1933–50). CBS's first television soap opera was *The First Hundred Years* (1950–52), a serial about marriage. ABC held out the longest, not debuting a TV soap until *The Road to Reality* (1960–61).

Since the dawn of the televised soap opera, in the United States, almost eighty shows have come, and all but eleven are gone. The genre has become a national institution—as the famed playwright William Inge noted in 1961, "I feel that soap opera is a [peculiarly] American form. People sneer at it, but it has the basis for a truer, more meaningful drama. Italian opera and drama grew out of the *commedia dell'arte*, and I feel that in soap opera we have the roots for a native American drama." Indeed, the soap opera is as much a part of American life as any other form of entertainment. Perhaps, more than we even realize.

• •

Firsts and Significant Dates in Daytime Television History

First (and only) Forty-Five-Minute Daytime Soap: *One Life to Live*—July 26, 1976

First (and only) Ninety-Minute Daytime Soap: *Another World*—March 5, 1979

First Day on Which Two Soaps Debuted: September 3, 1951 (*The Egg and I* and *Search for Tomorrow*, both on CBS)

First Day on Which Three Soaps Debuted: April 1, 1963 (NBC's *Ben Jarrod* and *The Doctors*, and ABC's *General Hospital*)

First Day on Which Four Soaps Debuted: September 27, 1965 (ABC's *Never Too Young* and *The Nurses*, and NBC's *Morning Star* and *Paradise Bay*)

First Day on Which Five Soaps Debuted: July 5, 1954 (CBS' *The Seeking Heart* and NBC's *A Time to Live, Golden Windows, Concerning Miss Marlowe*, and *First Love*)

First Day on Which Two Soaps Went Off the Air: January 8, 1954 (NBC's *The Bennetts* and *Follow Your Heart*)

First Day on Which Three Soaps Went Off the Air: September 18, 1962 (CBS' *The Brighter Day* and *The Verdict Is Yours*, and NBC's *Our Five Daughters*)

First Day on Which Five Soaps Went Off the Air: July 1, 1955 (NBC's *Hawkins Falls, Concerning Miss Marlowe*, and *The Greatest Gift*, and CBS' *Portia Faces Life* and *The Road of Life*)

First Daytime Soap on the ABC Network: *Road to Reality*—October 17, 1960

First Daytime Soap on the CBS Network: *The First Hundred Years*—December 4, 1950

First Daytime Soap on the NBC Network: *These Are My Children*—January 31, 1949

First Daytime Soap to Originate in Sixty-Minute Length: *Texas*—August 4, 1980

First Daytime Soap to Spin Off a Daytime Serial: *Another World*—spun off *Somerset* on March 30, 1970

First Daytime Soap to Spin Off a Nighttime Serial: *As the World Turns*—spun off *Our Private World* on May 5, 1965

First Daytime Soap to Spin Off Three Daytime Serials: *Another World*—*Somerset* (1970), *Lovers and Friends* (January 3, 1977), and *Texas* (1980)

First Daytime Soap to Win a Daytime Emmy: *The Doctors*—May 14, 1972

First Fifteen-Minute Daytime Soap, and First to Originate in Fifteen-Minute Length: *These Are My Children*—January 31, 1949

First Thirty-Minute Daytime Soaps, and First to Originate in Thirty-Minute Length: *As the World Turns* and *The Edge of Night*—both premiered on April 2, 1956

First Hour-Long Daytime Soap: *Another World*—January 6, 1975

First Soaps to Debut and Be Canceled on the Same Day: NBC's *Morning Star* and *Paradise Bay*—September 27, 1965 and July 1, 1966

Soaps That Went Off the Air on New Year's Eve: All of these NBC programs went off the air on December 31—*Three Steps to Heaven* and *A Time to Live* (1954), *The World of Mr. Sweeney* (1955), *Somerset* (1976), and *The Doctors* and *Texas* (1982)

* *

All of a Sudden, We *Can* See the Suds...

Each TV daytime drama that has aired, since 1949, has made its own personal statement, and in each serial memories are treasured. After a rich history of nearly fifty years, each TV soap opera, some defunct, some still airing, has keenly influenced the genre, and has helped to shape it as a unique entertainment form. Their story is a saga in itself—a continual, daily battle for ratings, a stretch for ever-interesting and exciting stories, and, at the heart of this book, a stage for powerhouse performances by talented and dedicated actors and actresses, many of whom have graduated from the genre to enjoy further stardom on a wider scale. From humble beginnings in black-and-white format, musical accompaniment by an in-studio organ, and live telecasts in lengths as short as fifteen minutes, the daytime TV soaps that have come and gone continue to be remembered.

Within three weeks in September 1951, CBS introduced two powerful serials, *Search for Tomorrow* and *Love of Life*, both created by Roy Winsor. The network soon added more programs to its daytime lineup, including the influential *As the World Turns* (1956–present). Created by the legendary Irna Phillips (considered by most the Mother of the Soap Opera), the show was one of the first major half-hour soaps, and revolutionized visual technique by showcasing closeups, sudden cuts between stories, and long conversations, emphasizing character rather than action.

Initially, NBC did not fare as well as CBS in its daytime offerings and had a number of short-run programs. Its early soaps (including *Three Steps to Heaven*, [1953–54], and *Concerning Miss Marlowe*, [1954–55]) dealt with the fantasies of career women, which were a fine subject matter for the imaginative medium of radio. However, with the advent of television, where one saw as well as heard, viewers preferred the authenticity of women who were like the viewers. By the mid-1960s, NBC got with the program, as it were, launching such big hits as *The Doctors* (1963–82), *Another World* (1964–present), and *Days of Our Lives* (1965–present), all of which featured characters with whom viewers could identify. ABC also hit pay dirt at this time with its airing of the still-running drama *General Hospital* (1963–present).

For many years, CBS and its soap company sponsor Proctor and Gamble ruled daytime television. Its shows were strong, conservative, and popular, and its collection of acting, writing and directing talent was legendary. Still, to this day, Proctor and Gamble remains a major advertising power in daytime TV, through the sponsorship of such soaps as *Guiding Light* (1952–present), *As the World Turns* (1956–present), and *Another World* (1964–present).

The first soap opera that incorporated prime time- and cinema-level production values was CBS' *The Secret Storm* (1955-74), another Roy Winsor creation. The show, which featured characters with tremendous emotional angst and story lines with dramatic impact (including a daring romance between young Laurie Hollister and Catholic priest Father Mark Reddin), had its production problems, not the least of which was sharing a studio with *Captain Kangaroo* (1955–84), with frequent visits onto the sets by uninvited animal guests from the Captain's menagerie.

In 1956, CBS offered a new kind of soap—the mystery serial *The Edge of Night* (1956–84), which was innovative both for its *Perry Mason*-like plot lines, and its unique late-afternoon time slot (4:30 P.M. on the East Coast). *The Edge of Night* debuted on the same day (April 2, 1956) as did another CBS offering *As the World Turns*; and they were the first thirty-minute long soaps.

The Guiding Light (as it was known until "The" was taken out of the title in 1977, in an attempt to "get hip"), debuted on CBS television in June 1952 (it continued on radio and TV until 1956). One of its writers in the early 1960s was a protégée of Irna Phillips, Agnes Nixon. Over the years—the show is still running—it has gone from a fifteen- to thirty- to sixty-minute format.

Nixon later wrote for NBC's *Another World* before being given the opportunity, by ABC, to create two new soaps: which she did with the 1968 introduction of *One Life to Live* (1968–present), the first and only serial to be expanded to an unusual forty-five-minute length (in 1976), and *All My Children* (1970–present). Both still-popular TV programs, with their emphasis on social topics, ethnic characters, comedy, and strong male figures, began a period of experimentation and great innovation in daytime TV.

In the mid-1960s, a serial debuted that took reality to a Gothic level: ABC's *Dark Shadows* (1966–71). With its supernatural theme, vampires, tragic female victims, and mystical sets and costuming, it soon became a cult hit, and was a particular favorite of former First Lady Jacqueline Kennedy. Yes indeed, "important" people were, and still are, watching the soaps.

As ABC was scoring big with soaps dealing with youth and social relevance, CBS countered with its 1973 offering, *The Young and the Restless*, which is still going strong today. Furthering the innovations, and reflecting the decade we were entering, the show featured a cast too-beautiful-to-believe, semi-nudity, social awareness, seamless production values, and a haunting musical score.

Again, reflecting the 1970s post–Vietnam War values and women's increased awareness of self, the soaps did what the early-1960s shows couldn't do: showcase career women and their lives, fantasies, and successes. Increasingly, soap women left the home, and entered the work world. In addition, female characters began to experience life's tragedies, illustrating that, while film and fictional writings have their own endings, daily life (and, yes, the soap opera) does, indeed, go on...

...On ABC's *Ryan's Hope* (1975–89), every adult female character held a job...on *The Young and The Restless*, the aftermath of Chris Brooks' rape was painstakingly studied...on *One Life to Live*, Cathy Craig struggled to support herself as a writer and raise her out-of-wedlock child...on *All My Children*, Erica Kane had the first televised legal abortion...and on *The Doctors*, good girl Greta Powers dealt with her teenage pregnancy without the support of the baby's father. However, no serial made as much initial impact as the women's lib soap *How to Survive a Marriage* (1974–75), which aired for fifteen months on NBC. This was a bold program, featuring new ideas, explicit philandering, life tragedies, but ultimately suffered from a lack of character focus. Its ninety-minute debut on January 7, 1974, featured a bedroom scene between a married male character and his mistress. One of its strongest characters, Fran Bachman, realistically dealt with the aftermath of her husband's death, complete with loneliness and bills. The reality of this, and other 1970s programs, left a few fans wondering what Ma Perkins would have said. Finally, daytime drama was fully meeting the needs of a varied contemporary audience.

Still, viewer ratings are the key, and many TV soaps have fallen victim to the Nielsen numbers. Longtime favorites that died in the 1980s were *Love of Life*, *The Edge of Night*, and *Search for Tomorrow*. Additions in that decade, *Loving* (1983–95) and *Santa Barbara* (1984–93), were both affected by ratings, and were canceled, though the popularity each show enjoyed was great (and, still is, as each soap continues to be honored with Web sites). One soap that made a great difference, *Generations* (1989–91), had a brief life but still has impact, owing to its place in history as the first soap (and only, thus far) to have at its center an African-American family. When the relatively short-lived "hip" series debuted, ad slogans for the show read "Black and White—In Color."

Ratings sometimes call for soaps to tap into popular cultural themes of the times. Such is the case of two entries, one defunct, one extant. *Capitol* (1982–87), a CBS offering created by former *The Young and the Restless* executive producer John Conboy, centered on Washington, D.C., with its politicking and power: the program lasted five years (one year longer than the average term of a Congressman!). *Capitol* was replaced in 1987 by a still-thriving addition to the CBS family: *The Bold and the Beautiful* (1987–present), the suds story of the fashion industry and its beautiful people, sister soap to *The Young and the Restless,* and emanating from the same source, the legendary Bell family: Husband and wife team William and Lee Phillip Bell were responsible for much of the best writing for soaps, and their daughter Lauralee is an acclaimed actress on *The Young and the Restless.*

Owing to the continuing popularity of *General Hospital,* which hit upon gold with the exciting adventures of wonder couple Luke and Laura, a spin-off, *Port Charles* (1997–present), was created. However, not all offspring of flourishing parent soaps succeed: *Another World* offshoots, *Somerset* (1970), *Lovers and Friends* (1977—later known as *For Richer, for Poorer*), and *Texas* (1980) lasted six, one, and two years, respectively. Each soap succumbed to low ratings; viewership numbers are essential to the life of any program, whether daytime or nighttime.

· ·

Love that *Love of Life*

Love of Life aired on CBS from September 24, 1951—February 1, 1980. At the time of its cancellation, the show played out its scripts as written, hoping to be picked up by another network. By the air date of its final episode (No. 7,316 over its almost thirty-year run), no interest was shown, and the series ended with the proverbial untied end: with Betsy fainting while testifying at Ben's trial for assault.

· ·

Soaps Go Nighttime

The genre of soap operas adapted quite comfortably to prime-time hours, with the debut of NBC's TV version of *One Man's Family* (1949–52), which later aired on NBC daytime (1954–55). Even at its inception, television recognized the soap format as a popular and viable offering for all audiences. The continuing story lines, familial angst, and intriguing characters were workable entities, attracting many kinds of viewers. The serial was therefore added to the nighttime schedules of the major TV networks (and, eventually, cable networks as well).

The first runaway hit was the nighttime soap *Peyton Place* (1964–69), based on the best-selling novel by Grace Metalious. Its popularity (up to sixty million viewers per episode!) was staggering, securing the soap opera format as a mainstay among nighttime programming schedules.

Since then, numerous serialized programs have enjoyed similar approval: CBS offered *Dallas* (1978–91), *Knots Landing* (1979–93), and *Falcon Crest* (1981–90). NBC presented *Flamingo Road* (1981–82), *Bare Essence* (1983), and *Emerald Point* (1983–84). ABC countered with *Dynasty* (1981–89), *The Colbys* (1985–87), and the half-hour comedy serial *Soap* (1977–81). Fox contributed *Beverly Hills, 90210* (1990–present), *Melrose Place* (1992–present), and *Pacific Palisades* (1997). The WB network aired *Savannah* (1996–97), and cable's Showtime network ran *A New Day in Eden* (1982–83).

Nighttime soaps used the same themes as their daytime equivalents, just on a grander scale. Budgets were bigger, sets were more lush, the cliffhangers were steeper, and the characters and situations more extreme. Just like their daytime counterparts, the nighttime soaps grew from humble roots to enjoy their current popularity—and many of the prime-time soaps showcased performers who also enjoyed daytime star status (see page 107).

Although the soap opera is not solely daytime fare anymore, the overwhelming popularity of daytime soaps has taken on almost mythical proportions. Consider, for instance, the sheer numbers of magazines currently dedicated to soaps, the widely attended soap opera festivals, the frequent segments about daytime television on syndicated magazine-style programs (such as *Entertainment Tonight* and *Access Hollywood*), and the now-standard prime-time airings of the Daytime Emmy Award programs.

This popularity is further demonstrated by a nighttime talk show, *Pure Soap*, created solely to fill the needs of the insatiable fans of the daytime serials. It aired on the E! Entertainment Television cable network from October 1993 to December 1994, hosted by *General Hospital* graduate Shelley Taylor Morgan (and, in its infancy, cohosted by *TV Guide*'s Michael Logan). The half-hour show devoted its air time to soap news and story plots, plus interviews with soap star guests and live call-in questions from fans. This innovative entry, which gave viewers an opportunity to catch up on the latest news and chat with their favorite daytime performers, is sorely missed by enthusiasts of the stars and the soaps.

At the Heart of It All

The soap opera would be nothing without its array of dynamic characters. The stories and the production values would have no meaning without the strong roles in the plot lines. The heart of the programs are the individuals that audiences grow to know, to love, or to hate. The viewer truly does see itself in the Erica Kanes (*All My Children*), the Victor Newmans (*The Young and the Restless*), the Laura Spencers (*General Hospital*), and the Bo Bradys (*Days of Our Lives*) of the soaps. As such, the plots that showcase the characters have, increasingly, grown to reflect not only real life, but the happenings, fantasies and tragedies of people everywhere. The medical breakthrough plots, socially aware story lines, and fascinating educational studies are reflections of what we, the viewing audience, need and want to know and learn from.

A Typical Week on the Soaps

The characters that are so pivotal to soap success are played, on a daily basis, by talented and hard-working performers who dedicate more hours to their craft than most viewers would believe. The audience for the average soap opera enjoys either a thirty-minute or sixty-minute episode daily. Daytime serials enjoy no hiatus as, generally, prime-time programs are allowed. This means an average of 313 new episodes are produced yearly by each soap. Multiplied by the eleven shows on American TV in 1998, that would mean 3,443 new soap opera installments in one year. Just getting those shows produced is no mean feat.

- Each soap employs an average of twenty-four full-time cast members, plus a bevy of extras (atmosphere, or background, players) and under-fives (players who speak five or fewer lines of dialogue, who are addressed individually by a principal player, who are alone in a scene, or who speak as part of a group).

- The actors get their scripts approximately one week in advance of shooting.

- The average script for an hour-long episode is eighty-five to ninety pages long. A performer with a front-burner story line could have as many as twenty to forty pages of his/her own dialogue to memorize per script.

- Memorization, rehearsal, and blocking (figuring out the physical action) happens during the week before taping.

- It takes an average of nine to twelve hours to shoot a one-hour episode, and five to eight hours to shoot a half-hour episode. Most shoots begin between seven and nine in the morning, and end between six and seven in the evening, depending on the story. Some soaps have been known to have sets open until midnight.

All of this happens nearly 313 times per year, per soap! With such a schedule, the performers who partake must really be dedicated, otherwise such time restraints could never be endured.

This dedication inspired this book, which applauds star soap performers, and primarily focuses on those who have risen from this demanding format to wider distinction in prime-time television, film, music, or stage. In addition, the contributions of established performers who, later in their careers, graced the soaps, will be noted. Much fine work has been done in daytime drama. But we already know that.

The names, you will know. Their roots in the soaps, however, might not be as widely recognized. Yet their origins should be brought to light, because these stars are graduates of perhaps the most challenging life an actor can know: the soap opera player. They worked, day by day, in an atmosphere of deadlines that had to be met, pressure for program ratings, and need for camaraderie with other performers. They grew into their stardom in a very demanding and difficult genre, which required them to perform their roles with uniform intensity, and with little rehearsal. The graduates who appear in this book, and the actors who continue to make their livelihoods in daytime dramas, are disciplined and well-trained, and their hard work has paid off, both in their enduring popularity on the soaps, and in their work in other media. Within these pages, some soap graduates will reveal the challenging nature of their work on daytime television serials, and share their stories of long hours, much memorization, and great fun.

This topic has been touched upon chiefly in appendices in prior soap book studies. It is now time for a sole book to feature the wonderful work that is being done in daytime drama, and elevate the genre from popular misconceptions (idle plaything of the bored housewife, etc.) to its rightful label as a thriving training ground for some of the best performers the world has known. That is not an overstatement: flip the pages, and see who has contributed talent and artistry to soap operas!

chapter 1

Biographies of Sixty of Daytime Television's Hottest Graduates

Kevin Bacon

If you define your whole personal life around your business life, once it takes a turn for the worse, it can kill you.

—Kevin Bacon, 1996

Troubled teen Tim "T. J." Werner was memorably portrayed by Kevin Bacon on Guiding Light *from 1980–81. Video screen photo, collection of author.*

Born: July 8, 1958, in Philadelphia, Pennsylvania, the youngest of six children of Mr. and Mrs. Edmund Bacon

Education: Manning Street Actor's Theatre (Philadelphia); Circle-in-the-Square (New York City)

Debuts: stage—*Forty Deuce* (off-Broadway, 1976); film—*National Lampoon's Animal House* (1978); television—*Search for Tomorrow* (1979) as Tod Adamson; Broadway—*Slab Boys* (1983); music—*Forosoco* (1997, CD with brother Michael)

Award: Obie Award, 1976, for *Forty Deuce*

Honors: Nominated for a Golden Globe in 1995 and a Screen Actors Guild Award in 1996

Marital Status: Married actress Kyra Sedgwick, September 4, 1988; children, Travis and Sosie

Worked with His Wife In: *Lemon Sky* (1987), *Pyrates* (1991), and *Losing Chase* (1996, he directed her)

Book: *Six Degrees of Kevin Bacon*, by Craig Fass, Mike Ginelli, and Brian Turtle, introduction by Bacon (1996)

Not many stars have a game named after them. The cultural curiosity *Six Degrees of Kevin Bacon*, created by three college fraternity brothers, reasons that any person who has been in a film during the last twenty or so years can somehow be linked to Kevin Bacon, via his wide array of movie costars. Initially not amused, Bacon came to accept this challenging game as a compliment to his prolific career.

Perennially young-looking and versatile, Bacon received acting training in New York—at the age of seventeen, he was the youngest student to appear at Circle-in-the-Square Theatre in Manhattan. His film debut, as a preppie fraternity recruit in *National Lampoon's Animal House* (1978), predated by one year his television debut, on *Search for Tomorrow*. In the course of his soap career, which also included a two-year stint on *Guiding Light*, he continued to appear on the big screen and in live theater performances. He left *GL* in 1981, when he began to receive offers for starring film and stage roles.

The vehicles that followed, boasting such roles as an alcoholic in *Diner* (1982), a dancin' fool in the hip musical *Footloose* (1984), a tough handyman in *Tremors* (1989), an after-life experimenter in *Flatliners* (1990), and an astronaut in the blockbuster hit *Apollo 13* (1995), established him as an actor capable of portraying an impressive array of characters without resorting to clichés. His youthful yet edgy quality made him adept at both comedy and drama, evidenced in flustered expectant father Jefferson "Jake" Edward Briggs in *She's Having a Baby* (1988), and in his powerful cameo as hustler Willie O'Keefe in *JFK* (1991). His rebellious longer-cropped hair, combined with steady performances, ensured a wide appeal and, no matter how well or how poorly his movies were received, Bacon often earned better notices than his higher-billed costars.

In addition to his acting, Bacon made his feature directorial debut in 1996 with *Losing Chase*, which featured his wife, actress Kyra Sedgwick. The two met in 1987 when both worked in an American Playhouse TV offering, *Lemon Sky,* and married a year later. The duo appeared together in *Pyrates* (1991) as a randy couple who started fires whenever they made love. Their children, Travis and Sosie, are the subject of one of the songs, "Brown Eyes," on the Bacon Brothers' (Kevin and his composer brother Michael) premiere CD, named in honor of their style of music—blending folk, rock, soul, and country influences, hence, Fo-ro-so-co.

Unwilling to raise their young family in Los Angeles, and wary of the often damaging "Hollywood" environment, Bacon and Sedgwick live with their children in suburban Connecticut. This is one star family that shines without the obvious glitter.

Films: 1978: *National Lampoon's Animal House*. 1979: *Starting Over.* 1980: *Friday the 13th*; *Hero At Large.* 1981: *Only When I Laugh.* 1982: *Diner*; *Forty Deuce.* 1983: *Enormous Changes at the Last Minute.* 1984: *Footloose.* 1986: *Quicksilver.* 1987: *Planes, Trains & Automobiles; End of the Line*; *Lemon Sky*; *White Water Summer.* 1988: *She's Having a Baby.* 1989: *The Big Picture; Criminal Law.* 1990: *Flatliners*; *Tremors.* 1991: *He Said, She Said*; *JFK*; *Pyrates*; *Queens Logic.* 1992: *A Few Good Men.* 1994: *The Air*

Up There; *The River Wild*. 1995: *Balto* (voice only); *Apollo 13*; *Murder in the First*. 1996: *Sleepers*; *Losing Chase* (director only). 1997: *Telling Lies in America*; *Picture Perfect*. 1998: *Wild Things* (also executive producer); *Digging to China*. Forthcoming: *Stir of Echoes*; *My Dog Skip*.

TV movies: 1979: *The Gift*. 1983: *The Demon Murder Case*. 1997: *Happy Birthday Elizabeth: A Celebration of Life*.

TV series: 1979: *Search for Tomorrow*. 1980–81: *Guiding Light*.

Video: 1997: *Destination Anywhere*.

Meet Tod and T. J.

On *Search for Tomorrow*, the role of Tod Adamson was originated in 1979, and played solely by Kevin Bacon.

Tod was the son of Ted Adamson (Wayne Tippit) and the brother of Sunny Adamson (Marcia McCabe), savvy blonde reporter for the Henderson town newspaper.

On *Guiding Light*, the role of Tim "T. J." Werner was played by T. J. Hargrave (1974–76), Kevin Bacon (1980–81), Christopher Marcantel (1981), and Nigel Reed (1981–82).

T. J. was the son of Doctors Joe (then Anthony Call) and Sarah McIntyre Werner (Millette Alexander). In his teenage years T. J. had a bad problem with alcohol and once even ran away. Most of his time was spent explaining away his habits. This was a role that struck a particular chord with the show's growing adolescent audience.

Two T. J.'s Got Their Kyra

On Guiding Light, Kevin Bacon portrayed Tim (T. J.) Werner. When he left the show in 1981, the role was taken over by Christopher Marcantel. A few years later, after Marcantel left *GL*, he joined the cast of *Another World* as Pete Shea, and soon began romancing a costar—Kyra Sedgwick (Julia Shearer), who married Bacon on September 4, 1988.

Alec Baldwin

The final of five actors to play unscrupulous Billy Aldrich on The Doctors *was Alec Baldwin, from 1980–82. Courtesy of Soap Opera Digest.*

A major revival of Tennessee Williams comes along once every generation, and I knew that I wouldn't get this chance again. What I wanted to do was to compete with the [Marlon] Brando Stanley [Kowalski], and to make them forget the film [1951] for just one night.

—Alec Baldwin, on starring in Broadway's
A Streetcar Named Desire *(1992)*

Born: April 3, 1958, in Massapequa, New York, to Alexander Rae Jr. and Carol Martineau Baldwin; birth name, Alexander Rae Baldwin III; second of six children, two sisters, three younger brothers (fellow actors William, Daniel, and Stephen)

Education: George Washington University (Washington, D.C.); New York University's Lee Strasberg Theatre Institute (Manhattan)

Debuts: television—*The Doctors* (1980) as Billy Aldrich; Broadway—*Loot* (1986); film—*Forever Lulu* (1987)

Awards: Theatre World Award, for *Loot*, 1986; Obie Award, as Best Actor for *Prelude to a Kiss*, 1991; nominated for a Tony in 1992

Honor: Chosen by *People* magazine as one of the Fifty Most Beautiful People in the world (1990)

Marital Status: Married actress Kim Basinger, August 19, 1993; daughter, Ireland

Worked With His Wife In: *The Marrying Man* (1991) and *The Getaway* (1994)

Literary Reference: *Alec Baldwin Doesn't Love Me and Other Trials of My Queer Life* by Michael Thomas Ford (1998)

His third-grade teacher wrote on Alec Baldwin's report card that he would "become famous or President of the U.S.—one or the other."

Alec's initial direction as a youngster was towards acting; however, upon entering college he decided to major in political science with intentions of becoming a lawyer. In the middle of his college career he realized that the theater was his real love, so he quit George Washington University, which he attended from 1976–79, moving from Washington, D.C., to New York to enroll in New York University's Lee Strasberg Theatre Institute, where he studied from 1979–80. In addition to his university course work he studied under Mira Rostova of the Moscow Art Theatre, New York.

In September 1980 he landed a role on TV's *The Doctors* as the final portrayer of longstanding character Billy Aldrich. He had been noticed: upon cancellation of the soap, he was quickly snapped up for prime-time work on the TV series *Cutter to Houston* in 1983 and the next year on the nighttime soap *Knots Landing*, for portraying evangelist Joshua Rush.

His small screen fame ensured, Alec then moved to the big screen. His roles in such films as the grim war picture *Full Metal Jacket* (1987), Tim Burton's whimsical *Beetlejuice* (1988), the satirical *Married to the Mob* (1988), and the thriller *The Hunt for Red October* (1990) showcased both his comic and dramatic abilities, and his equal ease with leads and character roles. It was widely expected that he would revive his part as CIA agent Jack Ryan when the sequel to *The Hunt for Red October* (which grossed $200 million worldwide), *Patriot Games* (1992), was announced. Surprisingly, he decided to forego the screen part in order to star on Broadway in 1992 as Stanley Kowalski in a major revival of *A Streetcar Named Desire*. Alec won popular acclaim and a Tony nomination for his efforts, but his successor in the Ryan role, Harrison Ford, reaped the financial and popular gains of the film sequel and its various sequels. For Baldwin it was the beginning of a downward career slide in Hollywood. He dropped out of *Henry & June* (1990), citing exhaustion, and was passed over for the role of Vincent Mancini (it went to Andy Garcia) in Francis Ford Coppola's *The Godfather Part III* (1990). In 1991, he had signed to play the lead in *The Fugitive* (based on the 1963–67 TV series), but script difficulties delayed the project for two years, with the role again slipping from Baldwin's grasp, and into Harrison Ford's hands once again. The 1993 picture was a huge box-office hit.

Baldwin, who supports his favorite causes with vigor, voiced this clever public service announcement that aired on radio on St. Valentine's Day, 1997: "What do Leonardo Da Vinci, Madonna, Tony LaRussa, and Gandhi all have in common with my wife Kim and me? We all learned to kick the meat habit, and you can, too."

Baldwin first met his future wife, actress (and 1998 Oscar winner) Kim Basinger, while filming Disney's unsuccessful comedy *The Marrying Man* (1991)—the two would later work together as on-the-run gangsters in *The Getaway* (1994), a lifeless remake of the Steve McQueen–Ali McGraw 1972 screen original. Their nuptials, quietly held on August 19, 1993, were not as secret as they had wished. Word leaked out of the pending sunset wedding, and by ceremony time helicopters overhead drowned out the marriage vows.

Ironically, since his marriage Alec Baldwin has neither enjoyed a hit film nor a starring role that has showcased successfully the many talents he first exhibited in his daytime and prime-time soap stints. Those abilities remain many, with much promise for the future.

Films: 1987: *The Alamo: Thirteen Days to Glory; Forever, Lulu.* 1988: *Married to the Mob; Beetlejuice; She's Having a Baby; Talk Radio; Working Girl.* 1989: *Great Balls of Fire!* 1990: *Miami Blues; The Hunt for Red October; Alice.* 1991: *The Marrying Man.* 1992: *Glengarry Glen Ross; Prelude to a Kiss.* 1993: *Earth and the American Dream* (voice only); *Malice.* 1994: *The Shadow; The Getaway.* 1995: *Two Bits; A Streetcar Named Desire; Wild Bill: A Hollywood Maverick.* 1996: *Ghosts of Mississippi; Looking for Richard; Heaven's Prisoners* (also executive producer); *The Juror.* 1997: *The Edge.* 1998: *Mercury Rising.* 1999: *Thick as Thieves.* Forthcoming: *Outside Providence; The Confession* (also producer).

TV movies: 1984: *Sweet Revenge.* 1985: *Love on the Run.* 1986: *Dress Gray.*

TV series: 1980–82: *The Doctors.* 1983: *Cutter to Houston.* 1984–85: *Knots Landing.*

Meet Billy

On *The Doctors*, the character of Billy Allison Aldrich was played by Bobby Hennessy (1971–72), David Elliott (1973–77), Shawn Campbell (1977–79), and Alec Baldwin (1980–82).

Said Baldwin of the soap experience: "I sometimes have a fantasy of going back and doing a soap opera for a week. For inspiration. Work is work. People who are in films and talk about returning to TV often have a slumming connotation to it—that's so inappropriate, because the only advantage of film over television is scheduling. The acting is just as good."

Billy was a prolific ladies' man, romancing young Greta Powers (Gracie Harrison, then Lori-Nan Engler), Nola Aldrich (Kim Zimmer), and Natalie Ball (Jane Badler), all at the same time. With Greta, he had a daughter, LeeAnn (Stacey Long), and he remained with Greta only because of an inheritance promised her by her wealthy aunt Theodora Van Alen (Augusta Dabney). He bedded Nola during her separation from husband Jason (Glenn Corbett), and his affair with Natalie was chronicled in her diary: someone was sending Billy copies of her most compromising entries, threatening to expose him if he did not get out of town. Billy did! In the final episode of *The Doctors*, which was canceled on December 31, 1982, Lieutenant Paul Reed (Mark Goddard) was arrested for Billy Aldrich's murder.

Amanda Bearse

I think the more commonplace we can make people being honest about their sexuality, the better off it will be for human rights and civil rights for everyone.

—Amanda Bearse, 1995

Born: August 9, 1958, in Winter Park, Florida

Education: University of Southern California (Los Angeles) and American Film Institute (Los Angeles)

Debuts: television—*All My Children* (1982) as Amanda Cousins; film—*Protocol* (1984)

Stage Highlights: performed off-Broadway in *St. Joan*, *Wilderness*, and *This Property Is Condemned*.

Life Off Screen: Lives in Los Angeles with her partner and her adopted daughter Zoe

Aware, brave, and honest are three adjectives that definitely fit Amanda Bearse, who brought to life the character of Marcy Rhoades D'Arcy, long suffering neighbor of the Bundys on the popular comedy series, *Married . . . . . .With Children* (1987–97). On the TV show, Marcy was married twice, crude, rude, and promiscuous. Marcy's portrayer is anything but such a person.

At an early age, Amanda knew the direction her career would take. She participated in numerous acting and community theater programs, and eventually moved to New York to pursue a professional acting career. It was in the Big Apple that she landed the first role that put her on the acting map: Amanda Cousins, a role she originated on *All My Children* in 1982. Before that time, she had appeared in a number of off-Broadway productions, which gave her the exposure and experience necessary for her demanding daytime role. This new work paid off, too, for Bearse injected into the portrayal of Cousins a dramatic approach which would later enhance her comedic abilities. After her two-year run on *AMC*, she guested on the ABC series *Hotel* and, ironically, played a soap opera actor in the Goldie Hawn feature *Protocol* (1984).

In 1986 she auditioned for the television series that would ensure her growth as an actor and, eventually, a director: *Married......With Children*. On this highly successful sitcom, Marcy's first husband, Steve Rhoades, left home to become a park ranger after losing his job (Steve's portrayer, wholesome David Garrison, left the show to appear in a play). Her remarriage to Jefferson D'Arcy, saw handsome actor Ted McGinley join the TV show ensemble, adding a new dimension to Marcy's character, that of the randy wife of the visibly virile stud. It was this light-hearted approach to life that endeared the show's characters to its faithful viewers.

In 1991, her professional career took a groundbreaking turn: she became one of the show's directors. Amanda directed episodes of *Married...... With Children* from 1991 until the show went off the Fox network in 1997. Her reasons for becoming a director (the first of the cast members to branch out into directing) were clear: "I thought with directing that, first of all, I might have the ability for it, because when I watched other people's performances, it stimulated me with ideas. And directing has expanded my life on *Married......With Children* in a way that wasn't going to happen for me on camera. When I step behind the camera it's a whole new world."

In 1993, Amanda adopted a newborn baby girl, whom she named Zoe. The decision to be a parent was an easy yet thoughtful one for the actress: "I had a career, and didn't want to leave my job, but also knew what the demands were going to be in time and energy. I can't even think of a better work environment than the one I have to bring up a child."

In October 1993, on National Coming Out Day, Amanda Bearse held a press conference, coming out publicly as a lesbian. For her, it was a multi-faceted decision: "My coming out was sort of initiated by the tabloids finding out about the adoption of my baby daughter. They had already known about my living in a gay relationship. I gave a press conference to say that, yes, there was some information that was put out there about me that I want to confirm, and I also want to confirm that I don't have any shame about being homosexual, and it doesn't affect the way I do my job." In 1995 she worked as a correspondent on a syndicated entertainment/lifestyle newsmagazine, *Freestyles*, which was geared towards gays and lesbians.

Her dedication to her craft, which is now centered around directing, is clear: "The opportunity to direct was a trial by fire—it always is, you just have to jump in and do it. But, if I hadn't done it well, I wouldn't have gotten a second chance." Obviously, Amanda Bearse understands how well suited she is for her role as a woman director, and as a woman of action.

Films: 1984: *Protocol*. 1985: *Fraternity Vacation*; *Fright Night*. 1995: *The Doom Generation*.

TV movies: 1983: *First Affair.* 1988: *Goddess of Love.* 1995: *Here Come the Munsters.*

TV series: 1982–84: *All My Children.* 1987–97: *Married . . . . . . With Children* (also director). 1995: *Freestyles.* 1997: *Pauly.* 1997–present: occasional director on such shows as *Veronica's Closet, Dharma & Greg, Alright Already.*

Meet Amanda

⬚ On *All My Children*, the character of Amanda Cousins was originated and played solely by Amanda Bearse (1982–84).

Amanda was best friends with legendary bad girl Liza Colby (then, and now, played by Marcy Walker). At the time, the love story of Jenny Gardner (*see* **Kim Delaney**) and Greg Nelson (Laurence Lau) was beset with complications, including Liza, who had her claws set on the handsome Greg. As an ever-faithful friend, Amanda not only helped Liza in her machinations to break up Jenny and Greg, but she also romanced Greg when he and Jenny split apart. She also dated another suds stud, Tad Martin (then, and now, played by Michael E. Knight).

Amanda's greatest act came while dating on-the-rebound Greg, who had broken up with Jenny after being paralyzed in an accident—Amanda discovered a love letter from Jenny to Greg, and gave it to him over his Aunt Enid's (Natalie Ross) objections. Realizing that Jenny still loved him, Greg saved Jenny from a loveless marriage. Poor Amanda: she did the right thing, but lost Greg.

Tom Berenger

He's as beautiful a person as he is in the movies, one of those men made by Michelangelo with very little extra help from God.

—Anne Rice, on Tom Berenger, 1995

He lost his life for the woman he loved: Tim Siegel, played by Tom Berenger on One Life to Live *from 1975–76. Courtesy of Soap Opera Digest.*

Born: May 31, 1950, in Chicago, Illinois; birth name, Thomas Michael Moore

Education: Rich East High School (Park Forest, Illinois); University of Missouri (Columbia)

Debuts: television—*One Life to Live* (1975–76) as Timmy Siegel; film—*Looking for Mr. Goodbar* (1977)

Awards: Golden Globe Award, as Best Supporting Actor, for his role as Sergeant Barnes in *Platoon*, 1986; Lone Star Film and Television Award, as Best Television Actor, 1998

Honor: Nominated for Academy Award, 1986; Distinguished Alumni Award, University of Missouri, 1988; Tom Berenger Acting Scholarship, University of Missouri

Marital Status: Divorced from first wife, Barbara; married second wife, Lisa, 1986, divorced; married Patricia Ann Alvaran, January 23, 1998; five children (one son and one daughter with first wife; three daughters with second wife)

Remember those lollypops that had something unexpected on the inside, like bubble gum or candy? That is Tom Berenger: you know how good he is on the outside, but go deeper, and you're in for interesting surprises.

Thomas Michael Moore was a good student who, at an early age, became fascinated with Civil War history (one of its generals would take on an important role in his non-acting life, for Tom once owned a North Carolina nightclub called General Longstreet's HQ). While in high school in the Midwest, he excelled in history and played football, besides being an active member of the Spanish National Honor Society. Tom graduated from Rich East High School, Park Forest, Illinois, in 1967.

Tom spent his college years at the University of Missouri at Columbia, where he began as a journalism major and he graduated in 1972 with a B.A. in speech and dramatic art. While in college, he was a flight attendant for Eastern Airlines, modeled men's clothes for the Wilhelmina Modeling Agency, and was cast in the campus stage production of *Who's Afraid of Virginia Woolf?* It was this last experience that changed not only his major but his life.

Before moving to New York in the mid-1970s, Tom changed his name, choosing the surname Berenger after the last name (Behringer) of his best friend in high school. Now, as Tom Berenger, he toured with various repertory companies before landing his first role in 1975: Tim Siegel on *One Life to Live*. His year on the show made him a fan favorite, mainly due to his sympathetic front-burner TV role, which honed both his dramatic abilities and his heartthrob appeal.

After a year in daytime TV he graduated to feature films, where he first gained notice as the psychotic pretty boy Gary in *Looking for Mr. Goodbar* (1977). Varied roles followed, taking him from hero to villain from movie to movie. He showed adeptness with all the characters he portrayed: Whether it was the strong, manly type, as in *The Big Chill* (1983); the sociopathic type, as in his Oscar-nominated role of Sergeant Barnes in the gripping *Platoon* (1986); or his friendly, fatherly type, as in *Major League* (1989), Tom seemed to surprise audiences with each new trip to the screen and versatility made him a sought-after character actor.

Tom is not the only member of his family with dramatic credits: his second wife, Lisa, acted with Tom in *Last Rites* (1988), as did their oldest daughter, Chelsea. Chelsea also appeared in *Avenging Angel* (a 1995 TV movie that was the debut of Tom's production company), as did daughter Chloe. (Incidentally, Tom and Lisa were married on the grounds of the house used in filming *The Big Chill*.)

Platoon, perhaps more than any other film assignment, stretched Berenger's acting abilities. For his extraordinary acting in this intense Vietnam War drama he received an Academy Award nomination, but it wasn't an easy role to play. "He shoots fast," said Berenger of demanding director Oliver Stone, "which is great for actors but very hard on the crew, especially in 110 degree heat."

In 1992, Tom took on the acting assignment that seemingly was closest to his heart, that of the Civil War's Lt. General James Longstreet, in *Gettysburg* (1992). The experience of playing Longstreet stayed with Tom: in 1995, he formed his own production company and called it First Corps Endeavors, so named after Longstreet who was a member of the First Corps. One of the latest productions to come out of Tom's company was a 1997 TNT cable miniseries, *Rough Riders*.

Tom found playing Theodore Roosevelt in this miniseries a welcome acting challenge. Berenger diligently worked on voice and breathing exercises in order to capture the effects of Roosevelt's asthmatic condition. *Rough Riders* was the second-highest rated miniseries in cable TV history.

Filmmaking and acting are his life, but beefy Tom Berenger has other interests. In particular, he is part owner (with twins Lisa and Debbie Ganz) of Twins Restaurant located on New York City's upper east side. The establishment is fully staffed by thirty sets of identical twins, with each pair working the same shift, in the same station, in the same uniform.

There is more to Tom Berenger the actor than his beefy exterior might lead one to believe. He is full of surprises, all of them pleasing.

Films: 1976: *Rush It.* 1977: *Looking for Mr. Goodbar; The Sentinel.* 1978: *In Praise of Older Women.* 1979: *Butch and Sundance: The Early Days.* 1980: *The Dogs of War.* 1982: *Beyond the Door.* 1983: *The Big Chill; Eddie and the Cruisers.* 1984: *Fear City.* 1985: *Rustlers' Rhapsody.* 1986: *Platoon.* 1987: *Someone to Watch Over Me.* 1988: *Betrayed; Shoot to Kill; Last Rites.* 1989: *Born on the Fourth of July; Major League.* 1990: *The Field; Love at Large.* 1991: *Shattered; At Play in the Fields of the Lord.* 1993: *Sliver; Sniper; Gettysburg.* 1994: *Chasers; Major League II.* 1995: *Last of the Dogmen.* 1996: *An Occasional Hell* (also executive producer); *The Substitute.* 1998: *The Gingerbread Man; A Murder of Crows; Shadow of a Doubt.* Forthcoming: *One Man's Hero* (also producer); *Takedown.*

TV movies: 1977: *Johnny, We Hardly Knew Ye.* 1979: *Flesh & Blood.* 1987: *Dear America: Letters Home from Vietnam* (co-narrator). 1995: *The Avenging Angel; Body Language.* 1997: *Rough Riders* (also producer). 1998: *The Agency.*

TV miniseries: 1986: *If Tomorrow Comes.*

TV series: 1975–76: *One Life to Live.*

Meet Tim

🗐 On *One Life to Live*, the character of Tim Siegel was played by William Fowler (1969), William Cox (1970–71), and Tom Berenger (1975–76).

The romantic story of Tim Siegel and Jenny Wolek (then played by Katherine Glass) was one of those stories that could only happen on daytime TV. Jenny, a novice nun, fell deeply in love with Tim. As could be expected, the young couple's romance sent shock waves through the town of Llanview. Mother Eileen (Alice Hirson) was vehemently opposed to Tim's relationship with Jenny because she felt it had been the reason Tim dropped out of law school. The Wolek family was equally upset, feeling that Jenny should not waver in her commitment to God. The two, nonetheless, married, but it was on Tim's deathbed that the duo exchanged their vows: Tim had gotten into a heated debate with Jenny's cousin Vince (Antony Ponzini) on a flight of stairs, over her decision to leave the convent. Tragically, Tim fell, hit his head, and survived long enough to make Jenny his bride. For her part, Jenny honored her commitment by moving to a third-world country to keep a promise to aid earthquake victims in San Carlos.

Yasmine Bleeth

Sultry Lee Ann Demarest (seen here with a costar) was winningly portrayed by Yasmine Bleeth on One Life to Live *from 1991–93. Courtesy of Soap Opera Digest.*

I do try to dispel any preconceived notions that I might not be able to form a sentence just because I'm on Baywatch. *If I go to a party where I know no one, I feel like people assume that I'm snotty or maybe I've nothing to say because of the way I look. That makes me uncomfortable.*

—Yasmine Bleeth, 1996

Born: June 14, 1968, in Manhattan, New York

Education: United Nations School (New York City)

Debuts: career—modeled as the Johnson & Johnson baby at six months; film—*Hey Babe* (1980); television—*Ryan's Hope* (1984) as Ryan Fenelli

Honors: Chosen by *People* magazine as one of the Fifty Most Beautiful People in the World (1995)

The program: NBC's TV sitcom *Friends*. The scene: roommates Joey and Chandler are discussing the latest happenings on *Baywatch*:

Joey: "You're in love with Yasmine Bleeth."

Chandler: "Isn't everybody?"

Joey: " . . . she's running! Run. . . . Run like the wind!"

One fictional repartee that catapulted Yasmine Bleeth to a very nonfictional fame.

Her fascinating roots, born to a French North African mother and a New York–born German, Russian, and Jewish father, dictated an exotic moniker ("I wouldn't change it for the world!"), and a career before the camera lens. After an advertising campaign that drew the attention of famed fashion photographer Francesco Scavullo, six-year-old Yasmine appeared in his 1972 book, *Scavullo's Women*. She had a career although, as she noted, "It wasn't my choice initially."

Want to be a soap star? Consider, before you do, Yasmine's description of a typical day on the set of *Ryan's Hope*, which she joined at age sixteen:

"I would show up to work about seven o'clock in the morning, have breakfast, study my lines. You would learn the lines the same day. Just have sittings and makeup. It was actually very leisurely. It saved me from going to college." Yasmine remained in this role until *Ryan's Hope* went off the air, on January 13, 1989. That year, too, she lost her mother, Carina, to breast cancer. Since that time, Bleeth has launched her own tireless breast cancer awareness campaign, in an effort to save other women from her mother's fate.

In 1991, Yasmine created the role of LeeAnn Demerest on *One Life to Live*, a part she played until 1993. Now twenty-three, with fully developed striking looks and talent to match, she became a fan favorite rather rapidly. She was noticed, in a big way. It was upon leaving the daytime soap that her career took a challenging new direction: westward ho, in *Baywatch* territory.

The fame that Yasmine garnered for her work in *Baywatch* was legendary. Above all, it was a welcome change as playing Caroline Holden on *Baywatch* was, in her words, "Usually really easy, and it's beautiful and we spend the day at the beach. We sit in our trailers until they are ready for us and then we have a wonderful lunch and then we go home."

All good things do end. Her decision to leave *Baywatch* in 1997 was a difficult one: "I think what I am trying to do right now is be Yasmine Bleeth as opposed to Yasmine Bleeth from *Baywatch*."

Life after "Caroline" has included a cinematic turn in the comedic romp *BASEketball* (1998), and a line of swimsuits called Yazwear, sold exclusively through the Newport News catalog. ("Thanks to *Baywatch*," she says, "it seemed apropos that I do a swimwear line.") In addition she has joined the ensemble of the hit CBS nighttime TV series *Nash Bridges*, costarring Don Johnson. Bleeth plays the bright, assertive head of an internal affairs unit who watches Johnson's Nash like a hawk.

Five years in soaps, three seasons on a hit prime-time series, and Yasmine Bleeth still gets excited about being recognized. The difference between the soap audience, and the prime-time fan base is, to her, clear: "People are a little more in awe now, the people who don't know me from the soap, but the people who do know me from the soap, it's like, 'Hey, girlfriend, what's up?' It's funny, different fans' reactions to different characters that they've, you know, spent their life with, they spend their afternoons with."

Seems as if soap fans are Yasmine's kind of people.

Films: 1980: *Hey Babe!* 1994: *The Force.* 1997: *Heaven or Vegas.* 1998: *BASEketball.* Forthcoming: *Coming Soon.*

TV movies: 1996: *A Face to Die For; Talk to Me.* 1997: *Crowned and Dangerous.* 1998: *The Lake.* 1999: *Ultimate Deception.* Forthcoming: *It Came from the Sky.*

TV series: 1985–89: *Ryan's Hope.* 1991–93: *One Life to Live.* 1994–97: *Baywatch;* 1998–present: *Nash Bridges.*

Interactive: 1998: *Maximum Surge.*

Video: 1995: *Baywatch: Forbidden Paradise.*

Meet Ryan and LeeAnn

📺 On *Ryan's Hope*, the role of Ryan Fenelli was played by Kerry McNamara (1979–80), Jenny Rebecca Dweir (1980–84), and Yasmine Bleeth (1985–89).

Ryan was the daughter of newspaper reporters Jack Fenelli (Michael Levin) and Mary Ryan (*see* **Kate Mulgrew**). In Yasmine's years on the TV show, her mother had already been killed (by organized crime, in 1979, after investigating the Mafia). Ryan, herself, became a reporter—first, her school newspaper, and then professionally—in keeping with family tradition.

📺 On *One Life to Live*, Bleeth created the sultry, misunderstood LeeAnn Demerest, who was involved with Max Holden (Nicholas Walker), Kevin Buchanan (Joey Thrower), who lost his virginity to the blue-eyed lass, and long-haired Jason Webb (Mark Brettschneider).

When Kevin discovered that LeeAnn was pregnant, he "did the right thing" and proposed to her: the two eloped. Upon returning to town, LeeAnn found herself growing closer to the rebellious Jason. When Kevin caught them kissing, he angrily demanded a divorce—then fought and won custody of her newborn son, Demerest "Duke" Buchanan. After the court decision was handed down, Jason and a desperate LeeAnn took Duke and fled town, but were eventually apprehended.

Kate Capshaw

I think it takes a great deal for him to allow me to pursue my career in a way that's not as controlling as he'd probably love it to be.

—Kate Capshaw, on husband Steven Spielberg, 1994

Kate Capshaw inaugurated the role of Jinx Avery Mallory on The Edge of Night in 1981. Courtesy of Archive Photo.

Born: November 3, 1953, in Fort Worth, Texas; birth name, Katherine Sue Nail

Education: University of Missouri (Columbia)

Debuts: television—*The Edge of Night* (1981) as Jinx Avery Mallory; film—*A Little Sex* (1982)

Marital Status: Divorced from Robert Capshaw; married director Steven Spielberg, October 12, 1991; seven children: Jessica (with ex-husband Robert), Destry Allyn, Mikaela George, Sasha, Sawyer, Theo (adopted), and (from Spielberg's prior marriage to actress Amy Irving) Max

If Given a Choice: "The truth is I prefer not working."

When Steven Spielberg came home from work one day, he asked his wife, actress Kate Capshaw, how her day went.

"Okay, hon," she answered, "Guess what I did? I have the Saran Wrap in the long boxes in the long drawer, and the short boxes in the short drawer. And how are those beautiful, talented people you see all the time?"

From a young age, little Kathy Sue Nail wanted to be an actress. However, realizing that the chances of achieving this goal were slim at best, she enrolled in the University of Missouri at Columbia. She emerged with a master's degree in special education and taught for two years. Challenging as that career was, Kathy decided to relocate to New York to seek out acting jobs. Now going by her married name of Kate Capshaw (surname of first husband Robert), she arrived in the Big Apple in 1981.

She soon landed a role: Jinx Avery on *The Edge of Night*. According to *Soap Opera Digest*, the casting people were completely wowed by her audition. It wasn't until she was on the air in the actual role that they realized that she wasn't right for the part (Susan McDonald was soon recast as Jinx).

After her brief soap stint ended, Kate's agent suggested that she do a prime-time television series. "She sent me a TV script," Kate said, "about a really, really smart woman on her way somewhere else but she gets stuck in this little job at a bar." She passed on the part. It went to Shelley Long. The NBC-TV show was *Cheers* (1983–93).

Undaunted by these professional setbacks, Kate appeared in a few little-remembered films, then auditioned for a role that would change her professional, and personal, life: *Indiana Jones and the Temple of Doom* (1984).

Landing the plum, high-profile assignment of Willie Scott did not come easy: she beat out 120 other actresses who strove for the screen part opposite Harrison Ford. Of equal importance to Kate: this was her initial introduction to the adventure film's director, Steven Spielberg, who was then involved with actress Amy Irving. Spielberg and Irving married in 1985, and divorced in 1989, with Irving receiving what is said to be the biggest divorce settlement ever between Hollywood personalities.

Indiana Jones and the Temple of Doom grossed $45,709,328 in its first week, topping the previous high-grosser, *Return of the Jedi* (1983), the third in the *Star War* trilogy. (Interestingly, the violent nature of some of the scenes in *Indiana Jones and the Temple of Doom* had much to do with the institution of the PG-13 rating, requiring that children under thirteen admitted to such rated films be accompanied by an adult.)

Again, in a repeat of that plum *Cheers* role that got away, after her fame was assured with *Indiana Jones and the Temple of Doom*, Kate received a script. "It was this film comedy about a woman who has her husband kidnap babies because she can't have any. I said that doesn't sound funny." She declined it, but Holly Hunter took the chance. The project was the Coen Brothers' well-received *Raising Arizona* (1987). Passing on good scripts has been an unfortunate feature of Capshaw's professional progress.

Kate married Steven Spielberg on October 12, 1991, at his Long Island estate, and it was assumed that, because of her high-profile marriage to perhaps the world's most celebrated contemporary director, her career would be a string of Spielberg-orchestrated vehicles. However, this has proved not to be the case. "In the same way that I would not rush to show him some great idea that would be shot in Zimbabwe," notes Capshaw, "he is not going to rush to show me that same idea."

However unpredicatable she is about her acting work, Capshaw remains very grounded in her life. "I believe that you do make choices between the nurturing side of your life and the professional side. It's not physically possible in the universe to be two places at once. You can't be home and at work at the same time."

Above all, her preference is the home, though she intends to keep working. The industry is a part of her life, as is her family. Case in point is adopted daughter Mikaela's initial introduction to her father, on television, days after her adoption at infancy. When mother Kate prompted, "Look, honey, there's your daddy!", Mikaela responded by burping. No doubt, Mommy wouldn't have had it any other way.

Films: 1982: *A Little Sex*. 1984: *Indiana Jones and the Temple of Doom*; *Best Defense*; *Dreamscape*; *Windy City*. 1986: *SpaceCamp*; *Power*. 1988: *Internal Affair*; *Private Affairs*. 1989: *Black Rain*. 1990: *Love at Large*. 1991: *My Heroes Have Always Been Cowboys*. 1994: *Love Affair*. 1995: *How to Make an American Quilt*; *Just Cause*; *Duke of Groove*; *No Dogs Allowed*. 1997: *Life During Wartime*; *The Locusts*. Forthcoming: *The Love Letter* (also producer/director).

TV movies: 1982: *Missing Children: A Mother's Story*. 1987: *Her Secret Life*; *The Quick and the Dead*. 1990: *The Earth Day Special*. 1994: *Next Door*. 1998: *The Alarmist*.

TV series: 1981: *The Edge of Night*. 1993: *Black Tie Affair*.

Meet Jinx

▢ On *The Edge of Night*, the character of Jinx Avery Mallory was played by Kate Capshaw (1981) and Susan McDonald (1981–82).

Jinx was married to the new Monticello police chief Derek Mallory (Dennis Parker). *The Edge of Night* made history on December 1, 1975, becoming the first daytime serial to switch networks. With the move from CBS to ABC, dictated primarily because of CBS' rescheduling of the program from late day (*edging*, as it were, into *night*time) to early afternoon, the soap also ended its twenty-one year run as the last serial to be aired live. *The Edge of Night* was broadcast on ABC until December 28, 1984.

Lacey Chabert

I want to do features. I want to go to college when I am older. I want to go to Paris to film school. That would be awesome. I would also like to do some directing.

—Lacey Chabert, on her ambitions, 1998

Born: September 30, 1982, to Tony and Julie Chabert, in Purvis, Mississippi; two older sisters, Chrissy and Wendy; younger brother, T. J.

Debuts: stage—*Les Miserables* (1991); television—*Star Search* '91 (1991); film—*Anastasia* (1997, voice only)

Award: Second Annual *Hollywood Reporter* Young Star Award, 1997, for her role as Claudia Salinger on *Party of Five*

On Her Big Break: "The first thing I did was I auditioned for *Star Search*. It was a fluke altogether. It was really my older sister who was auditioning and I just went along for the ride and I ended up getting on the show and she didn't."

Seventeen going on thirty—a fitting description of the mature young actress Lacey Chabert, whose role as violin prodigy Claudia Salinger on *Party of Five* (1994–present) has brought her legions of young fans. Yet, her ambitions and goals seem more suited to her parents' age group than her own. Combining youthful exuberance with a sense of reality is the trademark of "typical teenager" Lacey.

She knew, quite early, what her life would become: a joyous ride. "I used to always sing around the house and took part in school plays when I was a kid. It was something I always had a passion to do."

Noticing the talent in their young daughter, Lacey's parents took her to New York in 1987 where she coughed on camera for a Triaminic TV commercial. In 1991, while again on vacation in the Big Apple, she auditioned for, and won, the plum role of young Cosette (plus Young Eponine and a one-time performance as Gavroche thrown in) in the Broadway musical, *Les Miserables*. The show, still running at Broadway's Imperial Theatre, was her base until 1993. During that time, she appeared in a myriad of TV ads, most notably a Zest spot, in which she sang about being "Zest-fully clean!"

The year 1991 was not over yet for Lacey, as she had a successful turn on the former hit-maker *Star Search*, reaching the Junior Vocals finals, and appearing in her first made-for-TV movie, NBC's *A Little Piece of Heaven*.

Once her run in *Les Miserables* ended in 1993, Lacey was cast as the still-running character of Bianca Montgomery on *All My Children*. As the third actress to handle the role, Lacey played, for six months, the out-of-wedlock daughter of Erica Kane (Susan Lucci). Later that year, Lacey appeared in *Gypsy*, playing blonde Baby June opposite Bette Midler in a landmark airing that marked Midler's first TV movie appearance and CBS's first musical production since 1968.

In 1993, the Chabert family discovered that Lacey's older sister, Chrissy, had a rare form of muscular dystrophy. Lacey told *TV Guide* in 1996, "She realizes it could be something worse. I think it made me want to help people." It is this mature outlook that has drawn Lacey towards numerous charities, notably those concerned with pediatric AIDS.

In January of 1994, when casting directors Mary V. Buck and Susan Edelman began auditioning for an upcoming Fox network TV series, *Party of Five*, about five orphaned siblings in San Francisco trying to keep the family unit together amidst ever-tragic circumstances, Lacey sent an audition tape and was invited to Los Angeles, where she literally claimed the role of Claudia Salinger, a sassy and intelligent teenaged violin prodigy. And, yes, the fact that Lacey herself plays the violin didn't hurt her chances at all in the auditions.

The teen actress has described her part on *Party of Five* as, "Claud is so concerned with keeping the family together. I think she really doesn't have a specific person watching out for her as a parent, so she feels really responsible for herself."

Her 1990s TV series roles brought other work her way: besides being a sought-after voice-over artist, Lacey took a large career step with her part as Penny Robinson in the movie version of the 1960s TV series *Lost in Space*. Though the 1998 film was critically panned and had disappointing box-office response, she enjoyed the opportunity to create a different Penny than had Angela Cartwright: "She's far more independent and feisty than the TV character," Lacey observed. "There's no way it would have worked had we modeled her on the original."

There is no question that Lacey Chabert will be a force to be reckoned with. Whether it will be in movies ("I'd love to spend time in Paris at a film school or something") or directing ("I want to direct") or other areas ("I want to open a restaurant. I grew up on Cajun food, so I plan on opening Chabert's when I get old enough to do so"), only time—and definitely Lacey—will tell.

Films: 1997: *Anastasia* (voice only). 1998: *Lost in Space*; *The Prince of Egypt* (voice only); *Babes in Toyland* (voice only).

TV movies: 1991: *A Little Piece of Heaven*. 1993: *Gypsy*. 1996: *Educating Mom*. 1997: *When Secrets Kill*.

TV series: 1991: *Star Search '91*. 1993: *All My Children*. 1994–present: *Party of Five*. 1996: *Hey Arnold* (voice only). 1997: *The Wild Thornberries* (voice only).

Video: 1997: *Journey Beneath the Sea* (voice only). *Little Redux Riding Hood* (voice only). 1998: *The Lion King: Simba's Pride* (voice only).

Meet Bianca

📺 On *All My Children*, the character of Bianca Montgomery has been played by Jessica Leigh Falborn (1988–91), Caroline Wilde (1991), Lacey Chabert (1993), Gina Gallagher (1993–97), and Nathalie Paulding (1997–present).

Bianca was born, out of wedlock, to Erica Kane (Susan Lucci) and Travis Montgomery (Larkin Malloy), who eventually married, divorced, remarried, and divorced again.

While visiting Pine Valley in 1993, Bianca was nearly raped by Richard Fields (James A. Stephens), but was rescued by her half-sister Kendall (*see* **Sarah Michelle Gellar**)—ironically, it was Fields who had raped and impregnated Erica years earlier, resulting in Kendall.

Ted Danson

Once you have kids, and you realize you're not passing along to your children what was passed on to you by your parents, you start feeling very guilty and angry and confused.

—Ted Danson, environmentalist, 1996

From 1974–76, Ted Danson played womanizing scoundrel Tom Conway on Somerset. Courtesy of Soap Opera Digest.

Born: December 29, 1947, in Flagstaff, Arizona, to Edward and Jessica McMaster Danson; birth name, Edward Bridge Danson III

Education: Kent School (Connecticut); Stanford University (California) and Carnegie-Mellon University (Pittsburgh, Pennsylvania); Actor's Institute (Los Angeles); Beverly Hills Playhouse (California)

Debuts: television—*Somerset* (1974) as Tom Conway; film—*The Onion Field* (1979)

Awards: Golden Globe Award, for Best Performance by an Actor in a Miniseries or Motion Picture Made for TV, for *Something About Amelia*, 1985; Emmy Award, for Outstanding Lead Actor in a Comedy Series, for his role as Sam Malone on *Cheers*, 1990 and 1991; Golden Globe Award, for Best Performance by an Actor in a TV Series, for *Cheers*, 1990, 1991, and 1992

Honors: Nominated for Emmy Awards, 1983–89; nominated for Golden Globe Awards, 1986 and 1993

Marital Status: Married Randy Gosch, August 1970, divorced, 1975; married environmental designer Casey Coates, July 30, 1977, divorced, 1993; married Mary Steenburgen, October 7, 1995; two daughters, Kate, Alexis (both with second wife; one adopted)

First known in his role as a womanizing bartender and a sex symbol, Ted Danson is now known as an activist for environmental awareness. His visibility and name recognition have given support to a most worthwhile cause.

Born the son of Edward Bridge Danson II, a prominent archaeologist and museum director, Ted grew up near a Navajo reservation in Arizona. His love for the oceans can be traced back to his childhood, when he and his family enjoyed many summer days at the Pacific Ocean on the California coast. Years later, when he wanted to take his family on a similar trip, he found the beach closed—due to pollution.

Ted played basketball at Kent School in Connecticut (1961–66), and graduated to Stanford University. There, he dated an unnamed aspiring actress, who encouraged him to audition for a production. The bug bit, and bit hard. By the end of the year, he had transferred to Carnegie-Mellon University, in Pittsburgh, Pennsylvania (1968–72), where he changed his major to drama.

In 1970, Ted married Randy Gosch, a union that lasted five years. Being close to New York, he began auditioning for shows, and did much extra work in media productions. Commercials followed. Then Ted tried out for and won a recast role on TV's daytime drama *Somerset*. Soon, he began a two-year stint (1974–76) as rascally playboy Tom Conway. On this soap, Ted learned lessons of screen womanizing that he would use to great professional advantage later.

Leaving the soap, Ted married for the second time in 1977 to Casey Coates (to whom he was wed until 1993, and with whom he raised two daughters), and spent the next few years working in television (he appeared in a 1976 episode of *Laverne & Shirley* and a 1981 episode of the detective series *Magnum P.I.* with fellow soap alumnus **Tom Selleck**) and appearing in commercials before hitting upon his first feature film role, as murdered police officer Ian Campbell in *The Onion Field* (1979). Bigger things were on the horizon: the defining role in Danson's career was born on September 30, 1982.

"Sometimes you want to go where everybody knows your name." And, for eleven seasons, *Cheers* was the place. Based on a Beacon Street bar in downtown Boston, the NBC-TV series featured a marvelously witty cast. Danson was Sam Malone, former pitcher for the Boston Red Sox, skirt chaser, and reformed alcoholic who owned (for a time) and tended the bar. Danson's chemistry with both of his female foils, Shelley Long (playing Diane Chambers from 1982–87) and Kirstie Alley (playing Rebecca Howe from 1987–93) was splendid, visibly bringing out the best in Ted, who seemed to become a better actor with each passing season: after being nominated for Emmys for seven consecutive years, he won two of the coveted awards in 1991 and 1992. Danson and Alley would act together again, this time on her sitcom, *Veronica's Closet*, in 1998.

During *Cheers*' lengthy run, Danson kept busy outside of the bar set as well, parlaying his TV success into big feature film roles, most notably in the comedy *Three Men and a Baby* (1987) and its 1990 sequel, *Three Men and a Little Lady*. On the small screen, too, he was being noticed, as he won another Emmy in 1985, this time for his role as an incestuous child abuser in the TV movie *Something About Amelia*, costarring Glenn Close. The story held over sixty million shocked home viewers riveted.

The 1990s saw increasing appearances for Danson in theatrical films. On the set of *Made in America*, a 1993 comedy, he met and romanced costar Whoopi Goldberg, an interracial relationship that surprised fans, and eventually broke up his second marriage. On October 8, 1993, at a New York Friars Club roast honoring Whoopi, Ted appeared on stage in blackface, and proceeded to attempt humorous racial jokes. The publicity surrounding this was horrendous—and, less than a month later, on November 5, Whoopi and Ted broke up.

After the whirlwind of negative response surrounding the Friars Club roast, Danson found solace in his new relationship with actress Mary Steenburgen, who had been married to actor Malcolm McDowell from 1980–90. Ted and Mary married on October 7, 1995. Together, the two starred in a short-lived TV series (*Ink*) in 1996, in which he played a grizzled newspaper reporter. Ratings, after production overhauls, were good, but backstage executive woes killed the show in its debut season. Danson has rebounded from this mishap with a new series, *Becker*, which began fall 1998 on CBS-TV. In it, Ted plays an iconoclastic, drinking, and smoking doctor. Kind of like playing an alcoholic bartender...

However it is his commitment to his American Oceans Campaign that is now closest to Ted's heart. He is a vegetarian and has become very active politically by producing and starring in numerous videos, documentaries, and public service announcements on behalf of his ecological views. In a film shot for the National Audubon Society, which aired on CNN and PBS, he shared the screen with another celebrity conservationist, Kermit the Frog.

Ted Danson: happily married, environmentally aware, and proud of it.

Films: 1979: *The Onion Field*. 1981: *Body Heat*. 1982: *Creepshow*. 1985: *Little Treasure*. 1986: *A Fine Mess*; *Just Between Friends*. 1987: *Three Men and a Baby*. 1988: *She's Having a Baby*. 1989: *Cousins*; *Dad*. 1990: *Three Men and a Little Lady*. 1993: *Made in America*. 1994: *Getting Even with Dad*; *Pontiac Moon* (also executive producer). 1995: *Loch Ness*. 1998: *Saving Private Ryan*; *Homegrown*; *Jerry & Tom*. Forthcoming: *Mumford*.

TV movies: 1978: *The Chinese Web*. 1980: *Once Upon a Spy*; *The Women's Room*. 1981: *Our Family Business*; 1983: *Cowboy*. 1984: *Something About Amelia*, 1986: *When the Bough Breaks* (also executive producer). 1987: *We Are the Children*. 1990: *Down Home* (co-producer only). 1996: *Gulliver's Travels*.

TV miniseries: 1998: *Thanks of a Grateful Nation*.

TV series: 1974–76: *Somerset*. 1982–93: *Cheers*. 1996: *Ink* (also executive producer). 1998–present: *Becker*.

Video: 1996: *Grand Canyon: From Dinosaurs to Dams*.

Meet Tom

📺 On *Somerset*, Tom Conway was played by Michael Nouri (1974) and Ted Danson (1974–76).

Tom Conway was an attorney who worked for Ben Grant (Ed Kemmer). Conway had a rather persistent and, frankly, slimy way with the ladies: one of his conquests was the show's heroine, Eve Lawrence (Bibi Besch), who had just lost her true love, Julian Cannell (Joel Crothers) to wicked Kate Thornton (Tina Sloan). Eve needed cheering up, and Tom was just the guy who could provide her solace.

Kim Delaney

I keep reminding myself that no matter how long a relationship lasts, it's worth it.

—Kim Delaney, 1984

Popular heroine Jenny Gardner was played by Kim Delaney on All My Children *from 1981–84. Jenny made a post-mortem return to Pine Valley in 1994. Courtesy of Soap Opera Digest.*

Born: November 29, 1961, in Philadelphia, Pennsylvania, to Jack and Joan Delaney; four brothers

Education: Hallahan High School (Philadelphia, Pennsylvania)

Debuts: stage—*Loving Reno* (early 1980s); television—*All My Children* (1981) as Jenny Gardner; film—*That Was Then...This Is Now* (1985)

Award: Emmy Award, for Outstanding Supporting Actress in a Drama Series, for her role as Detective Diane Russell on *NYPD Blue*, 1997

Honors: Nominated for Emmy Award in 1982; nominated for Golden Globes in 1997 and 1998

Marital Status: Married actor Charles Flohe, 1985, divorced; married actor Joe Cortese, 1991, divorced, 1994; engaged to producer Alan Barnett; one son, Jack (with ex-husband Cortese)

In late 1984, known-to-be deceased Jenny Gardner Nelson was "spotted," roaming around *All My Children*'s Pine Valley. In actuality, a double had been hired by Jenny's former modeling agent to impersonate the dead beauty, thinking that the publicity would benefit the career of the lookalike. This plot reminded *AMC* devotees of how valuable an asset Kim Delaney was in her portrayal as Jenny. In three years on the soap, Kim made an impact: now, long after she left the daytime drama, Delaney is making a bigger splash, as an actress of great talent, and as a head-turning beauty.

Kim's radiance was evident early: she was a sought-after model in her days at Philadelphia's Hallahan High. Shortly after graduation, she moved to New York, signed with the Elite Modeling Agency, soon gracing the covers of such magazines as *Glamour* and *Seventeen*. She also began acting training with renowned coach Bill Esper.

In 1981, Kim joined the cast of *All My Children*, originating the role of popular teenage beauty Jenny Gardner. Her popularity was swift and sure, and her 1984 onscreen marriage was a high-rated, and long-awaited, event. Soon after the soap nuptials, however, Kim decided to try prime-time TV and feature films, so her contract was not renewed: to the horror of viewers, Jenny was killed off *AMC* in 1984 (she did "resurrect," so to speak, as the ghost of Jenny, for a 1994 cameo).

After a breakup with Bob McGowan, with whom she had been involved for five years, Kim entered into a relationship with actor Charles Flohe, then starring as Preacher on *The Edge of Night*, and the two married in 1985. They divorced quickly. Now known as Charles Grant, the actor is still active in daytime drama.

After appearing in such critically panned films as *That Was Then...This Is Now* (1985) and *Campus Man* (1987), Delaney returned to the small screen. A 1987 guest spot on *L.A. Law* (as a determined associate who, as research for her novel on high-powered law firms, bedded Arnie Becker) turned heads and got her a two-season role on the CBS Vietnam TV series *Tour of Duty* in 1988.

Kim took a hiatus from her career after giving birth to Jack (son of her second husband, actor Joe Cortese), then settled into a niche as a TV movie actress, before being cast for a four-episode stint on *NYPD Blue* as a love interest for Bobby Simone. Her portrayal of alcoholic detective Diane Russell was popular enough to earn her a regular turn on the police drama. Her talents were recognized with a 1997 Emmy Award.

Currently living with, and engaged to, television producer Alan Barnett, Kim Delaney is a spokesperson for Revlon Ultima II cosmetics. She enjoys spending time with her young son, and, judging by the busy nature of her rejuvenated career, that time is, indeed, most precious.

Films: 1985: *That Was Then...This Is Now*. 1986: *The Delta Force*. 1987: *Campus Man; Hunter's Blood*. 1988: *The Drifter*. 1991: *Body Parts; Hangfire*. 1994: *Dark Goddess; Darkman II: The Return of Durant; The Force*. 1995: *Closer and Closer; Project: Metalbeast*.

TV movies: 1983: *First Affair*. 1987: *Christmas Comes to Willow Creek; Cracked Up; Perry Mason: The Case of the Sinister Spirit*. 1988: *Take My Daughters, Please; Something Is Out There*. 1992: *Jackie Collins' "Lady Boss"; The Broken Cord*. 1993: *The Disappearance of Christina*. 1995: *Tall, Dark and Deadly*. 1997: *The Devil's Child; All Lies End in Murder*.

TV series: 1981–84, 1994: *All My Children*. 1988–90: *Tour of Duty*. 1992: *The Fifth Corner*; 1995–present: *NYPD Blue*.

Meet Jenny

On *All My Children*, Jenny Gardner was originated, and played solely, by Kim Delaney from 1981–84, and for a surprise cameo in 1994.

Jenny Gardner, a girl from the wrong side of the tracks, came to live in Pine Valley with her tacky mother, Opal (Dorothy Lyman). Greg Nelson (Laurence Lau), the boy most likely to succeed at Pine Valley High, was one of Jenny's classmates. Their romance blossomed when Greg, an amateur photographer, asked Jenny to pose for him. Soon his snobby girlfriend Lisa (Marcy Walker) tried to break them up. She frightened Jenny into leaving town—Jenny and her friend Jesse Hubbard (Darnell Williams) spent the summer on the run in New York's Spanish Harlem. In Manhattan, unsuspecting Jenny got trapped into appearing in a porn flick (*Jenny Does the Big Apple*). Later, when the movie was screened at a college frat party, Jenny ran out, humiliated. Greg tried to stop her from hiding on a scaffold in the college theater, but fell himself and was paralyzed.

The injured Greg rejected Jenny, mistaking her love for pity. So she buried her sorrows in her New York modeling career, moving into Erica's (Susan Lucci) penthouse and meeting a fellow aspiring model, Tony Barclay (Brent Barrett). For publicity purposes, Jenny and Tony feigned romance—actually, only Jenny pretended, as Tony was quickly smitten. But Jenny agreed to marry Tony, reasoning that she had lost her true love, Greg.

Jenny and Tony were *this close* to nuptials when, miraculously, Greg recovered, and reclaimed his lady love. Jenny and Greg wed on Valentine's Day, 1984—but their happiness was short-lived: Jenny Gardner Nelson died a few months after marriage, when a jet ski she was riding exploded. The "accident" was rigged by a jealous Tony, who intended to kill Greg.

In 1994, after Tad (Michael E. Knight) was seriously injured in a tornado, he took an out-of-body trip and there encountered his dearly departed sister, Jenny. For both the character of Tad and the audience, Jenny was certainly an intriguing sight to behold.

· ·

Show/Name Mix-up

China Beach and *Tour of Duty*, which debuted five months apart in 1988, were both centered around the Vietnam War. Its stars, Dana Delany (*Love of Life* and *As the World Turns*, later *China Beach*) and Kim Delaney (*All My Children*, later *Tour of Duty*), are frequently confused with one another, both for their names and their wholesome, brunette looks.

· ·

Dana Delany

I, as a teenager, was addicted to soap operas. I mean, I was one of those girls that, every day at lunch, would go into a side room with the other girls and we'd watch All My Children. *I mean, we wouldn't miss it every day at school.*

—Dana Delany, on soaps, 1997

Born: March 13, 1956, in New York City; birth name, Dana Welles Delany; one of four children

Education: Westhill High School (Stamford, Connecticut); Phillips Academy (Andover, Massachusetts); Wesleyan University (Middletown, Connecticut)

Debuts: career—commercial for Carefree sugarless gum (1978); television—*Love of Life* (1979) as Amy Russell; film—*The Fan* (1981)

Awards: Emmy Award, as Outstanding Lead Actress in a Drama Series, for her role as Lt. Colleen McMurphy on *China Beach*, 1988; Viewers for Quality Television Awards, as Best Actress in a Quality Drama Series, for *China Beach*, 1989, 1990, 1991

Honor: Chosen by *People* magazine as one of the Fifty Most Beautiful People in the World (1991)

On the December 17, 1990, edition of *The Joan Rivers Show*, Dana Delany shared a family secret with the TV talk show host. A deep secret. "My great grandfather started the family business, which was flush valves for toilets." To be precise, Delany Flush Valves. A rather noteworthy footnote in the career of one of the classiest actresses of our generation.

Dana Delany knew, as early as age three, that she wanted to be an actress. As a child she enjoyed Doris Day movies and musicals and as an adult does embody Day's qualities of perky, elegant attractiveness. In addition, Dana has a notable singing voice—obviously, she spent her childhood studying well.

After graduation from Wesleyan University in Middletown, Connecticut, she moved to New York, and spent the ensuing years honing her skills through stage work and two daytime TV stints: on *Love of Life* (1979) and *As the World Turns* (1981), both New York-based productions.

After leaving soaps, and New York, she complemented stage work with guest spots in TV series, TV movies, and some theatrical films. This young actress kept very busy. In 1988, her hard work paid dividends, as she earned the role of conscientious Lt. Colleen McMurphy, a nurse, on *China Beach*—a groundbreaking TV show, in that its perspective was an unflinching view of the Vietnam War through the eyes of the American women who were stationed there. The hour-long show also starred fellow soap graduate Marg Helgenberger.

To Delany, *China Beach* had the best qualities of the TV medium's potential, possessing "a moral viewpoint and a way of educating people and affecting lives." The program, however, was canceled in 1990, after only three seasons. For Dana, the quieting of the show's message was a troubling issue, for she felt strongly about what the series was accomplishing: "The women who were there were equally affected by it as men. And the only problem was they didn't have the fighting, the combat, as an outlet for their feelings. They couldn't get back at anybody."

After the show's cancellation came a stream of TV guest appearances and feature films, which showcased Dana's abilities as a versatile actress. Her stints, for example, on three episodes of HBO's *The Larry Sanders Show*—in each case, she played herself (no easy feat for a performer who is used to embodying a fictional character)—and her turn on the TV miniseries *Wild Palms* (1993) drew raves and praise.

One acting part that caused a bit of a stir was as birth control pioneer Margaret Sanger in the 1995 TV biopic *Choices of the Heart: The Margaret Sanger Story*—those who knew and respected Dana from her role as an Irish-Catholic nurse on *China Beach* were outraged by this portrayal. The actress received mail aplenty, including promises of boycotts from irate viewers, who vowed never to watch any Dana Delany vehicle again.

The role that got away? Margaret Colin's part as Chief-of-Staff in the 1997 blockbuster *Independence Day*. "Did I make a mistake?" she asked fans on a May 20, 1997, Prodigy chat session. "I chose *Fly Away Home*, which I thought was more life-affirming..."

Armed with a ferocious self-belief and talent to match, the never-married Dana Delany is an actress's actress: "I just believe what I'm doing, and I'm very clear about what my character wants. And, if I find myself acting, I quit." Well, she could always join the family business....

Films: 1981: *The Fan*. 1984: *Almost You*. 1986: *Where the River Runs Black*. 1988: *Masquerade*; *Moon Over Parador*; *Patty Hearst*. 1991: *Light Sleeper*. 1992: *House Sitter*. 1993: *Batman: Mask of the Phantasm* (voice only);

Tombstone. 1994: *Exit to Eden*; *Texan*. 1995: *Live Nude Girls*. 1996: *Fly Away Home*. 1998: *Wide Awake*; *The Curve*; *The Outfitters*.

TV movies: 1984: *Threesome*. 1986: *A Winner Never Quits*. 1988: *China Beach*. 1990: *A Promise to Keep*. 1993: *Donato and Daughter*. 1994: *The Enemy Within*. 1995: *Choices of the Heart: The Margaret Sanger Story*. 1996: *For Hope*. 1998: *The Patron Saint of Liars*; *Rescuers: Stories of Courage—Two Couples*.

TV miniseries: 1993: *Wild Palms*. 1997: *True Women*.

TV series: 1979–80: *Love of Life*. 1981: *As the World Turns*. 1988–91: *China Beach*. 1996: *Wing Commander Academy* (voice only); *Superman* (voice only). 1997–present: *New Batman/Superman Adventures* (voice only).

Meet Amy and Haley

On *Love of Life*, the role of Amy Russell was originated, and played solely by Dana Delany, from 1979–80.

Amy was a college student who became close to Vanessa (Audrey Peters) and Bruce Sterling (Ron Tomme), when Bruce taught law at Rosehill University, where Amy studied. There was a reason for that bond: as it turned out, Amy was Bruce's long-lost daughter. The exploration of this new relationship, however, never happened as the show was canceled, in limbo (expecting to be picked up by another network, it wasn't), on February 1, 1980.

On *As the World Turns*, the character of Haley Wilson was originated, and played solely, by Dana Delany in 1981.

Haley was a college student whose father, an archaeology professor, had been killed in a cave-in. She fell in love with Eric Hollister (Peter Reckell, who would find fame as Bo Brady on *Days of Our Lives*): the two married in 1981, and then left Oakdale.

* *

She Had to Rinse

Dana Delany, on her *As the World Turns* role of Haley, and her unique view of soap acting: "My character was a virgin, and that was, like, the whole basis of her character. Just as soon as she got married that was the end of my part. Because there was no character left. I got very lazy. I did as little as possible; I tried to see whatever I could get away with. I would stay out all night and I would go to work at seven in the morning without having slept the night before. When I finished on the soap, I had to go back to acting class for a year before I worked again, to re-learn and get rid of these habits."

* *

Leonardo DiCaprio

The best thing about acting is that I get to lose myself in another character and actually get paid for it. It's a great outlet. As for myself, I'm not sure who I am. It seems that I change every day.
—Leonardo DiCaprio, 1998

Popular Santa Barbara *character Mason Capwell was played, as a teenager in flashback, by Leonardo DiCaprio, in 1990. Courtesy of Ann Bogart.*

Born: November 11, 1974, in Los Angeles, California, to George and Irmelin DiCaprio; birth name, Leonardo Wilhelm DiCaprio; one stepbrother, Adam Farrar

Education: John Marshall High School and Center for Enriched Studies (Los Angeles)

Debuts: television—*Romper Room* (1979); film—*Critters 3* (1991)

Awards: New Generation Award from Los Angeles Film Critics Association, 1993; Blockbuster Entertainment Award, as Favorite Actor, Romance, for his role as Romeo in *William Shakespeare's Romeo & Juliet*, 1997; Silver Berlin Bear Award, as Best Actor, for *William Shakespeare's Romeo & Juliet*, 1997; MTV Movie Award, for Best Male Performance, for his role as Jack Dawson in *Titanic*, 1998; Blockbuster Entertainment Award, as Favorite Actor, Drama, for *Titanic*, 1998

Honors: Nominated for Academy Award, 1994; chosen by *People* magazine as one of the Fifty Most Beautiful People in the World, 1997; nominated for three MTV Movie Awards in 1997, and two in 1998; nominated for Golden Globe Awards, 1994 and 1998; nominated for Golden Satellite Award, 1998

Books: *Leonardo: A Scrapbook in Words and Pictures*, by Grace Catalano (1998); *Leonardo DiCaprio*, by Kieran Scott (1998); *Leonardo DiCaprio*, by Smithmark Publishing (1998); *Leonardo DiCaprio*, by Stacey Stauffer (1998); *Leonardo DiCaprio*, by Douglas Thompson (1998); *Leonardo DiCaprio: A Biography*, by Nancy Krulik (1998); *The Leonardo DiCaprio Album*, by Brian J. Robb and

John Berry (1997); *Leonardo DiCaprio: Modern-Day Romeo*, by Grace Catalano (1997); *Leonardo DiCaprio: Romantic Hero*, by Mark Bego (1998); *Leonardo DiCaprio Trivia Book*, by Nancy Krulik (1998); *Lovin' Leo: Your Leonardo DiCaprio Scrapbook*, by Scholastic Books Inc., Scholastic Staff, ed., (1998)

While she was admiring a Leonardo da Vinci painting at a museum in early 1974, the baby in the womb of Irmelin DiCaprio suddenly kicked. At that moment, she knew that, if the baby was a male, she would name him Leonardo. It was a boy.

He was always a performer. In school in Los Angeles, instead of concentrating on his studies ("I could never focus on things I didn't want to learn"), Leonardo would entertain classmates. Sometimes, such "problem students" emerge later as geniuses, and the teachers who punished them eat humble pie. Many such educators are likely now wondering what they missed in assessing Leonardo DiCaprio.

His first appearance on television was as one in a crowd of children: the kiddie show *Romper Room*. Five-year-old Leo fared no better on the set than he would in the classroom: he was booted from the set for bad behavior.

In 1988, at age fourteen, things began to pick up for the career of this blond teenager: he appeared in over thirty TV commercials, and such educational films as *Mickey's Safety Club* and *How to Deal with a Parent Who Takes Drugs*. At age sixteen, he got his first regular acting job, a limited role on the daytime drama *Santa Barbara*, portraying the young Mason Capwell in a dream sequence aired on May 30, 1990. Though a very brief run, the hard work, thick scripts, and limited rehearsal time proved to be a helpful experience for Leonardo, who rapidly overcame his discipline problems.

The next two years saw him appear in a forgettable film debut, in *Critters 3* (1991), and two prime-time TV series, *Parenthood* (1990) and *Growing Pains* (1991–92). On the last one, he played the homeless Luke Brower, a small part that became a regular role for a year—evidence of his charismatic potential. His good looks and flowing hair, coupled with his exotic name, made him stand out. Interestingly, one former talent agent had encouraged him to cut his hair and change his name to Lenny Williams.

DiCaprio beat out four hundred other hopefuls for the role of Tobias Wolff in *This Boy's Life* (1993), a coming-of-age movie set in the 1950s. Costarring Robert De Niro and Ellen Barkin, DiCaprio received the strongest notices of the heavyweight cast, despite the film's box-office fizzle. What he also gained from this experience was a sense of self as an actor, learning to carefully pick acting parts: "I want to take my time with each role, and that's how you plan a long career, rather than doing it all at once in a big explosion." (Long known for turning down roles that other actors would "die for," Leonardo refused the role of Robin in the 1995 hit *Batman Forever*, opting instead to appear in the disappointing 1995 gritty memoir *The Basketball Diaries*.)

His other 1993 offering, *What's Eating Gilbert Grape?*, almost slipped through DiCaprio's fingers, as his handsome appearance might have worked against him in the tricky role of mentally challenged Arnie Grape. Leo, however, made the character totally believable, and emerged with his first Oscar nomination.

The year 1994 started as a disappointment, as he lost the role of the young reporter in *Interview with the Vampire* (1994) to **Christian Slater**. However, DiCaprio rebounded, furthering his acclaim, garnering the supporting role, opposite Gene Hackman, of the witty cynic, The Kid, in the Sharon Stone western *The Quick and the Dead* (1995). His other 1995 big screen offering, *Total Eclipse*, called for him to portray young French poet Arthur Rimbaud, whose complex homosexual relationship with his older mentor Paul Verlaine (David Thewlis) stretched his acting skills even further. What next? Shakespeare?

Well, yes, actually. *William Shakespeare's Romeo & Juliet* (1996) offered an interpretation of the tragic lovers with a 1990s flavor. However, Leonardo's reputation as a screen lover was sealed with *Titanic* (1997), the highest-grossing film ever. As Jack, he set female hearts a-swooning, and answered, most definitively, that the hype directed his way was not a whim. The young Leonardo DiCaprio, who had been kicked off the set of TV's *Romper Room* all those years ago, was now a Hollywood talent with whom to be reckoned, with no semblance of flash-in-the-pan about him.

Films: 1991: *Critters 3.* 1992: *Poison Ivy.* 1993: *What's Eating Gilbert Grape?*; *This Boy's Life.* 1994: *The Foot Shooting Party.* 1995: *Total Eclipse*; *The Basketball Diaries*; *The Quick and the Dead.* 1996: *Marvin's Room*; *William Shakespeare's Romeo & Juliet.* 1997: *Titanic.* 1998: *The Man in the Iron Mask*; *Celebrity*; *Don's Plum.* Forthcoming: *The Beach*; *The Chet Baker Story.*

TV series: 1990: *Parenthood.* 1990: *Santa Barbara.* 1991–92: *Growing Pains.*

Meet Teenage Mason

On *Santa Barbara*, the role of teenage Mason Capwell was performed by Leonardo DiCaprio beginning on May 30, 1990.

Mason was played by Terry Lester at the time, and DiCaprio's role dealt with flashbacks of two decades earlier. Four men had grown up in an orphanage together. Twenty years earlier, a girl named Cassie who was also parentless was buried in an underground tunnel cave-in and presumed dead. The youths blamed Mason, the son of a wealthy oil tycoon, for Cassie's death. Cassie, though, turned up alive before the orphans could kill Mason in retaliation.

* *

A Titanic Connection

Leonardo DiCaprio's (*Santa Barbara*) character in Titanic (1997), Jack Dawson, fell in love (and into the sea) with Rose, the daughter of Frances Fisher's (*Edge of Night, Guiding Light*) character, Ruth Bukater. In addition, the richest man aboard the doomed ocean liner, John Jacob Astor, was portrayed by *The Young and the Restless'* Eric Braeden (Victor Newman).

* *

Roma Downey

If you had told me that I could have taken this journey to arrive at this place, I would have laughed and said, Haven't you got the great imagination?

—Roma Downey, on her career, 1998

Born: May 6, 1964, in Derry, Northern Ireland, to Patrick and Maureen Downey; youngest of six children

Education: Brighton Art College (England) and London Drama Studio (England)

Debuts: television—*One Life to Live* (1988) as Lady Joanna Leighton; Broadway—*The Circle* (1989); film—*The Last Word* (1994)

Award: Most Promising Student of the Year Award, London Drama Studio, 1984

Honor: Chosen by *People* magazine as one of the Fifty Most Beautiful People in the World (1997)

Marital Status: First marriage ended in divorce; married director David Anspaugh, November 24, 1985, estranged, 1998; one daughter, Reilly

Adopting the immortal words of painter Vincent Van Gogh, "It's no longer enough to be the painter, I want to be the paint!", Roma Downey began a path of life that has put her squarely in the middle of the canvas as a respected and gifted actress. Upon learning of her roots, however, one can be amazed at the survival instincts of this radiant talent.

The political unrest surrounding the British invasion of her Irish homeland was never far from her tiny corner of the world, the working-class community of Bogside. The disturbances became very personal in 1974, when she lost her forty-eight-year-old mother, Maureen, to a heart attack. That same year, her house was damaged by a tear gas canister which came in through the window and exploded in the living room. After that the windows were permanently shuttered: "The house was so dark after that. It was horrible," recalls the actress.

Her schoolmaster father, Patrick, insisted that young Roma leave home, to escape the horrors, particularly after her older brother, Lawrence, was shot and wounded by a rubber bullet. When Roma finished high school, her father sent her across the Channel to Brighton Art College, where she studied painting and complemented her studies by joining the drama society. She later transferred to the London Drama Studio.

While in London, twenty-one-year-old Roma lost her father to a heart attack. The next year, 1986, she married an unidentified fellow student, and the two of them relocated to New York so Roma could pursue an acting career. The marital union soon ended and she considered going back to Ireland. She eventually decided against such a move, choosing instead to participate in various stage productions in New York, and spending the next few years seeking work on television.

In 1988, Roma auditioned for, and won, a six-month role as vixenish Joanna Leighton on *One Life to Live*. After that busy, if brief, stint ended, she returned to the stage and enjoyed her Broadway debut, appearing in Rex Harrison's 1989 revival of W. Somerset Maugham's sophisticated comedy *The Circle*. In 1991, Roma was nominated for the Helen Hayes Best Actress Award for her stage role in *The Playboy of the Western World*. Later that season, she was cast in a pivotal acting assignment that would gain Roma her widest notice to date.

Playing as strong a woman as a First Lady is no mean feat: portraying the legendary Jacqueline Kennedy Onassis should have been near impossible for any performer. Cast as Jackie in the 1991 TV miniseries *A Woman Named Jackie*, Roma underwent tedious speech training to "lose her accent," voraciously read up on JFK's wife, and gained widespread recognition for her stunning performance. (Interestingly, in the role of Jackie in her teenage years was another future star, **Sarah Michelle Gellar**, of *Buffy the Vampire Slayer* fame). Such portrayals come with a cost: Downey quickly found herself characterized professionally as The Woman Who Played Jackie. "I didn't even have a name," she recalled.

The next two years consisted of one audition after another with few results, save for one theatrical film and three TV movies—life was hard. Then, in 1994, her personal and professional lives took a turn for the better in a series of sweeping steps.

Roma met feature film director David Anspaugh on a blind date—she beat him in a game of pool. Meanwhile, in Hollywood a new series, *Touched by an Angel*, began cast searches and Roma soon found herself starring in a groundbreaking TV series.

While filming the pilot, Anspaugh (right there, on the set) proposed marriage. The two were married on November 24, 1995, in Utah, in a ceremony conducted by *Touched by an Angel* costar and part-time minister Della Reese. It was the second marriage for both bride and groom. David had a daughter from his first union.

From the very beginning, *Touched by an Angel* endeavored to rebuild a bridge between television and its viewership that had been sorely lacking: spiritual awareness. With Downey as Monica, an angel who guides people at life's crucial crossroads, the show scored as CBS had hoped. Ratings soared, critics raved, and audiences were charmed.

Because of this role, which is so strongly devout, Downey found herself typecast in two subsequent telefeatures: the 1995 tearjerker *A Child Is Missing* touched chords for its theme of family bonds, and the charming 1997 fantasy *Borrowed Hearts: A Holiday Romance* (aired, "coincidentally," right after *Touched by an Angel*), in which her character taught a hardened business man the true meaning of family.

Roma became a mother in 1996, giving birth to daughter Reilly Marie. She and Anspaugh bought a house in Utah that year, and the working duo commuted between Los Angeles and Utah. However, the pressures of such a lifestyle took their toll and in March 1998 Roma filed for divorce after two and a half years of marriage.

Despite personal woes, her professional career continues to escalate, and it is likely that the glow of this angel will not soon fade away.

Film: 1994: *The Last Word*.

TV movies: 1992: *Devlin, Getting Up and Going Home*. 1994: *Hercules and the Amazon Women*. 1995: *A Child Is Missing*. 1997: *Borrowed Hearts: A Holiday Romance* (also executive producer). 1998: *Monday After the Miracle*.

TV miniseries: 1991: *A Woman Named Jackie*.

TV series: 1988: *One Life to Live*. 1991: *Disney Presents the 100 Lives of Black Jack Savage*. 1994–present: *Touched by an Angel*.

Meet Joanna

On *One Life to Live*, the role of Joanna Leighton was originated, and played solely, by Roma Downey, in 1988.

Joanna was married to former underworld prince Rob Coronal (Mark Arnold), who still had a thing for his ex-wife, Cassie Callison (Holly Gagnier). The Leightons, as it turned out, also had criminal ties and were in league with the evil Sanders family in an attempt to take over the fortune of Llanview's premier clan, the Buchanans.

Patty Duke

At the tender age of twelve in 1958, Patty Duke launched her portrayal of Ellen Dennis on the CBS soap The Brighter Day. Courtesy of Archive Photo.

Though I've been a professional actress since I was seven or eight, acting was never a dream of mine. What I really wanted to be was a nun; nuns were the only people I came in contact with who weren't drinking and screaming!

—Patty Duke, on ambition, 1987

Born: December 14, 1946, in Elmhurst, New York, to John Patrick and Frances Duke; birth name, Anna Marie Duke; older sister, Carol; older brother, Raymond

Debuts: television—*Armstrong Circle Theatre* (1956) in "The S.S. *Andrea Doria*"; film—*The Goddess* (1958); stage—*The Miracle Worker* (1959)

Awards: Theatre World Award, Most Promising Star, 1959–60; Academy Award, Best Supporting Actress, *The Miracle Worker*, 1962; Golden Globe Award, Most Outstanding Future Star, 1963; Golden Globe Award, Best Actress in a Musical or Comedy, *Me, Natalie*, 1969; Emmy Award, Best Actress (Single Performance), *My Sweet Charlie*, 1970; Emmy Award, Best Actress (Limited Series), *Captains and the Kings*, 1977; Emmy Award, Outstanding Actress (Limited Series or Special), *The Miracle Worker*, 1980; People's Choice Award, Most Popular Television Actress, *It Takes Two*, 1983

Honors: Nominated for Golden Globe in 1965–66; nominated for Emmy Awards in 1963, two in 1977, and 1983; has hamburgers named after her in two NYC restaurants (Twins Restaurant, Ellen's Starlite Diner)

Marital Status: Married television director Harry Falk, November 26, 1965, divorced, March 24, 1970; married rock promoter Michael Tell, May 11, 1970, separated June 1970, annulled, June 4, 1971; married actor John Astin, August 5, 1972, divorced, 1984; married Sgt. Michael Pearce, March 15, 1986; three sons, Sean and Mackenzie Astin, Kevin Pearce

Books: Autobiography: *Call Me Anna* (1987, Duke played herself in the 1990 TV movie based on her memoirs); *About: A Brilliant Madness*, by Patty Duke and Gloria Hochman (1992); *Patty Duke: A Bio-Bibliography*, by Stephen L. Eberly (1988)

In her touching 1987 autobiography, *Call Me Anna*, resilient, multitalented actress Patty Duke revealed a largely painful life story that reads almost like fiction. However, the ups and downs of this life as shared by she who lived it were very moving, sometimes disturbing, and very real.

Anna Marie Duke's pre-teen years were spent in Manhattan with her family. Her earliest recollections were of her parents' constant fights, culminating in John and Frances separating when Anna was six. Her dad moved into a bachelor apartment, eventually dying of alcoholism in a boarding house in 1962 at age fifty. Anna's mother, Frances, was depressed and often violent towards her children. She was first hospitalized for depression when Anna was about six, and would be institutionalized two more times before finally being diagnosed as a manic-depressive.

At age eight, in 1954, perhaps to create the life she wanted but didn't have, Anna decided to become an actress, which led to John and Ethel Ross being hired as her managers. The Rosses, ambitious to a fault, decided to "recreate" Anna—first, they decreased her official age from eight to six and then they gave her a new name. "Okay, we've finally decided, we're gonna change your name. Anna Marie is dead. You're Patty now." To Duke, this is remembered as "the beginning of the little by little murder of Annie Marie Duke and the rebuilding of the Frankenstein's monster that became Patty Duke."

Patty's memories of John and Ethel Ross are horrific: sexual molestation by an often-drunk John; the Rosses spending most of Patty's money; Frances Duke reduced to doing the Rosses' laundry; no friends or privacy, and alcohol and prescription drugs. Patty became an alcohol abuser in her mid-teens, drinking more heavily as she got older.

After being sent on audition after audition, ten-year-old Patty achieved her first speaking role onscreen, in 1956, on the television anthology series *Armstrong Circle Theatre*, as a young girl who is separated from her mother on "The S.S. *Andrea Doria*."

Two years later, after still more auditions, she landed a role on a fifteen-minute daytime soap opera, *The Brighter Day*. She played Ellen Dennis from 1958–59. In her autobiography, she shared a soap memory:

"It was done live, without a teleprompter, and one day I forgot my lines. I had a 104-degree fever.... I'd throw up just before I made an entrance and once again after I made an exit.... I was supposed to introduce Hal Hol-brook's character, the Reverend Dennis, but I was so sick I couldn't remem-ber even that much.... I looked over at Hal. He wanted to save me, but the terror was contagious. He had the same scared look on his face I did and now he couldn't remember his [character's] name either... then from nowhere he blurted out, 'She's been with—*me*!'." Such training was good for Patty: "I've always been grateful that I began acting during what's come to be known as the 'golden age' of live TV."

Her 1959 Broadway stage debut, in the story of Helen Keller and Anne Sullivan, *The Miracle Worker,* saw Patty deliver a splendid portrayal of blind-deaf-mute Keller. *The Miracle Worker,* costarring Anne Bancroft as Sullivan, ran 719 performances at the Playhouse Theatre. Bancroft and Patty would revive their characters in the 1962 film adaptation for which Patty won the Academy Award as Best Supporting Actress. In 1979, in a made-for-TV movie of the same name, a more mature Duke played Anne Sullivan.

In 1963, ABC debuted *The Patty Duke Show.* The frothy TV sitcom aired on Wednesday nights and lasted 104 episodes, through 1966. In it, Patty played the dual roles of "diff'rent as night and day" cousins Patty (who "loves her rock 'n' roll—a hot dog makes her lose control") and Cathy (who "adores a minuet, the *Ballet Russe*, and crepe Suzette") Lane, and won a 1963 Best Series Actress Emmy.

Patty has been married four times: to Harry Falk, thirteen years her sen-ior, in 1965; to Michael Tell, a thirteen-day union, in 1970; to actor John Astin, father of her sons Mackenzie and Sean; and, finally, on March 15, 1986, to Army sergeant Michael Pearce, eight years her junior.

Her career, as ever, kept on rolling through the decades, with a bounty of television and theatrical movies, as well as several series: *It Takes Two* from 1982–83, *Hail to the Chief* in 1985 (in which Duke played the first female U.S. president), and *Karen's Song* in 1987 (fellow soap alumna, **Teri Hatcher,** played Duke's daughter). Patty remains, perennially, a fixture on television, gracing the small screen with her dynamic, telling perform-ances, combining powerful technique with a sense of enjoyment. Aware of the public's delight in nostalgia, Duke revived what was perhaps her great-est TV success, reuniting with herself for the 1999 TV movie *The Patty Duke Show Reunion Movie.* The difference? Former twin teen idols Patty and Cathy Lane are now, of course, grandmothers!

The turning point for Duke was her 1982 diagnosis of bipolar disorder, or manic-depressive illness. It could have ruined her life. Instead, it brought her peace, relief, and a purpose. "I've survived," Patty Duke concludes, in the last line of her autobiography. "I've beaten my own bad system and on some days, on most days, that feels like a miracle."

Films: 1955: *I'll Cry Tomorrow.* 1956: *Somebody Up There Likes Me.* 1958: *The Goddess*; *Country Music Holiday.* 1959: *4-D Man*; *Happy Anniversary.*

1962: *The Miracle Worker*. 1965: *Billie*. 1966: *The Daydreamer* (voice only). 1967: *Valley of the Dolls*. 1969: *Me, Natalie*. 1971: *You'll Like My Mother*. 1978: *The Swarm* (billed as Patty Duke Astin). 1982: *By Design*. 1986: *Willy/Milly*. 1992: *Prelude to a Kiss*. 1996: *Harvest of Fire*.

TV movies: 1970: *My Sweet Charlie*. 1971: *If Tomorrow Comes*; *Two on a Bench*; *She Waits*. 1972: *Deadly Harvest*. 1974: *Nightmare*. 1976: *Look What's Happened to Rosemary's Baby*. 1977: *Killer on Board*; *Curse of the Black Widow*; *Fire!*; *Rosetti and Ryan: Men Who Love Women*; *The Storyteller*. 1978: *A Family Upside Down*; *Having Babies III*. 1979: *Before and After*; *Hanging by a Thread*; *The Miracle Worker*. 1980: *The Babysitter*; *Mom, the Wolfman and Me*; *The Women's Room*. 1981: *Please Don't Hit Me, Mom*; *The Violation of Sarah McDavid*. 1982: *Something So Right*. 1983: *September Gun*. 1984: *Best Kept Secrets* (billed as Patty Duke Astin). 1986: *A Time to Triumph*. 1987: *Fight for Life*. 1988: *Perry Mason: The Case of the Avenging Ace*; *Fatal Judgement*. 1989: *Everybody's Baby: The Rescue of Jessica McClure*; *Amityville: The Evil Escapes*. 1990: *Always Remember I Love You*; *Call Me Anna*. 1991: *Absolute Strangers*. 1992: *A Killer Among Friends*; *Grave Secrets: The Legacy of Hilltop Drive*; *Last Wish*. 1993: *A Matter of Justice, No Child of Mine*; *Family of Strangers*. 1994: *Cries from the Heart*; *One Woman's Courage*. 1995: *When the Vows Break*. 1996: *Race Against Time: The Search for Sarah*. 1997: *A Christmas Memory*; *The Disappearing Act*. 1998: *When He Didn't Come Home*. Forthcoming: *The Patty Duke Show Reunion Movie*.

TV miniseries: 1961: *The Power and the Glory*. 1976: *Captains and the Kings* (billed as Patty Duke Astin). 1984: *George Washington*. 1986: *George Washington II: The Forging of a Nation*.

TV series: 1958: *Kitty Foyle*. 1958–59: *The Brighter Day*. 1963–66: *The Patty Duke Show*. 1968: *Journey to the Unknown*. 1982–83: *It Takes Two* (billed as Patty Duke Astin). 1985: *Hail to the Chief*. 1987: *Karen's Song*. 1995: *Amazing Grace*.

Meet Ellen's *The Brighter Day*

✒ The character of Ellen Dennis on *The Brighter Day* (1954–62) was played by Patty Duke (1958–59) and Lanna Saunders (1960). Saunders would later go on to play Sister Marie Horton on *Days of Our Lives* from 1979–85.

Duke was not the only famous graduate of *The Brighter Day*: also in the ensemble cast over the years were Hal Holbrook, Lois Nettleton, Jack Lemmon, and William Windom. The CBS show, created by Irna Phillips, had been a thriving radio program since 1948 when it was transitioned to television.

From 1954–56, it was on both radio and television: the radio offering was an audio repeat of the day's video episode. The year the radio soap went off the air, 1956, was the year of the TV soap's greatest popularity: it was the number four soap, behind *Search for Tomorrow*, *The Guiding Light*, and *Love of Life*.

Each episode opened with the haunting words: "Our years are as the falling leaves. We live, we love, we dream, and then we go. But somehow, we keep hoping, don't we, that our dreams come true on that brighter day."

In 1961, *The Brighter Day* expanded from its original fifteen-minute length to a half-hour format, and had myriads of writers, producers, and time slots. Such changes are deadly to any TV program that needs to maintain an audience base. On September 28, 1962, the show went off the air, and actor Paul Langton, in his character as Walter Dennis, gathered his onscreen family around the camera and said to home viewers:

"The microphones can't pick up the voices, and soon the picture will fade. If, on occasion, you think of us, we hope your memory will be a pleasant one."

• •

Academy Award Winners Who Were on the Soaps

F. Murray Abraham (1984 Best Actor for *Amadeus*)—*How to Survive a Marriage*

Kathy Bates (1990 Best Actress for *Misery*)—*All My Children*

Warren Beatty (1981 Best Director for *Reds*)—*Love of Life*

Ed Begley Sr. (1962 Best Supporting Actor for *Sweet Bird of Youth*)—*Guiding Light*

Ellen Burstyn (1974 Best Actress for *Alice Doesn't Live Here Anymore*)—*The Doctors* (known at the time as Ellen MacRae)

Joan Crawford (1945 Best Actress for *Mildred Pierce*)—*The Secret Storm*

Robert De Niro (1974 Best Supporting Actor for *The Godfather Part II*; 1980 Best Actor for *Raging Bull*)—*Search for Tomorrow*

Sandy Dennis (1966 Best Supporting Actress for *Who's Afraid of Virginia Woolf?*)—*The Guiding Light*

Olympia Dukakis (1987 Best Supporting Actress for *Moonstruck*)—*Search for Tomorrow*

Patty Duke (1962 Best Supporting Actress for *The Miracle Worker*)—*The Brighter Day*

Jose Ferrer (1950 Best Actor for *Cyrano de Bergerac*)—*Another World*

Joan Fontaine (1941 Best Actress for *Suspicion*)—*Ryan's Hope*

Lee Grant (1975 Best Supporting Actress for *Shampoo*)—*Search for Tomorrow*

Eileen Heckart (1972 Best Supporting Actress for *Butterflies Are Free*)—*One Life to Live*

Charlton Heston (1959 Best Actor for *Ben-Hur*)—*The Bold and the Beautiful*

Dustin Hoffman (1979 Best Actor for *Kramer vs. Kramer*; 1988 Best Actor for *Rain Man*)—*Search for Tomorrow*

Celeste Holm (1947 Best Supporting Actress for *Gentleman's Agreement*)—*Loving*

Kim Hunter (1951 Best Supporting Actress for *A Streetcar Named Desire*)—*The Edge of Night*

Tommy Lee Jones (1993 Best Supporting Actor for *The Fugitive*)—*One Life to Live*

Kevin Kline (1988 Best Supporting Actor for *A Fish Called Wanda*)—*Search for Tomorrow*

Jack Lemmon (1955 Best Supporting Actor for *Mister Roberts*; 1973 Best Actor for *Save the Tiger*)—*The Brighter Day* and *The Road of Life*

Anne Revere (1945 Best Supporting Actress for *National Velvet*)—*Ryan's Hope*

Mercedes Ruehl (1991 Best Supporting Actress for *The Fisher King*)—*The Doctors*

Susan Sarandon (1995 Best Actress for *Dead Man Walking*)—*A World Apart* and *Search for Tomorrow*

Gale Sondergaard (1936 Best Supporting Actress for *Anthony Adverse*)—*Best of Everything* and *Ryan's Hope*

Beatrice Straight (1976 Best Supporting Actress for *Network*)—*Love of Life* and *Santa Barbara*

Elizabeth Taylor (1960 Best Actress for *Butterfield 8*; 1966 Best Actress for *Who's Afraid of Virginia Woolf?*)—*All My Children* and *General Hospital*

Ernest Thompson (1980 Best Writer for *On Golden Pond*)—*Somerset*

Marisa Tomei (1992 Best Supporting Actress for *My Cousin Vinny*)—*As the World Turns*

Christopher Walken (1978 Best Supporting Actor for *The Deer Hunter*)—*The Guiding Light*

Teresa Wright (1942 Best Supporting Actress for *Mrs. Miniver*)—*Guiding Light*

• •

Laurence Fishburne

When I was fourteen, people said I looked forty. But now maybe they'll reverse it and say I look twenty.

—Laurence Fishburne, 1998

From 1973–76 Laurence Fishburne played Joshua West, a young drug-dealing street kid, on One Life to Live. *Courtesy of Archive Photo.*

Born: July 30, 1961, in Augusta, Georgia, to Laurence John and Hattie Bell Crawford Fishburne; birth name, Laurence Fishburne III

Education: New York High School for the Performing Arts and Lincoln Square Academy (New York City)

Debuts: stage—*In My Many Names and Days* (1971); television—*If You Give a Dance You Gotta Pay the Band* (1972); film—*Cornbread, Earl and Me* (1975)

Awards: Tony Award, Drama Desk Award, Outer Critics Circle Award and Theatre World Award, all for his role as Sterling Johnson in *Two Trains Running*, 1992; Emmy Award as Best Guest Actor in a Drama for *Tribeca: The Box*, 1993

Honors: Nominated for 1994 Academy Award; nominated for 1996 Emmy Award

Marital Status: Married Hajna Moss, July 1, 1985, divorced, 1991; children, Langston Issa and Montana Isis

I know that people think I'm older, but, hey, I'm over letting that bother me." The rather comical plight of Laurence Fishburne is perhaps shared by all personalities who grew up on screen. Given the opportunity to chart his professional growth from age twelve, audiences have witnessed remarkable progress and diversity.

Laurence Fishburne III was raised in the Park Slope section of Brooklyn, New York, by his mother, Hattie, a divorced teacher of math and science;

his father, Laurence, was a social worker. In the sometimes tough neighborhoods, Larry was a good student who excelled at basketball and acting; his English professor godfather shared Hattie's opinion that Larry had real talent. Soon the youngster was being shuffled from one Manhattan audition to another. In 1971, he made his stage debut off-Broadway in the New Federal Theatre's production of Charles Fuller's *In My Many Names and Days*. The next year saw his television debut in an ABC Theatre presentation of *If You Give a Dance You Gotta Pay the Band*. One of this episode's viewers, soap opera maven Agnes Nixon, saw such potential in young Larry that she cast him on her ABC soap creation, *One Life to Live*, as Joshua West. Fishburne was in a professional haze through most of the 1973–76 soap experience, noting, "I didn't know who any of the people were I was working with.... They were just grown people to me." He left the daytime drama in 1976, having shown great depth and maturity in a challenging part.

Just seven days before his thirteenth birthday, *Daily Variety* reported that Larry had been signed for his movie debut in *Hit the Open Man*, later re-titled *Cornbread, Earl and Me* (1975). When he was fourteen, he began work on a film that would be released three years after principal shooting began: *Apocalypse Now* (1979). To gain the coveted part of Bronx-born sailor Clean, Larry lied about his age. The hardships endured by cast and crew during filming in the Philippines were formidable, headed by costar Martin Sheen's heart attack, and is chronicled in the documentary *Hearts of Madness: A Filmmaker's Apocalypse* (1991).

For the next several years, Larry was offered only small acting roles. He eventually landed the part of Cowboy Curtis in 1981 on, of all things, a bizarre children's TV series, *The Pee-wee Herman Show*. In 1983, he appeared in a biopic centered on the story of Medgar Evers, *For Us, the Living*, beginning a series of appearances in films which focused on African-American themes, including *The Cotton Club* (1984) and *The Color Purple* (1985). He married Hajna Moss in 1985 and the couple had two children—son Langston (b. 1987), daughter Montana (b. 1991)—before divorcing. After one more appearance on what was now called *Pee-wee's Playhouse*, in 1986, and after a spell of film appearances in forgettable vehicles, things started to perk professionally for the twenty-five-year-old Larry.

On the set of *Pee-wee's Playhouse*, Larry had met a young fellow film hopeful, John Singleton, who was at the time a studio security guard. Singleton would later direct Fishburne in his breakthrough screen role as Furious Styles in *Boyz N the Hood* (1991): Larry made his part, of a divorced father, look effortless. The grim movie, set in the ghetto section of south central Los Angeles, was marked by brilliant acting, yet its merits were overshadowed by violence related to its showings in twelve states, leaving three moviegoers dead. Nineteen theatres pulled the movie, which costarred another future soap star, Nia Long.

The next year, 1992, Larry conquered Broadway, sweeping all major awards, including the coveted Tony, as Best Actor for August Wilson's *Two Trains Running*, in which he revived the role of Sterling Johnson that he had played at the Yale Repertory Theatre years earlier.

His performance as talented, violent singer Ike Turner in *What's Love Got to Do with It* (1993) earned him an Oscar nomination. In 1994, he returned to the legitimate theater to write, direct, and star in the one-act play *Riff Raff*, which sold out its entire New York City run, even before being reviewed.

In 1995, Larry starred in the title role of Kenneth Branagh's *Othello*, the first African American to play Shakespeare's Moorish general on the big screen. The *San Francisco Bay Guardian* raved that Fishburne was the "possessor of the best frown, the angriest eyes, the biggest pores, and the most righteous indignation in the household-name industry."

Fishburne has made an actor's name for himself by not fitting into any mold. In 1995, he received much praise (Emmy, Golden Globe, and Cable Ace Award nominations and winner of the NAACP Image Award) for playing heroic Hannibal "Iowa" Lee Jr., in the HBO cable movie *The Tuskegee Airmen*, an account of America's first black combat pilots in World War II. In 1997, he served as both executive producer and star of *Hoodlum*, as Ellsworth "Bumpy" Johnson, the defiant ex-con who became the godfather of Harlem in the 1930s. He was joined in that film by another former soap star (now an even more famous film star), **Cicely Tyson**, who played the manager of the prostitute racket in Harlem, Madame Stephanie St. Clair.

Unlike many child stars who find difficulty in the transition to adulthood, Laurence Fishburne continues to redefine himself as an actor, impressing audiences in the process.

Films: 1975: *Cornbread, Earl and Me*. 1979: *Apocalypse Now**; *Fast Break* (billed as Laurence Fishburne III). 1980: *Willie and Phil*. 1981: *Death Wish II* (billed as Laurence Fishburne III). 1983: *Rumble Fish**. 1984: *The Cotton Club*. 1985: *The Color Purple*. 1986: *Band of the Hand*; *Quicksilver*. 1987: *Cherry 2000**; *Gardens of Stone*; *A Nightmare on Elm Street 3: Dream Warriors*. 1988: *Red Heat*; *School Daze*. 1990: *King of New York*. 1991: *Boyz N the Hood*; *Cadence**; *Class Action**. 1992: *Deep Cover**. 1993: *What's Love Got to Do with It?*; *Searching for Bobby Fischer*. 1995: *Othello*; *Just Cause*; *Bad Company*; *Higher Learning*. 1996: *Fled*. 1997: *Hoodlum* (also executive producer); *Event Horizon*. 1998: *Welcome to Hollywood*; Forthcoming: *Matrix*; *Once In the Life* (also producer/director). * billed as Larry Fishburne

TV movies: 1980: *A Rumor of War*. 1983: *For Us, the Living*. 1990: *Decoration Day*. 1995: *The Tuskegee Airmen*. 1997: *Miss Evers' Boys* (also executive producer). 1998: *Always Outnumbered, Always Outgunned* (also executive producer).

TV miniseries: 1993: *The Wild West.*

TV series: 1973–76: *One Life to Live.* 1980: *The Six O'Clock Follies.* 1981: *The Pee-wee Herman Show.* 1986: *Pee-wee's Playhouse*

Meet Josh

⎚ On *One Life to Live*, the character of Joshua West Hall was played by Laurence Fishburne (1973–76) and Todd Davis (1977).

Eileen Riley Siegel (Alice Hirson) lost her beloved husband Dave (Allan Miller) in 1972, and it seemed as if she would never stop mourning. Those around her tried to ease her pain: Dr. Dorian (Nancy Pinkerton), for instance, prescribed medication to alleviate the grief. She was soon hooked, and when the medication ran out, she turned to the streets to find more drugs. She found a source, in the person of young street kid Joshua West.

Josh, though, did clean up his act after being adopted by newlyweds Ed (Al Freeman Jr.) and Carla (Ellen Holly) Hall in 1974. Carla, who had once tried to pass for a white woman, soon became proud of her heritage, and settled into a contented happy family life.

Frances Fisher

Kinda hit a ceiling.

—Frances Fisher, on why she left soaps, 1994

Monticello's dynamic redhead, Deborah Saxon, played on The Edge of Night *by Frances Fisher, from 1976–81. Fisher also appeared on* Guiding Light *in 1985, as Suzette Saxon. Courtesy of* Soap Opera Digest.

Born: May 11, 1952, to Bill and Olga Fisher, in England

Education: Luther Stark High School and Orange Community Playhouse (Orange, Texas)

Debuts: television—*The Edge of Night* (1976) as Deborah Saxon; film—*Can She Bake a Cherry Pie?* (1983)

Marital Status: Married Billy Mack Hamilton, 1970, divorced, 1972; daughter, Francesca (from relationship with actor/director Clint Eastwood)

Her role as icy, snobbish Ruth DeWitt Bukater in the 1997 mammoth film *Titanic* catapulted Frances Fisher into unforeseen visibility. Yet, her over-twenty-year career has been filled with ups, downs, and much turmoil; her life, in its beginnings, reads like a daytime drama plot.

British-born Frances Fisher moved nine times by the time she was twelve, and her family settled in Orange, Texas, approximately one hundred miles northeast of Houston. In the process, she lived in such varied places as Brazil, Columbia, England, France, Iowa, Italy, and Turkey, due to her father's position as a supervising oil refinery construction executive. She changed schools virtually once a year, eventually settling down in Texas' Lutcher Stark High School, from where she graduated in 1970. Diverse, certainly, but hardly a stable lifestyle for a youngster.

She was fifteen when, in 1967, her mother Olga died of heart failure. Three years later, at eighteen, she wed her high school sweetheart, Billy Mack Hamilton. Their marriage lasted two years. In Orange, she undertook a hopeful acting career by beginning studies and performances at Orange Community Playhouse, while earning a living as a secretary at Firestone. Performances in local repertory shows convinced Frances that she had found her real passion and her true career path. She quit Firestone and moved to New York.

Frances lived in New York for nearly fourteen years, studying acting and appearing in local productions. After a few years of auditions and small shows, in 1976 she landed a role in *The Edge of Night*, as Deborah Saxon, whom she would play for five years. Soon thereafter, she began studying at the Actors Studio, where she appeared in, among other shows, Sam Shepard's *Fool for Love*.

Still living in New York in 1985, she accepted a six-month contract from another CBS soap, *Guiding Light*, playing, ironically enough, another Saxon: Suzette. The role allowed Frances to thoroughly exhibit her talents, creating a character that evolved from an ambitious record promoter to a murderess.

In 1988, Frances relocated to Los Angeles, where she found a consistent stream of acting jobs. In the coming years, she combined TV movie parts, guest roles in TV series, and feature film assignments (*Patty Hearst, Pink Cadillac, L.A. Story*), uniformly showing great promise in small parts, before making a big splash in a very challenging performance.

It is not easy playing a living legend: this Frances did, in the very difficult role of comedic superstar Lucille Ball in the made-for-TV movie *Lucy & Desi: Before the Laughter* (1991), a biopic which chronicled the Arnaz family prior to 1951's *I Love Lucy*. Frances' red hair and big, expressive eyes made her a very convincing Lucille. That performance was noticed, and taken into account when she auditioned for, and won, a role in a western feature to be directed by Clint Eastwood, *Unforgiven*, the 1992 Academy Award-winning Best Film. In it, Frances played Strawberry Alice, a frontier prostitute, and her performance was highly acclaimed by the critics.

Fisher had met fifty-five-year-old Eastwood in 1988 when he cast her as Dinah in the 1989 big screen comedy *Pink Cadillac*. She calls the meeting "one of those life-changing moments," for it culminated in a romantic relationship that lasted six years. Their involvement broke up Eastwood's thirteen-year relationship with actress Sondra Locke. In 1993, their daughter, Francesca Ruth, was born. A year later, involved in another intense relationship, Eastwood left Fisher. Eastwood, since remarried, still maintains a good rapport with Frances and Francesca, and though Eastwood "has no set schedule to see her," according to Fisher, Francesca "loves him. He's her Daddy."

Today, audiences know Frances Fisher best for her role as Ruth DeWitt Bukater in the 1997 Academy Award-winning Best Film, *Titanic*, in which she elevated the term "snob" to a whole new level. Dressed in elegant period costumes, limited makeup and sweeping hairstyles, Frances was utterly convincing as the cold mother of Kate Winslet's Rose, the latter falling in love with **Leonardo DiCaprio**'s Jack Dawson. Though overshadowed by the fictional/factual plot line, Frances' depiction of determination in preserving her family's "old money" was a shining moment in an overall powerful cinematic tour de force.

With Frances Fisher fully in charge of her own destiny and her own career, her involvement with a sinking ship will stay as just one more bookmark in her continuous cinematic memory.

Films: 1983: *Can She Bake a Cherry Pie?* 1987: *Heart*; *Tough Guys Don't Dance*. 1988: *Bum Rap*; *Heavy Petting*; *Patty Hearst*. 1989: *Lost Angels*; *Pink Cadillac*. 1990: *Welcome Home, Roxy Carmichael*. 1991: *L.A. Story*; *Frame Up*. 1992: *Unforgiven*. 1993: *Frame-Up II: The Cover-Up*; *Molly & Gina*. 1994: *Babyfever*. 1995: *The Stars Fell on Henrietta*. 1996: *Female Perversions*; *Striptease*. 1997: *Wild America*; *Burnhill*; *Titanic*. Forthcoming: *True Crime*; *Je M'Appelle Crawford*.

TV movies: 1987: *Broken Vows*. 1989: *Cold Sassy Tree*; *Elysian Fields*. 1990: *A Promise to Keep*; *Sudie and Simpson*. 1991: *Lucy & Desi: Before the Laughter*. 1992: *Devlin*. 1993: *Attack of the 50 Ft. Woman*; *Praying Mantis*. 1995: *The Other Mother: A Moment of Truth Movie*.

TV series: 1976–81: *The Edge of Night*. 1985: *Guiding Light*. 1995–96: *Strange Luck*.

Meet a Pair of Saxons

On *The Edge of Night*, the role of Deborah Saxon was originated, and played solely, by Frances Fisher, from 1976–81.

Deborah, a wealthy socialite, was married to Tony Saxon (Louis Turenne).

On *Guiding Light*, the part of Suzette Saxon was originated, and played solely, by Frances Fisher, in 1985.

Suzette was a record company promoter, who took an interest in Lujack (Vincent Irizarry), a former street-tough-turned-nice guy rock singer. Meanwhile, Suzette's boyfriend, the treacherous David Preston (John Martinuzzi), was helping the crime lord "Largo" try to assassinate multimillionaire Kyle Sampson (Larkin Malloy, who, like Fisher, began his career on *The Edge of Night*). Preston's lover, Suzette, fell out of love, in a big way: she was jailed, after confessing to David's murder.

Calista Flockhart

I always know when people are talking about me. My left fibula itches.

—*Calista Flockhart, as* Ally McBeal *(1998)*

Calista Flockhart played an ambitious teen on Guiding Light in 1989. Video screen photo, collection of author.

Born: November 11, 1964, in Freeport, Illinois, to Ronald and Kay Flockhart; one brother, Gary

Education: Shawnee High School (Medford, New Jersey); Rutgers University (New Brunswick, New Jersey)

Debuts: television—*Guiding Light* (1989); film—*Quiz Show* (1994); Broadway— *The Glass Menagerie* (1994)

Awards: Won Theatre World Award and Clarence Derwent Award, for her role as Laura in *The Glass Menagerie*, 1994; won Golden Globe Award, for Best Performance by an Actress in a TV Series—Comedy/Musical, for her starring role in *Ally McBeal*, 1998

Honors: Nominated for Emmy Award, 1998; nominated for People's Choice Award, 1998; Nominated for Screen Actors Guild Award, 1998; nominated for Viewers for Quality Television Q Award, 1998; chosen by *People* magazine as one of the Fifty Most Beautiful People in the World (1998)

If there were a pictorial definition of "overnight" success, the face of Calista Flockhart would be its embodiment. After more than a decade of stage work, resulting in semi-obscurity, a TV series named *Ally McBeal* came along in 1997 and made both face and name household fixtures.

Named after her Greek great-grandmother, Calista once reluctantly revealed the meaning of her unique first name as "most beautiful."

Brought up in Iowa, Minnesota, and New York, Calista and the Flockhart family finally settled in Medford, New Jersey, where she attended high school. Following graduation, she enrolled in Rutgers University in 1983, where she majored in fine arts. After studying acting, performing in numerous school and community theater productions, and attaining her degree in 1987, Calista moved to New York to pursue an acting career.

The first stop in the Big Apple was the stage, where Flockhart flexed her dramatic muscles in a bounty of dramatic and comedic roles off-Broadway. A bit part on *Guiding Light* in late 1989 started her television résumé; her character didn't even have a name. However, it was enough of a chance for her to be noticed: she soon received a supporting part in the telefeature *Darrow* (1991), a biographical study of famed lawyer Clarence Darrow (1857–1938). The next year found her in her first starring role, the very dramatic title character in HBO's *Lifestories: Families in Crisis* episode "The Secret Life of Mary-Margaret: Portrait of a Bulimic."

However whirlwind those two years might sound, they were followed by lean ones. At least her stage work was gaining notice, particularly her performance as Irina in Anton Chekhov's *Three Sisters* in Chicago. However, television was not beckoning, and at one point in 1993 she was reduced to managing on a $400 salary for eight weeks of work in an off-off-Broadway show: Calista survived on a case of ravioli, a present from her brother.

Happily, 1994 opened more optimistically with her Broadway debut as Laura in a revival of Tennessee Williams' *The Glass Menagerie*. Excellent reviews were capped by two major theater awards. In addition, her notices propelled her into three big-screen assignments: a bit part in Robert Redford's *Quiz Show* (1994), a supporting role in the cable movie *Drunks* (1995), and, after being noticed by director Mike Nichols, a part in his major comedy hit, *The Birdcage* (1996), as a bride-to-be.

In February 1997, Calista returned to Broadway, again to star in *Three Sisters*, but this time in the role of villainous Natasha. She was with the show for almost two months when she learned of a new TV series being developed for the Fox network by industry wunderkind David E. Kelley: *Ally McBeal*. Kelley, in turn, had heard of Calista, from her stage successes, and wanted her to try out for the lead. Understandably, Calista was a bit sour on television and scoffed at auditioning, until friends literally dragged her to meet Kelley. The writer-producer, married to movie star Michelle Pfeiffer to whom Calista bears a remarkable resemblance, offered Flockhart the title role after this first meeting. (Several hundred actresses had already been turned down for the pivotal part of Ally in the hour-long series.)

Ally McBeal, boasting a marvelous cast which includes fellow soap alumna Jane Krakowski, is a rare hour-long comedy (dealing with a Boston law firm) which received a whopping ten Emmy nominations in its freshman year, 1997. One of these nominations, for Best Actress in a Comedy, went to Calista, whose visualized thoughts, underlying sarcastic manner, and dance sequences with a computerized baby have embodied the show's quirky approach to life's everyday occurrences. As Ally, Flockhart won a Best Actress Golden Globe in 1998.

Owing to her small-screen success, Calista returned to the big screen, appearing opposite **Kevin Bacon** in *Telling Lies in America* (1997). Film releases for 1999 include the role of Helena in *A Midsummer Night's Dream* and a part in *Like a Hole in the Head*, as well as *Pictures of Baby Jane Doe*, a 1996 independent film with a delayed release.

Much like her favorite actress, Lucille Ball, Calista Flockhart's career only began to take flight with the right vehicle and the right role. In another parallel to Ball's acting profession, Flockhart attained her success after years of hard work with limited broad notice. And, like Lucy, Calista promises to be a name that is not likely to be forgotten.

Films: 1994: *Quiz Show*; *Getting In*; *Naked in New York*. 1995: *Drunks*. 1996: *The Birdcage*; *Pictures of Baby Jane Doe* (unreleased to date). 1997: *Telling Lies in America*; *Milk and Money*. Forthcoming: *Like a Hole in the Head*; *A Midsummer Night's Dream*.

TV movie: 1991: *Darrow*.

TV series: 1989: *Guiding Light*; 1997–present: *Ally McBeal*.

Calista's Bit

🖵 On *Guiding Light*, Calista Flockhart appeared in a bit part in late 1989, in a sequence involving wacko Sonni Lewis (Michelle Forbes). Calista's character complained about being tired, but grateful for the ten dollars an hour she would be receiving for her part in one of the many dastardly deeds Sonni committed in her whirlwind of amnesia, dual personality, and mental illness. Calista made her brief time on screen count: in a denim jacket and with longer blonde hair, her facial expressions were more telling than her lines.

Vivica A. Fox

My life changed in a day—Independence Day.
—Vivica A. Fox, 1997

Vivica A. Fox portrayed Maya on the groundbreaking soap Generations *from 1989–91. Fox also appeared on* Days of Our Lives *in 1988, and* The Young and the Restless *in 1994. Video screen photo, collection of author.*

Born: July 30, 1964, Indianapolis, Indiana; birth name, Vivica Anjanetta Fox; one older sister and two older brothers

Education: Golden West College (Huntington Beach, California)

Debuts: television—*Days of Our Lives* (1988) as Carmen; film—*Born on the Fourth of July* (1989)

Award: Won MTV Movie Award, for Best Kiss, in *Independence Day* (award shared with Will Smith), 1997

Honors: Chosen by *People* magazine as one of the Fifty Most Beautiful People in the World (1997); nominated for Image Award, 1998; nominated for MTV Movie Awards, 1997 and 1998

Marital Status: Married singer Sixx-Nine, December 29, 1998

When producers are looking for black and sassy, they call me. These characters are actually a reflection of me. I'm a sassy little thing." Strong and confident words from a most confident and strong young actress, Vivica A. Fox, who is enjoying success on both big and small screens.

Vivica Anjanetta Fox has fond memories of her childhood, with family all around, and lots of good smells emanating from the kitchen. "I'm a real mashed potatoes and macaroni-and-cheese kind of girl," Fox admitted. Years later, in *Soul Food* (1997), these aspects of home and family would be a pleasant launching place for Vivica.

Directly after her 1986 college graduation in Long Beach, California, she started the long climb up the performers' ladder that, at times, has rungs that seem to be set very far apart. Her ascent began with a recurring job on *Days of Our Lives* in 1988, playing the short-lived role of Carmen. Later came a spot on *Generations*. She played Maya on this soap, which ran until January 1991. At long last Vivica was noticed.

During that time, Fox made her feature film debut as a hooker in *Born on the Fourth of July* (1989). She also had guest spots on numerous TV shows, including *The Fresh Prince of Bel-Air*, where she first met and befriended the show's star, Will Smith.

The next years were quite a challenge for Vivica, who plugged away on failed TV series (*Living Dolls, In the House, Out All Night*), a brief 1994 role as Dr. Stephanie Simmons on *The Young and the Restless*, and minor participation in a cable TV movie, *The Tuskegee Airmen* (1995). She was ready to call it a career when friend Will Smith put in a word for her on something called *Independence Day* (1996). "I was unemployed, broke. But my parents were extremely supportive; my family lent me money. And I had an acting coach who said your life can change in a day, you've gotta stay focused."

When Fox auditioned for *Independence Day*, producer/director Roland Emerich immediately wanted to cast her. Vivica recalled, "Roland saw the chemistry I had with Will, but the studio wanted a better-known actress. Will went to bat for me. I'd had a guest spot on his TV show, so he knew I could handle the part."

The role of Smith's stripper girlfriend, who pulls herself, her son, and their dog through the debris of an alien invasion, was the kickoff to her busiest year—a season of employment that included the campy safe sex comedy *Booty Call* (1997). Her reasoning behind this role: "I didn't want to be known in Hollywood as Polly Pure Bread. I wanted to show I could be sexy and funny."

Vivica then garnered a costarring role on the short-lived sitcom, *Arsenio* (1997). "That show was dead in the water," Fox recalled. "I showed up, there were five Jewish people—all men—writing for an African-American couple of the '90s. Hello? You see somethin' wrong with that picture goin' in?"

Her next 1997 role got her excited: "I got to play Arnold Schwarzenegger's black babe in *Batman & Robin*," Vivica bubbled. "That makes me the first black woman in the *Batman* films."

Her next assignment was the charming *Soul Food* (1997), costarring Vanessa Williams and fellow soap alumna Nia Long. The movie centers around a bickering African-American family whose forty-year tradition of high-cholesterol Sunday dinners was threatened when the matriarch (Irma P. Hall) suffers a stroke. Director George Tillman Jr., had to tailor the shooting of *Soul Food* around *Batman & Robin*—hoops he was willing to jump through "because there was a sense that, with so many things going on, Vivica would be really hot by the time the movie came out."

Just when fans thought Vivica might be softening her image, she appeared in the riotous film *Why Do Fools Fall in Love* (1998), the story of the late singer Frankie Lyman (Larenz Tate), who wrote the title 1950s hit song, and died of a heroin overdose at age twenty-six. Vivica was seen as one of Lyman's three *simultaneous* wives, Elizabeth Waters.

At the same time that she was filming *Why Do Fools Fall in Love?*, Vivica was developing a new Fox (ironically enough) television series, *Getting Personal*. Vivica serves as both star and executive producer of the half-hour hit show, dealing with the antics in an advertising agency.

"I would love to be in a sitcom for five years—I could get married and have kids. Doing movies is hard work. I want to have regular hours."

The ball is rolling on the marriage part of that equation, as she married singer Sixx-Nine (his name refers to his height) on December 29, 1998, in Los Angeles.

Obviously, Vivica is a confident star-quality performer, whose memories of the lean years back in the late 1980s and early 1990s become more distant with each performance. "I'm definitely that sassy little actress, and a lot of people are diggin' on that vibe." In the case of Vivica A. Fox, we most assuredly dig.

Films: 1989: *Born on the Fourth of July*. 1996: *Set It Off*; *Independence Day*; *Don't Be a Menace to South Central While Drinking Your Juice in the Hood*. 1997: *Soul Food*; *Batman & Robin*; *Booty Call*. 1998: *Why Do Fools Fall in Love?* Forthcoming: *Killing Mrs. Tingle*; *Idle Hands*; *Thirty Wishes*.

TV movie: 1995: *The Tuskegee Airmen*. 1999: *A Saintly Switch*.

TV series: 1988: *Days of Our Lives*. 1989–91: *Generations*. 1992: *Out All Night*. 1994: *The Young and the Restless*. 1997: *Arsenio*. 1998–present: *Getting Personal* (also executive producer).

Meet Carmen, Maya, and Stephanie

⌗ On *Days of Our Lives*, the role of Carmen was played by Vivica A. Fox in 1988. This short-term part was recurring, and non-contract.

⌗ On *Generations*, the role of Maya was performed by Fox from 1989–91.

The show, created by Sally Sussman, was the first daytime serial in which one of the two major families involved in the story line was black. It ran on NBC from March 27, 1989, until its cancellation on January 25, 1991.

Vivica joined the cast line-up in late 1990, and quickly established herself as a beautiful young supporting actress. She played Maya, who was involved, off-and-on, with young college student Adam Marshall (Kristoff St. John).

🗹 On *The Young and the Restless*, Vivica A. Fox handled the recurring role of Dr. Stephanie Simmons, resident at Genoa City Memorial Hospital, in 1994.

Stephanie was a friend of another resident, Dr. Olivia Barber Hastings (Tonya Lee Williams), and was slated as a possible love interest for Olivia's eventual husband, new-to-town Malcolm Winters (Shemar Moore). Ironically, Malcolm's brother, Neil, is played by Kristoff St. John, temporarily reuniting the former *Generations* costars.

Jonathan Frakes

I knew this was a real part, a big one, and I had to get it.

—Jonathan Frakes, on Com. William Riker, 1997

Ten years before inaugurating the role of Commander Riker on Star Trek, *Jonathan Frakes spent 1977–78 as Tom Carroll on* The Doctors. *Video screen photo, collection of author.*

Born: August 19, 1952, in Bethlehem, Pennsylvania

Education: Pennsylvania State University (University Park); Harvard University (Cambridge, Massachusetts)

Debuts: television—*The Doctors* (1977) as Tom Carroll; film—*Gargoyles: The Heroes Awaken* (1994)

Marital Status: Married actress Genie Francis, May 28, 1988; two children, Jameson and Elizabeth

Book: *The Abductors: Conspiracy*, by Jonathan Frakes and Dean Wesley Smith (1996)

Each year, millions of self-professed "Trekkies" celebrate the phenomenon that is *Star Trek* at conventions and festivals worldwide. Previously the sole domain of William Shatner, Leonard Nimoy, and company, Jonathan Frakes joined the bandwagon in 1987, and, truly, the rest is continuing history.

Jonathan did undergraduate work at Pennsylvania State University and continued his education at Harvard, graduating in 1974, during which time he spent several seasons with the Loeb Drama Center. He then lived for five years in New York, appearing on and off-Broadway in several regional theater productions.

"I gave myself a five-year limit," Frakes recalls. "If I wasn't making a living at acting in five years, I would find something else to do. After a year and a half of being the worst waiter in New York and screwing up my back as a furniture mover, I got a role in *Shenandoah* on Broadway and then landed a part in *The Doctors*."

That TV part, as Tom Carroll, sustained the actor—gave him a living, so to speak—from 1977–78, when his less-than-powerful part was written out of the plot line.

In 1979, at the suggestion of his agent, Frakes moved to Los Angeles. "There's a cliché in this business," Jonathan noted, "that says the easy part of being an actor is doing the job. The hardest part is getting the job."

Perhaps his most memorable role from this early period was a two-episode stint on the popular CBS series *The Waltons* as Ashley Longworth Jr., in February and November of 1979. More television jobs followed, in movies (*Bare Essence*, *The Night the City Screamed*), in series (*Beulah Land*, *Bare Essence*, *Paper Dolls*), and in miniseries (*North and South*, *Dream West*). Two of these titles are very near and dear to the actor, not necessarily professionally, but definitely personally.

It was on the set of *Bare Essence*, the 1983 series, that Frakes first met Genie Francis, who had made perhaps soaps' greatest splash in the early 1980s, as half of super soap couple Luke and Laura on *General Hospital*. It was on the set of *North and South*, the 1985 miniseries about the Civil War, that the two reunited and fell in love. Jonathan and Genie married on May 28, 1988. They have two children, son, Jameson Ivor, born August 20, 1994, and daughter, Elizabeth, born May 30, 1997, and live in Los Angeles.

In 1987, Frakes accepted a role in, first, a TV movie, then a TV series, that changed his life and career: both called *Star Trek: The Next Generation*. He credits Gene Roddenberry, *Star Trek* creator, with giving him the initial insight necessary to make Riker as enduring a character as he is.

"Gene was so very non-Hollywood and quite paternal," Jonathan shares. "One of the things he said to me was, 'You have a Machiavellian glint in your eye. Life is a bowl of cherries.' I think Gene felt that way, which is why he wrote the way he wrote. He's very positive and Commander Riker will reflect that."

On the show, Jonathan Frakes portrayed Commander William Riker, the executive officer and second-in-command of the Starship *Enterprise*. During the third season (1989–90) of *Star Trek: The Next Generation*, Jonathan made his directorial debut with an episode entitled "The Offspring." He so impressed the executive producers with his efforts that he also directed two additional episodes in the fourth season, one in the fifth season, and two more in the sixth season.

Recently, Frakes has taken a more active role as a director, most notably on the *Star Trek* movies *First Contact* (1996) and *Star Trek: Insurrection* (1998), as well as in the sequel film *Total Recall 2* (1999). He also directed the video game *Star Trek: Klingon*, appeared in the video games *Multimedia Celebrity Poker* (1995) and *Star Trek: Generations* (1997), and hosted the popular TV series *Beyond Belief: Fact or Fiction*, which presented supernatural-based stories, challenging the audience to determine whether what they saw was factual or fictional.

With a thriving career, a happy family life, and a future place in *Star Trek* history assured, Jonathan Frakes can feel certain that he made the right decision not staying in the furniture moving business.

Films: 1987: *Star Trek: The Next Generation—Encounter at Farpoint.* 1994: *Star Trek: Generations; Camp Nowhere; Gargoyles: The Heroes Awaken* (voice only). 1996: *Star Trek: First Contact* (also director). 1998: *Star Trek: Insurrection* (also director). Forthcoming; *Total Recall 2* (director only).

TV movies: 1979: *Beach Patrol.* 1980: *The Night the City Screamed.* 1982: *Bare Essence.* 1989: *The Cover Girl and the Cop.* 1994: *Star Trek: The Next Generation—All Good Things....* (the final two-part airing of this series). 1996: *Brothers of the Frontier.*

TV miniseries: 1980: *Beulah Land.* 1985: *North and South.* 1986: *Dream West; North and South II.* 1987: *Nutcracker; Money, Madness & Murder.* 1994: *Heaven & Hell: North & South, Book III.*

TV series: 1977–78: *The Doctors.* 1983: *Bare Essence.* 1984: *Paper Dolls.* 1987–94: *Star Trek: The Next Generation* (also occasional director). 1993: *Star Trek: Deep Space Nine* (director only). 1994: *Gargoyles* (voice only); *University Hospital* (director only). 1995: *Star Trek: Voyager* (director only). 1996: *Gargoyles: The Goliath Chronicles* (voice only). 1998–present: *Beyond Belief: Fact or Fiction* (host).

Interactive: 1995: *Multimedia Celebrity Poker; Star Trek: The Next Generation—A Final Unity* (voice only). 1996: *Star Trek: Klingon* (director only). 1997: *Star Trek: Generations.*

Meet Tom Carroll

⊏╕ On *The Doctors*, the part of Tom Carroll was played by two prominent daytime alumni: James Rebhorn (1977) and Jonathan Frakes (1977–78). Rebhorn would later shine as incestuous stepfather Bradley Raines on *Guiding Light.*

Tom Carroll married popular character M. J. Match (Lauren White), who was a nurse at Hope Memorial Hospital, in 1978.

The Doctors was the first recipient of the then-new Daytime Emmy Award for Best Show, in 1972; ten years later, on December 31, 1982, the doors to Hope Memorial Hospital were permanently closed. *The Doctors* was canceled on the very same day as another NBC soap, *Texas.*

Morgan Freeman

He's got a credibility, and warmth, and humanity. He's like John Wayne and Gary Cooper. He comes on the screen, and you know who he is.
—Director Gary Fleder, on Morgan Freeman, 1997

During the early days of his diverse and illustrious career, Morgan Freeman played Bay City's dashing architect Roy Bingham on Another World *(from 1982–84). Courtesy of Photofest.*

Born: June 1, 1937, in Memphis, Tennessee to Grafton Curtis and Mayme Edna Revere Freeman

Education: Los Angeles City College; Pasadena Playhouse (California)

Debuts: stage—*Niggerlover* (1967); Broadway—*Hello, Dolly!* (1967); television—*The Electric Company* (1971); film—*Who Says I Can't Ride a Rainbow?* (1971)

Awards: Won Obie Awards for *Coriolanus* and *Mother Courage*, both in 1980, for *The Gospel at Colonus* in 1986, and for *Driving Miss Daisy* in 1988; won Golden Globe Award as Best Performance by an Actor in a Motion Picture—Comedy/Musical, for *Driving Miss Daisy*, 1990; won Silver Berlin Bear Award with Jessica Tandy for Best Acting Team for *Driving Miss Daisy*, 1990

Honors: Nominated for Academy Awards in 1988, 1990, and 1995

Marital Status: Married Jeanette Bradshaw, October 22, 1967, divorced, 1979; married Myrna Colley-Lee, June 16, 1984; four children, daughters Deena and Morgana (from his first marriage), sons Alfonso, Saifoulaye (from relationships with women he did not marry)

A late bloomer: the perfect label for actor Morgan Freeman. Late because his first leading role in a motion picture came in 1987, at age fifty. Bloomer because for that part he earned an Oscar nomination as Best

Supporting Actor. Yet, his is a career filled with diversity, strength, and still much potential.

Right out of high school in 1955, Morgan Freeman joined the U.S. Air Force, and stayed in the wild blue yonder for three years. "I'm just a born romantic," he noted of his experiences. "And, if you're a romantic, the military just beckons." After his service ended, he started studying at Los Angeles City College, and there recognized a yen for acting—he later transferred to performance study at the Pasadena Playhouse.

His earliest career work consisted of stage productions, including *Hello Dolly!* with Pearl Bailey in 1967. (That year, on October 22, Freeman married Jeanette Bradshaw. They were divorced in 1979.) He followed with a five-year stint (1971–76) on PBS's *The Electric Company*, an educational children's TV series, in the role of Easy Reader. He remembers the period with a quiet uneasiness:

"It was a great career booster. Doing it for five years, however, was not. I was terrified I was gonna wind up being Captain Kangaroo."

Morgan continued balancing stage and television work, with one feature film, his 1971 debut, *Who Says I Can't Ride a Rainbow?* He wouldn't appear in another feature film until the prison drama *Brubaker* (1980).

He started off the 1980s doing mostly stage work, complementing African-American–based vehicles with Shakespeare. His stage experience was an overwhelmingly positive one, as he shared in a *Filmweb* interview:

"When I was doing stage work I had total acceptance of myself as one of the chosen, the best, because I am looking at myself strictly through the eyes of the audience. I don't have to judge—they judge, and I come out looking real good."

In 1982, Morgan accepted a continuing role on *Another World*, as Roy Bingham. *AW* gave him his first real opportunity off the stage to make an impact with audiences, and he soon became one of the daytime drama's more popular leads. Freeman remained with the soap for seventeen months, and in that time refined his trademark creditable acting style. The same year he left, 1984, marked a beginning as well: on June 16, he married his second wife, Myrna Colley-Lee.

The next three years consisted of forgettable TV movies, and secondary roles in feature films like *Harry and Son* (1984) and *That Was Then...This Is Now* (1985). However, his career as a feature film actor really began with *Street Smart* (1987), in which he played shrewd, menacing pimp Fast Black, and earned his first Oscar nomination as Best Supporting Actor. With such recognition, his cinematic offers grew in stature and strength.

In 1989, Freeman revived a role he had acted on stage two years earlier: *Driving Miss Daisy*, as chauffeur Hoke Colburn alongside Jessica Tandy's Miss Daisy. The film was a huge success, winning Academy Awards for Best Film and Best Actress, and earning Freeman his second Oscar nomination, this time for Best Actor.

A bounty of choice roles in major films, seemingly one after another, followed: *Lean on Me* (1989), *The Bonfire of the Vanities* (1990), *Unforgiven* (1992), *The Shawshank Redemption* (1994, Oscar nomination for Best Actor), *Se7en* (1995), *Amistad* (1997), and *Hard Rain* (1998). All were strong, authoritative showcases, and in each Freeman commanded the screen.

Morgan is a very contemplative and complex man who has only one complaint at this point in his career: he feels typecast as a good guy, which is humorous since he earned his first Oscar nomination playing a tough street pimp. He has grown since. Now he is the owner of his own production company, Revelations Entertainment, and its premiere feature film, *Rendezvous with Rama*, was released in 1999.

"You ought to be glad about your life, whatever it is," Morgan Freeman concludes. "I've got all my fingers and toes. My eyesight is good. My smeller works. Of course, I'm happy about my life, because I'm still here."

Films: 1971: *Who Says I Can't Ride a Rainbow?* 1979: *Coriolanus*. 1980: *Brubaker*. 1981: *Eyewitness*. 1984: *Harry and Son; Teachers*. 1985: *Marie; That Was Then...This Is Now*. 1987: *Street Smart*. 1988: *Clean and Sober*. 1989: *Johnny Handsome; Driving Miss Daisy; Glory; Lean on Me*. 1990: *Bonfire of the Vanities*. 1991: *Robin Hood: Prince of Thieves*. 1992: *The Power of One; Unforgiven*. 1993: *Bopha!* (director only). 1994: *A Century of Cinema; The Shawshank Redemption*. 1995: *Se7en; Outbreak*. 1996: *Chain Reaction; Moll Flanders; Cosmic Voyage* (voice only). 1997: *The Long Way Home* (voice only); *Amistad; Kiss the Girls*. 1998: *Hard Rain; Deep Impact*. Forthcoming: *Rendezvous with Rama; Nurse Betty; Long Way to Freedom; Under Suspicion*.

TV movies: 1978: *Roll of Thunder, Hear My Cry*. 1979: *Hollow Image*. 1980: *Attica*. 1981: *The Marva Collins Story*. 1985: *Atlanta Child Murders; The Execution of Raymond Graham*. 1986: *Resting Place*. 1987: *Fight for Life*. 1988: *Clinton and Nadine*. Forthcoming: *Port Chicago Mutiny*.

TV miniseries: 1990: *The Civil War* (voice only).

TV series: 1971–76: The Electric Company. 1982–84: Another World.

Video: 1979: *Julius Caesar*.

Meet Roy

⧈ On *Another World*, the character of Roy Bingham was played by Morgan Freeman from October 1982 through April 1984.

Roy Bingham was an architect in Bay City. At first, he romanced secretary Quinn Harding (Petronia Paley). Meanwhile, Abel Marsh (Joe Morton) entered into a relationship with Quinn, while his brother Leo (Morton, in a dual role) swept Henrietta Morgan (Michele Shay) off her feet, despite the fact that Roy had fallen in love with her. Henrietta had been widowed when her husband, Lt. Bob Morgan (Robert Christian) died in 1983. Interestingly, previous to marrying Henrietta, Bob had been involved, too, with Quinn.

In 1984, Roy Bingham married Henrietta Morgan, and the two left Bay City that year.

• •

Where Did They Live?

The towns in which the soaps are set take on a very real meaning to daily viewers. Here are some of the names of the big, and small, cities that your favorite daytime television characters called home. (Missing from this list are those categorized as "the obvious": *Port Charles*, *Return to Peyton Place*, *Santa Barbara*, and *Somerset*—guess where these shows were set?!)

All My Children—Pine Valley
Another World—Bay City
As the World Turns—Oakdale
Ben Jarrod—Indian Hill
The Bennetts—Kingsport
Best of Everything—New York City
The Bold and the Beautiful—
    Los Angeles
Bright Promise—Bancroft
The Brighter Day—New Hope
Capitol—Washington, D.C.
The City—Soho
The Clear Horizon—Cape Canaveral
Concerning Miss Marlowe—
    New York City
Dark Shadows—Collinsport
A Date with Life—Bay City
Days of Our Lives—Salem
The Edge of Night—Monticello
For Richer, for Poorer—Point Clair
From These Roots—Strathfield
General Hospital—Port Charles
Golden Windows—New York City
The Greatest Gift—Ridgeton
Guiding Light—Springfield
Hawkins Falls—Woodstock
Hotel Cosmopolitan—New York City

Kitty Foyle—Philadelphia
Love Is a Many Splendored Thing—
    San Francisco
Love of Life—Barrowsville, then
    Rosehill
Lovers and Friends—Point Clair
Loving—Corinth
Miss Susan—Martinsville
Morning Star—New York City
Never Too Young—Malibu Beach
One Life to Live—Llanview
One Man's Family—San Francisco
Portia Faces Life—Parkerstown
The Road of Life—Merrimac
Ryan's Hope—New York City
Search for Tomorrow—Henderson
The Secret Storm—Woodbridge
Texas—Houston
Three Steps to Heaven—
    New York City
Today Is Ours—Bolton
Where the Heart Is—Northcross
Woman with a Past—New York City
The World of Mr. Sweeney—Mapleton
The Young and the Restless—
    Genoa City
Young Dr. Malone—Denison

• •

Sarah Michelle Gellar

In the first month alone, I tried to seduce my stepfather, burned my parents' divorce papers, slept with a stable boy and got arrested.
—Sarah Michelle Gellar, on her TV role as Kendall Hart, 1997

Her portrayal of conniving Kendall Hart on All My Children won Sarah Michelle Gellar an Emmy award in 1995. Video screen photo, collection of author.

Born: April 14, 1977, in New York City

Education: LaGuardia High School for the Performing Arts (New York City), Columbia Preparatory School (New York City), and Professional Children's School (New York City)

Debuts: television—*An Invasion of Privacy* (1983); film—*Over the Brooklyn Bridge* (1984); stage—*The Widow Claire* (1986)

Awards: Won Daytime Emmy Award, for Outstanding Younger Leading Actress in a Daytime Drama, for her role as Kendall Hart in *All My Children*, 1995; won Blockbuster Entertainment Award, for Favorite Supporting Actress—Horror, for her role as Helen Shivers in *I Know What You Did Last Summer*, 1998

Honors: Nominated for Daytime Emmy Award, 1994; chosen by *People* magazine as one of the Fifty Most Beautiful People in the World (1998)

Books: *Bite Me!; Sarah Michelle Gellar and Buffy the Vampire Slayer*, by Nikki Stafford (1998); *Buffy XPosed: The Unauthorized Biography of Sarah Michelle Gellar and Her OnScreen Character*, by Nadine Crenshaw (1998); *The Girl's Got Bite: The Unofficial Guide to Buffy's World*, by Kathleen Tracy (1998); *Sarah Michelle Gellar*, by Jennifer Baker (1998)

By day, she is a typical teenager coping with the traumas of being an outsider amidst the cliques at Sunnydale High School. By night, she is a martial arts master, battling to protect the world from the vampire armies of the dark. She is Buffy Summers—brought to spook-slaying life on TV by Sarah Michelle Gellar, whose martial arts acumen almost rivals her talent on the screen.

Raised on Manhattan's Upper East Side by her divorced school-teacher mother, Sarah displayed, early, a penchant for performance. At the age of three and a half, she was spotted by a talent agent while eating at a restaurant with her mother: within months, her show business career was under way.

Sarah appeared in over one hundred TV commercials, followed in 1983 by her TV debut in a Valerie Harper TV movie, *An Invasion of Privacy*. The next year, her feature film debut (*Over the Brooklyn Bridge*) was made, and, two years later, she had her stage bow in a Circle in the Square production of Horton Foote's *The Widow Claire*. Meanwhile, in 1985, Sarah got an extra role on TV's *Guiding Light*, playing a flower girl at the wedding of oncamera characters Mindy Lewis and Kurt Corday.

Gellar enrolled in the famous Professional Children's School in Manhattan, from which she graduated early, with honors. For Sarah, this school brought an end to a nagging problem she had endured previously: envy. "I didn't have anything in common with the kids," she recalled of her past experiences. "I never liked to talk about my acting because if I did, I was branded a snob, and if I didn't, I was still a snob. I would cry because I didn't understand why people didn't like me." It is, perhaps, this experience that helps Sarah so well understand the similar problems of socially outcast Buffy.

At age fourteen, Sarah won her first meaty role, that of teenaged Jacqueline Bouvier in the 1991 NBC miniseries *A Woman Named Jackie*, which costarred, as an adult Jackie, fellow soap alumna **Roma Downey**. The following year found Gellar starring in the syndicated TV series *Swan's Crossing*.

On February 24, 1993, at age sixteen, Sarah Michelle Gellar debuted in her first solid adult role, as Kendall Hart, long-lost daughter of Erica Kane (Susan Lucci), on *All My Children*. Sarah's ability to convince the world that she was the most evil person in Pine Valley earned her two daytime Emmy nominations, and a win in 1995.

After her first Emmy nomination for outstanding younger actress in 1994, the question of possible competition between Gellar and her onscreen mom, Lucci, was denied by Sarah: "I swear we are each other's biggest fan. Anything good that happens to one makes the other feel incredibly good." That year, both lost the Emmy prize.

The next year, on May 31, 1995, Gellar won her Emmy, and Lucci lost (after being nominated for a then-record seventeenth time). "It wasn't an easy time in my life," Sarah shared. "We didn't have a perfect working relationship. We, um, weren't going out to lunch." In the April 1998 *Rolling*

Stone magazine, Gellar further reflected, "I'm being polite by not saying what I'd like to say."

Twenty-four hours after the win, it was announced that Gellar was leaving *All My Children*. In 1996, she won the title role in the TV series *Buffy the Vampire Slayer*, based on the 1992 film of the same name that had starred Kristy Swanson and **Luke Perry**.

Buffy the Vampire Slayer is a cult favorite, and has afforded Sarah wide praise and critical attention, both for her charming, fresh approach to the role, and her uncanny ability to kick high while scantily clad. The program satisfied its audience's penchant for action, and, through its title character, brought to life both the pressures of high school and peer isolation. In addition, the fantasy elements (Buffy, social outcast, making her mark as a "vampire slayer" after hours) clicked with viewers. The show's popularity has also resulted in major film offers for its star. In 1997, Sarah appeared in two big-screen slasher thrillers, playing Helen Shivers, small-town-beauty-queen-with-a-damning-secret, in *I Know What You Did Last Summer*, and sorority girl Cici Cooper, who meets with a grisly end, in *Scream 2*. Both movies did quite well at the box office.

This is one young rising star with talent to match her potential. The promise she showed in her soap role continues to be realized, assuring that the name of Sarah Michelle Gellar will be seen on screens, small and big, for many kicks to come.

Films: 1984: *Over the Brooklyn Bridge*. 1988: *Funny Farm*. 1989: *High Stakes* (billed as Sarah Gellar). 1997: *Scream 2*; *I Know What You Did Last Summer*. 1998: *Small Soldiers* (voice only). 1999: *Simply Irresistible*; *Cruel Inventions*. Forthcoming: *Vanilla Fog*.

TV movies: 1983: *An Invasion of Privacy*. 1997: *Beverly Hills Family Robinson*.

TV miniseries: 1991: *A Woman Named Jackie*.

TV series: 1985: *Guiding Light*. 1989: *Girl Talk*. 1991: *Swans Crossing*. 1993–95: *All My Children*. 1997–present: *Buffy the Vampire Slayer*.

Meet The Flower Girl and Kendall

On *Guiding Light*, the role of one of the flower girls at the wedding of Kurt Corday (Mark Lewis) and Mindy Lewis (then Krista Tesreau) was played by Sarah Michelle Gellar for a two-day shoot in 1985. The nuptials were stunningly beautiful: however, it was never disclosed just who the two flower girls were (they were not Lewis relatives; possibly Corday family members). The marital union would be brief: Kurt died the next year.

📺 On *All My Children*, the role of Kendall Hart was originated, and solely played, by Sarah Michelle Gellar, from March 1993 through mid-1995.

Kendall got into no end of trouble in Pine Valley, beginning with deceiving Erica Kane (Susan Lucci) into hiring her as her television production assistant, gushing that she had idolized TV personality Erica all her life. Kendall knew that Erica was raped at fourteen, became pregnant, and gave the baby up for adoption. When Erica's mother Mona (Fran Heflin) noticed a telltale birthmark on Kendall, she knew that she was looking at Erica's daughter.

In Kendall's most wicked moment on *All My Children*, she bedded medical student Anton Lang (Rudolph Martin), telling Erica that her hubby Dimitri (Michael Nader) had raped her. Erica confronted her husband. Hallucinating back to the night years ago that Richard Fields (James A. Stephens) had molested her, Erica grabbed a letter opener, and in a moment of madness, plunged it into Dimitri's chest. He survived, but Erica went on trial nonetheless, explaining the delirium-driven motive. She was further implicated by a lying Kendall, who perjured herself by insisting that Dimitri had seduced her. Kendall eventually recanted, and went to jail for her crime.

Kendall later left town. Before departing Pine Valley, to return to Florida, Kendall apologized to Erica and the two made peace.

• •

Fast Food Fight

Sarah Michelle Gellar's (*Guiding Light, All My Children*) first commercial, in which she played a pint-sized pro-Burger King tot who chastised McDonald's for serving skimpy patties, resulted in the now-famous "Battle of the Burgers," a disparagement lawsuit between the rival fast-food giants, which was settled out of court in 1982. Even at age four, she had impact.

• •

Thomas Gibson

Well, I started as a kid—after swim meets I would do a Louis Armstrong impression.

—Thomas Gibson, on his acting habits, 1998

Born: July 3, 1962, in Charleston, South Carolina

Education: College of Charleston (South Carolina); Julliard School (New York City)

Stage Debuts: stage—*A Map of the World* (1985); television—*Lincoln* (1988); film—*Far and Away* (1992)

Marital Status: wife Cristina Gibson, 1993

You know, there is a certain amount of anonymity that actors have, but there is a trade-off. You know—you get better tables at restaurants." It is this tongue-in-cheek attitude, complementing a very serious actor, that characterizes Thomas Gibson. He takes himself very seriously... sometimes.

Thomas Gibson started acting at age ten, in children's theater, in his native South Carolina. He continued performing and studying with the Footlight Players at the Dock Street Theatre. His early roles were whimsical: Grumpy in *Snow White and the Seven Dwarfs*, The Mad Hatter in *Alice in Wonderland*, and Prince Charming in *Sleeping Beauty*. From 1979 to 1981, Thomas attended South Carolina's College of Charleston. During the summer of 1980, he interned at the Alabama Shakespeare Festival, where he was encouraged to apply to the famed Julliard School in Manhattan to continue his acting studies. He won a scholarship to that institution, and earned his Bachelor of Fine Arts degree there after what he categorized as "four very long years."

Gibson made his professional stage debut in David Hare's *A Map of the World* at the New York Shakespeare Festival Public Theatre in 1985. He later performed in such Shakespearean productions as *Twelfth Night, Two Gentlemen of Verona, Macbeth, Henry IV*, as well as revivals of Noël Coward's *Hay Fever* and Moliere's *The Miser*.

In 1988, he made his first television appearance, in Gore Vidal's TV movie *Lincoln*. The next year, he took a role as Derek Mason on *As the World Turns*. In a February 1998 chat session on the *TV Guide* Web site, Gibson noted how his daytime-drama alter ego met his end:

"Bomb explosion. You know, one of those great soap opera bomb explosions, in order to send Lily to Europe to have plastic surgery and become another actress." At the time, actress Martha Byrne decided to leave her role as Lily on *ATWT*, so the plastic surgery angle fit in beautifully with the eventual return of Lily in the person of actress Heather Rattray. Byrne has since returned to the show.

The next year, Thomas took a small fill-in part as Sam Fowler on *Another World*. He was on day-player status (on call while the regular was unavailable) when Robert Kelker-Kelly took time off from the series. In addition, in 1990, Gibson appeared in an ABC miniseries, *The Kennedys of Massachusetts*, playing family friend Peter Fitzwilliam.

Feature film work soon beckoned, with appearances in the period drama *Far and Away* (1992), in which he described his character as "The Anti-Cruise—The nemesis of Tom Cruise," and independent films *Barcelona* (1994) and *Sleep with Me* (1994). In a Canadian feature, *Love and Human Remains* (1993), Thomas was cast as a good-looking young gay man who gives up a successful acting career, fearing that his "fifteen minutes of fame" has passed. For the real-life Gibson, however, the fun was just beginning.

In 1996, he accepted a part on CBS's ongoing nighttime medical drama *Chicago Hope*, playing the pompous and rather obnoxious Dr. Daniel Nyland. He played the role until 1997 when a new program, and a fresh acting opportunity, emerged: *Dharma & Greg*.

Their screen pairing was highly unlikely: Dharma, madcap, earthy Bohemian, attracting the sole attentions of Greg, a privileged, if sometimes stuffy, attorney. However quirky, it clicked: Dharma and Greg Montgomery were voted "TV's Most Romantic Couple of 1998" by *TV Guide*. For good reason—the opportunities for slapstick and romantic comedy abound in this ABC series based in San Francisco, which has afforded Thomas a new brand of professional exposure.

Accordingly, Gibson has branched out, during his *Dharma & Greg* hiatus, into roles that cannot help but challenge him. Dark roles in TV movies like *The Devil's Child* (1997) and *Nightmare Street* (1998) stretch his acting possibilities. Gibson hosted a 1998 ABC-TV special, *Neighbors from Hell*, which featured horrific true stories of the people next door. Furthering the thrill was a wicked cable sequel miniseries, *More Tales of the City* (1998), in which he convincingly revived the role of bed-hopper-extraordinaire

Beauchamp Day, a character he had introduced in *Tales of the City* in 1993. *The Tales* were based on the stories of Armistad Maupin, and are delicious in their tartness.

Shakespearean roots, a hit comedy series, and spooky movies. Thomas Gibson does it all—from dark to funny to smarmy, and with each role, makes his name, his face, and his talent, increasingly unforgettable to a wide spectrum of viewers.

Films: 1992: *Far and Away*. 1993: *The Age of Innocence; Love and Human Remains*. 1994: *Barcelona; Men of War; Sleep with Me*. 1996: *To Love, Honor, and Deceive*. Forthcoming: *Eyes Wide Shut*.

TV movies: 1995: *Secrets*. 1996: *Night Visitors*. 1997: *The Devil's Child; Inheritance*. 1998: *Nightmare Street; A Will of Their Own*.

TV miniseries: 1988: *Lincoln*. 1990: *The Kennedys of Massachusetts*. 1993: *Tales of the City*. 1998: *More Tales of the City*. Forthcoming: *A Will of Their Own*.

TV series: 1989–90: *As the World Turns*. 1990: *Another World*. 1996–97: *Chicago Hope*. 1997–present: *Dharma & Greg*.

Meet Derek, and One-Time Sam

🗍 On *Another World*, Thomas Gibson filled in for an ill Robert Kelker-Kelly for a few episodes, on a day-to-day basis, in 1990. Sam Fowler, an artist, was written out of the story line in 1993. *Another World* fans did not see the last of Kelker-Kelly: he returned to the soap, in 1996, as Dr. Shane Roberts (masquerading as handyman Bobby Reno).

🗍 On *As the World Turns*, the character of Derek Mason was originated, and solely played, by Thomas Gibson, from 1989–90.

Lily (Martha Byrne), Lucinda Walsh's (Elizabeth Hubbard) adopted daughter, was wooed by and solely married the dashing-but-dangerous Derek Mason. He planned to kill her and inherit her fortune (which was sizable). Instead, the villain fell deeply in love with his victim—how that must have irked him!

Derek died in an explosion that he pre-planned for Lily. She left town, in her newly widowed horror. She came back with a new face (that of Heather Rattray), and resumed her seemingly-centuries-long infatuation with Holden Snyder (Jon Hensley).

Extra Beginners, Later Extraordinary

Courteney Cox tried out for the role of *As the World Turns'* Frannie Hughes when it was being recast in 1985. The part went to Julianne Moore. Cox did get a fleeting 1985 extra role, though, as young country club socialite Bunny.

Similarly, other performers who later had very successful film and/or TV careers languished in tiny and forgettable roles while in casts of various daytime soaps. Some of these include Leonard Nimoy, whose 1963 role as drug dealer Benny on *General Hospital* went nowhere, future Oscar winner Kathy Bates, who terrorized Erica Kane as a fellow prison inmate for a mere week on *All My Children* in 1984, and Brad Pitt, who never got past extra-status as high school jock Chris on *Another World* in 1987. Warren Beatty (on *Love of Life*), Robert De Niro and Dustin Hoffman (on *Search for Tomorrow*), John Travolta (on *The Edge of Night* and *The Secret Storm*), and Robert Urich (on *All My Children*), were likewise underused: proof that stardom only comes when the time is right.

Kelsey Grammer

Dr. Cunard (Kelsey Grammer) often had to defend his medical judgment in the emergency room on Another World *from 1984–85. Video screen photo, collection of author.*

Six months ago I was living in Boston. My wife had left me, which was very painful, then she came back to me, which was excruciating.
—Kelsey Grammer, *as Dr. Frasier Crane in* Frasier *(1993)*

Born: February 21, 1955, in St. Thomas, Virgin Islands, to Allen and Sally Grammer; birth name, Allen Kelsey Grammer; younger sister, Karen

Education: Julliard School (New York City)

Debuts: television—*Kennedy* (1983); film—*Runaway Brain* (1995)

Awards: Won Emmy Awards, as Outstanding Lead Actor in a Comedy Series, for his role as Dr. Frasier Crane on *Frasier*, 1994, 1995, and 1998; won Viewers for Quality Television Q Awards, as Best Actor in a Quality Comedy Series, for *Frasier*, 1995–97; won Golden Globe Award, for Best Performance by an Actor in a TV Series—Comedy/Musical, for *Frasier*, 1996

Honors: Nominated for Emmy Awards, 1988, 1990, 1996, and 1997; nominated for Golden Globe Awards, 1994, 1995, 1997, and 1998; nominated for Screen Actors Guild Awards, 1995–98; nominated for Q Award, 1998

Marital Status: Married Doreen Alderman, May 30, 1982, separated, 1984, divorced, 1990; married Leigh-Anne Csuhany, September 11, 1992, divorced, 1993; married model Camille Donatacci, August 2, 1997; three daughters, Spencer, Greer, and Kandace

Books: autobiography, *So Far* (1995); about, *Kelsey Grammer: The True Story*, by Jeff Rovin, with Kathleen Tracy and David Perrell (1995)

A quick quiz question: Who is the first actor in television history to be nominated for seven Emmy Awards (winning three) for playing the same role on three different shows? It's Kelsey Grammer, but before revealing all the details, it is important to learn how far this man has come to reach his current professional success.

Allen Kelsey Grammer was raised in New Jersey and Florida by his mother and grandmother. His father died when Kelsey was twelve, shot and killed by an assailant, who was later found not guilty by reason of insanity. The next year, 1968, his grandmother died. When Kelsey was twenty, his beloved sister Karen was kidnapped, raped, and murdered; five years later, in 1977, his two half-brothers died in a scuba-diving accident. By the age of twenty-five, tragedy was the cornerstone of this young man's life.

From his early teens, Kelsey was drawn to Shakespeare and the finer points of the English language, participating in stage performances in high school (coed prep school Pine Crest in Fort Lauderdale, Florida) and college (Julliard School, in New York City). He left Julliard after two years—*asked* to leave, chiefly due to Kelsey's lack of interest in any formal training (it is customary, at Julliard, to "prudently prune" the student body, retaining only the most promising apprentices). Kelsey knew that he wanted to be an actor, but he did not want to undertake an academic education to achieve his goals. He joined the Old Globe Theatre in San Diego, where he honed his skills in classic and comedic stage work. He spent most of his twenties in regional theater and off-Broadway, becoming an actor *his* way: by doing, rather than by studying. Then, television beckoned.

Grammer won a part in a 1983 TV miniseries, *Kennedy*, in which he portrayed Stephen Smith, husband of JFK's sister Jean Kennedy. He then spent six months on *Another World*, as Dr. Cunard, participating in many small-screen life-and-death emergency room dramas. It was his first steady work in this medium, but it was a far cry from the acclaimed doctor he would eventually portray on TV.

Psychiatrist Dr. Frasier Crane first saw life as an extra—playing a bar patron—on NBC's *Cheers* in 1986. The role of the acerbic, sometimes pompous Crane grew into a seven-year regular on the Boston-set sitcom. Grammer's chemistry with costars Shelley Long and Bebe Neuwirth made the character an instant hit with viewers, and a natural for a spin-off solo series when *Cheers* closed its doors in 1993 after eleven seasons. *Frasier* debuted that fall with psychiatrist Frasier Crane now in Seattle, Washington as home base, with both a newly divorced status, and a radio call-in show. *Frasier* was an immediate smash, eventually garnering Grammer three Emmys, a Golden Globe, and three Viewers for Quality Television Awards.

The actor made his starring debut in feature films in *Down Periscope* (1996) as Tom Dodge, the bumbling submarine commander in the slapstick military service comedy costarring **Lauren Holly**. Another Grammer big-screen portrayal of note is cynical Howard Spitz, a detective novelist-turned-children's book author, in *Writer's Block* (1998).

However satisfying his professional life was, the tragedies that hall-marked his early life stayed with Kelsey throughout the years. His first marriage, to Doreen Alderman, lasted from 1982–90, and produced one daughter, Spencer Karen (b. 1983). A relationship with Barrie Buckner produced a daughter, Greer, born in 1992. His second union, to Leigh-Anne Csuhany, lasted from September 1992 until their 1993 divorce and was tainted by her suicide attempt, which resulted in a miscarriage. In November 1994, a New Jersey girl alleged that in early 1993, at age fifteen, she had had sex with Kelsey Grammer. In October 1996, after a potentially fatal car accident the previous month, Grammer admitted himself to the Betty Ford Clinic in Rancho Mirage, California, for reported alcohol and drug abuse. However, the actor did rebound in August 1997 when he married his third wife, former *Playboy* model Camille Donatucci, in Malibu, California.

Recently, in addition to his series work, Kelsey has been a sought-after voice-over artist, lending his sonorous tones to several episodes of the animated Fox series *The Simpsons*, in the role of Sideshow Bob. His first appearance in a feature movie was also voice only, as Dr. Frankenollie in *Runaway Brain* (1995). He also vocalized Vladimir in the animated feature *Anastasia* (1997), and Captain Morgan Bateson in the theatrical release *Star Trek: First Contact* (1996), a role he had played, onscreen, in a 1992 episode, "Cause and Effect," of TV's *Star Trek: The Next Generation*.

Kelsey Grammer has been nominated for Emmy Awards, thus far seven times, all for the role of Frasier Crane, on three different TV sitcoms: *Cheers*, *Frasier*, and in a guest appearance on *Wings* during the 1991–92 season. With three victories to his credit, and years of Frasierisms still ahead, there is little doubt that the Grammer mantelpiece is not yet full.

Films: 1995: *Runaway Brain* (voice only). 1996: *Down Periscope*; *Star Trek: First Contact*. 1997: *Anastasia* (voice only). 1998: *The Real Howard Spitz*. 1999: *New Jersey Turnpikes*.

TV movies: 1988: *Dance 'Til Dawn*. 1989: *Top of the Hill*. 1992: *Galaxies Are Colliding*. 1993: *Beyond Suspicion*. 1994: *The Innocent*. 1996: *London Suite*. 1998: *The Pentagon Wars*.

TV miniseries: 1983: *Kennedy*. 1984: *George Washington*. 1986: *Crossings*.

TV series: 1984–85: *Another World*. 1986–93: *Cheers*. 1993–present: *Frasier* (also occasional director); 1997: *Fired Up* (executive producer only).

Meet Dr. Cunard

🗗 On *Another World*, the role of Dr. Cunard was played by Kelsey Grammer for six months in 1984–85.

An emergency room physician, Dr. Cunard (his first name was never revealed) often worked with fan favorite Dr. Alice Matthews Frame (Jacqueline Courtney), many times needing to defend his life-saving practices. The two often clashed in their medical diagnoses, and the audience, anxious as to whether the patient would survive, was left hanging with the doctors' arguments.

However small the soap role was for Grammer, it did afford him the opportunity, shortly after leaving *Another World*, to audition for the part that would make his career: Dr. Frasier Crane. The rest, as they say, is continuing history.

Larry Hagman

Who Shot J. R.?
—*The most asked question in America on March 21, 1980*

Trusted attorney Ed Gibson was played by Larry Hagman on The Edge of Night *from 1961–63. Courtesy of Soap Opera Digest.*

Born: September 21, 1931, in Weatherford, Texas, to Benjamin and Mary Martin Hagman

Education: Bard College (Annandale-on-Hudson, New York)

Debuts: television—*U.S. Steel Hour* (1958); film—*Fail-Safe* (1964)

Marital Status: Maj Axelsson, December 1954; two children, Kristina and Preston

Honors: Medal of Honor from the American Cancer Society for chairing the "Great American Smokeout" from 1981–92; Public Service Award from the National Kidney Foundation, 1996.

Books: *Larry Hagman*, by C. C. Risenhoover (1988); *Larry Hagman: A Biography*, by Leon Adams (1987)

Trusted nice guy or ruthless businessman—for which characterization is Larry Hagman better remembered? Hard to tell: it depends on whether you're thinking of aeronautics or oil.

Larry was born into performing royalty: his mother, legendary Broadway musical comedy superstar Mary Martin, dazzled stage audiences in such song-and-dance shows as *South Pacific* (1948) and *Peter Pan* (1955). His father, Ben Hagman, was an attorney. After his parents divorced in 1937, Larry moved to Los Angeles to live with his grandmother. After her 1943 death, when Larry was twelve years old, he returned to his mother who was by that time remarried (in 1940 to literary agent Richard Halliday) and just starting her stage career.

After a year at Bard College in Annandale-on-Hudson, New York, Hagman decided to follow in his mother's footsteps. He performed with the Margo Jones Theatre-in-the-Round in, *of all places*, Dallas. He also appeared in an early 1950s New York City Center production of *The Taming of the Shrew*, followed by a year in regional theater.

His mother, Mary Martin, was at this time starring in *South Pacific* in England—Larry soon joined her as a part of the ensemble, in the role of Herman Quayle, and stayed for five years. While in the United Kingdom, he enlisted in the U.S. Air Force where he produced and directed a number of productions for the troops. While stationed in England, Hagman met Maj Axelsson, a young Swedish designer. The two married in December 1954—she is called, by her husband, "the best thing that ever happened to me."

After he finished military service, Larry and Maj moved back to New York, where he appeared in a number of Broadway and off-Broadway plays. In New York, Larry began appearing on television, debuting in 1958 on the *U.S. Steel Hour* as an extra in the July 30 episode "Climate of Marriage." Three years later, he joined the cast of *The Edge of Night*. He stayed in the part of trusted lawman Ed Gibson for two and a half years, leaving in 1963. After eight years in New York, Larry decided to relocate his family, which now included daughter Kristina Mary (born February 17, 1958) and son Preston (born May 2, 1962), to Los Angeles.

In 1965, thirty-four-year-old Larry took a role in a new television series, *I Dream of Jeannie*. One of the in-vogue supernatural situation comedies of the 1960s, this charming program revolved around astronaut Tony Nelson, who inherits a blonde genie, played by fetching Barbara Eden. The popular show lasted for five seasons, with Genie and Tony marrying towards the end of the run.

In the early 1970s, Hagman played in two other TV situation comedies. In NBC's *The Good Life* (1971), Larry and costar **Donna Mills** portrayed a middle-class couple who hired themselves out as butler and maid to a wealthy couple. In ABC's *Here We Go Again* (1973), divorce was studied, sitcom-style. Neither series enjoyed his past, or future, success.

It was in 1978 that Hagman's career really went into high gear, as the result of a new CBS nighttime soap, *Dallas*. In the hour-long weekly drama, Larry was cast as wicked millionaire J. R. Ewing, the center of an oil-rich Texas family gushing with complex, never-ending problems. J. R.'s antics, in and out of multitudes of offices and bedrooms, made him the quintessential man viewers loved to hate, and catapulted *Dallas* into TV legend. Over the years, and especially since the 1991 cancellation of the long-running series, several TV movies have showcased the clan: *Dallas: The Early Years* (1986), *Dallas: J .R. Returns* (1996), and *Dallas: The War of the Ewings* (1998). Hagman also appeared, in the role of J. R., in a first-season episode of *Knots Landing* (1979–93), a spin-off from *Dallas*.

The March 1980 *Dallas* episode that asked "Who Shot J. R.?" was the second-highest rated U.S. TV show in the history of the medium. In the 1998 *Dallas* TV movie, when J. R. was shot yet again he survived, having learned a valuable lesson—a bullet-proof vest now bulked up his silk suit.

Since the high-profile TV role of J. R. Ewing, both a tycoon and a savvy, but corrupt, businessman, Hagman's career has taken a new direction. His roles have been powerful, influential, feared characters, such as Jack Jones in *Nixon* (1995), Judge Luther Charbonnet in the 1997 TV series *Orleans* (costarring fellow soap alumna Vanessa Bell Calloway), and Governor Fred Picker in the 1998 pseudo-fictional political study film *Primary Colors*.

From 1981–92, Hagman chaired the American Cancer Society's "Great American Smokeout." His efforts on behalf of organ donation are, perhaps, a bit closer to home. On August 23, 1995, he underwent sixteen hours of life-saving liver transplant surgery. In 1996, he received the National Kidney Foundation's Public Service Award for his work in heightening public awareness of the vital importance of donor programs.

Larry and Maj have a ranch in Ojai, California, a condo in Santa Monica, California, and a home in Santa Fe, New Mexico. To some degree, the Ewing lifestyle has defined Hagman. After two decades, off and on, as the personification of J. R., how could a little of the character's oversized way of life not have rubbed off on the man?

Films: 1964: *Ensign Pulver*; *Fail-Safe*. 1965: *The Cavern*; *In Harm's Way*. 1966: *The Group*. 1970: *Up in the Cellar*. 1973: *Antonio*. 1974: *Harry and Tonto*; *Stardust*. 1976: *The Big Bus*; *The Eagle Has Landed*; *Mother, Jugs and Speed*. 1977: *Checkered Flag or Crash*; *Cry for Justice*. 1978: *Superman*. 1981: *Jag Rodnar*; *S.O.B.* 1995: *Nixon*. 1998: *Primary Colors*.

TV movies: 1969: *Three's a Crowd*. 1971: *Vanished*; *Getting Away from It All*; *A Howling in the Woods*. 1972: *Beware! The Blob* (also director); *No Place to Run*. 1973: *The Alpha Caper*; *Blood Sport*; *What Are Best Friends For?* 1974: *The Big Rip-Off*; *Hurricane*; *Sidekicks*. 1975: *Sarah T.—Portrait of a Teenage Alcoholic*. 1976: *The Return of the World's Greatest Detective*. 1977: *Intimate Strangers*. 1978: *A Double Life*; *Last of the Good Guys*; *The President's Mistress*. 1982: *Deadly Encounter*. 1986: *Dallas: The Early Years*. 1993: *Staying Afloat* (also executive producer). 1994: *In the Heat of the Night: Who Was Geli Bendl?* (director only). 1996: *Dallas: J. R. Returns* (also executive producer). 1998: *Dallas: The War of the Ewings*.

TV documentary: 1985: *Lone Star*.

TV miniseries: 1977: *The Rhinemann Exchange*. 1997: *The Third Twin*.

TV series: 1961–63: *The Edge of Night*. 1964–65: *The Rogues*. 1965–70: *I Dream of Jeannie*. 1971–72: *The Good Life*. 1973: *Here We Go Again*. 1978–91: *Dallas* (also director and executive producer). 1988: *In the Heat of the Night* (director only). 1997: *Orleans*.

Meet Ed

⌨ On *The Edge of Night*, the character of Ed Gibson was originated, and solely played, by Larry Hagman, from 1961–63.

Ed Gibson was an attorney, the junior law partner of Monticello's District Attorney Mike Karr (John Larkin). No doubt they were busy: an early 1960s issue of *Time* magazine noted that, "Hell is a city much like Monticello."

Ed eventually married Judy Marceau (Joan Harvey), the daughter of Bill Marceau (Mandel Kramer), Monticello's chief of police.

• •

From Daytime to Nighttime (Soaps, That Is)

Ever wonder which of your favorite soap stars graduated from daytime, only to wind up on a nighttime soap? Here are four of the most popular after-dark serials that boast the most midday alumni—accompanying each star's names are the daytime soap(s) they appeared on, and the character and span of time they played on the nighttime program.

Dallas

David Ackroyd (*Another World, The Secret Storm*) Gary Ewing (1978)

Glenn Corbett (*The Doctors*) Paul Morgan (1983–84; 1986–88)

Susan Flannery (*Days of Our Lives*, currently of *The Bold and the Beautiful*) Leslie Stewart (1981)

Tom Fuccello (*Love Is a Many Splendored Thing, One Life to Live*) Dave Culver (1979–82; 1986–87)

Charles Grant (*The Edge of Night*, currently of *The Bold and the Beautiful*) David Shulton (1988)

Larry Hagman (*The Edge of Night*) J. R. Ewing (1978–91)

Alice Hirson (*The Edge of Night, One Life to Live*) Mavis Anderson (1982–88)

Barry Jenner (*Another World, Somerset*) Dr. Jerry Kenderson (1984; 1985–86)

Ken Kercheval (*Search for Tomorrow, The Secret Storm*) Cliff Barnes (1978–91)

Audrey Landers (*Somerset, One Life to Live*) Afton Cooper (1981–84; 1989)

Susan Lucci (currently of *All My Children*) Sheila Foley/Hillary Taylor (1990–91)

Donald May (*The Edge of Night, Texas*) Wes McDowall (1984)

Leigh McCloskey (*General Hospital, The Young and the Restless*) Mitch Cooper (1979–82; 1985)

Dack Rambo (*Never Too Young, All My Children, Another World*) Jack Ewing (1985–88)

John Reilly (*As the World Turns, General Hospital*) Roy Ralston (1983)

Ted Shackelford (*Another World*) Gary Ewing (1979–81)

Shari Shattuck (currently of *The Young and the Restless*) Kit (1991)

Joan Van Ark (*Days of Our Lives*) Valene Clements Ewing (1978–81)

Peter White (*The Secret Storm, All My Children*) Breslin (1990–91)

Michael Wilding Jr. (*Guiding Light*) Alex Barton (1989)

Ray Wise (*Love of Life*) Blair Sullivan (1982)

Dynasty

Deborah Adair (*The Young and the Restless, Days of Our Lives*) Tracy Kendall (1983–84)

Kathleen Beller (*Search for Tomorrow*) Kirby Anders Colby (1982–84)

Jack Coleman (*Days of Our Lives*) Steven Carrington (1982–88)

Terri Garber (*Texas, Santa Barbara*) Leslie Carrington (1987–88)

Richard Hatch (*All My Children*) Dean Caldwell (1984)

Leann Hunley (*Days of Our Lives*) Dana Waring Carrington (1986–88)

John James (*Search for Tomorrow*) Jeff Colby (1981–85, 1987–89)

Wayne Northrop (*Days of Our Lives*) Michael Culhane (1981; 1986–87)

Emma Samms (*General Hospital*) Fallon Carrington Colby/Randall Adams (1985–86; 1987–89)

Susan Scannell (*Another World, Ryan's Hope, Search for Tomorrow*) Nicole "Nikki" Simpson De Vilbis Colby (1984)

Gordon Thomson (*Ryan's Hope, Santa Barbara*) Adam Carrington/Michael Torrance (1982–1989)

Falcon Crest

Kristian Alfonso (currently of *Days of Our Lives)* Pilar Ortega (1988–90)

Ana Alicia (*Ryan's Hope*) Melissa Agretti Cumson Gioberti (1982–88) and Samantha Ross (1989)

Jane Badler (*The Doctors*) Meredith Braxton (1986–87)

Carla Borelli (*Days of Our Lives, Texas*) Connie Giannini (1985)

John Callahan (*General Hospital,* currently on *All My Children*) Eric Stavros (1986–88)

Jordan Charney (*Another World, Love of Life, One Life to Live, Somerset*) Norton Crane (1983–84)

Morgan Fairchild (*Search for Tomorrow, The City*) Jordan Roberts (1985–86)

Alan Feinstein (*The Nurses, The Edge of Night*) Malcolm Sinclair (1989)

Charles Frank (*All My Children*) Senator Ryder (1988)

Joe Lambie (*Guiding Light, The Edge of Night, Santa Barbara, Search for Tomorrow*) Sheriff Robbins (1982–85)

Donald May (*The Edge of Night, Texas*) Bradford Linton (1985–86)

Susan Sullivan (*Best of Everything, A World Apart, Another World*) Maggie Gioberti Channing (1981–89)

Roy Thinnes (*One Life to Live, General Hospital*) Nick Hogan (1982–83)

Knots Landing

David Ackroyd (*Another World, The Secret Storm*) Bill Medford (1980)

Alec Baldwin (*The Doctors*) Joshua Rush (1984–85)

Sam Behrens (*General Hospital*) Danny Waleska (1989–90)

Jane Elliot (*General Hospital, Guiding Light, The City, All My Children*) Judy Trent (1980–81)

Larry Hagman (*The Edge of Night*) J. R. Ewing (1979)

James Houghton (*The Young and the Restless*) Kenny Ward (1979–83)

Donna Mills (*The Secret Storm, Love Is a Many Splendored Thing*) Abby Cunningham (1980–89)

Kathleen Noone (*All My Children*) Claudia Whittaker (1990–93)

Peter Reckell (*As the World Turns, Days of Our Lives*) Johnny Rourke (1988–89)

Michael Sabatino (*Days of Our Lives, The Bold and the Beautiful*) Chip Roberts (1982–83)

Ted Shackelford (*Another World*) Gary Ewing (1979–93)

Doug Sheehan (*General Hospital*) Ben Gibson (1983–87)

Robin Strasser (*Another World, All My Children, One Life to Live*) Dianne Kirkwood (1990)

Joan Van Ark (*Days of Our Lives*) Valene Ewing (1979–92, 1993)

• •

Mark Hamill

A long time ago, in a galaxy far, far away...
—Introduction to Star Wars *(1977)*

Born: September 25, 1951, in Oakland, California, to William and Suzanne Hamill; birth name, Mark Richard Hamill; siblings Terry, Jan, Jeanie, William Jr., Kim, and Patrick

Education: Yokohama High School (Japan); Los Angeles City College

Debuts: television—*The Cosby Show* (1970); film—*Wizards* (1977); Broadway—*The Elephant Man* (1981)

Marital Status: Marilou York, 1978; three children, Nathan, Griffin, and Chelsea

Book: *The Black Pearl*, a five-part graphic novel co-written with Eric Johnson (1997)

Among science fiction devotees, the first three *Star Wars* (1977, 1980, 1983) big-screen epics rank among the most enduring of the genre. And one cannot think of the original *Star Wars* trio without its hero, Luke Skywalker, brought to life by Mark Hamill. That was the actor's first substantial role in a motion picture.

Mark's father, William, was a captain in the Navy and as a consequence his family moved extensively, to places such as California, Virginia, New York City, and Japan. After graduating from Yokohama High School in 1969, Mark moved with his family back to Southern California, where he enrolled in Theater Arts studies at Los Angeles City College.

While a student, Mark had his first role on a television program as a poetry-writing student on *The Cosby Show* (1970). He spent the next few years appearing in a number of TV series and movies, including a nine-month stint in fifty-one episodes of *General Hospital*. Soon after this daytime soap role ended, in 1973, he appeared in a distinctive episode of

TV's *The Partridge Family*: Mark gave character Laurie Partridge (Susan Dey) her first on-screen kiss.

In 1974, he was cast in a new television comedy series, *The Texas Wheelers*, which lasted on the ABC Friday night schedule for a mere four installments. The next year, 1975, he appeared in two powerful TV movies: *Eric*, based on Doris Lund's memoir of her son's leukemia, and *Sarah T.: Portrait of a Teenage Alcoholic*, costarring soap alumnus **Larry Hagman**. In this well-received drama Linda Blair starred as Sarah, a girl who turns to alcohol to escape family and school problems.

In 1976, Hamill portrayed David Bradford in the pilot TV film *Eight Is Enough*. In the regular ABC-TV series (1977–81), however, David, the oldest of the brood, was played by Grant Goodeve.

From March to June, 1976, Mark traveled to Tunisia and England for the eighty-two-day shoot for the feature film that would become his trademark: *Star Wars* (1977). In it, he portrays Luke Skywalker, a young farm boy on the planet Tatooine, who books passage to the planet Alderaan on the *Millennium Falcon*. In the epic final battle of the film, Luke fires the shot that destroys the *Death Star*, saving the rebellion and becoming a hero. This was the first of filmmaker George Lucas's trilogy, which included *The Empire Strikes Back* (1980) and *Return of the Jedi* (1983). (Incidentally, on January 11, 1977, Hamill got into a car accident, requiring facial plastic surgery; a special scene in *The Empire Strikes Back* was written to explain the changes in Mark's look.) In 1997, CGI (Computer-Generated Imaging)-enhanced re-releases of each film were issued, and the phenomenon that is *Star Wars* began anew.

In 1978, Hamill married Marilou York, and the couple have three children: sons Nathan Elias (born June 25, 1979), and Griffin Tobias (born March 4, 1983), and daughter Chelsea Elizabeth (born July 27, 1988).

After *Return of the Jedi*, with film roles hard to come by due to his *Star Wars* typecasting, Mark concentrated on stage acting. On Broadway, he brought to life the characters of John Merrick in *The Elephant Man*, which ran from June 9–28, 1981 at the Booth Theatre, and Wolfgang Amadeus Mozart in approximately three hundred performances of *Amadeus* between December 1982 and August 1983. Mark spent the next few years appearing in more plays, on stage-related TV and radio shows, and in guest spots on such TV series as *Amazing Stories* (1987) and *Alfred Hitchcock Presents* (1987).

In October 1992, Mark hosted the first *Star Wars*-devoted show on the cable shopping channel QVC. He would appear in similar programs in 1993 and 1995, pitching merchandise from various science fiction movies.

In recent years, Hamill has become a most sought-after voice-over talent, lending his sound to numerous TV cartoons. The youthful-sounding Mark was approaching age fifty, and the natural aging process necessitated branching out professionally (in much the same way that former sex-kitten **Kathleen Turner** expanded her career in a new direction as she grew older).

In a charming voice-only appearance on *Pinky and the Brain*, on September 27, 1997, Mark voiced Jimmy Joe Jr., in the episode "Brain Acres," a parody of the 1960s TV series *Green Acres*.

It might have been very easy for Mark Hamill to live off of both the reputation and the residuals of *Star Wars*: this hard-working and talented actor is doing anything but that.

Films: 1977: *Star Wars*; *Wizards* (voice only). 1978: *Corvette Summer*. 1980: *The Empire Strikes Back*; *The Big Red One*. 1981: *The Night the Lights Went Out in Georgia*. 1982: *Britannia Hospital*. 1983: *Return of the Jedi*. 1989: *Slipstream*. 1990: *Midnight Ride*. 1991: *Black Magic Woman*; *The Flash II: Revenge of the Trickster*; *The Guyver*; *Picture Perfect*. 1992: *Sleepwalkers*. 1993: *Batman: Mask of the Phantom* (voice only); *Time Runner*. 1994: *Silk Degrees*. 1995: *Village of the Damned*; *The Raffle*. 1997: *Gen 13* (voice only); *Laserhawk*. 1998: *Hamilton*. Forthcoming: *Sinbad: Beyond the Veil of Mists* (voice only).

TV movies: 1975: *Delancey Street: The Crisis Within*; *Eric*; *Sarah T.—Portrait of a Teenage Alcoholic*. 1976: *Mallory: Circumstantial Evidence*. 1977: *The City*. 1991: *Earth Angel*; 1993: *Hollyrock-a-Bye-Baby* (voice only); *Body Bags*. 1994: *Phantom 2040: The Ghost Who Walks* (voice only). 1997: *When Time Expires*.

TV series: 1972–73: *General Hospital*. 1973–75: *Jeannie* (voice only). 1974–75: *The Texas Wheelers*. 1977: *Eight Is Enough* (pilot only). 1992: *Batman: The Animated Series* (voice only). 1996: *Wing Commander Academy* (voice only); *B.R.U.N.O. the Kid* (voice only); *The Incredible Hulk* (voice only). 1997: *Batman: Gotham Knights* (voice only).

Interactive: 1994: *Gabriel Knight: Sins of the Fathers* (voice only); *Wing Commander III: Heart of the Tiger* (voice only). 1995: *Wing Commander IV: The Price of Freedom* (voice only). 1997: *Wing Commander: Prophecy* (voice only).

Meet Kent

On *General Hospital*, the role of Kent Murray was originated, and played solely, by Mark Hamill, from 1972–73.

When nurse Jessie Brewer's (Emily McLaughlin) widowed brother died, she became the guardian of two of his children, Carol (Anne Wyndham) and Kent (Mark Hamill) Murray.

Kent was a juvenile delinquent in his early days with Jessie but had a sudden personality change towards the end of the 1972 season, and became the perfect boy-next-door—how, we don't know (or nearly every parent in America would beg for the formula!). Kent left Port Charles when he was whisked off to military academy.

David Hasselhoff

The ladies swarmed around...yelling, "Hello, Snapper." A lot of them didn't even know my real name until I signed the autographs. They said, "David What?"

—David Hasselhoff, on the popularity
of his soap character, 1983

Females on The Young
and the Restless
looked forward to
house calls from
Dr. Snapper Foster,
portrayed by David
Hasselhoff from
1975–82. Video screen
photo, collection
of author.

Born: July 17, 1952, in Baltimore, Maryland, fifth child of Joe and Dolores Hasselhoff; sisters Diana, Lisa, Jean, and Joyce

Education: Lyons Township High School (La Grange, Illinois); Academy of Dramatic Arts (Chicago); California Institute of the Arts (Valencia, California)

Debuts: television—*The Young and the Restless* (1975) as Dr. Snapper Foster; film—*Revenge of the Cheerleaders* (1976)

Marital Status: Married actress Catherine Hickland, March 24, 1984; divorced, 1987; married Pamela Bach, 1989; two daughters: Taylor (b. 1990) and Hayley (b. 1992)—both with Pamela

Honors: Named "Most Popular and Best Selling Artist of the Year" in Germany, 1989; star on the Hollywood Walk of Fame, January 11, 1996

Albums: *Night Rocker* (1985); *Lovin' Feelings* (1987); *Looking for Freedom* (1989); *Crazy for You* (1990); *David* (1991); *Everybody Sunshine* (1992); *You Are Everything* (1993); *David Hasselhoff* (1995)

In the 1950s, beach movies were all the rage. Fun in the sun with Annette Funicello and Frankie Avalon, sipping soda pop, listening to transistor radios, and dancing in modest bikinis and shorts, kept many a teen giddily yearning for the ocean tides. The current small-screen counterpart for beach lovers is the markedly different *Baywatch*, with its revealing swimsuits and passion in the sun replacing the innocent '50s fare. Led by David Hasselhoff, the series not only has created a worldwide sensation, but has propelled its star into his third, and most successful, television incarnation.

David was the fifth child—first boy—born to Joe and Dolores Hasselhoff. As such, he was the continual center of attention; it was this captive audience that, most likely, inspired David in his choice of livelihood. From age seven, he knew he wanted to be a performer.

While in high school, David began acting seriously—maybe too seriously. "As a result," he shared with *TV Guide* in 1983, "I ended up with such terrible grades that the hotshot glory boy who played leads on the stage couldn't get into college. So, I went to California Institute of the Arts to study more acting."

In Los Angeles, Hasselhoff worked (as did many histrionic hopefuls) a survival job as a waiter. He eventually signed with talent agent Joyce Selznick, who got him his first meaty TV role: Dr. Snapper Foster on *The Young and the Restless*, a part David made his own from 1975–82. His popularity rose steadily, until leaving the daytime drama in 1982. He obviously felt the pressures inherent in soap acting: "I had been in *The Young and the Restless* for six years and I was going through the worst period of my life: tired of playing the part of dashing Snapper Foster; tired of devoting all my waking hours to learning twenty-five pages of script every day; tired of being turned down for parts in prime-time series."

Nonetheless, serendipity soon showed up. In March 1982, David was noticed, on a Los Angeles-bound plane, by then-NBC Entertainment President Brandon Tartikoff. The next day, Hasselhoff was asked to test for the role of Michael Knight on an upcoming series, *Knight Rider*. Many auditioned, but David won the series assignment he played for four years, earning an estimated $15,000 for each of the ninety episodes filmed. The plot: man and his car. But this man was different—Michael Long, undercover cop, was killed, and was brought back to life by mysterious millionaire Wilton Knight (thus, the new last name). The car, too, was special: a Pontiac Trans Am with a talking computer dubbed KITT (Knight Industries Two Thousand), which allowed it to converse and drive on its own. Together, KITT and Michael hunted down bad guys, assisted the good guys, and propelled David into prime-time stardom.

In 1982, David met soap actress Catherine Hickland. They became engaged in 1983, and married on March 24, 1984. They were divorced in 1987. Two years later, the second prime-time coming of Hasselhoff swept television viewers out of their armchairs.

The phenomenon that is *Baywatch* began in 1989, originally with a TV movie, *Baywatch: Panic at Malibu Pier*, which had such strong viewer ratings and appeal that a series was ordered immediately. A sister series later aired simultaneously—*Baywatch Nights* (1995–97)—and as lead actor and executive producer on both programs, Hasselhoff was named by *TV*

Guide as "one of the most powerful people in television." The number one American TV import overseas, *Baywatch* is watched, weekly, by an estimated one billion viewers. With a gorgeous cast, exotic locations, and exciting adventure story lines, there is no wonder why the show is so successful.

One would think, then, that David's childhood ambitions would have been met. Not quite. As a child, he had *two* dreams for his future: to be an actor and to be a pop music star.

In 1988, he achieved his other goal, releasing a number-one single, "Looking for Freedom," and a triple-platinum album of the same name. David performed his hit song on the Berlin Wall on New Year's Eve, 1989. Earlier that year, Hasselhoff married actress Pamela Bach; they have two daughters, Taylor Ann and Hayley Amber. In his spare time, David works for two charities: Race for Life and Camp Baywatch.

With both of his childhood goals—singing and acting—met, and with three major television characterizations on his résumé, David Hasselhoff has grown into, indeed, one of the tube's most powerful figures. Now in his late forties, he might not be characterized as *young* anymore . . . but he certainly is not *restless*.

Films: 1976: *Revenge of the Cheerleaders.* 1979: *Starcrash.* 1988: *Starke Zeiten.* 1989: *Witchery*; *W. B.*; *Blue and the Bean* (also producer). 1990: *The Final Alliance.* 1994: *Ring of the Musketeers.* 1996: *Dear God.* 1998: *Welcome to Hollywood*; *Legacy.*Forthcoming: *Je M'Appelle Crawford*; *Titanic Too: It Missed the Iceberg.*

TV movies: 1979: *Pleasure Cove.* 1982: *Knight Rider.* 1984: *The Cartier Affair*, 1985: *Bridge Across Time.* 1988: *Perry Mason: The Case of the Lady in the Lake.* 1989: *Fire and Rain*; *Baywatch: Panic at Malibu Pier.* 1991: *Knight Rider 2000.* 1994: *Avalanche.* 1996: *The Incredible Hulk*; *Gridlock.* 1997: *Nick Fury.* Forthcoming: *Shaka Zulu: The Citadel.*

TV miniseries: 1999: *The Diamond Hunters.*

TV series: 1975–82: *The Young and the Restless.* 1980: *Semi-Tough.* 1982–86: *Knight Rider.* 1989–present: *Baywatch* (also executive producer). 1995–97: *Baywatch Nights* (also creator and executive producer).

Video: 1993: *Behind the Scenes.* 1995: *Baywatch: Forbidden Paradise.* 1998: *Baywatch: White Thunder at Glacier Bay.*

Music Video: 1997: *Might Be Stars* (The Wannabes).

Meet Snapper

On *The Young and the Restless*, the character of William "Snapper" Foster was played by William Gray Espy (1973–75) and David Hasselhoff (1975–82).

Snapper was a doctor, brother to lawyer Greg (James Houghton) and beautician Jill (Brenda Dickson). Snapper fell in love and married Chris Brooks (Trish Stewart), who was adored, from not-so-far, by his brother Greg.

During the Hasselhoff years, Snapper worked in inner-city neighborhoods, bringing medical care to those who could least afford it. His marriage to Chris (later played by Lynne Topping) hit the skids when Dr. Casey Reed (Roberta Leighton) came to town. Oh, the gasps when Snapper and Casey demonstrated the Heimlich maneuver—and actually enjoyed it!

- -

The Days and Knights of Catherine

Catherine Hickland married David Hasselhoff (*The Young and the Restless*) in 1984, when he was playing Michael Knight on *Knight Rider*. They divorced, and she is now remarried to *All My Children* heartthrob, the real Michael E. Knight.

That Face! That Face!

In one of the strangest plots known to daytime, *The Young and the Restless* killer David Kimble (Michael Corbett) tried to evade capture by getting a new face. As part of that equation, Kimble held a plastic surgeon hostage, demanding David Hasselhoff's face. Hasselhoff, of course, had been on that show years earlier. (As a side note, Kimble died, in 1991, in one of daytime's most bizarre oncamera deaths. In a final attempt to avoid apprehension, David hid in a garbage chute, thinking it was a closet. His weight started the trash compactor: a death he could not *refuse*.)

- -

Teri Hatcher

People look at me now and think, oh, you've always been gorgeous and that makes your life great. But I was unpopular when I was an adolescent.

—Teri Hatcher, 1997

Born: December 8, 1964, in Sunnyvale, California, to Mr. and Mrs. Owen Hatcher; birth name, Teri Lynn Hatcher

Education: Fremont High School (Sunnyvale, California); American Conservatory Theatre (San Francisco); De Anza College (Cupertino, California)

Debuts: television—*The Love Boat* (1985); film—*The Big Picture* (1989)

Award: Golden Apple Award, as Female Discovery of the Year, 1996

Honor: Number Three of SciFi's Sexy Fifty, by *Femme Fatales* magazine (1997)

Marital Status: Married personal trainer Markus Leithold, June 4, 1988, divorced, 1989; married actor Jon Tenney, May 1994; daughter, Emerson (with Jon Tenney)

They're real, and they're spectacular." This statement, twice uttered on NBC's *Seinfeld* (once by the actress herself and once, in the series' final episode, by lawyer Jackie Chiles), has come to apply to more than one feature of actress Teri Hatcher. She has talent to match her physical dimensions.

Hatcher is the daughter of a physicist father and computer programmer mother. She winced at high school memories: "Up until my sophomore year, I was really nerdy and unpopular. I'd ask guys to dance and they'd find the cruelest high school way to say no."

Apparently, as she matured in her high school years, her "ugly duckling" status diminished. Graduated in 1982 from Fremont High School in Sunnyvale, California, Teri was captain of the cheerleading squad, a Featherette dance squad member, and was voted "Girl Most Likely to Become a Solid

Gold Dancer." The prognostication was close: she became a cheerleader for the San Francisco '49ers in 1984, at age twenty.

After graduation, she began undergraduate mathematics and engineering studies at De Anza College in Cupertino, California (1984–85). She soon left college to concentrate on acting, attending the American Conservatory Theatre of San Francisco. "Annette Bening was actually my acting teacher" for three months, Teri has recalled.

Hatcher attended an open casting call for TV's *The Love Boat*, and won a spot in a troupe of dancing mermaids in 1985. Later that year, a guest appearance as Penny Parker on ABC's *MacGyver* adventure series turned into a recurring role, initiating a three-year romantic involvement with its star, soap alum Richard Dean Anderson. Her recollection of that relationship is painful: "I got completely burned," Hatcher says.

Teri had a troublesome romance history—she had a ten-month marriage to personal trainer Markus Leithold, who reportedly dished to the tabloids every detail of their brief union. For a celebrity of Teri's stature, that must be the worst nightmare imaginable.

Despite her personal problems, she continued to focus on her acting career. In late 1985, she earned a role on *Capitol*, playing Angelica Clegg. She stayed briefly with the daytime drama, but quickly moved on from there, guesting on numerous TV shows, such as *Night Court*, *Star Trek: The Next Generation*, and *L.A. Law*, and starring in two short-lived series, *Karen's Song* (1987, playing the daughter of soap alumna **Patty Duke**), and the unsold pilot for *Sunday Dinner* (1991).

Hatcher won small roles in several feature films, notably as Sylvester Stallone's sister in *Tango & Cash* (1989) and as a big-coifed "ditz" in *Soapdish* (1991), before scoring in the role of sexy, spunky reporter Lois Lane in the 1993 TV series *Lois & Clark: The New Adventures of Superman*. She gained a loyal following for her portrayal, opposite Dean Cain in the title role, enjoying a legendary love affair with the Internet: for a long time, she held the title for the most downloaded female (most characteristically, in a photo showing her wrapped in Superman's cape).

In 1993, Teri made the first of three appearances on *Seinfeld* as Sidra, the woman with too-amazing-to-be-real physical dimensions. Her episode focus in "The Implant" (February 25, 1993) elevated her to star status, over and above her *Lois & Clark* following.

In May 1994, Teri married actor Jon Tenney. "Our first dinner together was at a party," Hatcher has recalled. "I was telling a story and everybody started talking among themselves. So I got up and started talking to the plant. Jon says that's the moment he fell in love with me." Tenney and Hatcher had their first child, daughter Emerson Rose, on November 10, 1997: the birth was an emergency cesarean section.

Roles in the James Bond entry, *Tomorrow Never Dies* (1997), and *Since You've Been Gone* (1998) show that Hatcher's talents are anything but artificial. A new venture, as a Mother's Day celebrity card designer, further proves that her talents go way beyond the histrionic. She joined Cheryl Tiegs and Stephen Baldwin in the designing, with proceeds benefiting the fight against breast cancer. It's a cause that is close to Hatcher's heart: she lost her grandmother to the disease.

In a further example of the actress's versatility, Hatcher signed on for the lead role of Sally Bowles in the national tour of the revival of the musical *Cabaret*, which will visit the cities of Los Angeles, Boston, Chicago, and Washington, D.C., beginning on February 23, 1999.

Real *and* spectacular: two adjectives that aptly describe Teri Hatcher.

Films: 1989: *The Big Picture*; *Tango & Cash*. 1991: *Soapdish*. 1992: *Straight Talk*. 1993: *Brain Smasher... A Love Story*. 1994: *All Tied Up*; *The Cool Surface*. 1996: *2 Days in the Valley*; *Heaven's Prisoners*. 1997: *Tomorrow Never Dies*. 1998: *Dead Girl*; *Since You've Been Gone*. Forthcoming: *Fever*.

TV movies: 1991: *Dead in the Water*.

TV series: 1985: *MacGyver*; *The Love Boat*. 1985–86: *Capitol*. 1987: *Karen's Song*. 1991: *Sunday Dinner*. 1993–97: *Lois & Clark: The New Adventures of Superman*.

Meet Angelica

On *Capitol*, the role of Angelica Clegg was originated, and solely played, by Teri Hatcher (1985–86).

Capitol was the first daytime drama to be introduced during prime time: a one-hour preview aired on March 26, 1982. This half-hour CBS soap, which debuted on March 29, 1982, was centered in Washington, D.C., and dealt with two powerful political families, the McCandlesses and the Cleggs. It went off the air, after a five-year run, on March 20, 1987.

Angelica was the second wife of Congressman Samuel "Trey" Clegg III (Nicholas Walker). His first wife was reporter Sloane Denning (Deborah Mullowney, later known as Debrah Farentino).

An Explosive Soap End

CBS's *Capitol* went off the air on March 20, 1987. At the time of its cancellation, much like CBS's *Love of Life*, it was expected that the show might be picked up by another network. It wasn't; and the show did not wrap up its story lines either. In the show's final episode, Sloane Denning Clegg, played by Deborah Mullowney, later known as Debrah Farentino, faced a firing squad in the fictional Mideastern country of Baracq, where her new hubby, Prince Ali (Peter Lochran) was held prisoner. The last words spoken on the show, as a blindfolded Sloane shook, were "Ready, aim..."

Anne Heche

I played twins on the soap Another World.
*Between the two characters I was either fucking
my sister's husband or stealing my own child or
getting abducted by insane people. But that's why
it was so much fun.*

— Anne Heche, on her big acting break, 1998

*Another World's
headstrong twins Vicky
and Marley Love were
dually handled by
Emmy winner Anne
Heche from 1987–91.
Video screen photo,
collection of author.*

Born: May 25, 1969, in Aurora, Ohio, to
Mr. and Mrs. Donald Heche

Debuts: television—*Another World*
(1987) as Vicky/Marley Love; film—*An
Ambush of Ghosts* (1993)

Awards: Daytime Emmy Award, for Outstanding Juvenile Female, for her role as
Vicky/Marley Love on *Another World*,
1989; Daytime Emmy Award, for Outstanding Younger Actress, for
Another World, 1991; Soap Opera Digest Award, for Outstanding Lead
Actress for *Another World*, 1992; National Board of Review Award,
for Best Supporting Actress for her roles in *Donnie Brasco* and *Wag
the Dog*, 1997

Honors: Chosen by *People* magazine as one of the Fifty Most Beautiful People in the World (1998)

Ellen [DeGeneres] and I 'came out' on *The Oprah Winfrey Show* in front
of fifteen million people. Now we've made it public. Now leave us alone."
Strong words from a strong person: Anne Heche. Her now-famous sexual
orientation change and great talent has Hollywood watching closely.

Anne's childhood was marked by survival in the midst of incredible odds.
Her father, Donald, was a choir director in a Baptist church who fre-
quented gay bars at night. At age twelve, Anne found out about her father's
dual life in horrific fashion: "I watched my dad disintegrate from AIDS,"
Anne has related, "because he was ashamed to be what he wanted to be."
Doubtless, this taught her a valuable lesson in self-esteem. Her father died

from the disease in 1982; three months after that tragedy hit again when her brother was killed in a car crash.

At age twelve, Anne had started acting in dinner theaters. After her father's death, performance became an economic necessity. By high school, acting became less of a need, and more of a hobby. While living in Chicago, and appearing in a production of *The Skin of Our Teeth*, fifteen-year-old Heche was approached by a talent scout from the New York-based *As the World Turns*. She was offered a role but turned it down, wanting to finish high school.

After she graduated, however, she did move to New York, having been offered a plum part on *Another World*. "The day I arrived," she remembered, "the producer said, 'Oh, by the way, you're playing twins, and one of them is a real sexpot. In your first scene you'll be naked in a bathtub and you've just lost a million dollars.'" As twins Vicky and Marley Love, Heche nabbed two Emmy Awards. During her soap tenure (1987–91), she lived with actor Richard Burgi, whom she met while he played an on-camera pimp on *Another World*.

Four years on the daytime drama gave Heche the experience necessary to embark on a movie career, and she soon relocated to the West Coast. Her first films were unmemorable, but a role in *A Simple Twist of Fate* (1994) led to a two-year romance with her costar, comedian Steve Martin. It broke up painfully, especially for Martin, whose friends reportedly took to calling Heche "The Heartbreak Kid" after she left the actor.

Anne was headed up the Hollywood visibility ladder in 1996, with a noticed performance in *Walking and Talking*, and a standout turn in *The Juror*, as fellow soap alumna **Demi Moore**'s vivacious friend. The next year, 1997, Anne costarred with such cinema heavy hitters as Johnny Depp (in *Donnie Brasco*), **Tommy Lee Jones** (in *Volcano*), and Robert De Niro (in *Wag the Dog*).

But it was her appearance, with comedienne Ellen DeGeneres, on the April 30, 1997, *Oprah Winfrey Show*, that made Anne Heche real water-cooler gossip material. The two, it was confirmed on air, were involved in a lesbian relationship.

In May 1997, seizing on the relationship, the film company Nulmage re-released a 1995 film, *Wild Side*, in which Anne's character had a lesbian affair. By June, Heche was on the cover of *The Advocate*, a national gay and lesbian publication. By September, Anne was listed as one of the "twenty most fascinating women in politics." Entering 1998, Anne was among the most talked-about stars in Hollywood, and received high notices for her roles in the romantic comedy *Six Days, Seven Nights* with Harrison Ford, and *Return to Paradise*. The filming of the latter was more notorious because of her alleged off-camera flirtation with costar Vince Vaughn (with whom she also appeared in the 1998's ill-received shot-by-shot color remake of the Alfred Hitchcock classic *Psycho*, also starring

Julianne Moore). By the end of 1998, Heche and DeGeneres announced that they would leave Hollywood and relocate to a less hectic locale (Santa Barbara), ostensibly to escape what they perceived to be overblown publicity coupled with sexual discrimination.

All the while, Anne has defended her lifestyle change. "I've been straight for a lot more years than I've been gay," Heche noted in the *Los Angeles Times*. "Why should they ask me if I can play a love scene with a man? I'm an actress. Maybe they should ask me if I could play a gay role?"

Seemingly, Anne Heche's lifestyle will be the subject of public attention. Her talent as an actress however will likely speak louder, and stronger.

Films: 1993: *The Adventures of Huck Finn*; *An Ambush of Ghosts*. 1994: *I'll Do Anything*; *Milk Money*; *A Simple Twist of Fate*. 1995: *Pie in the Sky*; *The Wild Side*. 1996: *Walking and Talking*; *The Juror*. 1997: *Wag the Dog*. *I Know What You Did Last Summer*; *Volcano*; *Donnie Brasco*. 1998: *Return to Paradise*; *Six Days, Seven Nights*; *Psycho*. Forthcoming: *The Third Miracle*; *Trixie*.

TV movies: 1992: *O Pioneers!* 1994: *Girls in Prison*. 1995: *Kingfish: A Story of Huey P. Long*. 1996: *If These Walls Could Talk*. 1997: *Subway Stories: Tales from the Underground*; *Against the Wall*.

TV series: 1987–91: *Another World*.

Meet Marley and Vicky

On *Another World*, the role of Marley was played by Ellen Wheeler (1984–86, 1998–present), Anne Heche (1987–91), and Jensen Buchanan (1991–98). The character first appeared on the program on May 14, 1984.

The role of Vicky was played by Ellen Wheeler (1985–86), Rhonda Lewin (1986–87), Anne Heche (1987–91) and Jensen Buchanan (1991–present). The character first appeared on the program on April 11, 1985.

Marley and Vicky are twin sisters, born to Donna Love (Anna Stuart) and Michael Hudson (Kale Browne) on July 19, 1967. Marley did not know she had a twin until Vicky came to Bay City in 1985, the year Marley developed leukemia—her life was saved by a bone-marrow transplant from newly-discovered sibling Vicky. As time wore on, the two sisters had numerous falling outs and reconciliations.

Marley was raped by Jake McKinnon on October 25, 1990. In 1991, their relationship strengthened when Vicky stood by Marley's side during her trial for shooting Jake. Vicky even impersonated Marley in court when Marley was unable to take the pressure.

Marley and Vicky, both still-running characters, have been romantically linked to most of the men in Bay City. Flirtations, marriages, and divorces are the twins' specialties. Active girls, these were, are, and continue to be.

● ●

Another World-iarchs

In the annals of *Another World*, two of its most popular female characters have been Alice and Rachel. The portrayers of their parents are equally noteworthy: Alice's father, Jim Matthews, was played from 1964–65 by Leon Janney, a child member of *Our Gang*, and from 1969–82 by Hugh Marlowe of radio/TV *Ellery Queen* fame; Rachel's mother, Ada Davis Downs McGowan Hobson, was played by TV and film veteran Constance Ford from 1967–93. In the early 1970s, Ada married Gil McGowan, a part originated by film perennial Charles Durning.

● ●

Lauren Holly

Julie's (Lauren Holly) wedding day in 1989 on All My Children. *Video screen photo, collection of author.*

I started on a soap as Julie on All My Children. *It was trauma city for this girl, because she found out that her father was an attacker and then she fell in love with a guy who pirated videos. To this day, it doesn't matter what I do, people still come up to me and ask, "Aren't you Julie?"*
—Lauren Holly, on her big career break, 1998

Born: October 28, 1963, in Bristol, Pennsylvania; birth name, Lauren Michael Holly

Education: Sarah Lawrence College (Bronxville, New York)

Debuts: film—*Seven Minutes in Heaven* (1985); television—*Love Lives On* (1985)

Award: Won Viewers for Quality Television Award as Best Supporting Actress in a Quality Drama Series for *Picket Fences*, 1994

Honor: Nominated for Daytime Emmy Award, 1988

Marital Status: Married Danny Quinn, 1991, divorced, 1993; married actor Jim Carrey, September 23, 1996, divorced, July 29, 1997, reconciled, May 1998, separated, October 1998

Jim was a great husband and an incredible father, but he was just unable to let me breathe . . . So, a relationship is hard to assume these times." As Lauren Holly has learned all too well, Hollywood marriages are, indeed, challenging.

Lauren Michael Holly was brought up in Geneva, New York, by professorial parents: Dad taught English literature, Mom taught Art History. Lauren lost her fourteen-year-old brother in a fire.

She studied English Literature, receiving her degree from Sarah Lawrence College. While on campus in Bronxville, New York, she roomed with another future performer, the former Mrs. Mike Tyson, Robin Givens.

Lauren used her lovely smile and good looks to get modeling jobs and a film debut in *Seven Minutes in Heaven* (1985). That next year, however, saw her first real acting stint: three years on *All My Children*, as Julie Cortlandt. She stayed on the soap until 1989, garnering an Outstanding Ingenue Emmy nomination that year.

In 1989, she began dating Danny Quinn, son of legendary actor Anthony Quinn. The two married in 1991, divorcing in 1993.

As the 1990s began, Lauren appeared in a number of less-than-memorable movies, such as *The Adventures of Ford Fairlane* (1990), starring in-your-face comedian Andrew Dice Clay. In 1992, Lauren took the role that gained her the experience, and the notice, that makes a career: Deputy Maxine Stewart in the Emmy-winning TV series *Picket Fences*. She spent four years on this exceptional weekly show and, in 1994, won a Q Award for her role.

During her *Picket Fences* tenure, Holly took the feature film part of Linda Lee Caldwell, the wife and widow of martial arts legend Bruce Lee in *Dragon: The Bruce Lee Story* (1993). In an interview with *Movieline* magazine, Lauren voiced her pleasure at finally receiving mature onscreen roles, shedding the previous stereotypical assignments of tomboys and vapid young ingenues.

Lauren rejected the Courteney Cox role in *Ace Ventura: Pet Detective* (1994), which, for Jim Carrey, was the first of many vehicles establishing him as one of this generation's most unique screen comics. "Back then, we were both just a couple of relative unknowns," Holly admitted. "I turned the role down. In retrospect it was the wisest thing I ever did. Everything worked out better for me, both professionally and personally."

Lauren did accept the next role offered her opposite Carrey, in a riotous 1994 comedy: "Jim and I dated on and off for two years after we met on *Dumb & Dumber*," recalled Holly. "That's a pretty long time for adults to be dating. I guess we were both leery of making that commitment to marriage."

Jim flew to San Francisco, to the set of Lauren's upcoming film, *A Smile Like Yours*, and proposed in July 1996. The two were married on September 23, 1996. It was to be a seesaw union.

On July 29, 1997, it was announced that Holly had filed for divorce from Carrey, citing the standard irreconcilable differences. She then became romantically linked with Edward Burns, her costar/director on *No Looking Back* (1998). That relationship fizzled and, seven months after she and Carrey had officially split, the pair were seen together at Hollywood parties and restaurants. By May 1998, it was announced that they, Holly and Carrey, had rented a house in Malibu for the summer, and had reconciled. This rapprochement too ended and the couple are now living apart.

Amidst all this personal tumult, Lauren Holly's career is swimming along just fine. Her 1997 appearances in *Turbulence*, as a flight attendant in peril, and *A Smile Like Yours*, as Greg Kinnear's love who wants a baby, brought excellent notices, even if both films were bombs. And the roles keep on coming. After all, half of Hollywood is Holly.

Films: 1985: *Seven Minutes in Heaven*. 1986: *Band of the Hand*. 1990: *The Adventures of Ford Fairlane*. 1993: *Dragon: The Bruce Lee Story*. 1994: *Dumb & Dumber*. 1995: *Sabrina*. 1996: *Down Periscope; Beautiful Girls*. 1997: *A Smile Like Yours; Turbulence*. 1998: *No Looking Back*. Forthcoming: *The League; Entropy*.

TV movies: 1985: *Love Lives On*. 1990: *Archie: To Riverdale and Back Again*. 1992: *Fugitive Among Us*. 1994: *Dangerous Heart*. 1998: *Vig*.

TV series: 1986–89: *All My Children*. 1991: *The Antagonists*. 1992–96: *Picket Fences*.

Meet Julie

On *All My Children*, the character of Julie was played by Stephanie Winters (1985–86), and Lauren Holly (1986–89).

Julie Rand was a spunky young girl who was adopted by newlyweds Ross Chandler (Robert Gentry) and Ellen Dalton (Kathleen Noone).

Julie witnessed a passionate kiss between Ross and nurse Natalie Hunter (Kate Collins), and recorded exactly what she saw in her diary. Later, after Natalie married Palmer Cortlandt (James Mitchell), Ross raped Natalie, whose cries for help long haunted Julie.

Julie later found out that her natural mother, Elizabeth Carlyle (Lisa Eichorn), had conceived Julie while a prostitute, and that the father was Mark Dalton (Mark LaMura). Devastated, Julie fled to New York and befriended Creed Kelly (James Horan) and his nephew, Nico (Maurice Bernard). In reality, Creed was Elizabeth's sworn enemy. Creed's plan to rape Julie in front of her mother was thwarted by Nico. Creed fled, and Julie apologized to Nico for misjudging him. Nico Kelly was later apprehended and imprisoned, but by then he and Julie were in love.

Later, Ellen and Ross's marriage ended in divorce; Ellen eventually married Mark Dalton. However, Julie was not as quick to accept Mark as her father. Julie turned all her attentions to Nico after his release from prison. By year's end, Julie and Nico wed, but their union was invalid because the small-town mayor who officiated at the ceremony was not authorized to perform marriages. Not long thereafter, Julie left Pine Valley for Washington, D.C.

James Earl Jones

I'm a stutterer. And once a stutterer, always a stutterer; we just learn how to work around it.
—James Earl Jones, 1996

On The Guiding Light *in 1966, Dr. Jim Frazier was played by two legendary actors: Billy Dee Williams and, seen here, James Earl Jones. Courtesy of Photofest.*

Born: January 17, 1931, in Arkabutla, Mississippi, to Robert Earl and Ruth Williams Jones; birth name, Todd Jones

Education: Kaleva-Norman-Dickson High School; University of Michigan (Ann Arbor)

Debuts: Broadway—*Egghead* (1958); film—*Dr. Strangelove; or How I Learned to Stop Worrying and Love the Bomb* (1963); television—*Guiding Light* (1966) as Dr. Jim Frazier

Awards: Won Tony Awards, for *The Great White Hope*, 1959, and for *Fences*, 1987; won Golden Globe Award, for *The Great White Hope*, 1970; won Emmy Award, for Best Actor, for *Gabriel's Fire*, 1991; won Emmy Award, for Best Supporting Actor, for *Heat Wave*, 1991

Marital Status: Married Cecilia "Ceci" Hart Jones, March 15, 1982; one son, Flynn

Books: autobiography: *James Earl Jones: Voices and Silences*, by Jones and Penelope Niven (1994). other: *The Art of the Lion King*, by Jones and Christopher Finch (1994); *Contest Problem Book III: Annual High School Contest of the Mathematical Association of America*, by Jones and Charles T. Salkind (1973); *Othello (Everyman Paperback Classics)*, foreword by Jones (1995); *The People Could Fly*, by Jones and Virginia Hamilton (1988); *Poetry Out Loud*, by Robert Alden Rubin, ed., introduction by Jones (1996). about: *James Earl Jones (Overcoming Adversity)*, by Judy L. Hasday (1998)

That voice! Powerful, distinguished, almost magisterial. James Earl Jones has worked steadily in both theater and film since the Truman Administration, with no end in sight.

Raised in the little town of Dublin, Michigan, Todd Jones was the son of a prize fighter who later became an actor. As a child, Todd was a boy of very few words, due to a crippling stutter, which is a recurring problem for the actor to this day. His conquering of this physical ailment is all the more notable, when it is considered that, perhaps, Jones's greatest asset is his *basso profundo* voice.

Jones graduated with a drama degree from the University of Michigan in 1953, later receiving a diploma from the American Theatre Wing in 1957, and an Honorary Doctorate of Letters from the University of Michigan in 1960. In the years that followed his graduation, he balanced stage work, notably in the title role of *Othello* in 1964, with a film debut, as Lieutenant Zogg in the Peter Sellers movie classic *Dr. Strangelove; or How I Learned to Stop Worrying and Love the Bomb* (1963). He remained in stage work until 1966, when he joined the cast of *Guiding Light*, appearing in the recurring role of Dr. Jim Frazier. Later that year, he moved to another CBS soap, *As the World Turns*, as Dr. Jerry Turner.

Jones's soap assignments were the initial widespread presentation of this multitalented performer. His two physician roles introduced his qualities of strength and power to the viewing public at large, and led to multiple successful careers in stage, television, and film. Whether the part called for him to be physically strong (as in his celebrated 1966–68 Broadway role as heavyweight champion Jack Jefferson in *The Great White Hope*, which he revived in the 1970 film version), or vocally mighty (as the voice of Darth Vader in the *Star Wars* film trilogy; 1977, 1980, 1983), Jones has made his presence known.

From September 1979 to January 1980, James played the title role of Detective Captain Woodrow *Paris* in the CBS crime series *Paris*, a show created specifically for him. This began a very busy decade for Jones, who appeared in five television movies and seventeen feature films, including the hit fantasy *Field of Dreams* (1989), in which he portrayed reclusive 1960s author Terrence Mann, modeled after J. D. Salinger.

As the 1990s unfolded, James found himself professionally busier, and in more demand, than ever. Besides screen roles that mark Jones's versatility, and his adeptness at comedy, drama, farce, and fantasy, Jones is the spokesperson voice of CNN cable network and Bell Atlantic. He also lent his voice to the original opening to the NBC-TV series *3rd Rock from the Sun* in 1996. His role as the Mountain King in the 1998 TV miniseries *Merlin* seems a fitting one for shy, stuttering Todd Jones, who grew to become a king amid the Hollywood royalty.

Films: 1963: *Dr. Strangelove or: How I Learned to Stop Worrying and Love the Bomb*. 1967: *The Comedians*. 1970: *End of the Road; The Great White Hope; King: A Filmed Record...Montgomery to Memphis* (voice only). 1972: *Malcolm X* (voice only); *The Man*. 1974: *Claudine*. 1976: *The Bingo Long Traveling All-Stars & Motor Kings; Deadly Hero; The River Niger; Swashbuckler*. 1977: *The Greatest; Star Wars* (voice only); *The Last Remake of Beau Geste; A Piece of the Action*. 1978: *Exorcist II: The Heretic*, 1979: *The Bushido Blade*. 1980: *The Empire Strikes Back* (voice only). 1981: *Conan the Barbarian*. 1982: *Blood Tide; The Flight of Dragons*. 1983: *Return of the Jedi* (voice only). 1985: *City Limits*. 1986: *My Little Girl; Soul Man*. 1987: *Gardens of Stone; Allan Quatermain and the Lost City of Gold; Matewan; Pinocchio and the Emperor of the Night* (voice only). 1988: *Coming to America; Lone Star Kid*. 1989: *Field of Dreams; Three Fugitives; Best of the Best*. 1990: *The Ambulance; The Hunt for Red October; Convicts; Grim Prairie Tales*. 1991: *Scorchers; True Identity*. 1992: *Sneakers; Patriot Games; Excessive Force*. 1993: *Sommersby; Dreamrider; The Meteor Man; The Sandlot*. 1994: *Clear and Present Danger; Naked Gun 33 1/3: The Final Insult; Africa: The Serengeti* (voice only); *Clean Slate; The Lion King* (voice only). 1995: *Judge Dredd* (voice only); *Jefferson in Paris; Cry, the Beloved Country*. 1996: *Looking for Richard; A Family Thing; Good Luck*. 1997: *Gang Related*. 1998: *Diary of an American Family*. Forthcoming: *Quest for Atlantis*.

TV movies: 1975: *The UFO Incident*. 1977: *The Greatest Thing That Almost Happened*. 1978: *Paul Robeson*. 1980: *The Golden Moment: An Olympic Love Story; Guyana Tragedy: The Story of Jim Jones*. 1981: *Amy and the Angel*. 1984: *The Vegas Strip War*. 1985: *The Atlanta Child Murders*. 1990: *Ivory Hunters; Heat Wave; Last Flight Out; By Dawn's Early Light*. 1992: *Lincoln* (voice only); *Diamonds on the Silver Screen* (voice only). 1993: *Hallelujah, Percy & Thunder*. 1994: *Twilight Zone: Rod Serling's Lost Classics; Confessions: Two Faces of Evil; The Vernon Johns Story*. 1996: *Rebound: The Legend of Earl 'The Goat' Manigault; Timepiece*. 1997: *What the Deaf Man Heard; The Second Civil War*. 1999: *Summer's End*.

TV miniseries: 1977: *Jesus of Nazareth*. 1979: *Roots: The Next Generations*. 1995: *Signs and Wonders*. 1998: *Merlin*.

TV series: 1966: *As the World Turns; The Guiding Light*. 1973: *Black Omnibus*. 1979–80: *Paris*. 1985: *Me and Mom*. 1990–91: *Gabriel's Fire*. 1991–92: *Pros and Cons*. 1995: *Under One Roof*. 1996: *3rd Rock from the Sun* (voice only).

Interactive: 1998: *Command & Conquer: Tiberian Sun*

Video: 1977: *King Lear*. 1997: *Casper: A Spirited Beginning* (voice only). 1999: *My Friend, Martin*.

Meet Jim and Jerry

⊟ On *Guiding Light*, the role of Dr. Jim Frazier was played by **Billy Dee Williams** and James Earl Jones, both in the year 1966, the only time span that the character appeared. Jim's wife, Martha, was portrayed by **Cicely Tyson** in 1966, and by Ruby Dee in 1967.

Dr. Jim and his nurse wife Martha both were on the staff of Cedars Hospital in Springfield.

⊟ On *As the World Turns*, the character of Dr. Jerry Turner was originated, and played solely, by James Earl Jones, in late 1966.

Dr. Jerry was a staff physician at Oakdale's Memorial Hospital.

- -

Who Was That Again?

Soap recasts can, at times, make fans dizzy, particularly for fans of two CBS soaps. Among the whopping eleven actresses to portray Patti Barron on *Search for Tomorrow* was veteran Trish Van Devere, in 1965. Two of the thirteen actors to play Tom Hughes on *As the World Turns* were Richard "John Boy" Thomas (1966–67) and Gregg Marx (1984–87), a descendant of a Marx Brother.

- -

Tommy Lee Jones

One of the best films I've ever appeared in.

—Tommy Lee Jones, on the video of a 1968
Yale/Harvard football game he was in
(which ended in a 29-29 tie), 1996

Llanview's bad penny: troubled Dr. Mark Toland, moodily portrayed by Tommy Lee Jones on One Life to Live *from 1971–75. Courtesy of Photofest.*

Born: September 15, 1946, in San Saba, Texas, to Clyde C. and Lucille Marie Scott Jones

Education: St. Mark's Prep School for Boys (Dallas, Texas); Harvard University (Cambridge, Massachusetts)

Debuts: Broadway—*A Patriot for Me* (1969); film—*Love Story* (1970); television—*One Life to Live* (1971) as Dr. Mark Toland

Awards: Won Emmy Award, as Outstanding Lead Actor in a Limited Series or Special, for his role as Gary Gilmore in *The Executioner's Song*, 1983; won Academy Award, as Best Supporting Actor, for his role as U.S. Marshal Sam Gerard in *The Fugitive*, 1994; won Golden Globe, as Best Performance by an Actor in a Supporting Role, for *The Fugitive*, 1994

Honors: Nominated for a Golden Globe Award in 1981, an Emmy Award in 1990, an Academy Award in 1992, a Screen Actors Guild Award in 1996, MTV Movie Awards in 1996 and 1998, and a Golden Satellite Award in 1998

Marital Status: Married Katherine Lardner, 1974, divorced, 1980; married Kimberlea Cloughley, May 30, 1981, divorced, 1995; children Austin and Victoria (with second wife)

Book: *The Films of Tommy Lee Jones*, by Alvin H. Marill (1998)

It's more fun than polo. It's like going undefeated in football." The words of Tommy Lee Jones on his profession. He loves acting, and it shows.

Tommy's parents had a seesaw relationship: they married, had Tommy, divorced, remarried, and divorced again. Father Clyde was often too tough on his son, making for a less-than-happy childhood. Tommy sought sanctuary in football, a welcome diversion from seventh grade through college.

When Tommy was fifteen, he received a football scholarship to St. Mark's School of Texas, a prestigious boys' prep school in Dallas. Initially, his school superiors called Tommy "sullen, morose, and belligerent." However, by graduation, he was a superior student, a stage performer, and a gridiron star. Tommy later attended Harvard on another football scholarship and graduated *cum laude* in English literature. While there, he roomed with a Tennessee blue blood by the name of Al Gore.

Tommy began his theatrical career on Broadway no less than ten days after graduating Harvard, in *A Patriot for Me in* 1969 (costarring Maxmillian Schell). In 1970, Jones made his film debut in *Love Story*, playing a small part as Ryan O'Neal's college roommate, ironically enough, at Harvard.

Tommy continued to appear in plays, both on and off-Broadway, balancing stage work with his first regular television job, on *One Life to Live*, where he portrayed troubled Dr. Mark Toland from 1971–75.

Jones was married twice, from 1974–80 to Kate Lardner, granddaughter of short story writer/columnist Ring Lardner, and to Kimberlea Cloughley, whom he wed on May 30, 1981. They had two children, Austin Leonard and Victoria Kafka, before divorcing in 1995.

Tommy Lee Jones has made his professional name by appearing in projects that mixed heavy and brooding harshness with a sense of moral ambiguity. He quickly gained a fast reputation as a powerful, contemplative actor, who could handle supporting as well as leading roles. He played the title part of the eccentric billionaire in the 1977 TV movie *The Amazing Howard Hughes*; an escaped convict in his first starring role in a feature film, *Jackson County Jail* (1976); Loretta Lynn's husband in *Coal Miner's Daughter* (1980); murderer Gary Gilmore in the TV drama *The Executioner's Song* (1982); a Texas Ranger in the acclaimed TV miniseries *Lonesome Dove* (1988); and the unflinching mobster Cosmo in *Stormy Monday* (1988). Jones was the bright spot in the title role in the dimly received baseball biopic *Ty Cobb* (1994), and costarred with comic Jim Carrey in *Batman Forever* (1995), and funnyman Will Smith, in the mega-hit *Men In Black* (1997).

Jones won an Academy Award for his role as hardened lawman Sam Gerard in the big-screen adaptation (1993) of the 1960s TV series *The Fugitive*. For the revival of his Oscar-winning role in the *Fugitive* sequel, *U.S. Marshals* (1998), Jones received a $10,000,000 salary.

All of this adulation is noteworthy, considering Jones has yet to take an acting class.

In 1998, Jones noted, "It's no mean calling to bring fun into the afternoons of large numbers of people. That too is part of my job, and I'm happy to serve when called on." Obviously, Tommy Lee Jones enjoys his work as much as his audiences do.

Films: 1970: *Eliza's Horoscope*; *Love Story* (billed as Tom Lee Jones). 1973: *Life Study*. 1976: *Jackson County Jail*. 1977: *Rolling Thunder*. 1978: *The Betsy*; *Eyes of Laura Mars*. 1980: *Barn Burning*; *Coal Miner's Daughter*. 1981: *Back Roads*. 1983: *Nate and Hayes*. 1984: *The River Rat*. 1986: *Black Moon Rising*. 1987: *The Big Town*. 1988: *Stormy Monday*. 1989: *The Package*. 1990: *Fire Birds*. 1991: *JFK*. 1992: *Under Siege*. 1993: *Heaven & Earth*; *The Fugitive*; *House of Cards*. 1994: *Cobb*; *Natural Born Killers*; *The Client*; *Blown Away*; *Blue Sky*. 1995: *Batman Forever*. 1997: *Men in Black*; *Volcano*. 1998: *Small Soldiers* (voice only); *U.S. Marshals*. 1999: *Double Jeopardy*; *Rules of Engagement*.

TV movies: 1976: *Charlie's Angels*; *Smash-Up on Interstate 5*. 1977: *The Amazing Howard Hughes*. 1978: *Outside Chance*. 1982: *The Executioner's Song*; *The Rainmaker*. 1985: *Cat on a Hot Tin Roof*. 1986: *The Park Is Mine*; *Yuri Nosenko, KGB*. 1987: *Broken Vows*. 1988: *April Morning*; *Gotham*; *Stranger on My Land*. 1995: *The Good Old Boys* (also director and writer).

TV miniseries: 1989: *Lonesome Dove*.

TV series: 1971–75: *One Life to Live*.

Meet Mark

◻ On *One Life to Live*, the role of Dr. Mark Toland was originated, and solely played, by Tommy Lee Jones, from 1971–75.

Emotionally scarred Julie Siegel (Lee Warrick) married Dr. Mark Toland in 1972. When Dr. Dorian Cramer (Nancy Pinkerton) arrived in Llanview in 1973, she entered into an affair with Toland. With a sexually frigid wife, Dr. Mark was more than willing.

In 1975, Larry Wolek (Michael Storm) was unjustly convicted for the mercy killing of patient Rachel Wilson (Nancy Barrett). Dorian had given Rachel an injection, but forgot to record it on the patient's chart. Later that night, Mark unknowingly administered a second, ultimately fatal, dose. Mark fled town in disgrace.

While hiding out in San Francisco, Mark found out that Victor Lord (Sheppard Strudwick) was searching for his long-lost son. Quite by accident, Mark met a woman who claimed to be the mother of Victor's son, Tony (George Reinholt). However, Mark was murdered by Susan Barry (Lisa Richards) before he could sell the information to Victor.

Soapster Collegiate Roommates

While a student at the State University of New York, Sherry Stringfield (*Guiding Light*) roomed with another future soap graduate, Parker Posey (*As the World Turns*). At Julliard, Christopher Reeve (*Love of Life*) roomed with Robin Williams. At Harvard, Tommy Lee Jones (*One Life to Live*) roomed with the future Vice-President of the United States, Al Gore. At Sarah Lawrence College, Lauren Holly (*All My Children*) was the roommate of Robin Givens.

Kevin Kline

Kevin has all the attributes of what you would call a nineteenth-century actor—proper bearing, tremendous agility, a sense of style, and a command of the language that very few American actors have.

—Joseph Papp, on Kevin Kline, 1988

Soap acting—
"something I vowed I
would never do."
However, he did it:
Kevin Kline played
Woody Reed on Search
for Tomorrow *in 1977.*
Courtesy of Photofest.

Born: October 24, 1947, in St. Louis, Missouri, to Robert and Peggy Kirk Kline; birth name, Kevin Delaney Kline; older sister, Kate, and younger brothers, Chris and Alex

Education: St. Louis Priory School (Missouri); Indiana University (Bloomington); Julliard School (New York City)

Debuts: stage—*Richard III* (1970); television—*Search for Tomorrow* (1977) as Woody Reed; Broadway—*On the Twentieth Century* (1978); film—*Sophie's Choice* (1980)

Awards: Won Tony Awards, for his role as Bruce Granit in *On the Twentieth Century*, 1978, and for his role as the Pirate King in *The Pirates of Penzance*, 1981; won Academy Award, as Best Supporting Actor, for his role as Otto West in *A Fish Called Wanda*, 1988

Honor: Number thirty-four of *Entertainment Weekly*'s Fifty Funniest People Alive

Marital Status: Married actress Phoebe Cates, March 5, 1989; two children, Greta and Owen

Worked with His Wife In: Feature films: *I Love You to Death* (1990), *Princess Caraboo* (1994); Stage: *Much Ado About Nothing* (1988)

Book: *Shoptalk: Conversations About Theater and Film with Twelve Writers, One Producer and Tennessee Williams' Mother*, by Kline and Dennis Brown (1992)

A friend of mine cut a little thing from *Parade*, one of those letters in *Parade* magazine, that says, 'Geez, I thought Kevin Kline's career had taken off. Now I read that he's back to doing free Shakespeare in the park. What happened?'" Such impressions amuse him, for Kline finds equal ease with classics as he does with contemporary satire.

Kevin's dad wanted him to be a musician. "My father was passionate about music," Kline has recalled. "Our house was always filled with music." Father's love rubbed off on his son: Kevin demonstrated his adeptness with the piano ivories in *Sophie's Choice* (1982), in which he played a selection from Robert Schumann's *Kinderscenen*.

From grades six through twelve, Kline attended St. Louis Priory School, run by Benedictine monks. He was, as might be expected, the class clown; he excelled in all things academic and athletic, plus something else. "I went to Mass every day for six years," he remembered. "I calculated that if you work out the number of Sundays over a lifetime, I'm all paid up. But, I'm still religious. I still pray."

After graduating from the Priory School in 1966, he moved on to Indiana University, where he majored in music for two years, before changing his focus to drama. "It was at Indiana where I tried this acting thing, and I really loved it," he remembered.

In 1970, Kevin graduated and received, as a commencement gift, a plane ticket to New York. There he earned a spot in the newly established Julliard Drama Center in Manhattan. Two years later, he and other actors in the class formed John Houseman's Acting Company, named after the actor/producer who founded the Drama Center.

By 1977, Kevin needed to find steady, paying work. He told *TV Guide Online* about his first television experience, playing Woody Reed on *Search for Tomorrow*:

"It was something I vowed I would never do. I was a trained classical actor, and I would never cheapen myself or sell myself out by doing commercials or soap operas. And the year after I left John Houseman's The Acting Company, someone said, 'You know, an artist's first—one of his first—duties is to eat,' which I was on the verge of not doing, and I got offered this part on a soap opera and a couple of commercials, and I was able to eat by day and do theater at night. That turned out to be very worthwhile."

In 1978, producer/director Hal Prince cast him in the role of outrageously vain movie star Bruce Granit in the Broadway musical *On the Twentieth Century*. His performance earned him his first Tony Award. By next summer, he was playing the Pirate King in *The Pirates of Penzance* off-Broadway. Kevin and his costar, Linda Ronstadt, were such a hit that the show was sent to Broadway—and his role as the sarcastic swashbuckler was a marvelous showcase for his talents, showing audiences what he could, and would, offer on stage. One who was impressed was film director Alan J. Pakula, who cast Kevin in his film debut, *Sophie's Choice* (1982). By the time that movie was released, Kline had won his second Tony award, for *The Pirates of Penzance*. In 1983, he revived his swashbuckler role in the film version.

In 1983 he appeared in *The Big Chill*, his first of now five films under the direction of Lawrence Kasdan. Amidst the excellent cast were fellow soap alums **Tom Berenger** and **JoBeth Williams**.

In 1988, Kline won an Academy Award for his role, opposite John Cleese, Michael Palin, and Jamie Lee Curtis, in the comedy *A Fish Called Wanda*. Kevin played Otto West, whose grunts of "Don't call me stupid!" combined with his torturing of costar Palin (by eating live goldfish one by one) and taking deep, erotic sniffs from his own armpits before making love to Curtis, provided pure, unadulterated farcical joy.

In March 1989, Kline married actress Phoebe Cates, fifteen years his junior. They met on the set of *The Big Chill* in 1983, with little fanfare—until they saw each other again three years later. "Phoebe was so beautiful, I just liked looking at her," Kline said of his wife. "And she was funny. This was ten years ago. She was very young, and that was very scary to me. I could have adopted her or dated her. Those seemed to be the options." The Kline family became four with the 1991 birth of Owen, and the 1994 arrival of Greta.

In 1991, he took on the role of Jeffrey Anderson in the big-screen soap opera, *Soapdish*. This amusing poke at TV's daily serial genre, costarring Sally Field and Robert Downey Jr., furthered the common stereotypical views of daytime drama.

His roles in *Dave* (1993) and *The Ice Storm* (1997) were box-office successes, but neither of them set off the amount of sparks and controversy that *In & Out* (1997) created. In that entry, costarring **Tom Selleck**, Kline played a firmly closeted gay drama teacher from the Midwest who is accidentally "outed," on national TV no less, by a bumbling former student (Matt Dillon).

Kline's emphasis on quality over quantity in his movie roles has left him with a shorter résumé than others with his years of experience—he finds himself, sometimes, with months and up to a year between projects.

"I've been very fortunate," concludes Kevin Kline. "I'm doing work that I want to do. I enjoy going to my job every day. And, I'm told I'm in the minority. A lot of people go to work, and it's not their favorite thing that they do." Not a bad way to go, indeed.

Films: 1982: *Sophie's Choice*. 1983: *The Big Chill*; *He Makes Me Feel Like Dancin'*; *The Pirates of Penzance*. 1985: *Silverado*. 1986: *Violets Are Blue . . . .* 1987: *Cry Freedom*. 1988: *A Fish Called Wanda*. 1989: *The January Man*. 1990: *I Love You to Death*. 1991: *Soapdish*; *Grand Canyon*. 1992: *Chaplin*; *Consenting Adults*. 1993: *Dave*; *The Nutcracker* (voice only). 1994: *Princess Caraboo*. 1995: *French Kiss*. 1996: *Looking for Richard*; *The Hunchback of Notre Dame* (voice only); *Shakespeare's Children*. 1997: *Fierce*

Creatures; The Ice Storm; In & Out. Forthcoming: *The Wild, Wild West; A Midsummer Night's Dream; The Road to El Dorado* (voice only).

TV movies: 1990: *Hamlet* (also director).

TV series: 1977: *Search for Tomorrow*.

Meet Woody

📺 On *Search for Tomorrow*, the role of Woody Reed was originated, and solely played, by Kevin Kline, in 1977.

The character of Woody was added at a time when a ratings-inspired youth movement had just begun on TV's longest running soap. This was, no doubt, inspired further by *The Young and the Restless*, which then boasted daytime's most beautiful cast.

Kline has noted, "Working in a soap opera was the first time I got to work with cameras. I got to work with no rehearsal. You learn to be loose in front of the camera, or three or four cameras, as the case may be in a soap opera. So I learned all of these kind of new techniques with less than stellar material albeit, but that was part of it, too, rewriting. I learned to rewrite."

• •

Pepperoni or Sausage?

For their roles in *I Love You to Death* (1990), Kevin Kline (*Search for Tomorrow*) and Tracey Ullman had to bone up on their pizza twirling acumen: they learned from Joe Lando (*One Life to Live, Guiding Light*), who was a pizza chef previous to his soap work, and who got credit as technical advisor on the film.

• •

Ray Liotta

The sweetest guy in Bay City: Joey Perrini, portrayed by Ray Liotta on Another World *from 1978–81. Video screen photo, collection of author.*

I started off on the soap Another World, *and my character was such a sweet guy it was ridiculous. Towards the end of the show I married this beautiful blonde nurse who turned out to be one of the richest women in America. But instead of enjoying the money, I got an annulment from her, just because she lied to me. That's how goofy it got. When I quit the show, they had us remarry and I guess we're still in Switzerland skiing.*

—Ray Liotta, on his big acting break, 1998

Born: December 18, 1955, in Newark, New Jersey; adopted at six months old by Alfred and Mary Liotta

Education: University of Miami (Florida)

Debuts: television—*Another World* (1978) as Joey Perrini; film—*The Lonely Lady* (1983)

Honor: Nominated for Golden Globe Award, 1987

Marital Status: Married former model Michelle Johnson Grace, February 15, 1997; one daughter, Karsen.

It doesn't matter what everyone else is saying, just do what you got to do." This is Ray Liotta's credo, both in life and in work. Once considered one of Hollywood's most sought-after newcomers, the now-veteran Liotta's half-demonic/half-heroic presence still has immediate impact, regardless of any other virtues in the particular film in which he has a part.

Liotta was adopted at age six months. Though his adoptive surname is Italian, Ray does not consider himself belonging to any particular heritage.

Ray attended Union High School in Union, New Jersey—he had trouble drawing an analogy between his school years and his eventual career: "It's funny I play violent guys, because in life I've only had one fight," he has recalled. "A boy at school claimed that I was sitting in his seat. Nothing happened to me. But he got hurt."

After high school graduation, he was unsure about his direction. "I didn't even want to go to college," he once recalled. "But I went down to the University of Miami, and I didn't want to do a lot of math and science; so I thought, why don't I just take theater and breeze around for a year?"

He studied theater and fine arts, taking part in several stage productions. "I played a dancing waiter in *Cabaret*, and then I did *West Side Story*, *The Sound of Music*—and I was just this jock from Jersey, so it was an alien world to me." While in college, he earned spending money by working in a local Florida cemetery.

After college, Liotta moved to New York, working in commercials, and then, in 1978, landing a three-year stint on *Another World*, in the role of ultra-sweet Joey Perrini. Playing a too-lovable hero would prove an ironic twist to his later penchant for gangster and tough-guy acting roles. His soap days ended in December 1981, beginning a particularly slow next four years: three TV movies and one theatrical film (his debut, *The Lonely Lady*, 1983).

His acquaintance Melanie Griffith (wed, at the time, to Liotta's college friend, actor Stephen Bauer) suggested Ray to director Jonathan Demme for a part alongside her in *Something Wild* (1986). Ray won critical praise and a Golden Globe nomination in the role of ex-con Ray Sinclair.

Liotta has continued to draw raves for his acting. He played opposite Tom Hulce and Jamie Lee Curtis in *Dominick and Eugene* (1988) in a characterization that earned him standing as an actor's actor. He was soon cast in the pivotal role of Shoeless Joe Jackson in *Field of Dreams* (1989). A splendid performance and the film's Academy Award nomination for Best Picture solidified Liotta's ascent into the ranks of his generation's most respected actors.

Even Robert De Niro noticed, suggesting Liotta for a starring role in Martin Scorsese's disturbing gangster pic *GoodFellas* (1990), and Ray provided an excellent performance as reluctant mobster kingpin Harry Hill. As Ray recalled, "I got the part because I frightened Scorsese. I went up to him at a film festival and his bodyguards thought I was an assassin. It was perfect casting."

In his films, Liotta suggests a dark nature made more menacing by startling good looks. His steely blue eyes have charmed many a female: over the years his name has been connected with Cher and Brooke Shields, but he settled down to a post-forty first marriage with Michelle Johnson, ex-wife of baseball's Mark Grace, on February 15, 1997. The couple welcomed their first child, daughter Karsen, on December 21, 1998.

Ray's movie career has had a seesaw motion. He appeared with Whoopi Goldberg in *Corrina, Corrina* (1994), and then shared the screen with Danny Glover and a hovering pachyderm in *Operation Dumbo Drop* (1995). The not-exactly-memorable *Unforgettable* (1996), and *Turbulence* (1997, considered by many the worst film of the year), were followed up with the high-profile *Cop Land* (1997), which reinstated Liotta's big-screen respectability.

His reputation was furthered by a stellar turn as Frank Sinatra in the cable TV biopic *The Rat Pack* (1998). Playing the newly departed Chairman of the Board was no mean feat, but Liotta perfectly captured Sinatra's all-too-human complexity.

Ray Liotta continues to refine and reestablish his screen personalities, surprising viewers with each appearance; in the process, he makes his audiences increasingly happy that he ditched his collegiate cemetery career.

Films: 1983: *The Lonely Lady*. 1986: *Something Wild*. 1988: *Arena Brains*; *Dominick and Eugene*. 1989: *Field of Dreams*. 1990: *GoodFellas*. 1991: *Article 99*. 1992: *Unlawful Entry*. 1994: *Corrina, Corrina*; *No Escape*. 1995: *Operation Dumbo Drop*. 1996: *Unforgettable*. 1997: *Cop Land*; *Turbulence*. 1998: *Phoenix*. Forthcoming: *Muppets in Space*.

TV movies: 1980: *Hardhat and Legs*. 1981: *Crazy Times*. 1983: *Casablanca*. 1985: *Our Family Honor*. 1991: *Women & Men 2: In Love There Are No Rules*. 1998: *The Rat Pack*.

TV series: 1978–81: *Another World*.

Meet Joey

On *Another World*, the character of Joey Perrini was played by Paul Perri (1978) and Ray Liotta (1978–81).

Joey was the son of single mother Rose Perrini (Kathleen Widdoes), and brother of Angie Perrini Frame (then Maeve Kinkead). He was married to perky Eileen Simpson (Vicky Dawson), who died in 1979. He found happiness with Kit Farrell Halloway (Bradley Bliss). Joey and Kit were wed in April 1980, but were divorced the following year. They eventually reunited, and the two left Bay City in December 1981.

Donna Mills

I eat oatmeal or Raisin Bran for breakfast, just like everybody else. What else would I have? Quail?

—Donna Mills, 1996

Born: December 11, 1943 in Oak Park, Illinois; birth name, Donna Jean Miller

Education: University of Illinois (Urbana)

Broadway Highlight: *Don't Drink the Water* (1966)

Debuts: television—*The Secret Storm* (1966) as Rocket; film—*The Incident* (1967)

Personal Status: never married; adopted daughter Chloe

Abby Fairgate Cunningham Ewing Sumner: homewrecker, sleazy businesswoman, bombshell. From 1980–89 on the nighttime drama *Knots Landing*, Donna Mills gave a most wicked life to this glorious character. In this assignment, she offered one of the most memorable vixens television has ever known.

Donna Jean Miller grew up in Illinois, with aspirations of becoming a dancer. She soon leaned towards acting, changing her name to Donna Mills, moving to New York, and finding quick work as a model and actress. Her first assignment was on stage, with an early role in Woody Allen's Broadway debut, *Don't Drink the Water* (1966), followed by a recurring role as Rocket on the long-running *The Secret Storm*. She stayed with the soap for six months in 1966, and was noticed.

She soon nabbed her first big-screen role, as Alice in the New York–filmed *The Incident* (1967), following that with the role of Laura Donnelly on *Love Is a Many Splendored Thing*. Mills found the work in daytime TV particularly challenging: "I was so new to the city then," she has recalled. "New York was just like a wonderland to me. But [*Love Is a Many Splendored Thing*] was very hard work, because the show sort of ended up resting on my shoulders and Leslie Charleson's shoulders. We played sisters and all the story lines seemed to revolve around us—which was very flattering, but also, very draining." Donna stayed with the soap for three years, leaving in 1970.

Two jobs necessitated a 1971 move to Los Angeles, where the animal-loving Mills is said to have chosen her first apartment because it was next to a stable. First was a big-screen turn in *Play Misty for Me*, in support of Clint Eastwood, and next was a short-lived TV series, NBC's *The Good Life*, which aired from September 1971 to January 1972. This one, and numerous other roles in TV series and movies, culminated in her crowning achievement: Abby.

December 27, 1979 saw the premiere of a prime-time TV series. It was *Knots Landing*, the spin-off of the long-running *Dallas* (1978–91). The heated drama was set in a fictional Knots Landing, California, cul-de-sac. A 1980 addition to the continuing saga was Abby Fairgate Cunningham, who, in her ten-year reign, added surnames Ewing and Sumner to her moniker, breaking hearts and business deals along the way. Mills' striking blonde looks and commanding screen presence made Abby an unforgettable character. Since leaving the cul-de-sac in 1989, she has done double-duty behind the camera, serving as executive producer on her numerous TV movies, and founding Donna Mills Productions.

Offscreen, Mills is the picture of tranquil domesticity. She has never married, despite a long relationship with beau Richard Holland, and shares her Beverly Hills home with daughter Chloe, whom she adopted in 1994, four days after birth. Her life is utterly normal; yet she is continually amazed that Donna Mills, soap vixen and sex symbol, can participate in the daily chores of parenthood. She once sighed, "The other day, I was with Chloe and somebody asked if I changed diapers. I was like, 'Um . . . yeah!'"

Such confusion is understandable. We can't imagine Abby tolerating spent diapers. Often, the result of strong acting is the creation of unforgettable and human characters. So when audiences confuse Abby with the real Donna Mills, it is actually a high compliment to her powerful small-screen talents.

Films: 1967: *The Incident*. 1971: *Play Misty for Me*. 1975: *Live a Little, Steal a Lot*. 1995: *Dangerous Intentions*.

Television: movies—1972: *Haunts of the Very Rich*; *Night of Terror*; *Rolling Man*. 1973: *The Bait*; *Someone at the Top of the Stairs*. 1974: *Live Again, Die Again*. 1975: *Beyond the Bermuda Triangle*; *Who Is the Black Dahlia?* 1976: *Bunco*; *Look What's Happened to Rosemary's Baby*; *Smash-Up* *on Interstate 5*. 1977: *The Hunted Lady*; *Curse of the Black Widow*; *Fire!* 1978: *Superdome*; *Doctors' Private Lives*. 1979: *Hanging by a Thread*. 1980: *Waikiki*. 1982: *Bare Essence*. 1984: *He's Not Your Son*. 1985: *Alice in Wonderland*. 1986: *Intimate Encounters*. 1988: *Outback Bound*. 1989: *The Lady Forgets*. 1990: *The World's Oldest Living Bridesmaid* (also executive producer). 1991: *False Arrest*; *Runaway Father* (also executive producer). 1992: *The President's Child*; *In My Daughter's Name* (also executive producer). 1993: *Barbara Taylor Bradford's 'Remember'*. 1994: *My Name Is Kate* (also executive producer). 1995: *An Element of Truth*. 1996: *The Stepford Husbands*.

TV miniseries: 1997: *Knots Landing: Back to the Cul-de-Sac*

TV series: 1966: *The Secret Storm*. 1967–70: *Love Is a Many Splendored Thing*. 1971–72: *The Good Life*. 1980–89: *Knots Landing*.

Video: 1986: *Donna Mills: The Eyes Have It*; *Nancy Friday's "Intimate Sex"*

Meet Rocket and Laura

On *The Secret Storm*, the character of Rocket was played by Donna Mills for six months in 1966.

The show, which aired on CBS from February 1, 1954, to February 8, 1974, dealt with the comings and goings of residents of fictional Woodbridge, New York. The series was originally entitled *The Storm Within*: when it was learned that an antacid was one of the show's sponsors, producers wisely renamed the program.

Mills' character of Rocket was a short-lived, and very sporadic, part of the program. For it, Donna used her theatrical background to good use: Rocket was a nightclub singer.

On *Love Is a Many Splendored Thing*, the character of Laura Donnelly was played by Donna Mills (1967–70), Veleka Gray (1970–71), and Barbara Stanger (1972–73).

The show, which aired on CBS from September 18, 1967, to March 23, 1973, began as a continuation of the 1955 film of the same name, starring Jennifer Jones and William Holden. The movie, in turn, had been based upon the 1952 novel, *A Many Splendored Thing*, by Han Suyin.

The Donnelly family was comprised of Dr. Will (Judson Laire) and his daughters Iris (then Leslie Charleson) and Laura. In Mills' tenure, Laura was a confused young girl, initially seen in a convent, in tortuous conflict over whether or not to take her final vows. She didn't, as the religious overtones were seen as too controversial for the war-torn late 1960s. Laura eventually got married, to Mark Elliott (then David Birney).

A Not-So-*Secret Storm*

The Secret Storm is, perhaps, best remembered today for a guest stint by legendary actress Joan Crawford. Her daughter, Christina Crawford, played Joan Borman Kane on the show from 1968–69. One day in October 1968, Christina fell ill, and "Mommie Dearest" suggested her daughter's program replacement: herself. So, Joan Crawford was paid $585 for her four half-hour show appearances (a bit lower than the usual A.F.T.R.A. contract scale rate of, at that time, $165 per half-hour stint). Crawford gave the money to her hairdresser. Despite the thirty-three-year age difference between mother and daughter, sixty-year-old Joan gave a ratings-boosting performance as the twenty-something Joan, playing opposite Keith Charles who, as Nick Kane, was then in his mid-twenties.

Demi Moore

One day I had forty pages to learn. It gets a lot easier as time goes on. I really enjoy improvisation. It's an exciting way to work. It adds a spark to the performance and keeps the energy flowing.
—Demi Moore, from Who's Who in Daytime TV *(1982)*

Fresh-faced Demi Moore played reporter Jackie Templeton on General Hospital *from 1982–83; her debut was one of the most widely covered in soap history. Courtesy of Shooting Star.*

Born: November 11, 1962, in Roswell, New Mexico, to Virginia Guynes and Charles Harmon; birth name, Demetria Guynes; two half-brothers, Morgan Guynes and James Craig Harmon; stepfather Danny Guynes

Name Root: Her mother got the name Demetria from a beauty product she saw in a magazine

Education: Fairfax High School (Los Angeles)

Debuts: television—*Quincy* (1982); film—*Young Doctors in Love* (1982); stage—*The Early Girl* (1987)

Award: Won Theatre World Award, for her role in *The Early Girl*, 1987; won ShoWest Award as Female Star of the Year, 1994

Honors: Nominated for Golden Globe Awards in 1991 and 1997; chosen by *People* magazine as one of the Fifty Most Beautiful People in the World (1996); nominated for MTV Movie Awards in 1996 and 1998

Marital Status: Married musician Frederick G. "Freddy" Moore, February 1981, divorced, 1984; married actor Bruce Willis, November 21, 1987, separated, June 24, 1998; three children, Rumer, Scout, Tallulah (all with second husband Bruce Willis)

Books: *Pearls of Wisdom from Grandma*, by Jennifer Gates Hayes, ed., introduction by Moore (1997); *Practical Intuition: How to Harness the Power of Your Instinct and Make It Work for You*, by Laura Day, introduction by Moore (1996); *Starring Demi Moore As Hester Prynne: Hollywood's All-Time Worst Casting Blunders*, by Damien Bona (1996)

Back in 1982, she received the most publicity ever afforded to a daytime newcomer. Currently, she commands the highest base salary of any actress in the world. Yet, the road to worldwide fame that Demi Moore has traveled has been highlighted by many peaks and valleys.

Demetria Guynes was the first child of mother Virginia, who remarried Danny Guynes after being abandoned by Demi's birth father, Charles Harmon, after a two-month marriage. Danny's frequent gambling necessitated over thirty family moves throughout the west, and sent the family into poverty.

Demi's early years were marked by kidney disease at ages five and ten, two operations to correct a crossed right eye at age twelve, the divorce of Danny and Virginia in 1977, and the suicide of Danny Guynes in 1980. By age sixteen, Demi had dropped out of Fairfax High School in Los Angeles, moved into her own apartment, started acting studies, modeled for the Elite Agency, and worked for a debt collection agency.

At age eighteen, in February 1981, she married rock musician Freddy Moore, twelve years her senior. She quickly took her new husband's name, becoming Demi Moore. The couple divorced in 1984.

In 1982, Demi beat out a thousand other actresses for the role of Jackie Templeton on ABC's *General Hospital*. Initially slated to play a new love interest for soap superstar Anthony Geary, Demi was an instant sensation. In her first month on the afternoon show, she appeared on the cover of *Us* magazine (February 16, 1982) with Geary. "She had street smarts," recalled former *GH* costar Norma Connolly. "She learned fast."

Perhaps, too fast. During her days on the daytime drama, having gained a quick celebrity and a growing salary, she reportedly began abusing alcohol and cocaine. One year after Demi left *General Hospital,* in 1984, she began work on the feature film *St. Elmo's Fire* (1985), playing cocaine addict Jules. To play the role, she reportedly signed a contract stipulating that she would stop her own substance abuse. When she backslid, she received an ultimatum from the film's director Joel Schumacher: clean up, or be fired. Two weeks later, she returned to the studio, substance-free. It was a major turning point in her young life.

Demi rounded out the 1980s in little-remembered film vehicles, but struck gold with the mega-hit *Ghost* (1990). With that one magical turn, Demi was thrust to the top of the Hollywood A-List. Screen roles in *A Few Good Men* (1992), *Indecent Proposal* (1993), *Disclosure* (1994), *The Juror* (1995), *Striptease* (1996), and *G.I. Jane* (1997) placed Demi squarely in the public eye, and laughing all the way to her bank. Now the highest-paid actress in the world, she currently commands $12,500,000 per film. Her one serious misstep (*Striptease* to one side) was giving *The Scarlet Letter* (1995) a happy ending, contrary to author Nathaniel Hawthorne's morality-drenched conclusion. Her justification? "Not many people have read the book."

On the personal relationship front, Demi has not fared well. After her divorce from Freddy Moore, Demi entered into a three-year relationship with actor Emilio Estevez. After their 1987 breakup she met Bruce Willis, then costarring on ABC-TV's series *Moonlighting*. Following a short three-month courtship, Moore and Willis married on November 21, 1987, in a ceremony (officiated by Little Richard!) that cost a reported $875,000. The two have three daughters, Rumer Glenn (b. 1988), Scout Larue (b. 1991), and Tallulah Belle (b. 1994). On June 24, 1998, Demi and Bruce's estrangement was announced amid rumors of Willis's infidelity. Since October 1998, the tabloids have alternately insisted that the couple is divorcing, or reuniting. This story's ending has yet to be concluded.

Over recent years, two magazine cover appearances brought Demi celebrated notoriety: on the August 1991 cover of *Vanity Fair*, she posed very pregnant and nude, covering key spots with her arms. On the August 1992 cover of *Vanity Fair*, she wore a man's suit: of paint. *Allure* magazine called Demi a "famously buff mother of three [who] is despised by unbuff mothers of three everywhere." Despite this "rebuff," Moore has suffered not one bit professionally.

Her mother, Virginia Guynes, adding to a reportedly long record of arrests for drunken driving and arson, posed nude for a 1993 magazine spread, parodying Demi's 1991 *Vanity Fair* pregnancy cover. Demi placed her mother in a Minnesota rehabilitation center. When Virginia left rehab, Demi began a five-year estrangement from her, only ended during Virginia's battle with lung cancer, which she lost on July 2, 1998.

Today, after experiencing the inevitable highs and lows of extended Hollywood superstardom, Demi Moore continues to impress, having come a long way, and having successfully battled a lifetime's worth of demons, to reach the top, her way.

Films: 1981: *Choices*. 1982: *Parasite*; *Young Doctors in Love*. 1984: *Blame It on Rio*; *Master Ninja I*; *No Small Affair*. 1985: *St. Elmo's Fire*. 1986: *About Last Night . . .*; *One Crazy Summer*; *Wisdom*. 1988: *The Seventh Sign*. 1989: *We're No Angels*. 1990: *Ghost*. 1991: *Mortal Thoughts*; *The Butcher's Wife*; *Nothing But Trouble*. 1992: *A Few Good Men*. 1993: *Indecent Proposal*. 1994: *Disclosure*; *A Century of Cinema*. 1995: *Now and Then* (also producer); *The Scarlet Letter*. 1996: *Striptease*; *The Hunchback of Notre Dame* (voice only); *The Juror*; *Beavis and Butthead Do America* (voice only). 1997: *G.I. Jane* (also producer); *Austin Powers: International Man of Mystery* (producer only); *Deconstructing Harry*. 1998: *Passion of Mind*. Forthcoming: *Airframe*.

TV movies: 1996: *If These Walls Could Talk* (also executive producer)

TV series: 1982–83: *General Hospital*

Video: 1985: "St. Elmo's Fire (Man In Motion)". 1988: *The New Homeowner's Guide to Happiness*. 1997: *Destination Anywhere*

Meet Jackie

On *General Hospital*, the role of Jackie Templeton was originated, and played solely, by Demi Moore (1982–83).

In Port Charles, two Lauras mysteriously disappeared: Spencer (Genie Francis) and Templeton (**Janine Turner**). Joining in a search for the missing women were Laura's husband, Luke Spencer (Anthony Geary), his friends Robert Scorpio (Tristan Rogers) and Tiffany Hill (Sharon Wyatt), and Laura Templeton's sister, Jackie, a sassy investigative reporter. Eventually, Luke and Jackie discovered that both disappearances were engineered by David Gray (Paul Rossilli), a mystery man who intended to steal the treasures of Malkuth from the Port Charles Museum. Laura Templeton returned, unharmed.

Luke sadly came to accept the fact that his beloved Laura was never coming back (at least, not for a few years; Francis eventually returned in 1993, and she and Geary are still with *GH*). Scorpio fell in love with Jackie Templeton. Soon thereafter, David was killed in a fight with Luke.

Bratty Roots

In 1985, a group of several young and promising stars were labeled the "Brat Pack." Included in this group were Molly Ringwald, Ally Sheedy, Tom Cruise, Matt Dillon, Patrick Swayze, Keifer Sutherland, Phoebe Cates, Lou Diamond Phillips, Rob Lowe, Emilio Estevez, and Demi Moore (*General Hospital*).

Julianne Moore

It kind of gives you a different perspective on everything. It's wonderful. Although you don't want to make it important, everybody's talking about it.

—Julianne Moore, on her Oscar nomination, 1998

Julianne Moore won a 1988 Emmy Award for her dual portrayal of twins Frannie and Sabrina Hughes. Video screen photo, collection of author.

Born: December 3, 1960, in Boston, Massachusetts; birth name, Julie Smith

Education: Boston University (Massachusetts)

Debuts: television—*The Edge of Night* (1984) as Carmen Engler; film—*Tales from the Darkside: The Movie* (1990)

Awards: Won Daytime Emmy Award, as Outstanding Ingenue in a Daytime Drama Series, for her role as Frannie/Sabrina Hughes on *As the World Turns*, 1988; won Los Angeles Film Critics Association Award as Best Supporting Actress (1997), and National Society of Film Critics Award as Best Supporting Actress (1997), Florida Film Critics Circle Award as Best Supporting Actress (1998), Golden Satellite Award as Best Actress in a Supporting Role in a Motion Picture (1998), all for her role as Amber Waves in *Boogie Nights*

Honors: Nominated for Academy Award, Golden Globe, and Screen Actors Guild Award, 1998

Marital Status: Married John Gould Rubin, 1986, divorced, 1995; one son, Caleb (with beau Bart Freundlich)

A self-professed Army brat whose father's military livelihood moved the family twenty-three times before 1978, Julianne Moore honed her skills in college and on television, and in 1998 became one of the most honored Hollywood actresses.

After earning her Bachelor of Fine Arts from Boston University's School of the Performing Arts, she settled in Manhattan in 1982, quickly finding work off-Broadway. Two years later, in 1984, she made her television debut in a short-term part on *The Edge of Night*. The next year, however, came the role that was to endear her to soap fans: half-sisters Frannie and Sabrina Hughes on *As the World Turns*. As is common with actresses who play multiple roles (such as Erika Slezak on *One Life to Live*, and Ellen Wheeler and **Anne Heche** on *Another World*), Moore scored a Daytime Emmy Award for her work in 1988, the year she left the show.

Moore's level of name recognition did not transcend her soap stint until 1993, when three of her screen roles, in *The Fugitive, Body of Evidence*, and especially *Benny & Joon*, were well-received. In her assignment as Marian Wyman in Robert Altman's *Short Cuts* (1993) Moore provided perhaps the year's most talked-about scene. As Matthew Modine's artist-wife, she delivered a plucky monologue standing before him, and the audience, nude from the waist *down*.

Two subsequent independent films increased Moore's notice. In Louis Malle's critically acclaimed *Vanya on 42nd Street* (1994), she played the beguiling Yelena, a performance called by one reviewer "her most prestigious and perfect performance to date." In her first movie lead, in *Safe* (1995), Julianne portrayed a wealthy Los Angeles housewife plagued by a mysterious allergic reaction: Moore calls this her best and favorite role to date.

Her three-minute performance in *The Fugitive* (1997) prompted Steven Spielberg to cast her, *without an audition*, as Dr. Sarah Harding in *The Lost World*, the 1997 sequel to *Jurassic Park* (1993). She followed with *Boogie Nights*, an odd story of a family of adult entertainment filmmakers in the late 1970s seeking to elevate the industry to a form of art. Moore played the sensitive Amber Waves, and scored a Best Supporting Actress Oscar nomination, her first.

It is doubtful that it will be her last. Strong 1998 roles in the Coen Brothers' *The Big Lebowski* and *Chicago Cab*, and a costarring turn with Anne Heche in the remake of *Psycho* (1998), earned kudos.

Moore became a mother on December 4, 1997 (one would have thought that she was rehearsing for this milestone with her frantic comedic role in 1995's *Nine Months*), giving birth to Caleb, son of director/boyfriend Bart Freundlich. (Moore had been married, in 1986, to actor John Gould Rubin; they divorced in 1995.) Julianne became pregnant while shooting *The Big Lebowski*, which is ironic because, in that film, her character Maude, tries unsuccessfully to conceive.

With her personal and professional lives in such an upward positive spiral, it is certain that the great promise shown in Julianne Moore's dual role on *As the World Turns* will continue to be realized. Here, Moore *is* more.

Films: 1990: *Tales from the Darkside: The Movie*. 1992: *The Gun in Betty Lou's Handbag; The Hand That Rocks the Cradle*. 1993: *Short Cuts; The*

Fugitive; Benny & Joon; Body of Evidence. 1994: *Vanya on 42nd Street.* 1995: *Assassins; Nine Months; Safe; Roommates.* 1996: *Surviving Picasso.* 1997: *The Lost World: Jurassic Park; Boogie Nights; The Myth of Finger-prints.* 1998: *The Big Lebowski; Chicago Cab; Psycho.* Forthcoming: *An Ideal Husband; Cookie's Fortune; The End of the Affair; Magnolia; A Map of the World.*

TV movies: 1989: *Money, Power, Murder.* 1991: *Cast a Deadly Spell; The Last to Go.*

TV miniseries: 1987: *I'll Take Manhattan.*

TV series: 1984: *The Edge of Night.* 1985–88: *As the World Turns.*

Meet Carmen, Frannie, and Sabrina

◻ On *The Edge of Night*, the minor role of Carmen Engler was played, in the soap's last year on the air, 1984, by Julianne Moore.

◻ On *As the World Turns*, the role of Frannie Hughes was played by Kelly Campbell (1973), Maura Gilligan (1975–79), Tracy O'Neil (1987–89), Helene Udy (1983), Terri Vandenbosch (1983–84), Julianne Moore (1985–88), and Mary Ellen Stuart (1989–92). The role of Sabrina Hughes was played by Julianne Moore (1987–88) and Claire Beckman (1990–92).

Frannie was the daughter of Jennifer Ryan (Gillian Spencer) and Bob Hughes (Don Hastings), with half-sister Sabrina the product of an affair between married Bob and Kim Reynolds (Kathryn Hays). Kim, mistakenly, thought she had miscarried. Jennifer died in a 1975 car crash.

As can sometimes happen in daytime drama, prior history is altered to fit a later story line. Years after the "miscarriage," Kim and Bob discovered that the baby in question was born alive (yet they had been told the baby had died at birth), was swapped at Memorial Hospital, and that the child, daughter Sabrina, was sold on the black market, adopted, and raised in England. While studying in England in 1987, Frannie met Sabrina Fullerton, whose parentage was revealed soon thereafter.

Moore has recalled her soap stint with tongue-in-cheek: "I was on *As the World Turns* for three years; it was my first big job. I played Frannie Hughes, and her half-sister Sabrina, who was English. And mean. Frannie was the daughter of the chief of staff at the hospital . . . she was the good girl. I was raped, kidnapped; I had five boyfriends die; I was like the black widow of daytime; then they had me an evil half-sister who took my fiancé. It just went on and on."

Patrick Muldoon

Austin Reed and Carrie Brady (Patrick Muldoon and Christie Clark) remained sweethearts against all odds on Days of Our Lives *from 1992–95. Courtesy of Shooting Star.*

Austin represents everything that is good in me. He's faithful to one girl, he's committed to his family, he loves his mother, and Austin is a very honorable, honest person.

—Patrick Muldoon, on his Days of Our Lives *character, 1994*

Born: September 27, 1969, in San Pedro, California, to Patrick and Deanna Muldoon; birth name, William Patrick Muldoon III; one sister, Shana

Education: Loyola High School (Los Angeles) and University of Southern California (Los Angeles)

Debuts: television—*Who's the Boss?* (1990); film—*Rage and Honor II* (1993)

Award: Soap Opera Digest Award, as Best Male Newcomer of the Year, for his role as Austin Reed on *Days of Our Lives*, 1994

Honor: Chosen by *People* magazine as one of the Fifty Most Beautiful People in the World (1996)

Beauty is all in the lid [i.e., head of hair] for a guy. I mean, just look at Elvis Presley and James Dean. They had great hair. That's what I've got going for me, my lid." Be not mistaken: there's more to Patrick Muldoon than he readily admits.

Upon graduation from Loyola High School in Los Angeles, Patrick entered the University of Southern California on a partial football scholarship. His academic majors were English and communication; his gridiron talents (he played tight-end) earned Patrick two Rose Bowl rings as a member of the U.S.C. Trojans.

In his freshman year, he posed for the 1989 school calendar, *Men of U.S.C.*, gaining him a tremendous amount of exposure, a modeling contract with the prestigious Wilhelmina Agency, and an eventual campaign as a

Calvin Klein jeans model. He also had a budding career as an actor: in 1990 he landed guest gigs on TV sitcoms *Who's the Boss?* and *Saved By the Bell*, spelling an end to his football days. As Patrick noted, "When I walked into my first acting class at U.S.C., I thought, 'This is it.' I wasn't good at anything else."

Patrick approached acting in a very mature and realistic manner: "Acting is not about being young and cute," he informed *Cosmopolitan*. "And, if that's the only reason you're hired, you'll have a short career, because looks go fast. Like in football: the next young punk is right behind you."

It was with this healthy approach that he graduated U.S.C. in 1991 and landed a role the next year on *Days of Our Lives*. He originated the role of Austin Reed, a sweet and hunky all-American. In his three years in that TV part, Patrick gained legions of female admirers, and a Soap Opera Digest Award in 1994. He found the work rewarding, yet challenging: "You're locked up in a studio for about ten to fifteen hours a day for three years," Patrick told an Internet chat group on America Online. "You're either gonna become like family or you're gonna become like enemies. So, luckily, it worked out the right way."

With a few months left on his *Days* contract, Hollywood TV producer Aaron Spelling approached Muldoon, offering him a unique "holding contract," stipulating that Patrick would remain under Spelling's wing until an appropriate acting job could be found for him. Such opportunities shouldn't be ignored! Thus, Muldoon did not renew his contract with *Days of Our Lives*. "As much as I loved working there," he reasoned, "I always had something in the back of my head that made me curious about what other forums I could work in."

The initial forum as promised by Spelling was a stint on the nighttime drama *Melrose Place* (1992–present). As Richard Hart, fashion designer, he toyed with the hearts of a number of the show's females. "The pace of nighttime is slower, but it's not really easier," Patrick told America Online. "The thing that made daytime difficult was definitely the pace of it." He was on *Melrose Place* from 1995–96, after which he went on to explore a new medium: feature films.

His 1997 turn was a starring role in Paul Verhoeven's ninety-million-dollar sci-fi, high-tech thriller *Starship Troopers*. In the special effects showcase, costarring fellow soap alum **Casper Van Dien**, alien insects, trying to destroy the world, come up against the young heroes who, in turn, compete for the female element. "If we had women like that now in the military," Muldoon shared, "it would inspire enlistment."

After the visibility of *Starship Troopers*, Patrick suddenly found himself a sought-after actor. In *Wicked* (1998) he played alcoholic Lawson Smith, one of many suburban psychos in a pristine gated California community. Thereafter, Muldoon appeared in *The Arrival Agenda* (1998), as a computer scientist who received information that allowed him the ability to combat the alien infiltration of the Earth, thus saving the planet. *Toby's Story* (1998), his next offering, concerned the troubled life of a Vatican investigator.

Just as it seemed that Patrick's cinematic forte might be his (type)casting as Earth's great savior, he was seen in the HBO cable feature film *Black Cat Run* (1998) as race car driver Johnny, wrongly accused of the murder of his girlfriend's (former soapster Amelia Heinle) father.

Still-single Patrick Muldoon maintains a refreshing attitude about being a "hunk" ("If I am someone's heartthrob, I'm flattered"), and appears grounded in reality. "My family and my faith are the two things I fall back on when the going gets tough. My faith gets tested, just like anybody else's." This is the same guy who thinks that his *lid* is what he's got going for him?

Films: 1993: *Rage and Honor II*. 1997: *Starship Troopers*. 1998: *The Arrival Agenda*; *Wicked*. Forthcoming: *Toby's Story*.

TV movies: 1995: *Dead Weekend*. 1998: *Black Cat Run*; *Deadly Pursuits*.

TV series: 1992–95: *Days of Our Lives*. 1995–96: *Melrose Place*.

Meet Austin

📺 On *Days of Our Lives*, the role of Austin Reed was played by Patrick Muldoon (1992–95) and Austin Peck (1995–present).

In 1992, Kate Roberts (Deborah Adair) arrived in Salem with her son, Lucas (Bryan Datillo). Two young people, Billie (Lisa Rinna) and Austin Reed came to town around that time, as did their evil father, Curtis (Nicholas Benedict). Kate realized that Billie and Austin were the two children she had lost after escaping from her marriage to Curtis years earlier. Austin soon bonded with his mother.

During Muldoon's tenure, Austin Reed found love with sweet Carrie Brady (Christie Clark), sister of the evil Sami (Alison Sweeney). Sami loved Austin, and Lucas loved Carrie, resulting in havoc in love land. Sami stopped Austin and Carrie's wedding in late 1995 with the shocking news that she was pregnant: by Austin!

A Post-Soap Career Twist

Anne-Marie Martin (*Days of Our Lives*) retired from acting in 1988. She then moved on to another profession, screenwriting. Martin co-wrote the screenplay to *Twister* (1997) with her husband, *Jurassic Park* creator Michael Crichton, whom she married in 1989.

Kate Mulgrew

Captain Kathryn Janeway is the quintessential woman of the future... both commanding and discerning in her warmth; she's authoritative while remaining accessible.

—Kate Mulgrew, on her Star Trek: Voyager *character, 1995*

The long-awaited wedding of Mary Ryan (Kate Mulgrew) and Jack Fenelli (Michael Levin) aired on Ryan's Hope *from June 28–July 1, 1976. Courtesy of* Soap Opera Digest.

Born: April 29, 1955, in Dubuque, Iowa, to Thomas James and Joan Virginia Kiernan Mulgrew; birth name, Katherine Kiernan Mulgrew

Education: New York University and Stella Adler's Conservatory (New York City)

Debuts: stage—*The Widower's House* (1974); television—*Ryan's Hope* (1975) as Mary Ryan; film—*Lovespell* (1979)

Awards: Won the Tracey Humanitarian Award, for her one-time role as alcoholic reporter Hillary Wheaton on *Murphy Brown*, 1992; Honorary Doctorate of Letters for Artistic Contribution from Seton Hall University, New Jersey

Marital Status: Married Robert Harry Egan, 1982, divorced, 1993; two sons, Ian and Alexander James

On Her Home Town: "Dubuque, Iowa. Built on a bluff and run that way ever since."

The first female commander of a *Star Trek* space vessel. Not a bad claim to current fame for actress Kate Mulgrew, whose characters seem to always have the admirable characteristics of headstrong ambition, high aspirations, and grand success. The portrayer of these parts shares those traits.

Kate is the oldest girl in a family of eight, based in Dubuque, Iowa. From a very early age, she knew what future career path she wanted to take: she wanted to act. Following that goal, she left Dubuque at age seventeen, relocating to New York and entering New York University. At the same time, she enrolled in Stella Adler's Conservatory, and soon found that her studies were taking a back seat to her real love. Thus, in 1976, at the end of her junior year she left N.Y.U., after earning an Associate of Arts degree, to pursue acting full-time, balancing her Conservatory training with regional theater work.

Her career began with a 1974 debut at New York's Cyrano Repertory in *The Widower's House*. After that run, she took on television, accepting a role in 1975 on *Ryan's Hope*. The 1976 *Day TV Annual* described Kate's character, Mary Ryan: "She is vital, intense, passionate, stubborn, opinionated and impatient." While playing on the soap, she also performed in a Stamford, Connecticut, stage production of *Our Town*, in the pivotal role of Emily. By the end of 1977, her time on the soap had come to an end, with the role of Mary recast (Mulgrew would return to the show, briefly, in 1983). However, Kate had been noticed.

In 1978, she was approached by then-NBC Head of Programming Fred Silverman. He had developed a new network TV series with her in mind: *Mrs. Columbo*. The show ran from February–December, 1979, and featured Mulgrew as part-time reporter and amateur super sleuth Kate Columbo, the wife of Lieutenant Columbo (played by Peter Falk on his own series, *Columbo*; Falk was never seen on Mulgrew's show, and vice versa). The program underwent excessive name changes, from its original title to *Kate Columbo* to *Kate the Detective*, finally resting upon *Kate Loves a Mystery*. Though unsuccessful, the series did afford Mulgrew valuable prime-time visibility.

She was soon cast in a guest spot on *Dallas*, and in her feature film debut, as Iseult in *Lovespell* (1979), an adaptation of the classic tale of Tristan and Isolde, costarring Richard Burton. Afterwards, Kate appeared in a TV movie as the first American-born Saint, Mother Elizabeth Bayley Seton, in *A Time for Miracles* (1980), and on a TV historical miniseries, *The Manions of America* (1981), as Rachel Clement.

In 1982, Kate married Robert Egan, adding to the family in successive years, with son Ian, born in 1984 and son Alexander, born in 1985. The Egans divorced in 1993.

Through the years and the various performing media, Kate has stayed passionate about live stage performance, most notably appearing in *The Philadelphia Story* (1983), in the part of Tracy Lord, made famous in the 1940 film by Katharine Hepburn. Actually, Mulgrew bears a striking resemblance to a younger Hepburn. The two also share a cool and classy style, which Mulgrew developed in her soap tenure. She brings to her characters a sense of control and responsibility, qualities she would need in her most famed role to date.

In 1995, when a new series, UPN's *Star Trek: Voyager*, was added to the legacy of *Star Trek* franchises, a new element was introduced: a *female* Starfleet Captain. Kate nabbed the prized role of Kathryn Janeway, commander of the U.S.S. *Voyager* which, along with an enemy vessel, is thrown into the far reaches of the galaxy. Her continuing mission: bring the two crews together and get home.

In the opinion of fans of this legendary saga, this *Star Trek* ship, truly, could not be in better hands than those of Kate Mulgrew.

Films: 1979: *Lovespell.* 1982: *A Stranger Is Watching.* 1985: *Remo Williams: The Adventure Begins....* 1987: *Throw Momma from the Train.* 1992: *Round Numbers.* 1994: *Camp Nowhere.* 1995: *Captain Nuke and the Bomber Boys.*

TV movies: 1979: *Jennifer: A Woman's Story*; *Kate Loves a Mystery.* 1980: *A Time for Miracles.* 1987: *Roses Are for the Rich.* 1988: *Roots: The Gift*, *Heartbeat.* 1991: *Fatal Friendship*; *Daddy.* 1993: *For Love and Glory.* 1995: *Star Trek: Voyager—Caretaker.* 1998: *Nightworld: Riddler's Moon.*

TV miniseries: 1978: *The Word*; 1981: *The Manions of America.*

TV series: 1975: *Alien Lover*; *Ryan's Hope* (1975–77, 1983). 1979: *Kate Loves a Mystery.* 1988–89: *Heartbeat.* 1991: *Man of the People.* 1995–present: *Star Trek: Voyager.*

Meet Mary

On *Ryan's Hope*, the role of Mary Ryan Fenelli was played by Kate Mulgrew (1975–77, 1983), Mary Carney (1978), Kathleen Tolan (1978–79), and Nicolette Goulet (1979).

Mary was a headstrong, aspiring journalist who fell in love with, and married, hard-boiled reporter Jack Fenelli (Michael Levin). Their legendary arguments on feminism and social mores provided both humorous tension and important issue-raising.

After Mulgrew left the daytime show, and while Nicolette Goulet was in the role, Mary gave birth to a daughter, Ryan, who would later be played by **Yasmine Bleeth**.

In 1979, Mary Ryan Fenelli was killed by organized crime after investigating the Mafia. For years, her parents, Johnny (Bernard Barrow) and Maeve (Helen Gallagher), and her husband Jack, struggled to accept Mary's tragic and violent passing: in 1983, Kate Mulgrew returned to the role, in a guest appearance, visiting and comforting Maeve and Jack in daydreams.

Luke Perry

Luke Perry appeared on Ryan's Hope, Loving, *and* Another World *before moving to nighttime drama* Beverly Hills, 90210. *Courtesy of Shannon Van Meter.*

I don't worry about it. You know, before I had success I was just going along, living my life and doing my thing. I'm doing the same thing now, except I have a measure of success behind me that allows me more room to move within this business. But the objective is still the same: to find great parts and play them.

—Luke Perry, on success, 1997

Born: October 11, 1966, in Mansfield, Ohio, to Coy and Ann Perry; birth name, Coy Luther Perry III; brother, Tom; sister, Amy; stepsister, Emily

Education: Fredericktown High School (Ohio)

Debuts: television—*Loving* (1987) as Ned Bates; film—*Scorchers* (1991)

Honor: Chosen by *People* magazine as one of the Twenty-Five Most Intriguing People of 1991

Marital Status: Married former paralegal Minnie Sharp, November 20, 1993; one son, Jack

Books: *Loving Luke,* by Randi Reisfeld (1991); *Luke Perry (Reaching for the Stars),* by Rosemary Wallner (1992); *Luke Perry (Start Shots Collector's Book, 1),* by Sonia Black (1992); *Luke Perry (Who's Hot!, No. 1),* by Evan Keith (1992)

In the annals of television history, few performers have achieved the level of fan adulation, true over-the-wall frenzy, as has Luke Perry in his five-year turn (and now return) as heartthrob Dylan McKay on the Fox network smash nighttime drama *Beverly Hills, 90210.* Yet, such hero worship comes with a very high price tag, as this young actor found out.

As a youngster, Coy Luther Perry III was a rambunctious and active boy. At age five, Coy watched a rerun of the 1967 Paul Newman classic, *Cool Hand Luke.* After seeing that prison drama, he decided that, from then on, he was to be called Luke. It stuck.

It was at Fredericktown High School, where he was a mediocre student, that he first tasted the enjoyable aspects of performance: donning yellow tights, red feathers, a cape, and webbed feet, he was "Freddie Bird," the school mascot.

Following graduation, he moved to the West Coast. He earned needed money for acting classes in Hollywood by laying asphalt, selling shoes, and working in a doorknob factory. He did get his training, going out on a reported 216 failed auditions before landing an acting role that required a move to New York: his television debut, in 1987, as Ned Bates, on *Loving*. "That was my first break," Perry has remembered.

In his year on the daytime drama, he developed a romance with **Yasmine Bleeth**, then playing Ryan Fenelli on *Ryan's Hope*. The two lived together in Manhattan until shortly before he departed New York in 1990. Previous to that, after leaving *Loving*, he got a recurring role on another New York-based soap, *Another World*, as Kenny. When that brief assignment concluded in 1988, he found work in Levi's 501 TV commercials. "Then," according to Perry, "a year and a half of unemployment."

That was before he moved back to Los Angeles in 1990 and gained the favor of TV mogul Aaron Spelling, who wanted Perry to join the cast of his new series, *Beverly Hills, 90210*, costarring Shannen Doherty, Jason Priestley, and fellow soap alumnus **Ian Ziering**. Perry's salary was paid directly out of Spelling's pocket until 1992, when it was assured that Perry's character of Dylan McKay had caught on with audiences.

Perry was soon receiving almost three thousand fan letters a week. In a celebrated May 1991 episode of Dylan fever, Perry escaped four thousand female fans by hiding in a laundry hamper. Through his moody, heartthrob prime-time character, Luke was now one of the television industry's hottest commodities.

During his six-season *90210* tenure, Luke appeared in a number of feature films, including *Buffy the Vampire Slayer* (1992), inspiration for the current TV series starring soap grad **Sarah Michelle Gellar**. On the small screen, he was heard on the animated comedy series *The Simpsons*, playing himself via voice-over in the May 13, 1993, episode "Krusty Gets Kancelled." In 1994, he appeared in what he calls his favorite film appearance thus far: *8 Seconds*, the biopic about the late rodeo champion Lane Frost. The sincere little film did not fare well at the box office, but it did influence Perry's wardrobe. Afterwards, Luke was commonly spotted in cowboy boots and ten-gallon hats.

During the filming of *8 Seconds*, romance blossomed in Perry's personal life, and shortly after production on the picture wrapped in 1993, Luke married former paralegal Minnie Sharp. On June 15, 1997, the Perrys welcomed their first son, Jack. The family settled in the San Fernando Valley, all *six* of them: six, if you include their pets, three Vietnamese pot-bellied pigs!

In 1995, after six years on *Beverly Hills, 90210*, Luke determined that he needed to change his professional zip code and left the show. Not yet thirty, Perry found that his frequent label of "the next James Dean," was quite a cross to bear. "Even Michael J. Fox got called the next James Dean," Perry would comment. "They just want him to be alive and kicking, and he isn't. So get over it!"

Though he founded his own production company, Midwest Productions, Perry could not escape the role that made him a household name. He languished for three years in voice-over guest spots, and some theatrical films, TV movies and miniseries, capturing little of that "Dylan" brand of magic. In August 1998, *Variety* announced that Perry would return to *Beverly Hills, 90210*, starting with the November 12, 1998, episode, for at least twelve entries in the 1998–99 season, in a new development deal with Twentieth Century Fox TV. Luke Perry knew it was his destiny: "You just don't get that many shots in this world," he concluded. "Those opportunities don't come along often."

Films: 1991: *Scorchers.* 1992: *Buffy the Vampire Slayer*; *Terminal Bliss.* 1993: *The Webbers.* 1994: *8 Seconds.* 1996: *American Strays*; *Normal Life.* 1997: *The Fifth Element*; *Lifebreath.* 1998: *The Florentine.* Forthcoming: *Storm.*

TV movies: 1997: *Riot.* 1998: *Indiscreet.*

TV miniseries: 1997: *Robin Cook's Invasion.*

TV series: 1987–88: *Loving.* 1988: *Another World.* 1990–95, 1998–present: *Beverly Hills, 90210.* 1995: *Mortal Kombat: The Animated Series* (voice only). 1996: *The Incredible Hulk* (voice only).

Video: 1993: *For Our Children.*

Meet Ned and Kenny

⊏ On *Loving*, the character of Ned Bates was originated, and played solely, by Luke Perry (1987–88).

Ned was the brother of Lottie (Judith Hoag), and briefly dated April Hathaway (Alexandra Wilson).

Loving was created in 1983, and in its twelve-year tenure was one of the few half-hour series left on network daytime television. On November 13, 1995, the show was cancelled, but in a most unique way: months earlier, a serial killer began systematically exterminating major characters on the show. Some survived, transplanted from fictional Corinth, Pennsylvania, to Soho, New York, and saw new life through a revamped soap: when *Loving* died, *The City* was born. Despite its upgraded production values, and soap superstars Morgan Fairchild and Jane Elliot in its cast, *The City* was cancelled sixteen months after its premiere, on March 28, 1997.

⊏ On *Another World*, the small recurring role of Kenny was played by Luke Perry during a brief period in 1988.

Brad Pitt

You want to get to where you have the pick of films you want to do. You want people to be entertained. You want your work to be respected. To accomplish all that, all this comes with it.
—Brad Pitt, on fan frenzy, 1997

High school athlete Chris (Brad Pitt), ready to sink the basketball on Another World *in 1987. Video screen photo, collection of author.*

Born: December 18, 1963, in Shawnee, Oklahoma, to William and Jane Pitt; birth name, William Bradley Pitt; eldest of three children

Education: Kickapoo High School (Missouri); University of Missouri (Columbia)

Debuts: television—*Dallas* (1987); film—*Cutting Class* (1989)

Awards: Won ShoWest Award, as Male Star of Tomorrow, 1993; won MTV Movie Awards as Best Male Performance and Most Desirable Male, both for his role as Louis in *Interview with the Vampire*, 1995, and as Most Desirable Male, for his role as David Mills in *Se7en*, 1996; won Golden Globe Award as Best Supporting Actor for his role as Jeffrey Goines in *Twelve Monkeys*, 1996; won Blockbuster Entertainment Award, as Favorite Supporting Actor, Science Fiction, for *Twelve Monkeys*, 1997; won Rembrandt Award for Best Actor for his role as Heinrich Harrer in *Seven Years in Tibet*, 1998

Honors: Named Sexiest Man Alive by *People* magazine, 1994; nominated for Golden Globe Award in 1995; nominated for Academy Award and two MTV Movie Awards, 1996; chosen by *People* magazine as one of the Fifty Most Beautiful People in the World, 1996 and 1997

Books: *Brad Pitt*, by Holly George-Warren, Mark Seliger, and Chris Mundy (1997); *Brad Pitt*, by Paula Guzzetti (1998); *Brad Pitt*, by House of Collectibles (1996); *Brad Pitt*, by Chris Nickson (1995); *Brad Pitt*, by Matt Zoller Seitz (1996); *Brad Pitt: Hot and Sexy*, by Grace Catalano (1995); *Brad Pitt: Superstars of Film*, by Amy

Dempsey (1997); *Brad Pitt: Tear-Out Photo Book* (1996); *Brad Pitt: The Illustrated Story*, by Caroline Westbrook (1996); *Brad Pitt: The Rise to Stardom*, by Brian J. Robb (1996); *Brad Pitt (Who's Hot!)*, by Regan Shay (1992)

Females the world over adore him. The film industry reveres him. His name is household. Brad Pitt, though, came from the humblest of roots, worked the typical jobs, and built his career despite hard, if sometimes comical, circumstances.

Oldest of three children in a churchgoing, respectable Missouri family, William Bradley Pitt graduated from Kickapoo High School in 1981, excelling in debate, sports, and theatrics. He majored in advertising and graphic design at the University of Missouri, but had bigger plans. Two weeks, and two credits, short of graduation, Pitt crammed all his worldly goods into his Datsun (he dubbed the auto "Runaround Sue") and headed for California, telling his parents he was transferring to the Art Center College of Design in Pasadena. That was not altogether true.

He did arrive in California. However, his acting classes by day were balanced by night jobs such as waiting tables, driving a limousine, and donning a chicken costume for the El Pollo Loco restaurant chain. Soon, in 1987, his real ambitions were met, with a recurring role on TV's *Dallas*, playing the randy boyfriend of Charlie Wade (played by Shalane McCall). After that came a week-long stint as high school student Chris on *Another World*, in May 1987. The still very boyish-looking Pitt was noticed, sort of, in this role. Nevertheless, he spent the next three years languishing in guest roles, on such TV shows as *Growing Pains*, *thirtysomething*, and *Head of the Class* (in 1988, Pitt began a short-term interracial romance with *Head of the Class* costar Robin Givens). He was also involved, for three years, with his sixteen-year-old *Too Young to Die* (1990) costar Juliette Lewis.

It was in 1991, however, that Pitt was first universally noticed, as the horny hitchhiker J. D. in *Thelma & Louise*. Pitt briefly dated older costar Geena Davis, whose screen character Thelma received her first orgasm at J. D.'s hand. Hollywood recognized Brad as not just another pretty face, but as an actor of merit. He gained roles as the doomed golden boy in Robert Redford's *A River Runs Through It* (1992), and in rather forgettable vehicles such as *Johnny Suede* (1992) and the kinky *Kalifornia* (1993), before his life changed, monumentally.

He earned the romantic lead in the beautiful *Legends of the Fall* (1994), which led to *People* magazine naming Pitt "The Sexiest Man Alive" in 1994. Such adulation might be flattering, but Pitt aimed to show the world that he was more than the moniker described. He took the role of Louis in the screen adaptation of Anne Rice's *Interview with the Vampire* (1994), winning praise as the tortured blood-sucker. His next film, the sci-fi entry *Twelve Monkeys* (1995), costarring Bruce Willis, earned Pitt his first Oscar nomination. He was effective as cross-eyed psychotic mental patient Jeffrey Goines. In the gloomy *Se7en* (1995), Brad seemed out of place as a cop in search of a serial killer: even in a less-than-fitting part, he succeeded in garnering awards, fans, *and* a new girlfriend. During production, he entered into a two-and-a-half-year relationship with costar Gwyneth Paltrow, ten years his junior. Their engagement was mutually broken in June 1997.

Pitt was banned from entering China as the result of his effective role as an Austrian journeyman in *Seven Years in Tibet* (1997), a performance called by many his best thus far. That year he was named, for the second year in a row, one of the fifty most beautiful people in the world by *People* magazine.

His recent salary of $17,500,000, for the dark *Meet Joe Black* (1998), shows that behind Brad Pitt's face and form is a hot Hollywood commodity. It can be safely stated that his earlier role as a chicken for El Pollo Loco will never be revived.

Films: 1989: *Cutting Class; Happy Together.* 1991: *Thelma & Louise; Across the Tracks.* 1992: *Cool World; Johnny Suede; Contact; A River Runs Through It.* 1993: *True Romance; Kalifornia.* 1994: *Interview with the Vampire; The Favor; Legends of the Fall.* 1995: *Se7en; Twelve Monkeys.* 1996: *Sleepers.* 1997: *The Dark Side of the Sun* (filmed in 1988); *The Devil's Own; Seven Years in Tibet.* 1998: *Meet Joe Black.* Forthcoming: *Ambrose Chapel; Fight Club.*

TV movies: 1988: *A Stoning in Fulham County.* 1990: *Too Young to Die; The Image.*

TV series: 1987: *Another World; Dallas.*

Meet Chris

⌨ On *Another World*, the part of Chris was played by Brad Pitt for one week in May 1987.

Chris was a high school student who gained valuable experience on the basketball courts from brothers Michael (Kale Browne) and John Hudson (David Forsyth).

Phylicia Rashad

It was beyond my greatest dream that I would work with Bill Cosby once, much less twice.
—Phylicia Rashad, on her career, 1997

Phylicia Rashad was known by her maiden name, Phylicia Ayers-Allen, when she portrayed Courtney Wright on One Life to Live *from 1983–84. Courtesy of Shooting Star.*

Born: June 19, 1948, in Houston, Texas; birth name, Phylicia Ayers-Allen; mother Vivian; sister Debbie

Education: Howard University (Washington, D.C.)

Debuts: Broadway—*The Wiz* (1975); film—*The Wiz* (1978); television—*One Life to Live* (1983) as Courtney Wright

Awards: Won People's Choice Award as Favorite Female Television Performer for her role as Clair Huxtable on *The Cosby Show*, 1985; won Image Award, for Outstanding Lead Actress in a Comedy Series for her role as Ruth Lucas on *Cosby*, 1997

Honors: Won Harvard University's Foundation Award; honorary doctorate degrees from Providence College (Rhode Island), Morris Brown College (Atlanta, Georgia), and Barber-Scotia College (Concord, North Carolina)

Marital Status: Divorced William Lancelot Bowles Jr., 1975; married musician Victor Willis, 1978, divorced, 1980; married sportscaster Ahmad Rashad (né Bobby Moore), 1985; two children, Bill Bowles and Condola Phylea Rashad

Album: *Josephine Superstar* (1978)

Book: *The African American Family Album,* by Dorothy Hoobler and Thomas Hoobler, introduction by Rashad (1995)

You don't get anywhere without the people's grace, and so I'd like to thank the people for their grace." This was the acceptance speech of Phylicia Rashad, accepting a 1985 People's Choice Award as Favorite Female TV Performer for her role as Clair Huxtable on *The Cosby Show*. This is one actress who can always be counted upon to give her audiences healthy doses of her own brand of grace.

Phylicia graduated from Howard University, *magna cum laude*, with a Bachelor of Arts in fine arts. She is one of a long and distinguished list of Howard alumni, including Nobel Prize-winning author Toni Morrison, former U.S. Supreme Court Justice Thurgood Marshall, and opera star Jessye Norman.

In an industry that can make it a challenge for African-American performers to achieve headlining stardom, Phylicia has made a name for herself through exuberant stage and television performances, combining gifts in straight acting, singing, and dancing. She is an all-encompassing talent.

Phylicia Ayers-Allen first began as a musical stage headliner in 1975, joining an all-African-American cast in the *The Wiz*, based upon *The Wizard of Oz*, the classic L. Frank Baum story. Phylicia later appeared in the big-screen adaptation of *The Wiz* (1978). Costarring Diana Ross, Michael Jackson, Nipsey Russell, Lena Horne, and Richard Pryor, the film had Phylicia playing two supporting roles, a Munchkin and a Field Mouse.

Furthering her musical success, Phylicia appeared on Broadway in *Dreamgirls* (1981), *Into the Woods* (1987), and *Jelly's Last Jam* (1992). She appeared on stage in Atlanta, Washington, D.C., and Boston in *Blues for an Alabama Sky*, the Pearl Cleage drama set in 1930s Harlem.

Phylicia was divorced in 1975 from her first husband, dentist Bill Bowles, with whom she had a son, William Jr. In 1978, Phylicia married Victor Willis, the original cop in the Village People. Phylicia, a singer of note, opened for the band when they toured mid-size auditoriums. That year, too, she released her only singing album, *Josephine Superstar*. Her album was produced by the Village People's producer, Jacques Morali; the backup vocals on the offerings were provided by the Village People and the Ritchie Family, including famed future solo singer, Lionel Ritchie. Phylicia and Victor divorced in 1980.

In 1983, Ayers-Allen got her first regular television acting job, on the daytime soap *One Life to Live*, portraying Courtney Wright until 1984. She was noticed.

The next year saw her career-making break: she joined the cast of *The Cosby Show*, the consistently high-rated and wildly influential sitcom which aired for eight years on NBC. On the show, Phylicia played attorney Clair Huxtable against Cosby as obstetrician Dr. Heathcliff "Cliff" Huxtable. The show's portrayal of wholesome family values, coupled with fun-loving pokes at social mores, made it an overnight success, and one of the most watched programs of the 1980s. It also made Phylicia Ayers-Allen a household name and celebrity.

On Thanksgiving Day, 1985, sportscaster Ahmad Rashad shocked Phylicia, and most of the viewers watching the holiday football fare, by making an important personal statement during the game.

"I proposed on the set," Ahmad Rashad has recalled. "She didn't know it was coming. That's probably my single biggest moment on TV. I meet people that I know aren't sports fans who have seen copies of it and say 'that was such a wonderful thing.' She was in the Thanksgiving Day parade in New York, so the parade ended and she was at Macy's. I had told her when she got off the float to go in and look at TV. She went nuts." The couple married in 1985; they have a daughter, Condola Phylea. Phylicia Ayers-Allen, after marriage, became Phylicia Rashad.

During her tenure on *The Cosby Show*, she appeared in a number of TV movies, including *Uncle Tom's Cabin* (1987), *False Witness* (1989), *Polly* (1989), and *Polly: Comin' Home!* (1990), the latter two directed by her famous (and also talented) sister, Debbie Allen.

Post–*Cosby Show* appearances included the feature film *Once Upon a Time...When We Were Colored* (1995), costarring fellow *One Life to Live* alumnus Al Freeman Jr. The film earned her an NAACP Image Award nomination, in 1995.

The NAACP presented Phylicia with its Image Award, as Outstanding Lead Actress in a Comedy Series, in 1996, the year Phylicia re-joined former costar Bill Cosby on a new series, *Cosby*. She was very supportive when, in July 1997, Cosby learned his only son, Ennis, was killed by a young Russian immigrant on a Los Angeles freeway. No doubt that having his long-time costar and friend by his side helped, a great deal.

True, Phylicia Rashad is proud to be working with Bill Cosby again. Her audiences, too, can enjoy her on a weekly basis once again.

Films: 1978: *The Wiz.* 1995: *Once Upon a Time...When We Were Colored*

TV movies: 1987: *Uncle Tom's Cabin.* 1989: *Polly*; *False Witness.* 1990: *Polly: Comin' Home!* 1991: *Jailbirds.* 1993: *Hallelujah.* 1994: *David's Mother.* 1995: *The Babysitter's Seduction*; *The Possession of Michael D.* 1999: *Free of Eden.*

TV series: 1983–84: *One Life to Live.* 1984–92: *The Cosby Show.* 1996–present: *Cosby*

Meet Courtney

✂ On *One Life to Live*, the role of Courtney Wright was originated, and played solely, by Phylicia Ayers-Allen (1983–84).

Courtney was a public relations executive who dated Police Captain Ed Hall (played by later movie costar Al Freeman Jr.). When Ed went back to his ex-wife Carla (Ellen Holly), Courtney dated Carla's ex-boyfriend, a professional football player.

Christopher Reeve

Back in intensive care three years ago, I certainly wondered what the future would bring. I rarely have those days anymore because I'm so busy with so many projects.

—Christopher Reeve, on his paralysis, 1998

Before moving on to Superman *fame, Christopher Reeve played Ben Harper on* Love of Life *from 1974–76. Courtesy of Soap Opera Digest.*

Born: September 25, 1952, in New York City, to Franklin D'Olier and Barbara Johnson Reeve

Education: Princeton Day School (New Jersey); Cornell University (Ithaca, New York); Julliard School (New York City)

Debuts: stage—*A Month in the Country* (1969); television—*Love of Life* (1974) as Ben Harper; Broadway—*A Matter of Gravity* (1976); film—*Gray Lady Down* (1978)

Award: British Academy Award as Best Actor for his role in *Superman: The Movie*, 1979

Marital Status: Married singer/actress Dana Morosini, April 11, 1992; three children, Matthew and Alexandra (from relationship with Gae Exton), William (with wife Dana)

Books: autobiography: *Still Me* (1998); about: *Christopher Reeve: Actor & Activist*, by Margaret L. Finn (1997); *Christopher Reeve (Taking Part)*, by Libby Hughes (1997); *Man of Steel: The Career and Courage of Christopher Reeve*, by Adrian Havill (1996)

Christopher Reeve is *Superman* personified. With rugged good looks and pumped-up body, he graduated from soaps into one of the more storied cinematic roles, and made the Man of Steel screen character his own. Despite a crippling 1995 accident, Reeve has continued to demonstrate that the man is more like his alter-ego character than the other way around.

Christopher Reeve's interest in the theater began early. At age eight, Christopher had begun appearing in school plays, and was also very interested in music. By age sixteen, he had an agent; by age seventeen, in 1969, he made his stage debut in *A Month in the Country*, with the American Repertory Company in Cambridge, Massachusetts.

After finishing high school, he began English and music studies at Cornell University (where he received his B.A. in 1974), still dabbling in theater. His talent got him admitted to New York City's Julliard School in the fall of 1974. While studying under John Houseman there, his roommate was Robin Williams. Also that year he began a two-year stint as bigamous Ben Harper on *Love of Life*. Reeve used his good looks and acting training to make a real impact on the daytime soap.

After his film debut as Ensign Phillips in *Gray Lady Down* (1977), he was signed to the plum role of Clark Kent/Superman in the first feature movie chronicling *Superman* (1978). The popularity of that entry spurred three sequels, in all of which Reeve portrayed the caped Man of Steel. Reeve's looks, build, and boyish yet mature nature made him a natural for the oncamera dual role.

Throughout the 1980s, Reeve was very active socially, mainly romancing British-born advertising agent Gae Exton, whom he had met while shooting *Superman* in England in 1977. The two never married, but share a son, Matthew (b. 1981) and a daughter, Alexandra (b. 1985). The relationship ended in 1987. On April 11, 1992, Reeve married Dana Morosini, a cabaret singer and actress he had met in Williamstown, Massachusetts. The two have one child, William, born in 1993.

Reeve has always loved athletics and the outdoors: he earned his pilot's license in his twenties, did his own film stunts—some quite dangerous—and was expert at such sports as hang gliding, scuba diving, skiing, golf, and horseback riding. It was a freak accident resulting from his love for equestrian sport that was a tragic (and near fatal) definitive moment in Reeve's life.

On May 27, 1995, Christopher Reeve fell headlong, off his thoroughbred horse, Eastern Express, during a Culpepper County, Virginia, equestrian exhibition, causing multiple fractures, and leaving him a quadriplegic. He was instantly paralyzed from the neck down, and unable to breathe: surgeons performed emergency surgery, stabilizing his shattered C1-C2 vertebrae and, literally, reattaching his head to his spine.

Through speeches at the Academy Awards, the Chicago Democratic Convention, and the Paralympics, all in 1996, Reeve began using the strong international interest in his situation to increase public awareness of spinal cord injury and the need for increased research funds towards finding a cure. He also returned to acting, appearing on *Touched by an Angel* and a TV film, *A Step Toward Tomorrow* (1996), and directed a TV movie, *Into the Gloaming* (1997), followed in 1998 by a new version of the famed 1954 Alfred Hitchcock suspense film, *Rear Window*, in which Christopher took on the role originally portrayed by Jimmy Stewart.

In his 1998 autobiography, *Still Me*, Reeve disclosed the fact that, after his tragic accident, he was far closer to death than the public realized. According to Christopher, his mother was so pessimistic about his medical condition that "she became distraught and began arguing strenuously that the doctors should pull the plug." Attending physicians were able to convince her that he would survive. And he has!

Christopher Reeve has been characterized, much like his screen character, as a Man of Steel. His attitude mirrors the moniker. "My spinal cord is ready below the injury," he concluded. "I'm realistically optimistic. I don't plan to spend the rest of my life like this."

Films: 1978: *Gray Lady Down; Superman.* 1980: *Somewhere in Time; Superman II.* 1982: *Deathtrap; Monsignor.* 1983: *Superman III.* 1984: *The Bostonians.* 1985: *The Aviator.* 1987: *Superman IV: The Quest for Peace* (also story writer and second unit director); *Street Smart.* 1988: *Switching Channels.* 1992: *Noises Off.* 1993: *The Remains of the Day; Earth and the American Dream* (voice only). 1994: *Above Suspicion; Speechless.* 1995: *Village of the Damned.* 1996: *A Step Toward Tomorrow.*

TV movies: 1985: *Anna Karenina.* 1988: *The Great Escape II: The Untold Story.* 1990: *The Rose and the Jackal.* 1991: *Death Dreams; Bump in the Night.* 1992: *Nightmare in the Daylight; Mortal Sins.* 1993: *The Sea Wolf; Morning Glory.* 1994: *Black Fox: The Price of Peace.* 1995: *Black Fox: Blood Horse; Black Fox: Good Men and Bad.* 1997: *In the Gloaming* (director only). 1998: *Christopher Reeve: A Celebration of Hope; Rear Window.*

TV series: 1974–76: *Love of Life.* 1991: *Hollywood Stuntmakers.*

Meet Ben

On *Love of Life*, the character of Ben Harper was played by Dennis Parnell (1951–57), Tommy White (1957–58), Christopher Reeve (1974–76), and Chandler Hill Harben (1976–80).

Ben was the handsome and selfish son of Meg (then Tudi Wiggins) and Charles Harper (Paul Potter), who divorced when their son was just a tyke. Alternately known as either "Beanie" or the ever-popular "Beano," during the Reeve years, he was called Ben.

Ben returned to the small town of Rosehill after sixteen years "away." The cad, unbeknownst to all, was leading a dark double life: married to two women at the same time, *and in the same town*, no less! Eventually, both women, Bride A, wicked Arlene Lovett (Birgitta Tolksdorf), and

Bride B, sweet socialite Betsy Crawford (then Elizabeth Kemp), decided to expose him. At the time of Reeve's departure from the role, Ben Harper was sentenced to a prison term for his bigamous activities. Reeve must have anticipated the coming "activities": Harben's first scene as Ben was as the victim of a prison rape.

Super*er*

Christopher Reeve (*Love of Life*) beat out, for the big-screen role of *Superman*, the following competition for the plum part: Charles Bronson, James Caan, Clint Eastwood, Bruce Jenner, Steve McQueen, Robert Redford, and Sylvester Stallone.

Meg Ryan

Completely adorable. It's so annoying.

—Sleepless in Seattle costar Rosie O'Donnell
on Meg Ryan, 1997

Life was filled with ups and downs for Betsy Montgomery on As the World Turns, played by Meg Ryan from 1982–84. Courtesy of Soap Opera Digest.

Born: November 19, 1961, in Fairfield, Connecticut, to Harry and Susan Hyra; birth name, Margaret Mary Emily Anne Hyra

Education: Bethel High School (Connecticut); University of Connecticut (Storrs); New York University

Debuts: television—*Amy and the Angel* (1981); film—*Rich and Famous* (1981)

Awards: Won Golden Apple Award as Female Discovery of the Year (award shared with Pauline Collins), 1989; won the Harvard Hasty Pudding Award as "Woman of the Year," 1994

Honors: Nominated for Golden Globe Award in 1990 and 1994; chosen by *People* magazine as one of the Fifty Most Beautiful People in the World, 1994; nominated for Screen Actors Guild Award, 1995; ranked number ninety-four in *Empire* magazine's "Top One Hundred Movie Stars of All Time" list (1997); ranked number seventy-four in *Premiere* magazine's "One Hundred Most Powerful People in Hollywood" list (1998)

Marital Status: Married actor Dennis Quaid, February 14, 1991; one son, Jack Henry

I never intended to be an actress," Meg Ryan told the July 1984 *Daytime TV* magazine. "My first goal was to be a writer. What I really wanted, and still do, is to be a reporter and travel." Well, at least she got to travel.

A popular student at Bethel High School in Connecticut, where she was voted "cutest" girl and homecoming queen in 1979, Meg enrolled at the University of Connecticut to study journalism. She secured a Screen Actors Guild card under her mother's maiden name, Ryan, and began doing TV ads in New York. "My main reason for doing commercials," Meg recalled in 1984, "was simply to earn money for college."

Two years into her degree, Ryan won the role of Candice Bergen's daughter in veteran director George Cukor's last movie, *Rich and Famous* (1981). "I was thoroughly petrified," Meg admitted of her screen debut. "It was the first time I'd ever been on a plane, not to mention a movie set."

Encouraged by the experience, then-twenty-year-old Meg left the University of Connecticutt. She turned to television, first appearing in a 1991 ABC *Afterschool Special*, *Amy and the Angel*, and then, in 1982, as Betsy on *As the World Turns*. At the same time, she studied journalism at New York University, part-time, at night. She took both roles, actress and student, seriously, but seemed to be leaning towards one over the other.

"Every once in a while," Meg said in 1984, "I'll do a scene that I'm really proud of, and that makes all the pressure and exhaustion worth it. It's times like that when I think, 'Wow, I'm really beginning to be an actress!'"

Departing the soap, to great fan dismay, in 1984, Ryan relocated to Los Angeles, and gained her first post-soap notice for a solid supporting turn in the action flick *Top Gun* (1986), playing the wife of Tom Cruise's naval fighter co-pilot (Anthony Edwards). Ryan and Edwards' tragedy-tinged fictional romance translated into a short-lived offscreen relationship.

Ryan's winsome talents were optimized in her first leading movie role, in Rob Reiner's romantic comedy *When Harry Met Sally...* (1989), which featured Ryan's now-famous simulated-orgasm scene. Based on that one sequence, Meg was catapulted into the spotlight, a true comic/romantic heroine.

On Valentine's Day, 1991, Meg married actor Dennis Quaid; the two had first met during filming of the 1987 sci-fi vehicle *Innerspace*, and became a couple when they re-teamed for the mis-hit 1988 noir remake *D.O.A.* The couple's son, Jack Henry, was born in April 1992.

Ryan can seemingly make any role her own: Jim Morrison's druggy girlfriend in *The Doors* (1991), an alcoholic wife to Andy Garcia in *When a Man Loves a Woman* (1994), a captivating supporting turn in the hip period-piece *Restoration* (1995), or a Medevac helicopter pilot in *Courage Under Fire* (1996). However, it is in Betsy-type roles, romantic, sentimental, and imaginative, that Ryan is best regarded, as in Nora Ephron's romantic hit *Sleepless in Seattle* (1993), in *Anastasia* (1997, voice only), in the transcendent tearjerker *City of Angels* (1998), and the romance-on-the-Internet romp *You've Got Mail* (1998).

John Patrick Shanley, Meg's director in *Joe Versus the Volcano* (1990), recalled a cameraman's reminiscence, after lighting a scene for Ryan's stand-in: "He put up the light meter up to Meg's face and said, 'Do you see that? Her face reflects two hundred times more light than the other girl's!'" No offense to the stand-in, but, yes, we did notice.

Films: 1981: *Rich and Famous*. 1983: *Amityville 3-D*. 1986: *Top Gun*; *Armed and Dangerous*. 1987: *Innerspace*. 1988: *The Presidio*; *D.O.A.*; *Promised Land*. 1989: *When Harry Met Sally...* 1990: *Joe Versus the Volcano*. 1991: *The Doors*. 1992: *Prelude to a Kiss*. 1993: *Flesh and Bone*; *Sleepless in Seattle*. 1994: *When a Man Loves a Woman*; *A Century of Cinema*; *I.Q.* 1995: *Restoration*, 1996: *Courage Under Fire*; *French Kiss* (also producer). 1997: *Anastasia* (voice only); *Addicted to Love*; *Two for the Road* (also producer). 1998: *City of Angels*; *Hurlyburly*; *You've Got Mail*. Forthcoming: *Hanging Up*.

TV movies: 1981: *Amy and the Angel*. 1997: *Northern Lights* (executive producer only).

TV series: 1982: *One of the Boys*. 1982–84: *As the World Turns*. 1985: *Wildside*.

Meet Betsy

On *As the World Turns*, the role of Betsy Stewart Montgomery Andropolous was played by Patricia McGuiness (1971), Suzanne Davidson (1972–80), Lisa Denton (1981–82), Meg Ryan (1982–84), Lindsay Frost (1984–88), and Jordan Baker (1994).

During the Ryan years, Betsy fell in love with the married Steve Andropolous (Frank Runyeon) in 1980. Though she married Craig Montgomery (Scott Bryce), Betsy could never forget Steve: they found each other anew, in Europe, and consummated their love.

Several weeks later, Craig found out that Betsy was pregnant. Knowing that the child couldn't be his (he was sterile), Craig realized that Steve was back in the picture. Betsy gave birth to a daughter, Danielle, and left Craig.

Betsy and Steve married in a spectacular outdoor wedding: their honeymoon was short-lived, as Betsy's corpse was found in a fiery auto wreck. Or, *was* it?

It wasn't: in reality, Betsy was alive, in a New England hospital, suffering from amnesia. Just like real life, no?

Antonio Sabato Jr.

He's human. I'm that way too, very human. Jagger is me. You never become the character: you are the character.

—Antonio Sabato Jr., on his General Hospital *role, 1993*

From 1992–94, many a female General Hospital *viewer swooned at this sight: Antonio Sabato Jr., as Jagger Cates. Courtesy of Ann Bogart.*

Born: February 29, 1972, in Rome, Italy, to Antonio and Yvonne Sabato; one sister, Simonne

Education: Beverly Hills High School (California); Palisades High School (California)

Debuts: film—*Arizona Road* (1990); television—*Malcolm Takes a Shot* (1992)

Honor: Chosen by *People* magazine as one of the Fifty Most Beautiful People in the World (1994)

Marital Status: Married actress Tully Jensen, 1992, divorced; one son, Jack (with actress Virginia Madsen)

The scene: a restaurant. One of the diners: Miss Piggy. Her fantasy dinner partner: Antonio Sabato Jr. For millions of females, seeing Miss Piggy sharing Lay's potato chips with Antonio was like living their own fantasy. Yet, this is one truly reluctant heartthrob, amazing as it sounds.

The son of prominent European actor Antonio Sabato, leap-year baby Antonio moved with his family to the United States when he was twelve. The child spoke Italian, and it took him twelve months of ESL (English as a second language) classes to master his new vernacular. "It was certainly a challenge," he has recalled.

Antonio graduated from legendary Beverly Hills High School and immediately found his first job: in a Janet Jackson music video, "Love Will Never Do (Without You)." He was already a known commodity to ABC, from a TV appearance in a 1992 *Afterschool Special*, "Malcolm Takes a

Shot," when he originated the role of Jagger Cates on *General Hospital*. During his highly-touted tenure on the soap, he was nominated for Hottest Male and Outstanding Newcomer awards from *Soap Opera Digest*, was on the cover of *TV Guide*, produced his own 1994 sell-out calendar, and was named to *People* magazine's 1994 list of the fifty most beautiful people in the world. He also appeared in a number of TV movies, including *Moment of Truth: Why My Daughter?* (1993) and *Jailbreakers* (1994).

With both adulation and experience under his belt, he felt ready to explore his chances on the big screen, leaving the soap in 1994. "I had a great time on *General Hospital*," he explained. "It was like going to high school. Now, I'm graduating and going to college."

The *Calgary* (Alberta, Canada) *Herald* summed up his *General Hospital* impact best: "The Romanesque profile and smoldering passion of Antonio Sabato Jr., made Jagger the kind of brooding lover boy who could send female viewers into cardiac arrest..."

His first post-Jagger character was Alonzo Solace, on *Earth 2*, a 1994–95 sci-fi TV series produced by Steven Spielberg's Amblin Entertainment. Solace was a rocket pilot, recruited to help ferry Earthlings to a distant planet in the year 2125, with a polluted Mother Earth gasping her last breaths. The program was canceled due to its losing in the time slot competition with *60 Minutes* and the costly weather-dictated shoots in Santa Fe, New Mexico.

In 1992, Antonio was briefly married to, and as quickly divorced from, actress Tully Jensen. He moved directly into a relationship with actress Virginia Madsen, nine years his senior. The couple met in late 1993, and on August 6, 1994, Madsen gave birth to their son, Jack. By early 1995, they separated, never having married. "I was terribly in love with her," Sabato said later. It was another sad episode in his personal life.

The year 1996 was his busiest to date: besides his TV work, Antonio began appearing in a battery of advertisements for Calvin Klein underwear. His success was not "brief," thanks to a ninety-foot billboard over Manhattan's Times Square. "It's so overwhelming that I don't think it's me," he told *People* magazine in June 1996. "Thinking it's somebody else helps me look at it."

Sabato is a cautious heartthrob, who smoldered in five 1998–99 pictures, including the action adventure *The Big Hit*, with Mark Wahlberg (another former Calvin Klein underwear model), the number one box-office film for the weekend of April 24–26, 1998.

Antonio Sabato Jr., is worlds apart from the stereotypical actor-on-his-looks-only label. "Sometimes I can be a serious person, but I try not to be. Life is a joke, and you just live it. Even if you have bad times, you just move on and try to be happy. There's no secret to it. You have to make yourself happy: nobody else can do it for you." Except if you're Miss Piggy, and you're dining on chips *du jour* with your dream man.

Films: 1990: *Karate Rock*; *Arizona Road*. 1998: *The Big Hit*; *High Voltage*; *Circles*.

TV movies: 1992: *Malcolm Takes a Shot*. 1993: *Moment of Truth: Why My Daughter?* 1994: *Jailbreakers*; *Earth 2*. 1995: *Her Hidden Truth*. 1996: *Thrill*; *If Looks Could Kill*. 1998: *The Perfect Getaway*. Forthcoming: *Fatal Error*.

TV miniseries: 1995: *Padre, Papa*.

TV series: 1992–94: *General Hospital*. 1994: *Earth 2*. 1996: *Codename: Wolverine*.

Video: 1989: "Love Will Never Do (Without You)." 1997: *Happily Ever After: Fairy Tales for Every Child* (voice only).

Meet Jagger

On *General Hospital*, the role of John "Jagger" Cates was originated, and played solely, by Antonio Sabato Jr. (1992–94).

Jason Quartermaine (Steve Burton) and Karen Wexler (Cari Shayne) went out for an afternoon picnic on one of the Quartermaine boats. Jagger Cates, a smoking, boxing, street rogue who was also interested in Karen, had stowed away on board with them. The three got caught in a severe storm and the boat was destroyed. They found their way to a deserted island, and were eventually rescued.

On Valentine's Day, 1994, Karen got together with Jagger. The couple embarked on a search for Jagger's long-lost brother and sister, and found brother, Stone (Michael Sutton), who later contracted AIDS.

After a stormy relationship, Karen and Jagger finally married, moving to the Midwest.

Susan Sarandon

A pensive Susan Sarandon played Patrice Kahlman on A World Apart *from 1970–71, and Sarah Fairbanks on* Search for Tomorrow *in 1972. Video screen photo, collection of author.*

I believe in using words, not fists.... I believe in my outrage knowing people are living in boxes on the street.... I believe in honesty. I believe in a good time. I believe in good food. I believe in sex.
—Susan Sarandon, 1997

Born: October 4, 1946, in New York City to Phillip Leslie and Lenora Marie Criscione Tomalin; birth name Susan Abigail Tomalin; oldest of nine children

Education: Catholic University of America (Washington, D.C.)

Debuts: film—Joe (1970); television—*A World Apart* (1970) as Patrice Kahlman; Broadway—*An Evening with Richard Nixon and...* (1974)

Awards: Won Genie Award, as Best Actress, for her role in *Atlantic City*, 1981; won Honorary Award of the City of Locarno at the San Sebastian International Film Festival, 1995; won Hasty Pudding Award as Woman of the Year, 1996; won Academy Award, as Best Actress, and Screen Actors Guild Award, for Outstanding Performance by a Female Actress in a Leading Role, for her role as Sister Helen Prejean in *Dead Man Walking*, both 1996; won Blockbuster Entertainment Award as Favorite Actress in a Drama for *Dead Man Walking*, 1997

Honors: Nominated for Academy Awards in 1982, 1992, 1993, 1995; nominated for Golden Globe Awards in 1989, 1991, 1992, 1993, 1996; nominated for Screen Actors Guild Award in 1995; ranked number thirty-five in *Empire* magazine's "Top One Hundred Movie Stars of All Time" list (1997); chosen by *People* magazine as one of the Fifty Most Beautiful People in the World (1997)

Marital Status: Married actor Chris Sarandon, September 16, 1967, divorced, 1979; relationship with actor/director Tim Robbins; children Eva Maria (with Franco Amurri), Jack and Miles (with Tim Robbins)

In the early 1970s, before the ban on television advertising of cigarettes, Virginia Slims coined the slogan, "You've come a long way, baby." In the annals of cinema, perhaps no career has personified that phrase better than that of Susan Sarandon.

She has always been a free thinker. Pronounced by her third grade Catholic school teachers as boasting an "overabundance of original sin," and later arrested for her involvement in Civil Rights protests while still in high school, Susan Tomalin later double-majored in drama and English at Catholic University of America, Washington, D.C. While there, she fell in love with fellow thespian Chris Sarandon; they married during her senior year, in the fall of 1967.

Sarandon's saucer-eyed beauty instantly landed her modeling work through New York's prestigious Ford Agency. When she accompanied hubby Chris to an audition, her own movie career was launched, as she was cast in a small role in *Joe* (1970). Susan debuted on television, also in 1970, on the soap *A World Apart*, portraying Patrice Kahlman. She returned to daytime in 1972, with the brief, but critical, role of Sarah Fairbanks on *Search for Tomorrow*.

Sarandon's characters over the years have uniquely blended sexy coolness and believability. With equal ease she has scored in wacky screen comedies—*The Rocky Horror Picture Show* (1975), *The Witches of Eastwick* (1977), and *Thelma & Louise* (1991); in dramatic tearjerkers—*Pretty Baby* (1978), *Lorenzo's Oil* (1992), and *Dead Man Walking* (1995) and in seductive love narratives—*The Great Waldo Pepper* (1975), *Bull Durham* (1988), and *Twilight* (1998), with equal ease, optimally defining herself as sexually uninhibited, a manner typically denied older actresses.

After being nominated for four Academy Awards—for *Atlantic City* (1981), *Thelma & Louise*, *Lorenzo's Oil*, and as a tough-as-nails lawyer in *The Client* (1994)—Sarandon finally acquired a coveted gold statue for her superb turn as Sister Helen Prejean in *Dead Man Walking*.

Sarandon divorced her college-sweetheart husband in 1979, and has been involved romantically since with director Louis Malle, Sean Penn (fourteen years her junior), director Franco Amurri (father of Sarandon's out-of-wedlock daughter, Eva Maria, born in 1981), and Tim Robbins (her *Dead Man Walking* director). It is Robbins who fathered Sarandon's two late-in-life sons, Jack Henry, in 1986, and Miles Guthrie, in 1989. Susan and Tim have been together long enough, under California common law, to be considered married.

As Susan has said, "Sexuality... is something that develops and becomes stronger and stronger the older you get." Without question, Susan Sarandon has aged most gracefully, and has, in the process, come a long, long way.

Films: 1970: *Joe*. 1971: *Fleur bleue*. 1972: *Mortadella*. 1974: *The Front Page*; *Lovin' Molly*. 1975: *The Great Waldo Pepper*; *The Rocky Horror Picture Show*. 1976: *The Great Smokey Roadblock* (also co-producer); *One Summer Love*. 1977: *The Other Side of Midnight*; *Checkered Flag or Crash*.

1978: *Pretty Baby*; *King of the Gypsies*. 1979: *Something Short of Paradise*. 1980: *Loving Couples*. 1981: *Atlantic City*. 1982: *Tempest*. 1983: *The Hunger*. 1984: *The Buddy System*. 1985: *Compromising Positions*. 1987: *The Witches of Eastwick*. 1988: *Bull Durham*; *Sweet Hearts Dance*. 1989: *A Dry White Season*; *January Man*. 1991: *Thelma & Louise*; *White Palace*; *Light Sleeper*. 1992: *Bob Roberts*; *The Player*; *Lorenzo's Oil*. 1994: *The Client*; *Little Women*; *Safe Passage*. 1995: *Dead Man Walking*; *The Celluloid Closet*. 1996: *James and the Giant Peach* (voice only); *Tell the Truth and Run: George Seldes and the American Press* (voice only). 1997: *187: Documented* (voice only); *Father Roy: Inside the School of Assassins* (voice only). 1998: *Twilight*; *Illuminata*; *Stepmom* (also producer). Forthcoming: *Anywhere But Here*; *The Cradle Will Rock*.

Television: movies—1974: *F. Scott Fitzgerald and 'The Last of the Belles'*. 1981: *Who Am I This Time?* 1985: *Mussolini: The Decline and Fall of Il Duce*. 1986: *Women of Valor*.

TV miniseries: 1985: *A.D.*

TV series: 1970–71: *A World Apart*. 1972: *Search for Tomorrow*.

Video: 1999: *My Friend, Martin*.

Meet Patrice and Sarah

On *A World Apart*, the role of Patrice Kahlman was originated, and solely played, by Susan Sarandon for the entire run of the show, from March 30, 1970, to June 25, 1971.

The show was created by Irna Phillips' adopted daughter, Katherine, and as such, mirrors many of the events in the elder Phillips' own life. Case in point is the show's focus on central heroine, Betty Kahlman Barry (Elizabeth Lawrence, then Augusta Dabney) and her two adopted children, Patrice and Chris (Matthew Cowles).

On *Search for Tomorrow*, the role of Sarah Fairbanks was originated, and solely played, by Susan Sarandon, in 1972.

Sarah and her cohort, George Joslyn (Kipp Osborne), were young drifters who murdered Sam Reynolds (originated by Robert Mandan, then played by George Gaynes, and finally by Roy Shuman) in 1972. Sam's murder ended a long on-again, off-again romance with the show's heroine, Joanne (Mary Stuart). Jo grieved, but recovered, and soon—her marriage to Dr. Tony Vincente (Anthony George) aired on October 22, 1972.

Name's the Same

Both Susan Sarandon (*A World Apart*, *Search for Tomorrow*) and Meg Ryan (*As the World Turns*) have a son named Jack Henry.

Tom Selleck

I can't control whether people see me as a sex symbol or a doofus, and I can't control who finds me attractive and who doesn't.

—Tom Selleck, 1995

This smile made many a female heart swoon in daytime: Tom Selleck as Jed Andrews on The Young and the Restless, *from 1974–75. Video screen photo, collection of author.*

Born: January 29, 1945, in Detroit, Michigan, to Robert D. and Martha Selleck; brothers Bob and Danny; sister Marti

Education: University of Southern California (Los Angeles)

Debuts: television—*The Movie Murderer* (1970); film—*Myra Breckinridge* (1970)

Awards: Won Hollywood Women's Press Club Award as Male Star of the Year, 1983; won Emmy Award, as Outstanding Leading Actor in a Drama Series, for his role as Thomas Sullivan Magnum on *Magnum P.I.*, 1984; won Golden Globe Award, for Best Performance by an Actor in a TV Drama Series, for his role on *Magnum P.I.*, 1985

Honor: Chosen by *People* magazine as one of the Fifty Most Beautiful People in the World (1998)

Marital Status: Married model Jacquelyn Ray, 1970, separated, 1979, divorced, 1982; married actress Jilly Joan Mack, August 7, 1987; daughter, Hannah (with Jilly)

Book: *Tom Selleck,* by Jason Bonderoff (1983)

When the term "aging gracefully" comes to mind, the image of Tom Selleck cannot help but be conjured. This is a man whose appeal is universal, and an actor whose talent has taken him from steamy shower scenes to private investigating to kissing men—and beyond.

Tom Selleck was raised in Sherman Oaks, California, but his Motor City roots never really left him: that is why his future breakthrough character, Thomas Magnum, always wore a Detroit Tigers cap.

He won a basketball scholarship to the University of Southern California, and joined the Sigma Chi fraternity. "I was planning to go into architecture," Selleck noted. "But when I arrived [to sign up for courses] architecture was filled up. Acting was right next to it. So I signed up for acting instead."

Three classes short of attaining his bachelor's degree, Tom dropped out of U.S.C. "I decided if I didn't try acting," Tom has recalled, "I'd wonder ten years later how I would have done."

Selleck began his career under contract to Twentieth Century-Fox. His debut was a TV thriller, *The Movie Murderer* (1970). That year, too, he made his feature film debut, playing a secretary in Mae West's *Myra Breckinridge*, as well as marrying aspiring actress and model Jacquelyn Ray. The two would separate in 1979, divorcing in 1982.

In 1974, Tom achieved his first steady work as recurring character Jed Andrews on the Los Angeles-filmed soap *The Young and the Restless*. His character had the distinction of being in one of daytime's most erotic (for the time) sequences, as Jed stepped out of a shower into the awaiting arms of Lauralee Brooks (Jaime Lyn Bauer). Ironically, Tom Selleck was dismissed from *Y&R*, in 1975, reportedly because show co-creator Bill Bell didn't like the pitch of Selleck's voice.

After that unceremonious end to his soap career, Selleck worked in a battery of TV films and theatrical movies before assuming the role of private eye Lance White on James Garner's *The Rockford Files* from 1979–80.

On December 11, 1980, CBS premiered the new TV series *Magnum, P.I.*, starring Selleck in the role of Thomas Sullivan Magnum, a Vietnam veteran who becomes a private investigator in Hawaii. The TV show was a huge success, winning Selleck two Emmy Awards and catapulting him into sex symbol/superstar status. It was thought that the 1986–87 season would be the series' last (even after a February 1987 guest appearance by Frank Sinatra to boost the sagging ratings), so Magnum was shot, apparently killed. However, the show *was* renewed for yet another season, and Magnum's "death" was explained in true soap opera fashion: he imagined his own death (reminiscent of *Dallas*'s Fall 1986 opener.) After 162 hour-long action episodes, *Magnum, P.I.* finally ended on September 12, 1988.

On August 7, 1987, Selleck married Jilly Mack. He successfully transferred into starring roles in feature films with the comedic *Three Men and a Baby* (1987), and its sequel, *Three Men and a Little Lady* (1990). Selleck parlayed his screen success with children into his own married life: Tom and Jilly welcomed a daughter, Hannah Margaret Mack Selleck, on December 16, 1988. Tom was an American cowboy in Australia in the delightful Western comedy *Quigley Down Under* (1991), an American ballplayer in Japan in *Mr. Baseball* (1992), and a wildly put-upon family man in the bizarre would-be comedy *Folks!* (1992).

Selleck made seven guest TV appearances on NBC's *Friends* from February 8, 1996, through January 30, 1997, as Dr. Richard Burke, older love interest to Courteney Cox. Later, in 1997, Selleck lost his mustache, and broke barriers (and many hearts) as gay television reporter Peter Malloy in *In & Out*, costarring **Kevin Kline**. For the film, Selleck and Kline shared a *forty*-second onscreen kiss.

In 1998, Selleck returned to the TV series ranks, with a sitcom, *The Closer*, teamed with Ed Asner. In it, Tom played Jack McLaren, cutthroat advertising executive who, in Selleck's words, "has to move forward or he can't breathe." Ten episodes were filmed: only nine aired; *The Closer* was canceled in May 1998.

True staying power, and continued heartthrob status: Tom Selleck still has it—he can still take the breath away.

Films: 1970: *Myra Breckinridge*. 1971: *The Seven Minutes*. 1972: *Daughters of Satan*. 1973: *Terminal Island*. 1976: *Midway*. 1977: *The Washington Affair*. 1978: *Coma*; *The Gypsy Warriors*. 1983: *High Road to China*. 1984: *Lassiter*; *Runaway*. 1987: *Three Men and a Baby*. 1989: *Her Alibi*; *An Innocent Man*. 1990: *Three Men and a Little Lady*. 1991: *Quigley Down Under*. 1992: *Christopher Columbus: The Discovery*; *Folks!*; *Mr. Baseball*. 1996: *Open Season*. 1997: *In & Out*. Forthcoming: *The Love Letter*.

TV movies: 1970: *The Movie Murderer*. 1974: *A Case of Rape*. 1975: *Returning Home*. 1976: *Bunco*; *Most Wanted*. 1978: *Superdome*. 1979: *The Concrete Cowboys*; *The Sacketts*. 1980: *Magnum P.I.* 1982: *Divorce Wars: A Love Story*; *The Shadow Riders*. 1990: *Revealing Evidence: Stalking the Honolulu Strangler* (executive producer only). 1995: *Broken Trust*. 1996: *Ruby Jean and Joe* (also executive producer). 1997: *Big Guns Talk: The Story of the Western*; *Last Stand at Saber River* (also executive producer).

TV series: 1974–75: *The Young and the Restless*. 1979–80: *The Rockford Files*. 1980–88: *Magnum P.I.* 1989: *B. L. Stryker* (executive producer only). 1998: *The Closer* (also executive producer).

Meet Jed

On *The Young and the Restless*, the role of Jed Andrews was originated, and solely played, by Tom Selleck, in 1974–75.

Jed was responsible for Lauralee "Lorie" Brooks' (Jaime Lyn Bauer) first manuscript, and got her a lucrative publishing contract. Jed, a married man, comforted Lorie when her engagement to Brad (Tom Hallick) broke up.

(Remember who played his wife, Barbara, from 1973–75? It was Deidre Hall, who later gained fame as Dr. Marlena Evans Brady on *Days of Our Lives*.) Jed toured with Lorie to promote her first book and later negotiated her second book deal: the autobiographical exposé, *In My Sister's Shadow*, which dealt with her difficulties coping with a famous older sister, concert pianist Leslie (then Janice Lynde).

Presidential Connections

Steven Ford (*The Young and the Restless*) is the son of former U.S. President Gerald R. Ford. Olympia Dukakis (*Search for Tomorrow*) is the cousin of 1988 Democratic Presidential candidate Michael Dukakis.

Charles Shaughnessy

The great thing a soap has to offer is this: It teaches you a facility to come up with [acting] choices very fast, and to be able to change them very fast, and not get too stuck on a particular thing.

—Charles Shaughnessy, on soap acting, 1998

Days of Our Lives'
Kimberly Brady
(Patsy Pease) and
Shane Donovan
(Charles Shaughnessy)
were one of the
most popular super
couples in soap opera
history. Courtesy of
Shooting Star.

Born: February 9, 1955, in London, England, United Kingdom, to Mr. and Mrs. Alfred Shaughnessy

Education: Eton College (England) and Cambridge University (England)

Debut: television—*General Hospital* (1983) as Alistair

Awards: Won Soap Opera Digest Awards, for Outstanding Male Newcomer, 1985, for Outstanding Super Couple (with Patsy Pease), 1986, and for Favorite Super Couple (with Patsy Pease), 1988

Honor: Nominated for 1992 Soap Opera Digest Award

Marital Status: Married actress Susan Fallender, May 21, 1983; two daughters, Jenny and Madelyn

Accent! That double-meaning word is aptly applied to the long-running sitcom *The Nanny* (1993–99), both for its *emphasis* on family values, however quirky, and in the varying *inflections* of its chief characters: Fran Fine (Fran Drescher), the streetwise Queens nanny-turned-wife to "Mis-tuh Sheffield," and Broadway producer Maxwell Sheffield himself, played by Charles Shaughnessy, suave Brit whose enunciation could redefine "propah" elocution.

Charles Shaughnessy was born into a prominent British show business family: his father, Alfred, was the script editor and principal writer for the BBC series *Upstairs, Downstairs*. His mother was an actress. So it was no surprise when, as a youngster, Charles began acting in school productions:

his first stage experience was at the age of seven, in a fourth grade production of *The Wicked Wizard*.

After graduating from Eton College, he was accepted to the Cambridge University law program. Charles noted, "Despite a lifelong love of the theater, I thought it was about time someone in my family did something sensible." He also joined the University's famed "Footlights Revue" comedy group. After graduation, he enrolled in a drama school in London. After touring in repertory for a year, he played the lead role in a BBC drama series, *Jury*. That was, alas, as close as he would get to being a barrister.

In 1983, he moved to Los Angeles, both to get acting work in America, and to marry Susan Fallender, an American actress he had met years earlier in drama school, when she was an exchange student in England. They have two daughters, Jenny Johanna, and Madelyn Sarah.

His first acting gigs in the United States were L.A.-based performances in repertory companies. Charles spent a fleeting four days portraying Alistair, cousin to Holly Scorpio (Emma Samms), on *General Hospital*, in late 1983. However, his real step towards stardom was accepting a role on *Days of Our Lives*, playing secret agent Shane Donovan from 1984–92. During that lengthy period, he won three Soap Opera Digest Awards, and countless legions of fans. His romantic and adventurous story lines on air kept viewers riveted to their sets.

During his tenure on *Days*, he appeared in the TV movie *Till We Meet Again* (1989), in guest spots on *Murphy Brown* (1992), and on the Fox network situation comedy *Harry and the Hendersons*, as Lord Bertram Moseley. Sitcom acting was, for Charles, a wonderful experience: "interesting," he noted, "because it was a lot slower-paced than *Days*, yet the day seemed very full. It's amazing how your work expands."

In a 1991 *Daytime TV* magazine, Charles noted that the only familial downside to the long hours on the soap was that "the only time [wife] Susie and I have is when [our daughter] Jenny is taking a nap."

Maybe he needed a nanny. Well, after his soap *Days* concluded in 1992, he found one, garnering a role on a new sitcom, *The Nanny*, developed by actress Fran Drescher and her husband, Peter Mark Jacobson. In it, Drescher played Fran Fine, whose microscopic outfits and gruff charm made her an unlikely nanny-turned-wife to wealthy widower Maxwell Sheffield, played solidly by Shaughnessy. Though hardly the formula for a likely hit, it caught on with audiences, who were puzzlingly charmed by the off beat prime-time series.

What did he enjoy better, daytime or nighttime acting? Hard to say: "On a soap, you spend all day working on a show that, in the end, is mostly very dramatic and very serious, especially Shane, the character that I played," shared Shaughnessy. "Usually, there was not a lot of humor. Digging your way out of collapsed tunnels or whatever it might be. And we used to just have such a blast during the day, working on the stuff."

Proof that soap actors, like daytime graduate Charles Shaughnessy, can enjoy providing fans with the dazzle that lights up our *Days*.

TV movies: 1989: *Till We Meet Again.* 1992: *Day-O.* 1996: *A Kiss So Deadly.* 1997: *A Degree of Deception.* 1998: *Denial.*

TV miniseries: 1997: *Everything to Gain.*

TV series: 1983: *General Hospital.* 1984–92: *Days of Our Lives.* 1993–99: *The Nanny*

Meet Alistair, Shane, and Drew

On *General Hospital,* Charles Shaughnessy briefly played the character of Alistair Crawford in 1983. Alistair was the cousin of long-running soap favorite Holly Scorpio (Emma Samms).

On *Days of Our Lives,* the role of Shane Donovan was originated, and solely played, by Charles Shaughnessy (1984–92). Drew was Shane's evil doppelganger, who appeared briefly in 1988. Shane, a secret agent, was the perfect soap opera hero: suave, romantic, and adventurous. His romances with two Brady sisters thrilled audiences, and the additional intrigue of his international spy agency career established the character as one of the most popular in daytime history.

Initially, Shane fell in love with former prostitute Kimberly Brady (Patsy Pease) while on a case. After the popular couple was married, Kim helped Shane to gather information on known drug trafficker Victor Kiriakis (John Aniston) by pretending to be blind (after her eyesight recovered from an accident). After seducing Victor (to stop him from killing Shane), Kim became pregnant. Confused, yet convinced that Victor was the father, Kim left Shane, and Salem.

Newly single Shane reluctantly found himself falling in love with Kim's sister, recently widowed Kayla Brady Johnson (Mary Beth Evans). Both were torn because of their growing feelings—she was Kim's sister, after all. When Kim returned to Salem, she found that Shane was newly involved with Kayla. Heartbroken, Kim left Salem, yet again.

Shortly after Shane and Kayla consummated their love, Shane was crippled in an explosion, unable to walk. Depressed, he pushed Kayla away, however much he loved her. Even after surgery repaired his injured legs, the damage to the relationship had been done: Kayla left Salem. So did Shane, in October 1992.

Family Connections

Anne Heche's (*Another World*) sister, Susan Bergman, wrote two books, *Anonymity: The Secret Life of an American* (1995) and *Martyrs: Contemporary Writers on Modern Lives of Faith* (1998).

Susan Sarandon's daughter, Eva, played mama Susan's Sister Helen Prejean character as a child in *Dead Man Walking* (1995).

Charles Shaughnessy's (*General Hospital, Days of Our Lives*) brother, David, is a producer for *The Young and the Restless*.

Sigourney Weaver's uncle, Winstead Sheffield "Doodles" Weaver was also an actor, a member of Spike Jones' troupe, best remembered for his "Professor Feitlebaum" character.

Christian Slater

Always wear shoes that taste good, 'cause they usually end up in your mouth.

—*Christian Slater, 1997*

Troubled teen D. J. LaSalle was played by Christian Slater on Ryan's Hope *in 1985. Courtesy of* Soap Opera Digest.

Born: August 18, 1969, in New York City, to Mary Jo Slater and Michael (Gainsborough) Hawkins; birth name, Christian Michael Leonard Hawkins; half-brother, Ryan Slater

Education: Dalton School, Children's Professional School of Manhattan, and High School for the Performing Arts (New York City)

Debuts: television—*One Life to Live* (1976) as an extra; Broadway—*The Music Man* (1978); film—*The Legend of Billie Jean* (1985)

Award: Won MTV Movie Award, for Best Kiss in *Untamed Heart* (shared award with costar Marisa Tomei), 1993

Honor: Nominated for MTV Movie Award, 1996

Book: *Christian Slater (Who's Hot!)*, by Burke Bronwen (1992)

Born to be in show business: the label pinned on Christian Slater, virtually from birth. However, as sadly happens to so many young Hollywood stars, the responsibility and glamour of show business comes with a big price to pay.

Christian Michael Leonard Hawkins' mother, Mary Jo Slater, is a prominent casting director; his father, Michael Hawkins (*né* Gainsborough) is an actor who dabbled significantly in soaps, notably on *Ryan's Hope* (as the original Frank Ryan, 1975–76). Ten years after father debuted on *Ryan's Hope*, son would, too.

Christian started acting professionally at the age of nine when his mother, Mary Jo, was a guest on *The Joe Franklin Show*, and the talk show host, spotting Christian in the wings, called him onto the set. Director Michael Kidd, who happened to be watching the TV program, cast the youngster in a Broadway revival of *The Music Man* (1978), starring Dick Van Dyke. Prior to this appearance, Mary Jo cast her seven-year-old son in an extra role on *One Life to Live*. Christian complemented his elementary school work with modeling jobs for Pierre Cardin and numerous stage experiences in musicals, comedies, and tragedies: he grew into a very versatile performer, even before he hit it big in feature films.

A funny highlight about Christian Slater's unique look: he is a major *Star Trek* fan. His unusual eyebrows are the result of him shaving them when dressing up as Spock for Halloween as a youngster; they never grew back in properly.

In 1985, Christian made his feature film debut, in the supporting role of Binx in the teen-rebellion study *The Legend of Billie Jean*, and also started a stint as D. J. LaSalle on *Ryan's Hope*, in which he worked extensively with **Yasmine Bleeth** (Ryan), Grant Show (Rick), and Marg Helgenberger (Siobhan).

For his sophomore film outing, Slater played a teenager with his own share of difficulties, as the young novice to Sean Connery's monk/detective in the medieval murder mystery *The Name of the Rose* (1986). He continued his adolescent-angst screen characterizations with the under-appreciated black comedy *Heathers* (1989), playing a young anarchist killer who encouraged Winona Ryder (with whom he had a real-life fling) to poison the ringleader of a high school clique. His *Pump Up the Volume* (1990) character whipped the entire student body of his high school into a frenzy via his own pirate radio station.

Unfortunately, the trials and tribulations in Slater's life weren't all fictional. He was arrested in 1989 reportedly for evading the police, assault with a deadly weapon (Christian's cowboy boots), and driving with a suspended license while under the influence. In 1994, he was arrested at a New York airport for allegedly attempting to board the craft with a gun in his luggage. On August 11, 1997, he was arrested on alleged charges of battery and two counts of assault with a deadly weapon. A subsequent blood alcohol test reportedly revealed a level of .24 percent, three times California's legal limit. Slater voluntarily checked himself into a drug rehabilitation clinic, and was sentenced to a ninety-day jail term, fifty-nine days of which he served, at California's La Verne County Jail.

Surprisingly, all the bad press didn't seem to seriously impact Christian's box-office drawing potential. He graduated from troubled-teen to moody-adult dramatic roles in *True Romance* (1993), *Interview with the Vampire* (1994), and *Murder in the First* (1995). In the action entry *Broken Arrow* (1996), one scene called for John Travolta and Slater to box, without mouthpieces or helmets. Christian explained, "We tried it with the headgear. We both looked like dweebs, so they were history. As for the mouthpieces, we had to talk, so they went early."

In 1997, Slater attempted to recover from the unsatisfying release of the black comedy *The Tears of Julian Po* (1997) with producer duties in *Hard*

Rain (1998) and an executive producer role in *Very Bad Things* (1998), both in addition to acting.

"You know, I've spent my life trying to live up to a projected image, and you know, I think I've lost myself," Slater told reporters and fans upon leaving the La Verne County jail in March 1998. "I've made some mistakes; I'm in the process of cleaning the mess up and taking responsibility for that."

Christian Slater grabbed Hollywood for all it was worth—maybe too much, too soon. Much talent, many diversions, and more to come.

Films: 1985: *The Legend of Billie Jean.* 1986: *The Name of the Rose; Twisted.* 1988: *Tucker: The Man and His Dream.* 1989: *Beyond the Stars; Gleaming the Cube; Heathers; The Wizard.* 1990: *Pump Up the Volume; Young Guns II; Tales from the Darkside: The Movie.* 1991: *Mobsters; Star Trek VI: The Undiscovered Country; Robin Hood: Prince of Thieves.* 1992: *Kuffs; FernGully: The Last Rainforest* (voice only); *Where the Day Takes You.* 1993: *True Romance; Untamed Heart; The Last Party.* 1994: *Interview with the Vampire; Jimmy Hollywood;* 1995: *Murder in the First; Catwalk.* 1996: *Broken Arrow; Bed of Roses; Museum of Love* (director only). 1997: *The Tears of Julian Po; Austin Powers: International Man of Mystery.* 1998: *Basil* (also co-producer); *Hard Rain* (also producer); *Very Bad Things* (also executive producer).

TV movies: 1983: *The Haunted Mansion Mystery; Living Proof: The Hank Williams Jr. Story.* 1986: *Secrets.* 1989: *Desperate for Love.* 1997: *Merry Christmas, George Bailey.*

TV series: 1976: *One Life to Live.* 1985: *Ryan's Hope.*

Meet D. J.

◻ On *One Life to Live*, Slater played a brief extra role, at age seven, in 1976.

◻ On *Ryan's Hope*, the role of D. J. LaSalle was originated, and solely played, by Christian Slater, in 1985.

D. J. was the troubled son of an alcoholic maid. He was involved in a love triangle surrounding Ryan Fenelli (Yasmine Bleeth) and Rick Hyde (Grant Show).

Like Father, Like Son

Christian Slater's father, Michael Hawkins (*né* Gainsborough) is an actor who dabbled significantly in soaps, having starred on *As the World Turns* (as Dr. Paul Stewart, 1968), *Love Is a Many Splendored Thing* (as Mark Elliott, 1970–71), *How to Survive a Marriage* (as Larry Kirby, 1975), and *Ryan's Hope* (as the original Frank Ryan, 1975–76). It is interesting that, ten years after father debuted on *Ryan's Hope*, son would too, as D. J. LaSalle.

Richard Thomas

Good-night, John-Boy.

The fourth of, to date, thirteen actors to portray Tom Hughes on As the World Turns *was Richard Thomas, from 1966–67. Courtesy of Photofest.*

Born: June 13, 1951, in New York City to Richard and Barbara Fallis Thomas; birth name, Richard Earl Thomas

Education: Columbia University (New York City)

Debuts: Broadway—*Sunrise at Campobello* (1958); television—*1, 2, 3 Go* (1961); film—*Last Summer* (1969)

Awards: Won Television Champion Award for Most Promising New Star for his role as John-Boy Walton on *The Waltons*, 1972; won Emmy Award for Best Actor in a Drama Series, for *The Waltons*, 1973

Honor: Nominated for Emmy Award, 1974; nominated for Golden Globe Award, 1974

Marital Status: Married Alma Gonzales, February 14, 1975, divorced; married Georgiana Bischoff, November 20, 1994; five children, triplet daughters Pilar, Barbara and Gwyneth, son Richard (all with ex-wife Alma), and son Montana (with present wife Georgiana)

Rarely does a role become so distinctly associated with an actor that audiences cannot picture anyone else in that role. Mention *As the World Turns'* Tom Hughes, and Richard Thomas does not immediately come to mind. Mention *The Waltons'* John-Boy, however, and the connection is instant, so enduring was his TV characterization.

Richard Earl Thomas attended private schools in Manhattan, while his talented parents performed with the New York City Ballet. At the age of seven, Richard made his professional acting debut as John Roosevelt, son of

President Franklin Delano Roosevelt, in Broadway's *Sunrise at Campobello*. Three years later, in 1961, ten-year-old Richard became co-host (along with Jack Lescoulie) of a brief NBC educational TV series for children, *1,2,3 Go*.

Richard took two soap-induced breaks from school: first, at age thirteen, to appear on *A Flame in the Wind*, playing Chris Austen, and then, at age fifteen, to assume the part of teenager Tom Hughes on *As the World Turns*. Yes, Eileen Fulton *was* playing Lisa at that time (she created the role in 1960).

After graduating high school, Richard immersed himself in acting for the next three years, appearing in TV and feature films, which led to the defining character of Richard's show business résumé.

On December 19, 1971, the TV movie *The Homecoming* introduced one of the most popular families in television history: *The Waltons*. This closely knit brood of seven children, parents, and grandparents, lived in rural Virginia during the Depression. Eldest son and aspiring writer John-Boy, played by Thomas, was patterned after the show's creator, Earl Hamner. The series debuted on September 14, 1972, becoming a national Thursday evening institution until its final airing, on August 20, 1981. Richard had left the series in 1977 to pursue other interests, but appeared in eight subsequent *Waltons*-inspired TV movies and specials.

Richard married Alma Gonzales on February 14, 1975. Their son, Richard Francisco, arrived in 1976; five years later, Alma gave birth to triplet daughters (Pilar, Barbara, and Gwyneth). After his divorce from Alma, Richard married store manager Georgiana Bischoff on November 20, 1994; their son, Montana James Thomas (named after Richard's grandfather) was born, at their Los Angeles home, on July 28, 1996.

Richard's career was established by *The Waltons*, but he certainly could not live on the reputation of one role. He played strong parts in such TV movies as *Getting Married* (1977), *All Quiet on the Western Front* (1979), and the lead in *Living Proof: The Hank Williams Jr. Story* (1983), and in miniseries, including *Roots: The Next Generation* (1978), and *Glory! Glory!* (1988).

As the 1990s dawned, Richard was as busy as ever, complementing television work with live stage performances, including the title role of the Shakespeare Theatre's touring production of *Richard II*. In a 1993 review for the *New York Times*, critic Ben Brantley stated, "Surely no Richard II has ever given up the throne of England with quite the deviltry or vigor that Richard Thomas brings to that Shakespeare production."

Still busy in TV movies, in an acting capacity as well as producing and directing, he has even written some poetry. Maybe Richard Thomas got the yen for the pen from the writer in his TV alter-ego, John-Boy.

Films: 1969: *Winning*; *Last Summer*. 1970: *Cactus in the Snow*. 1971: *Red Sky at Morning*; *The Todd Killings*; *You'll Like My Mother*. 1978: *September 30, 1955*. 1980: *Battle Beyond the Stars*. Forthcoming: *Fortune Hunters*.

TV movies: 1971: *The Homecoming*. 1973: *The Thanksgiving Story*. 1974: *The Red Badge of Courage*. 1975: *The Silence*. 1978: *Getting Married*. 1979: *All Quiet on the Western Front*; *Bloody Kids*; *No Other Love*. 1980: *To Find My Son*. 1981: *Berlin Tunnel 21*. 1982: *Fifth of July*; *Johnny Belinda*. 1983: *Hobson's Choice*; *Living Proof: The Hank Williams Jr. Story*. 1984: *The Master of Ballantrae*. 1985: *Final Jeopardy*. 1988: *Go to the Light*; *Andy Colby's Incredible Adventure*. 1989: *Glory! Glory!*. 1990: *It*; *Common Ground*; *Andre's Mother*. 1991: *Yes, Virginia, There Is a Santa Claus*; *Mission of the Shark: The Saga of the U.S.S. Indianapolis*. 1992: *Lincoln* (voice only); *I Love You to Death: The Laura Black Story*; *Crash Landing: The Rescue of Flight 232*. 1993: *A Walton Thanksgiving Reunion*; *Precious Victims*; *I Can Make You Love Me, Linda*. 1994: *To Save the Children*. 1995: *The Christmas Box*; *A Walton Wedding*; *Death in Small Doses*; *Down, Out & Dangerous*. 1996: *Timepiece*; *What Love Sees* (also co-producer). 1997: *A Thousand Men and a Baby*; *A Walton Easter*; *Flood: A River's Rampage*. 1998: *Beyond the Prairie: The True Story of Laura Ingalls Wilder*.

TV miniseries: 1979: *Roots: The Next Generations*. 1995: *The Invaders*.

TV series: 1961–62: *1, 2, 3 Go*. 1964: *A Flame in the Wind*. 1966–67: *As the World Turns*. 1972–77: *The Waltons* (also director).

Meet Chris and Tom

On *A Flame in the Wind*, the role of Chris Austen was originated, and solely played, by Richard Thomas, in 1964.

This half-hour serial debuted in December 1964, and lasted through December 1966. In June 1965, its title was changed to *A Time for Us*. Set in the fictional town of Havilland, its stories centered around young people, including Chris Austen and his mother, widow Kate Austen (Kathleen Maguire).

On *As the World Turns*, the role of Tom Hughes has been played by James Madden (1963), Jerry Schaffer (1963), Frankie Michaels (1964–66), Richard Thomas (1966–67), Paul O'Keefe (1967–68), Peter Link (1969), Peter Galman (1969–73), C. David Colson (1973–78), Tom Tammi (1979–80), Justin Deas (1981–84), Jason Kincaid (1984), Gregg Marx (1984–87), and Scott Holmes (1987–present).

Tom is the son of Bob Hughes (Don Hastings) and Lisa Miller (Eileen Fulton). When played by Richard Thomas, Tom was a mere teenager, who couldn't have imagined that, someday, he'd be the District Attorney of Oakdale.

Marisa Tomei

I think I've never been an ingenue. I've never wanted to be an ingenue, even when I was a little girl. I've always liked the sidekick roles. I've never wanted to be the prissy, one-note lead who always had to be perfect and look pretty.

—*Marisa Tomei, 1997*

Born: December 4, 1964, in Brooklyn, New York, to Gary A. and Patricia Tomei; younger brother, Adam

Education: Boston University (Massachusetts); New York University

Debuts: television—*As the World Turns* (1983) as Marcy Thompson Cushing; film—*Sweet Ginger Brown* (1984); stage—*Daughters* (1986)

Awards: Won Theatre World Award for her role of Cetta in *Daughters*, 1986; won Academy Award, as Best Supporting Actress, for her role as Mona Lisa Vito in *My Cousin Vinny*, 1993; won MTV Movie Award, for Breakthrough Performance in *My Cousin Vinny*, 1993; won MTV Movie Award, for Best Kiss in *Untamed Heart* (shared award with costar **Christian Slater**), 1993

Honor: Nominated for Screen Actors Guild Award, 1997

In 1996, Marisa Tomei observed, "I began, and I got a lot of attention early on. I'm now learning about film acting." She lived the American film dream, winning an Oscar at a point in her career in which she felt she was just beginning. What a launch!

In her youth, archaeology was Marisa Tomei's unique career goal. However, after seeing the play *A Chorus Line* on Broadway at age twelve, she became star-struck, setting her sights on being an actress. While in junior high school, she began studying dancing and acting, and appearing in school productions. During her summers, she traveled to upstate New York, performing in plays at the Golden Bridge Colony.

She entered Boston University in 1982. The summer after freshman year, she became a waitress at Tony Roma's restaurant in New York. Sophomore year loomed: her father, naturally, wanted her to return to college. Her best friend, Allison, encouraged Marisa to explore her acting career. Allison won.

Marisa began auditioning in Manhattan, and soon made her professional debut on *As the World Turns*, as Marcy Thompson. She was a strong supporting player on the soap for eighteen months, during which time she made her feature film debut in *Sweet Ginger Brown* (1984), and also appeared in *The Flamingo Kid* (1984), starring Matt Dillon.

After leaving daytime TV in 1985, she won a role in the feature film *Playing for Keeps* (1986), and made her off-Broadway debut in 1986, as Cetta in the John Morgan Evans play *Daughters*. Marisa won a Theatre World Award for her performance.

Marisa moved to California to become a cast member in the sitcom *A Different World*, playing Maggie Lawton from 1987–88. Stage performances kept Marisa busy for the balance of the decade.

Marisa used her Brooklyn roots to good advantage in big-screen roles as floozy Remi in Nicolas Cage's erotic thriller *Zandalee* (1991) and as Sylvester Stallone's daughter Lisa Provolone in the comic *Oscar* (1991). However, it was in *My Cousin Vinny* (1992), as sassy, gum-chewing Mona Lisa Vito, resplendent with automotive proficiency and stereotypical Brooklynese twang, that Marisa scored, winning a surprise 1993 Academy Award. However, such major honors come with a big hitch: heightened expectations.

Her Oscar did not necessarily guarantee that her screen career was set. She appeared in a string of disappointing vehicles, first as a dead-ringer for exuberant, yet unflatteringly drawn, Mabel Normand in *Chaplin* (1992), then as Rosie Rivers in *Equinox* (1992). Roles in *Untamed Heart* (1993), *The Paper* (1994), and *Only You* (1994), while showcasing quality Tomei performances, did not pack the punch of *My Cousin Vinny*. Long known for giving her every effort to all her parts, she added eighteen pounds to her petite frame for her role as Cuban refugee Dottie Perez in Mira Nair's *The Perez Family* (1994). Marisa felt the continued pressure of the responsibility of being a member of the elite Oscar family. "I had really just started," she admitted. "Sometimes, it was like, 'Oh, I have to learn how to live in public and under a microscope.'"

In 1996, Marisa Tomei developed a career link to fellow soap alumna **Teri Hatcher**, celebrated *Seinfeld* TV series siren. In the February 8, 1996, episode of the popular sitcom, "The Cadillac," Marisa became the obsession of George Castanza (Jason Alexander)—so smitten was he that, in a later episode (in which Tomei did not appear), George called Marisa for a date on the very evening of the death of his fiancée, Susan Biddle Ross (Heidi Swedberg).

The big-screen spark in Marisa returned with strong roles in *Unhook the Stars* (1996), *Welcome to Sarajevo* (1997), *The Slums of Beverly Hills* (1998), and *Since You've Been Gone* (1998). In a return to the live theater, she played opposite Quentin Tarantino (in his Broadway debut) in a 1998 revival of the Frederick Knott suspense drama *Wait Until Dark*.

Still on the upswing, Marisa Tomei continues to show that her 1993 Academy Award was far from a one-hit wonder.

Films: 1984: *Sweet Ginger Brown*; *The Flamingo Kid*. 1986: *Playing for Keeps*. 1991: *Oscar*; *Zandalee*. 1992: *My Cousin Vinny*; *Chaplin*; *Equinox*. 1993: *Untamed Heart*. 1994: *The Paper*; *Only You*. 1995: *The Perez Family*; *Four Rooms*. 1996: *Unhook the Stars*. 1997: *A Brother's Kiss*; *Welcome to Sarajevo*. 1998: *The Slums of Beverly Hills*; *My Own Country*. Forthcoming: *King of the Jungle*.

TV movies: 1990: *Parker Kane*. 1998: *Only Love*; *Since You've Been Gone*.

TV series: 1983–85: *As the World Turns*. 1987–88: *A Different World*.

Meet Marcy

◻ On *As the World Turns*, the role of Marcy Thompson Cushing was originated, and solely played by, Marisa Tomei (1983–85).

Marcy was a troubled young pal of Frannie Hughes (then Terri Vandenbosch), who spent time living with the Hughes family in Oakdale. She was most notable for mistaking Bob Hughes' (Don Hastings) fatherly concerns for romantic overtures, making vicious accusations against him.

Marcy had a long friendship with Frannie, Kirk McColl (Christian J. LeBlanc), and Jay Connors (Breck Jamison), and at different times, Marcy dated both Kirk and Jay.

In 1985, Marcy won a "Cinderella" sweepstakes, sponsored by the town newspaper, *The Argus*. In a fairytale fog, Marcy met Lord Stewart Markham Cushing (Ross Kettle), a world-renowned tennis player, and aristocratic son of a fictional British stage actress. Their unlikely romance turned into marriage, with the Cushings settling in merrie old England.

• •

Fictional and Real Soap Mom and Sons

It's fictional: Judith Light's (*One Life to Live*) son on prime time's *Who's the Boss?* was played by Daniel Pintauro, who portrayed Paul Stenbeck on *As the World Turns* from 1983–84.

It's real: Elizabeth Taylor (*All My Children, General Hospital*) is the mother of Michael Wilding, who played Jackson Fremont on *Guiding Light* from 1985–87.

• •

Janine Turner

A career is wonderful, but having a baby and a family is the most important thing one can do.
—Janine Turner, 1998

Blonde and sultry, Janine Turner debuted on General Hospital, *in the role of Laura Templeton, on January 14, 1982. Courtesy of Archive Photo.*

Born: December 6, 1963, in Lincoln, Nebraska; birth name, Janine Gauntt; one brother, Tim

Education: Professional Children's School (New York)

Debuts: television—*Dallas* (1982); film—*Young Doctors in Love* (1982)

Honors: Nominated for Golden Globe Awards in 1993 and 1994

Personal Status: Never married; one daughter, Juliette

She is half of one of the most famous oncamera sister teams in the history of daytime soaps. Janine Turner, who played sibling to future superstar **Demi Moore** on *General Hospital* in 1982–83, soared to sky-high stardom on her own.

When Janine Gauntt was three years old, her family relocated to Euless, Texas, where the youngster began dance studies. In her early teens, while an apprentice with the Fort Worth Ballet, she developed an interest in acting as well. Janine's mother sent pictures of her fifteen-year-old daughter to the prestigious Wilhelmina Agency; the teen was soon signed on as the firm's youngest model.

After two years of studies at New York's famed Professional Children's School, Janine moved back to Texas to finish high school. One day, while Janine was in a grocery store, TV producer Leonard Katzman spotted her standing in line, and asked the eighteen-year-old to read for a small part on *Dallas*. She was soon cast, for three 1982 episodes of the prime-time series, as Susan, a friend of Lucy Ewing (Charlene Tilton). From that auspicious TV debut, Janine would go on to make a big splash in the soap world.

Her first suds were late-night, in the short-lived *Behind the Screen*, which aired on CBS from October 1981 through January 1982. Janine played starlet Janie-Claire Willow in the story of the cast and crew of a fictional daytime soap opera called "Generations." (Ironically, seven years later, an actual soap, *Generations*, would debut on NBC.) This serial-within-a-serial idea had been used thirty-two years earlier, in the 1949 TV soap, *A Woman to Remember*.

In 1982, coincident with a *General Hospital* story line surrounding the departure of Genie Francis from her popular role as Laura Spencer, Janine was hired as Laura Templeton, sister of Demi Moore's Jackie Templeton. Sporting long, wavy hair dyed blonde for the part, Janine appeared on the show for two seasons, with a resemblance, integral to the saga, to the "mistaken for dead" Laura Spencer.

While on the soap, Janine joined seven other cast members of *General Hospital*, in addition to actors from *All My Children* and *The Young and the Restless*, in the parody flick *Young Doctors in Love* (1982). The film included many spoofs of *GH*-esque story lines, and was great fun, in particular, for fans of *General Hospital*.

In the years after leaving the soap, Janine was busy, but in unwisely chosen films (*Knights of the City* and Dino DeLaurentis' *Tai-Pan* in 1986), and in TV guest spots. She returned to the daytime TV ranks with a minor role as Patricia Kirkland on the NBC soap *Another World*, from December 1986–March 1987.

After a hapless 1988 film appearance in *Monkey Shines: An Experiment in Fear*, it was *Steel Magnolias* (1989) that redeemed her—a charming film, boasting a talented ensemble cast, including Janine as Nancy Beth Marmillion, lively daughter of Belle (Bibi Besch), and niece of Clairee Belcher (Olympia Dukakis).

July 12, 1990, saw the debut of the quirky CBS nighttime series *Northern Exposure*. On the show, Janine starred as Mary Margaret "Maggie" O'Connell, a bush pilot, daughter of the youngest CEO in automotive history ("Do you remember the hatchback? That's my Dad"), and Mayor of Cicely, Alaska. Men she had slept with had a tendency to die: such knowledge kept her at a distance from Rob Morrow's character of Dr. Joel Fleischman. While on the show, she became famed for her short brunette hairstyle, which inspired a craze of similar coifs nationwide (markedly contrasting her *General Hospital* look). The show, resplendent with a graceful moose in the opening credits and a popular musical soundtrack, was a fan favorite until it was canceled, on July 26, 1995.

During her solid run on *Northern Exposure*, Janine appeared in *Cliffhanger* (1993), costarring as Jessie Deighan opposite Sylvester Stallone, in an action flick which marked Stallone's cinematic return to success after consecutive film flops.

In 1997, Janine took on the role of June Cleaver opposite Christopher McDonald as Ward in *Leave It to Beaver* (1997), a big-screen remake of the popular 1950s–1960s TV series in which she played the part made famous by Barbara Billingsley. She also filmed the TV movie *Circle of Deceit* (1998), in which she both co-produced and played Terry, a woman who fakes her own death after discovering that her husband was unfaithful.

Directly after the TV film's shooting session closed, Janine took time off from her film career to enjoy her pregnancy, keeping strictly hush-hush on the identity of the father. On November 22, 1997, the never-married Janine gave birth to daughter Juliette Loraine, after a twenty-seven-hour labor.

Janine returned to acting at the end of March 1998, in a TV movie, *Beauty*, which put a modern spin on the classic *Beauty and the Beast*, and in a series of classy car advertisements, in which she sported a sleekly elegant look that easily put her former bulky wool plaid *Northern Exposure* garb to shame.

She may have been billed as a duplicate on *General Hospital*, but there is no doubt that Janine Turner is nobody's carbon copy today.

Films: 1982: *Young Doctors in Love*. 1986: *Knights of the City*; *Tai-Pan*. 1988: *Monkey Shines: An Experiment in Fear*. 1989: *Steel Magnolias*. 1990: *The Ambulance*. 1993: *Cliffhanger*. 1997: *Leave It to Beaver*; *The Curse of Inferno*.

TV movies: 1997: *Stolen Women*; *Captured Hearts*. 1998: *Beauty*; *Circle of Deceit* (also co-producer).

TV series: 1981–82: *Behind the Screen*. 1982–83: *General Hospital*. 1986–87: *Another World*. 1990–95: *Northern Exposure*.

Meet Laura and Patricia

On *General Hospital*, the role of Laura Templeton was originated, and solely played, by Janine Turner (1982–83).

Port Charles was rocked by the disappearance of two of the town's Lauras, Spencer (Genie Francis) and Templeton. Among those who took part in the search for the missing women were Laura's husband Luke (Anthony Geary), and Laura Templeton's sister, investigative reporter Jackie (Demi Moore). After an exhaustive search, Laura Templeton returned, unharmed, but Laura Spencer would not resurface for years.

On *Another World*, the role of Patricia Kirkland was originated, and played solely, by Janine Turner, from December 1986–March 1987.

Patricia Kirkland was the old lover of fellow Bay City resident Scott LaSalle (Hank Cheyne).

Kathleen Turner

You could do things with the rate at which you open and close your eyes. Things that in a theater would be lost except to the first ten rows, and things with your voice that you could never do on stage.

—Kathleen Turner, on the differences between TV and stage, 1978

Born: June 19, 1954, in Springfield, Missouri; birth name, Mary Kathleen Turner

Education: Central School of Speech and Drama (London, England); Southwest Missouri State College (Springfield); University of Maryland (College Park)

Debuts: Broadway—*Gemini* (1978); television—*As the World Turns* (1977) as a court stenographer; film—*Body Heat* (1981)

Awards: Won Golden Globes, for Best Performance by an Actress in a Comedy/Musical Motion Picture, for her role as Joan Wilder in *Romancing the Stone*, 1985, and for her role as Irene Walker in *Prizzi's Honor*, 1986

Honors: Nominated for Golden Globes in 1982, 1987, and 1990; named Star of the Year by the National Association of Theatre Owners, 1985; nominated for Academy Award in 1987; named Woman of the Year by the Hasty Pudding Theatricals, 1989

Marital Status: Married businessman Jay Weiss, August 1984; one daughter, Rachel

Book: *Kathleen Turner*, by Rebecca Stefoff (1987)

She owned the 1980s. The persona that she developed in daytime television transferred with sizzling success to the big screen, making the name of Kathleen Turner one of true cinematic magic.

Mary Kathleen Turner grew up the daughter of a United States foreign service officer, whose occupation required numerous moves. Places where the

Turner family lived included Canada, Cuba, London, Venezuela, and Washington, D.C. While in England, Mary Kathleen studied at London's Central School of Speech and Drama. When the family returned to the United States, she attended Southwest Missouri State College, before receiving her Master of Fine Arts from the University of Maryland in 1977.

At the age of twenty-three, she shed her first name and debuted on television in a 1977 extra appearance as a court stenographer on *As the World Turns*. The next year saw her big break: the role as Nola Dancy on NBC's *The Doctors*. Her soap character, vampy, trampy, and campy, gave Kathleen a wide array of performance skills during her run on the show, 1978–79.

Two years later, on August 28, 1981, saw Kathleen's sizzling big-screen debut, in Lawrence Kasdan's *Body Heat*, costarring William Hurt. It was quite a career launch, bringing back into vogue the brand of temptress which hadn't been seen since the *film noir* tradition of 1940s Hollywood.

Film after film brought one Turner success after another. She played opposite Steve Martin in *The Man with Two Brains* (1983). Her comedic role of Joan Wilder in *Romancing the Stone* (1984), opposite Michael Douglas and Danny DeVito, spurred a sequel, *Jewel of the Nile* (1985). It showed Kathleen as a versatile performer, adept at many acting levels. Her style, combining a deep, sultry voice with classy sex appeal, her mysterious presence, and her true knack for comedy, catapulted her to popular heights, and established her as one of the decade's true stars.

Kathleen married businessman Jay Weiss in August 1984; they have one daughter, Rachel Ann, born in the fall of 1987.

On June 14, 1985, *Prizzi's Honor* opened, and was one more triumph for Kathleen, who earned raves and a Golden Globe for Best Actress in a Comedy (her second; her first was for *Romancing the Stone* in 1984) for her role as Irene Walker in this capital black comedy with Jack Nicholson. By 1986, Kathleen Turner was the ninth of ten top box-office draws in the world, joining such company as Tom Cruise, Sylvester Stallone, Clint Eastwood, and Whoopi Goldberg. In February of that year, Debra Winger, who was scheduled to star in *Peggy Sue Got Married* (1986), was in traction from a back injury: Kathleen took on the title role, and received an Oscar nomination.

The voice of sexy Jessica Rabbit in the mixed-live-and-cartoon-noir *Who Framed Roger Rabbit?* (1988) was that of Kathleen, bringing to animated life the sexpot unaccountably wedded to the nebbishy Roger. At number ten, Turner was the only woman in the top ten among the world's top 1989 box-office draws, a list which boasted Jack Nicholson, Robin Williams, Tom Hanks, and Mel Gibson. Her inclusion was, in large part, due to her splendid Barbara Rose opposite Michael Douglas in *The War of the Roses* (1989), a delicious disintegrating-marriage comedy.

On March 27, 1990, Kathleen gave the live stage a try, and opened to rave reviews in a Broadway revival of *Cat on a Hot Tin Roof*. Marring the triumph was a controversy involving Kathleen's husband: Weiss held the lease on the Happy Land Social Club in the Bronx, New York, which, on March

25, 1990, burned down due to allegedly insufficient sprinklers and eighty-seven people died inside.

The next years marked a slip in Kathleen's popularity, what with middle age hampering her sex-kittenish persona, a weight gain, etc. Nor did her film choices help matters: in *V. I. Warshawski* (1991), she not only earned poor notices in the detective caper, but broke her nose during filming. She was not to have a major screen hit until 1994, with John Waters' dark suburban satire *Serial Mom*, in which she portrayed crafty murdering mama Beverly Sutphin. This mature role not only brought back to the fore the wacky comedy technique that had so endeared her to 1980s audiences, but clearly defined her future career path.

Her voice is, currently, her great strength, and she has lent it to a February 17, 1994, episode of *The Simpsons*, entitled "Lisa vs. Malibu Stacy," and a 1997 voice-over in *Bad Baby*, playing the voice of Mom.

Most actors cannot sustain sex-kitten status for very long: Kathleen Turner did, and for much longer than most. Now, she is creating a whole new persona for the cinematic world to notice.

Films: 1981: *Body Heat.* 1983: *The Man with Two Brains.* 1984: *Romancing the Stone; A Breed Apart; Crimes of Passion.* 1985: *Prizzi's Honor; The Jewel of the Nile.* 1986: *Peggy Sue Got Married.* 1987: *Julia and Julia.* 1988: *Switching Channels; Who Framed Roger Rabbit?* (voice only); *The Accidental Tourist.* 1989: *Tummy Trouble* (voice only); *The War of the Roses.* 1991: *V. I. Warshawski.* 1992: *John Barry—Moviola.* 1993: *House of Cards; Undercover Blues.* 1994: *Naked in New York, Serial Mom.* 1995: *Moonlight and Valentino.* 1997: *A Simple Wish; Bad Baby* (voice only); *The Real Blonde.* Forthcoming: *Baby Geniuses; The Virgin Suicides; Love and Action in Chicago; Prince of Central Park.*

TV movies: 1987: *Dear America: Letters Home from Vietnam.* 1994: *Leslie's Folly* (director only). 1995: *Friends at Last* (also producer). 1997: *Love in the Ancient World.* 1998: *Legalese.*

TV series: 1978–79: *The Doctors.*

Meet Nola

✄ On *The Doctors*, the role of Nola Dancy Aldrich was played by Kathryn Harrold (1976–78), Kathleen Turner (1978–79), and Kim Zimmer (1979–82).

Nola was one of the other-side-of-the-tracks Dancy clan, the sister of Luke Dancy (Frank Telfer). She married Jason Aldrich (Glenn Corbett), twice, making a fast enemy in the Aldrich matriarch, wealthy and elegant Mona Croft (Meg Mundy). Their long feud was delicious in its tartness.

Cicely Tyson

Life for me ain't been no crystal stairs... But, all the time, I've been climbing on, reaching landings, turning corners, and sometimes going in the dark where there ain't been no light.

—Cicely Tyson, in The Autobiography of Miss Jane Pittman *(1973)*

Cicely Tyson was one of two renowned actresses to portray Martha Frazier on The Guiding Light in the mid-1960s. The other? Ruby Dee. Courtesy of Photofest.

Born: December 19, 1933, in New York City to William and Theodosia Tyson

Debuts: stage—*The Dark of the Moon* (mid-1950s); film—*Odds Against Tomorrow* (1959); television—*East Side, West Side* (1963)

Awards: Won Emmy Award, as Best Lead Actress in a Drama, for her role in *The Autobiography of Miss Jane Pittman*, 1974; won Special Emmy Award, as Actress of the Year, 1974

Honors: Nominated for Academy Award in 1973; nominated for Golden Globe Award in 1973; nominated for Emmy Awards in 1977, 1978, and 1995; nominated for Screen Actors' Guild Awards in 1995 and 1997; nominated for Image Awards in 1996, 1997, and 1998; received a Star on the Hollywood Walk of Fame, August 21, 1997; Honorary Doctorates, Atlanta University, Loyola University, Lincoln University

Marital Status: Married jazz musician Miles Davis, November 1981; separated, December 1988; divorced, 1989

She is one of the most honored and beloved actresses of all time. Her portrayals have inspired and stretched the boundaries of acting possibilities. Cicely Tyson, indeed, is a superstar.

She grew up in Harlem, where her parents settled after leaving the Island of Nevis in the Caribbean. Her mother was a domestic; her father operated a pushcart. Cicely's parents soon divorced, with Cicely staying with her mother. Before long, they were on welfare. Cicely earned extra money by selling shopping bags in the street.

She graduated from high school in 1950, and became a typist for the Red Cross. Cicely was at a beauty parlor having her hair done when the owner asked her to model at a hairstyle show. That appearance led to modeling assignments and, eventually, a role in an underfinanced independent film that was never completed. She so much enjoyed the experience that she decided to become an actress.

Her acting debut was in a Harlem YMCA production of *Dark of the Moon*. In 1959, Cicely made her film debut, in an uncredited turn as Fran in *Odds Against Tomorrow*. The movie, which dealt with racial overtones surrounding a thwarted bank robbery, starred Robert Ryan, Harry Belafonte, Ed Begley, Shelley Winters, and Gloria Grahame.

Her career was just beginning, but, because she is African American, her Cinderella story might have ended with the coach turning back into a pumpkin. However, as Tyson noted, "I was among the initial group of actors fortunate enough to be around at that time, especially because of the kind of social atmosphere we were involved in, the whole Civil Rights era."

Her television debut was in the 1963–64 dramatic series, *East Side, West Side*. Cicely was seen as Jane Porter, secretary to Neil Brock, played by George C. Scott. By appearing in this program, Tyson broke ground as the first African-American female performer cast in a regular role in a non-comedic role in a series, and as one of the first known sporters of an Afro hair style.

In 1966, Cicely began a six-month stint on *The Guiding Light*, playing Nurse Martha Frazier. She was noticed in this role, for she next appeared in the big-screen entry, *The Comedians* (1967), which dealt with the Haitian regime under Papa Doc Duvalier. Its stellar cast included Richard Burton, Elizabeth Taylor, Alec Guinness, Peter Ustinov, and Lillian Gish.

Cicely returned to the small screen for a number of series guest appearances: among them, *The F.B.I.*, *Mission: Impossible*, and the premiere episode of *Medical Center*, on September 24, 1969, in which she costarred with O. J. Simpson in "The Last Ten Yards." On TV, as elsewhere, she was a visible, and very dependable, multitalented actress. However, she realized the challenges both behind her, and ahead of her.

"There's not a black woman who exists in this world—particularly in this business—who has not been discriminated against," Tyson has admitted. "Roles were not written for black women. And I was not considered for roles simply because I was a good actress. I was considered for roles because I was a black actress who was good." Landing the role of Rebecca in *Sounder* (1972), about a black sharecropper family in Louisiana during the Depression, was a career turning point. For playing Rebecca Morgan, Cicely received her only Oscar nomination to date, for Best Actress.

The acclaim was far from over. In 1974, she dazzled TV audiences with a stunning performance in *The Autobiography of Miss Jane Pittman*, portraying the activist from young adulthood to her post-centennial. Cicely earned an unprecedented two Emmy Awards for this performance, for both Best Actress in a Drama and for Actress of the Year.

The coming years saw Cicely appearing in important vehicles, dealing with African-American women of strength: TV movies (1978's *A Woman Called Moses*, 1989's *The Women of Brewster Place*, 1994's *The Oldest Living Confederate Widow Tells All*, and 1998's *Mama Flora's Family*), miniseries (1977's *Roots* and 1978's *King*, both of which earned her Emmy nominations) and feature films (1976's *The River Niger*, 1978's *A Hero Ain't Nothin' But a Sandwich*, and 1997's *Hoodlum*, in which she played the wicked Madame Stephanie St. Clair, better known as "The Queen").

In 1989, she was divorced from her husband, jazz musician Miles Davis. The two had been married in November 1981, at comedian Bill Cosby's farm near Amherst, Massachusetts.

Her voice was lent to the 1994 TV miniseries *A Century of Women*—such a study of noted females could not have succeeded without the participation of Cicely Tyson, one of this century's most celebrated and distinctive actresses.

Films: 1959: *Odds Against Tomorrow*. 1966: *A Man Called Adam*. 1967: *The Comedians*. 1968: *The Heart Is a Lonely Hunter*. 1972: *Sounder*. 1976: *The Blue Bird; The River Niger*. 1978: *A Hero Ain't Nothin' But a Sandwich*. 1979: *Airport '79*. 1981: *Bustin' Loose*. 1991: *Fried Green Tomatoes*. 1997: *Hoodlum*.

TV movies: 1971: *Marriage: Year One*. 1974: *The Autobiography of Miss Jane Pittman*. 1976: *Just an Old Sweet Song*. 1977: *Wilma*. 1978: *A Woman Called Moses*. 1981: *The Marva Collins Story*. 1982: *Benny's Place*. 1985: *Playing with Fire*. 1986: *Acceptable Risks; Intimate Encounters; Samaritan: The Mitch Snyder Story*. 1989: *The Women of Brewster Place*. 1990: *Heat Wave; The Kid Who Loved Christmas*. 1992: *When No One Would Listen; Duplicates*. 1993: *House of Secrets*. 1994: *The Oldest Living Confederate Widow Tells All*. 1996: *Road to Galveston*. 1997: *Ms. Scrooge; The Price of Heaven; Riot; Bridge of Time*. 1998: *Always Outnumbered, Always Outgunned*.

TV miniseries: 1977: *Roots*. 1978: *King*. 1994: *A Century of Women* (voice only). 1998: *Mama Flora's Family*.

TV series: 1963–64: *East Side/West Side*. 1966: *The Guiding Light*. 1994: *Sweet Justice*.

Meet Martha

🏳 On *The Guiding Light*, the role of Martha Frazier was played by Cicely Tyson (1966) and Ruby Dee (1967).

The Guiding Light was one of the first, if not *the* first, soap to realistically portray an integrated workplace: Cedars Hospital in Springfield, where nurse Martha Frazier and her husband, Dr. Jim Frazier (**Billy Dee Williams**, then **James Earl Jones**) worked.

Casper Van Dien

I'm an actor, I'm a salesman, my product is me. I've got to constantly improve it, constantly promote it, and do the best job possible. I don't want to have any regrets in twenty years.
—Casper Van Dien, 1998

Casper Van Dien sizzled on One Life to Live *in the role of Ty Moody from 1993–94.* Courtesy of Soap Opera Digest.

Born: December 18, 1968, in Ridgefield, New Jersey; birth name, Casper Van Dien XI; three sisters, Debbie, Sudi, and Kristin

Education: Admiral Farragut Academy (St. Petersburg, Florida); Florida State University (Tallahassee)

Debuts: television—*Dangerous Women* (1991); film—*Night Eyes 4* (1995)

Marital Status: Married actress Carrie Mitchum, 1993, divorced; two children, Casper and Grace

On Filming *Starship Troopers* (1997): "Yeah, we had some bruises. I chipped two teeth. I bruised my ribs. My whole body was smashed up. I hurt my wrist, my knees. I coughed up blood after that tanker bug scene."

He went from military school to pre-med college studies. He went from sci-fi trooper to Tarzan. He is the eleventh of twelve named Casper Van Dien, and he's getting set to swing into film stardom.

Casper Van Dien XI comes from a long line of regulation crew-cut Caspers. Descended from Dutch colonists, Van Dien's father, Casper X, is a retired naval commander and fighter pilot who served in Korea and Vietnam. His grandfather, Casper IX, was a Marine who fought in both World Wars. Casper himself spent his early years in Florida and Okinawa, Japan. When he was four, his family settled into their ancestral hometown of Ridgefield, New Jersey, on Van Dien Avenue, the street named after Casper's great-great-grandfather.

No surprise then, when Casper dropped out of a formal high school education, opting instead for Admiral Farragut Academy, in St. Petersburg, Florida, where he graduated Third in Command in his class. After that, he went on to Florida State University as a pre-med student, with sights on becoming a field surgeon. He decided on a lark to take a Theater Arts class ("I studied theater to meet women"), and became instantly hooked on acting. This led to his dropping out of Florida State in 1988, and moving to Los Angeles, where he pursued an acting career.

Once in Los Angeles, he began the audition process. His first parts were on the TV series *Dangerous Women* (1991), on which he played Brad Morris, and *Freshman Dorm* (1992), where he played Zack. He also had guest roles on *Beverly Hills, 90210* (1992) and in *Dr. Quinn, Medicine Woman* (1993).

In late 1992, Casper went to a script reading where he met actress Carrie Mitchum, granddaughter of film superstar Robert Mitchum. She was a former soap actress, having appeared on *The Bold and the Beautiful* as Donna Logan, Brooke's sister. The two hit it off romantically. Before their 1993 nuptials, Carrie took Casper to Santa Barbara, to meet her legendary granddad. According to Casper, the crusty veteran told him, "You're the only boyfriend of Carrie's I've ever liked." Later in the year, Carrie gave birth to their first child, a son: Casper Robert Mitchum Van Dien XII.

In late 1993, Van Dien relocated to New York for a spell, having garnered the role of Ty Moody on *One Life to Live*. The best part of the soap experience, according to Casper, was that he "loved taking my clothes off and having sex with Tonya Walker." He stayed with the show for six months, returning to his young family in Los Angeles, where he had big career plans.

In 1995, he made his feature film debut in the softcore romance drama *Night Eyes 4*, and followed that with the low-caliber *Beastmaster III: The Eye of Braxus* (1995).

Casper and Carrie had a daughter, Grace, in 1996, before their relationship ended, in the middle of 1997. "It was a horrible thing because we had kids," he told *People* magazine. "We tried to make the marriage work."

Van Dien, still relatively new to the feature film business, takes his work very seriously, and completely immerses himself in his characters. In *James Dean: Race with Destiny*, made in 1997 but released in February 1999, in which he portrayed the celebrated screen idol, Casper not only watched Dean's TV and film appearances, but read fifteen books on Dean, "and skimmed twelve more." Of his role as Johnny Rico, the perfect soldier, leader of a squadron of bug-fighting warriors opposite **Patrick Muldoon** in *Starship Troopers* (1997), Van Dien noted, "I was amazed with the similarities I shared with Johnny. I don't quit at anything I do. I like to win and I don't like to lose at anything. That's the way I am, and that's the way Johnny Rico is." As with his James Dean characterization, for his title role in *Tarzan and the Lost City* (1998), Van Dien studied up a *bit*: he read all the Edgar Rice Burroughs novels, spoke with the author's grandson, boned up on Zulu language and customs, and studied Jane Goodall's work with the Gambe chimpanzees.

Whew! This from an actor who excuses his hyperactive personality thusly: "I'm always that way. I bounce off four walls, twenty-four hours a day, seven days a week."

He kills bugs, he swings from trees, and breaks a few hearts in the process. Handsome, chisel-chinned Casper Van Dien is, without question, a man on a mission.

Films: 1995: *Night Eyes 4*; *Beastmaster III: The Eye of Braxus*. 1997: *Starship Troopers*. 1998: *Cross Country*; *Dream True*; *On the Border*; *The Revenant*; *Tarzan and the Lost City*; Forthcoming: *Meltdown*; *Shark Attack*; *Romantic Moritz*; *The Collector*; *Sleepy Hollow*.

TV movie: 1997: *Nightscream*. 1999: *James Dean : Race with Destiny*.

TV series: 1991: *Dangerous Women*. 1992: *Freshman Dorm*. 1993–94: *One Life to Live*.

Video: 1997: *Casper: A Spirited Beginning*.

Interactive: 1995: *Wing Commander IV: The Price of Freedom*.

Meet Ty

⌨ On *One Life to Live*, the role of Ty Moody was originated, and solely played, by Casper Van Dien (1993–94).

Alex Olanov (Tonya Walker) came across Luna Moody's (Susan Batten) brother Ty, who was in town for a visit. Ty fell instantly for Alex's charms. Flattered, Alex led him on for a while, but told him her name was "Zan," because she knew that Luna hated her, and that she would be unflatteringly portrayed in the translation. Alex and Ty had a brief, passionate love affair, before he left Llanview.

Jack Wagner

A talented rock singer with the homespun look: Frisco Jones, played by Jack Wagner on General Hospital. *Courtesy of* Shooting Star.

Millions of people read this stuff in the magazines and they believe what you tell them. . . . I've had more things told to me by fans that I didn't know about and just weren't true. It's a shame.
—Jack Wagner, on the press, 1997

Born: October 3, 1959, in Washington, Missouri, to Peter and Scotty Wagner; birth name, Peter John Wagner II; two half-brothers and one half-sister

Education: St. Francis Borgia High School (Washington, Missouri); University of Missouri (Columbia); East Central College (Union, Missouri); University of Arizona (Tucson)

Debuts: stage—*Oliver!* (1975); television—*A New Day in Eden* (1982); film—*Play Murder for Me* (1990)

Honor: Nominated for Daytime Emmy Award, 1985

Marital Status: Married actress Kristina Malandro, December 18, 1993; two sons, Peter and Harrison

Worked with His Wife In: *General Hospital* (1984–87, 1989–91, 1994, 1995) and *Weddings of a Lifetime* (1995)

Albums: *All I Need* (1984), *Lighting Up the Night* (1985), *Don't Give Up Your Day Job* (1987), *Alone in a Crowd* (1993)

Few performers have as eclectic an array of interests and talents as does Jack Wagner. He acts. He sings. He plays golf. He's not a doctor, but he plays one on TV.

As a child in Missouri, Jack became passionate about golf, often caddying for his father at their local country club. By age twelve, he was winning against adult members of the club, and became Junior State golf champion as a teenager; he would later become a pro at the Bel Air

Country Club in Los Angeles, winning two Bel Air championships, in 1989 and 1990.

At age sixteen, Jack played Mr. Bumble in a high school production of *Oliver!*, his first taste of performance. After graduating high school, he began studies at East Central College, transferring, in 1980, to the University of Arizona at Tucson, hoping to land a golf scholarship. However, he received a full tuition grant from the drama department. While in college, he appeared in such shows as *The Grass Harp* and *Picnic*.

Jack graduated in 1982 and moved to Los Angeles. His first job was as a tour guide at Universal Studios. Before long, he had an agent and started modeling. He got his first acting gig on Showtime cable's nighttime soap *A New Day in Eden*, which aired between 1982 and 1983. During that period, too, he made two guest appearances on *Knots Landing*, as a senatorial aide to Greg Sumner (William Devane).

In December 1983, Jack joined the cast of *General Hospital*, creating the role of Frisco Jones. An ABC press conference at the time touted him as the show's new heartthrob: he was an instant hit, was nominated for a Daytime Emmy in 1985, and enjoyed a love affair with his audiences for more than a decade, during which he left and returned to the show three times, in 1989, 1994, and 1995. His chiseled matinee idol looks and adventurous story lines made Jack one of daytime's true superstars.

And his talents are not exclusive to television: in 1984, he had a number two hit single, "All I Need," and had onstage successes with a 1987 national trek of *West Side Story*, in which he played Tony, and in *Grease,* touring the country as Danny Zuko.

During his 1989 return to *General Hospital*, onscreen sparks with costar Kristina Malandro flew off the camera as well: on September 4, 1990, Kristina gave birth to Peter John Wagner III. On December 18, 1993, Jack and Kristina married in Lake Tahoe, Nevada. Upon marriage, Kristina officially changed her surname to Wagner. On December 1, 1994, their second son, Harrison Hale Wagner, was born.

In June 1991, Jack shocked the industry by announcing that he was leaving *General Hospital* to join the low-rated *Santa Barbara*. He was in the integral role of Warren Lockridge for less than two years when, in January 1993, NBC canceled the show. Nevertheless, his loyal fans would not be Wagner-less for long.

In August 1994, Jack joined the cast of *Melrose Place*. His character, Dr. Peter Burns, might be the most promiscuous medical practitioner in the history of television, having slept with no less than seven *Melrose Place* characters to date. To complement his nighttime Hippocratic shenanigans, Jack returned to daytime in 1997, in a guest spot on *Sunset Beach*. However, to soap enthusiasts, he will forever be Frisco.

His talents have long been known by his fans, who agree that whether it is the actor, the singer, or the golfer, it will be the best Jack Wagner he can offer.

Films: 1990: *Play Murder for Me.* 1993: *Trapped in Space.* 1998: *Dirty Little Secret.*

TV movies: 1988: *Moving Target.* 1989: *Swimsuit.* 1995: *Lady Killer.* 1996: *Frequent Flyer.* 1998: *Echo.*

TV series: 1983–87:, 1989–91:, 1994:, 1995: *General Hospital.* 1991–93: *Santa Barbara.* 1994–present: *Melrose Place.* 1995: *Weddings of a Lifetime.*

Meet Frisco and Warren

On *General Hospital*, the role of Frisco Jones was originated, and solely played, by Jack Wagner (1983–87, 1989–91, 1994, 1995).

Rock musician Frisco Jones arrived in Port Charles, and immediately fell for Tania Roskov (Hilary Edson), who promptly fell for Frisco's brother Tony (Brad Maule). Frisco later became involved with Aztec princess Felicia Cummings (Kristina Malandro), with whom he had two children, after a tortuous courtship.

On *Santa Barbara*, the role of Warren Lockridge was played by John Allen Nelson (1984–86), Scott Jenkins (1986–87), and Jack Wagner (1991–93).

Lifeguard and aspiring journalist Warren Lockridge was the son of Augusta (Louise Sorel). In his earliest incarnation, Warren became a compulsive gambler who was caught stealing cash from a local casino. He later taught journalism and started a newspaper, the *Santa Barbara Conscience*. He married his former student, B. J. Walker (Sydney Penny), on the show's final episode.

Sigourney Weaver

My uncle's name was Doodles, and my father's name is Sylvester, but they call him Pat. My mother's name is Desiree, but they call her Liz. My brother's name is Trajan, after the warrior. I guess with a name like Susan, I felt left out.

—Sigourney Weaver, on her birth name, 1997

Born: October 8, 1949, in New York City, to Sylvester and Desiree Weaver; birth name, Susan Alexander Weaver; one brother, Trajan

Education: Stanford University (California); Yale University School of Drama (New Haven, Connecticut)

Debuts: stage—*Watergate Classics* (1973); television—*Somerset* (1977) as Avis Ryan; film—*Annie Hall* (1977)

Awards: Won the Academy of Science Fiction, Horror and Fantasy Films' Saturn Award, as Best Actress, for her role as Lt. Ellen Ripley in *Aliens*, 1987; won Golden Globe Award, as Best Supporting Actress, for her role as Katherine Parker in *Working Girl*, 1989; won Golden Globe Award, as Best Actress in a Drama, for her role as Dian Fossey in *Gorillas in the Mist*, 1989

Honors: Nominated for Golden Globes in 1987 and 1998; nominated for Academy Awards in 1987 and two in 1989; ranked number seventy-one in *Empire* magazine's "Top One Hundred Movie Stars of All Time" list, October 1997; ranked number thirteen of Sci-Fi's Sexy Fifty, by *Femme Fatales* magazine, 1997; named Woman of the Year by the Hasty Pudding Theatricals, 1998; nominated for Screen Actors Guild Award in 1998

Marital Status: Married director Jim Simpson, October 1984; one daughter, Charlotte

Book: *Sigourney Weaver*, by T. D. Maguffee (1989)

How That Salary Has Grown!: *Annie Hall* (1977) $50; *Alien* (1979) $30,000; *Alien: Resurrection* (1997) $11,000,000

She is best known onscreen as an astronaut who fought drooling, man-eating aliens. However, Sigourney Weaver's life and background indicate much more wide-scoped talent.

Susan Alexander Weaver was born to NBC network President Sylvester "Pat" Weaver and his wife, actress Desiree "Liz" Weaver. Pat wanted to call his daughter Flavia, after a character in Roman history. ("Flavia is a lovely name. I don't know what you'd call a person for short. Flay?" mused Sigourney at a later date.) At the age of fourteen, Susan read the classic F. Scott Fitzgerald novel, *The Great Gatsby*. She decided to adopt the name of one of the book's minor characters: Susan was, from then on, known as Sigourney.

She began her college education at Stanford University, where she graduated with a Bachelor of Arts degree in English in 1971. She later earned a Master of Arts degree in drama in 1974 from Yale University's School of Drama (which has also graduated, among others, Stacy Keach, Paul Newman, and Meryl Streep). While at Yale, Weaver was horrified when her professors told her that she had no talent whatsoever.

In 1976, Sigourney got her first professional acting role, on *Somerset*, as Avis Ryan. In this small TV role, she was noticed, as she received, during that time, her first part in a feature film, as Alvy's theater date, in Woody Allen's celebrated *Annie Hall* (1977). It was a fleeting debut for Sigourney, flashing across the screen for all of six seconds.

Undaunted, she soon auditioned for an upcoming science fiction film, which she initially thought to be somewhat silly and unintelligent. Urged on by fellow auditioning actress Jill Eikenberry, she stuck with the plan and won the role over initial first choice, Veronica Cartwright. In June 1978, Weaver left for London to begin shooting *Alien*.

A combination science fiction and horror film, *Alien* (1979) introduced moviegoers to Lt. Ellen Ripley, one of a battery of astronauts returning to Earth after a tough mission. Along the way, they visited an apparently dead planet, only to be infected, and almost totally exterminated, by a violent, drooling creature with a rather nasty temperament. Weaver was instantly catapulted to movie star status with this strong character. The picture, so far, has spurred three sequels: *Aliens* (1986), *Alien 3* (1992), and *Alien Resurrection* (1997). With *Aliens*, directed by James (*Titanic*) Cameron, Sigourney became the first actress in a science fiction film to be nominated for an Academy Award.

Through the hits and the less-than-hits in her career, Weaver has established herself as one whose talents run much further than her science-fiction acumen. Her intelligence, marked by piercing eyes and expressive face, found her adept at comedy (1984's *Ghostbusters*, 1988's *Working Girl*, and 1993's *Dave*), intrigue (1981's *Eyewitness*), and drama (1983's *The Year of Living Dangerously*, 1994's *Death and the Maiden*, and 1997's *The Ice Storm*). However, it was her role in *Gorillas in the Mist* (1988), in which she portrayed scientist Dian Fossey (whose research into the lives of gorillas in

Africa so antagonized local poachers that she was murdered), that marked Sigourney's most important non-*Alien* success. She won a Best Actress Golden Globe, and her second Oscar nomination.

In 1984, Sigourney married stage director Jim Simpson. Their daughter, Charlotte, was born in April 1990. In 1994, when Sigourney was passed up for an Oscar nomination (for her portrayal of Paulina Escobar in *Death and the Maiden*), husband Jim carved an Academy Award out of wood for her, and the statue graces the mantelpiece of the Simpsons' Los Angeles home.

Sigourney Weaver has had a distinctive career, quite a step up from the young actress who hesitated auditioning for that sci-fi flick in 1979. "Once I get that engine going," she has noted, "I can work for an eternity." Her fans hope so.

Films: 1977: *Annie Hall*. 1978: *Madman*. 1979: *Alien*. 1981: *Eyewitness*. 1983: *The Year of Living Dangerously*; *Deal of the Century*. 1984: *Ghostbusters*. 1985: *One Woman or Two*. 1986: *Aliens*; *Half Moon Street*. 1988: *Gorillas in the Mist*; *Working Girl*. 1989: *Frames from the Edge*; *Ghostbusters II*. 1992: *1492: Conquest of Paradise*; *Alien 3* (also co-producer). 1993: *Dave*. 1994: *Death and the Maiden*. 1995: *Copycat*; *Jeffrey*. 1997: *Snow White*; *Alien: Resurrection* (also co-producer); *The Ice Storm*. Forthcoming: *A Map of the World*.

TV series: 1976: *Somerset*.

Meet Avis

On *Somerset*, the role of Avis Ryan was originated, and solely played, by Sigourney Weaver, in 1976. The character of Avis appeared at a time when *Somerset* boasted a staggering number of once and future greats, including Audrey Landers (Heather Lawrence), **JoBeth Williams** (Carrie Wheeler), Molly Picon (Sarah Briskin), **Ted Danson** (Tom Conway), Jameson Parker (Dale Robinson), and Weaver. Ironic, then, that low ratings canceled the show, one of three spin-offs of *Another World* (along with *Lovers and Friends* and *Texas*), on December 31, 1976.

Oh, What a Tangled Web We Weaver

For her 1989 roles in *Gorillas in the Mist* and *Working Girl*, Sigourney Weaver (*Somerset*) was nominated for Best Actress and Best Supporting Actress Academy Awards. Four previous times, an actor or actress who had been nominated in both Best and Supporting categories won a Supporting Award. Weaver broke the spell, as she lost both the 1989 Best Actress Oscar to Jodie Foster, for *The Accused*, and the Best Supporting Actress Oscar to Geena Davis, for *The Accidental Tourist*.

Ming-Na Wen

My philosophy is that if you're in the limelight, and you're becoming a celebrity, one of your responsibilities is portraying a more positive outlook; giving energy, as opposed to being someone who just keeps taking.

—Ming-Na Wen, 1998

Tom Hughes (played by Scott Holmes) gained a daughter when Lien (Ming-Na Wen) arrived on As the World Turns in 1988. Video screen photo, collection of author.

Born: November 20, 1963, in Macao, China, to Soo Lim Kee and Linchan Wen; two brothers, Johnathan and Leong

Education: Mt. Lebanon High School (Pennsylvania); Carnegie-Mellon University (Pittsburgh, Pennsylvania)

Debuts: stage—*South Pacific* (1979); television—*As the World Turns* (1988) as Lien Truong Hughes; film—*The Joy Luck Club* (1993)

Honor: Chosen by *People* magazine as one of the Fifty Most Beautiful People in the World (1994)

Marital Status: Married Kirk Aanes, 1990, divorced; married actor Eric Michael Zee on June 16, 1995

She is an actress of impressive diversity, able to portray a wide scope of emotions and personalities, making it all appear effortless. Ming-Na Wen, soap graduate, television alumna, stage veteran, and film siren, can do it all.

Ming-Na Wen, whose first name means "enlightenment," moved, along with her divorced mother, Linchan, and brothers, Johnathan and Leong, to Mt. Lebanon, Pennsylvania, a suburb of Pittsburgh, when Ming-Na was a youngster. Now a resident of an all-American town, the only link to her Asian heritage was, of all things, a television commercial. Wen identified it as "the embarrassing Calgon lady who said, 'Ancient Chinese secret.' I would dive for the remote control when she came on TV." The Wens spoke Chinese at home. Ming-Na recalled, "English was a language I had to learn in those special classes. I always felt the need to excel in school, because I never felt smart enough...always had to prove myself." Part of that process was in performance: she played "Thumpy the Rabbit" in her third-grade play.

She went to Mt. Lebanon High School. While she was a student, at age sixteen, she made her professional stage debut, as Lia in a production of *South Pacific*, costarring Maureen McGovern. Until her graduation in 1981, she continued acting in school shows. Her uniqueness, being one of, if not *the* only, Asian in the school then, created a hurtful distance from her classmates. "Growing up, I always knew that I never belonged and never fit in. Instead of dealing with the pain, I just immersed myself in a lot of school, classes, and theater, and just ignored it for a long time." Such trials did provide for Wen a sense of self and purpose which would prove therapeutic.

At Carnegie-Mellon University, she studied drama, graduating in 1988. Soon afterward, she joined the cast of *As the World Turns*, as Lien Truong, later revealed to be the long-unknown daughter of Oakdale's District Attorney Tom Hughes (Scott Holmes). It was a part singularly suited to Ming-Na, combining high drama and forbidden romance. She played it to the nines, and received much notice for her acting talents. Years later, she would still be getting fan mail addressed to "Lien." Wen left the part in 1991, one year after she married Kirk Aanes.

Ming-Na went on many Manhattan and Hollywood auditions after she left the soap, finally nabbing the plum role of introspective June in *The Joy Luck Club* (1993), based upon the best-selling novel of the same name by Amy Tan. The five-hankie hit not only redefined Asian performers as viable American commodities, but also gave Wen the widest audience exposure since her soap days. She stole the show. After that, work became steadier, and equally as fulfilling.

In 1994, she appeared opposite Jean-Claude Van Damme, and fellow soap alum Raul Julia, in *Street Fighter*. Her other roles that year, as Mai in the TV movies *Vanishing Son II* and *Vanishing Son IV*, as Han in *Terminal Voyage*, and as Katie Chun in *Hong Kong 97*, were equally predictable unlimited-bullet shootouts, with decidedly Asian overtones.

Starting in 1995, her parts would broaden, giving her significantly wider opportunities to branch out professionally. Her role on *ER*, as overachieving medical student Deborah Chen, was a step in that direction. Said Wen: "Her ethnicity was not a vital issue to her character."

After another feature film, portraying Han in *Starquest* (1995), she got the role that broke a barrier: sharp-talking gallery owner Trudy Sloan on *The Single Guy*. The TV sitcom costarred Jonathan Silverman and Ernest Borgnine. Much like her character on *As the World Turns*, Trudy was attached, in this case married, to a Caucasian.

For the TV part, Wen tried to make Trudy as "totally American" as possible. Her reasoning, again, was sound: "I don't want to fall into those stereotypical Asian topics for the sitcom; those are the grounds that I want to break."

On June 16, 1995, now-single Ming-Na married actor/producer Eric Michael Zee, after a two-year courtship. She had met him, initially, when she needed a ride to a screening of *The Joy Luck Club*. Now, together, they run a production company, Imerg, Inc., and have already produced a play, *Exit the Dragon*, which played to packed theaters in Berkeley, California. Together, someday, they hope to produce feature films.

In the days since *The Single Guy* went off the air in 1997, she has done TV, feature films, and voice-over work, most notably in Disney's animated version of the famous Chinese legend, *Mulan* (1998), in which she voiced Fa Mulan. She also returned to the live stage, playing Elizabeth Kwong/Eng Eling in *Golden Child*, a play by David Henry Hwang, in April 1998 at the Longacre Theatre, New York City.

Still, after climbing up a very steep ladder to a growing level of success, Ming-Na Wen continues to dream of the ideal role. "I'd love to portray a romantic woman in a beautiful story...that will lead this actress to the ultimate dream, the Oscar." Perhaps she was voicing her very future.

Films: 1993: *The Joy Luck Club*. 1994: *Hong Kong 97*; *Street Fighter*; *Terminal Voyage*. 1995: *Starquest*. 1997: *One Night Stand*. 1998: *Mulan* (voice only); *12 Bucks*.

TV movies: 1993: *Blind Spot*. 1994: *Vanishing Son II*; *Vanishing Son IV*. 1998: *Tempting Fate*.

TV series: 1988–91: *As the World Turns*. 1995: *ER*. 1995–97: *The Single Guy*. 1997: *Spawn* (voice only).

Interactive: 1995: *Street Fighter: The Movie*.

Meet Lien

⌨ On *As the World Turns*, the role of Lien Truong Hughes was originated, and solely played, by Ming-Na Wen (1988–91)

Lien was the daughter of Tom Hughes (Scott Holmes), from a relationship with a young Asian woman while he served in Vietnam. Lien began studies at Oakdale University and soon became involved with one of John Dixon's (Larry Bryggman) sons, other-side-of-the-trackster Duke Kramer (Michael Louden).

Billy Dee Williams

I look inside and outside simultaneously. My paintings define what I understand about life and what I don't understand.

—*Billy Dee Williams, on his* other *career, 1997*

Suave, debonair Billy Dee Williams appeared on two soap operas: The Guiding Light, as Dr. Jim Frazier in 1966, and Another World, as the Assistant District Attorney from 1966–67. Courtesy of Soap Opera Digest.

Born: April 6, 1937, New York City; birth name, William December Williams

Education: National Academy of Fine Arts and Design (New York City)

Debuts: film—*The Last Angry Man* (1959); television—*The Guiding Light* (1966) as Dr. Jim Frazier

Honor: Nominated for Emmy Award, 1972

He's suave. He's cool. He's debonair. He is one of the most revered African-American actors of this generation. He mastered stage, television, and film. And he has taken to a whole new canvas, redefining himself as a painter of renown. He is the very talented Billy Dee Williams.

Growing up in Harlem, he knew immediately that he wanted to master both film and fine art. Both interests long battled for Billy Dee's sole attention, and each got his attention, at different times in his life.

Early artistic talent led to a prestigious Hallgarten Award Scholarship to New York's National Academy of Fine Arts and Design. There, the teenager studied the classical principles of painting under Robert Phillip and Boris Ollensky.

He also trained at Sidney Poitier's acting workshop, and from there, performance took center stage in Billy Dee's life. In 1959, he appeared in his first feature film, in the role of Josh in *The Last Angry Man*. He spent the next years honing his craft in various New York-based stage productions.

In 1966, he joined the cast of *The Guiding Light*, playing Dr. Jim Frazier. At the time he played Jim, **Cicely Tyson** played the role of his wife, Martha. **James Earl Jones** took over for Billy Dee when he left the daytime program, in Fall 1966. Soon after, he joined the cast of *Another World*, playing the Assistant District Attorney until early 1967. Both roles, minor, yet authoritative, gave Billy Dee a wide television visibility.

From there, Williams toiled as a guest on such TV programs as *Coronet Blue*, *The F.B.I.*, *The New People*, and *Mission: Impossible*, and in the 1969 TV movies *Lost Flight* and *Carter's Army*. He also did feature film work, including an extra role, as a man in the Lost Property office, in the hilarious Jack Lemmon/Sandy Dennis romp, *The Out-of-Towners* (1970).

On November 30, 1971, the ABC movie-of-the-week was the poignant *Brian's Song*, the biographical story of Chicago Bears halfback, and cancer victim, Brian Piccolo (James Caan). The telefeature, which was also released theatrically in 1972, costarred Williams as Piccolo's best friend, Gale Sayers. For this role, Billy Dee was nominated for a Best Supporting Actor Emmy Award.

In 1972, Williams appeared in the first of two movies costarring Diana Ross: *Lady Sings the Blues*, in which he played Louis McKay to Ross' Billie Holiday (in her film debut). Later, in 1975, the two were reunited in *Mahogany*, with Williams cast as Ross's love interest. These music-related portrayals were followed by the plum title role in the story of ragtime's *Scott Joplin* (1977). These three roles established Williams as one of the premier African-American actors in the world.

Williams maintained this status with strong feature film parts, notably as freelance mercenary Lando Calrissian in *The Empire Strikes Back* (1980) and *Return of the Jedi* (1983), and as lawman Harvey Dent in *Batman* (1989). However, his prime work has been on television.

The small screen has seen a very diverse Williams. He portrayed suave thief Billy Diamond in a short-lived 1985 series, *Double Dare*, randy husband Brady Lloyd in *Dynasty* (1984–85), and legendary musical mogul Berry Gordy in *The Jacksons: An American Dream* (1992).

Williams began painting again after replacing James Earl Jones in the Broadway play, *Fences*, in 1988—evidently the creative juices inherent in the live stage inspired his ingenuity with the brush. He paints primarily in acrylics: The Dutch Masters, Edward Hopper, and Frida Kahlo are among his greatest influences. His pieces are included in the permanent collection of the Smithsonian's National Gallery in Washington, D.C., and highlighted the Platinum gallery of Artexpo, held in 1997 at the Los Angeles Convention Center. Private collectors of his work include General Alexander Haig, saxophonist Kenny G, and Motown Records founder Berry Gordy.

Rarely does a person get an opportunity to thoroughly investigate a way of life, and enjoy it along the way. Billy Dee Williams has done just that, twice.

Films: 1959: *The Last Angry Man.* 1970: *The Out-of-Towners.* 1972: *The Final Comedown; Lady Sings the Blues.* 1973: *Hit!* 1974: *The Take.* 1975: *Mahogany.* 1976: *The Bingo Long Traveling All-Stars & Motor Kings.* 1977: *Scott Joplin.* 1980: *The Final Countdown; The Empire Strikes Back.* 1981: *Nighthawks.* 1983: *Return of the Jedi; Marvin and Tige.* 1984: *Fear City.* 1987: *Deadly Illusion; Number One with a Bullet.* 1989: *Batman.* 1990: *Secret Agent OO Soul.* 1992: *Driving Me Crazy; Giant Steps.* 1993: *Alien Intruder.* 1996: *Mask of Death; Moving Target; The Prince; Steel Sharks.* 1998: *The Contract.*

TV movies: 1969: *Carter's Army; Lost Flight.* 1972: *Brian's Song; The Glass House.* 1979: *Christmas Lilies of the Field.* 1980: *The Hostage Tower; Children of Divorce.* 1983: *Shooting Stars.* 1984: *The Imposter; Time Bomb.* 1986: *Courage; Oceans of Fire; The Right of the People.* 1988: *The Return of Desperado.* 1990: *Dangerous Passion.* 1992: *The Jacksons: An American Dream.* 1993: *Message from Nam; Percy & Thunder; Marked for Murder.* 1995: *Falling for You, Triplecross.* 1998: *Hard Time.*

TV miniseries: 1983: *Chiefs.* 1994: *Heaven & Hell: North & South, Book III.*

TV series: 1966: *The Guiding Light.* 1966–67: *Another World.* 1984–85: *Dynasty.* 1985: *Double Dare.* 1992: *Lonesome Dove: The Series.*

Meet the D.A. and Jim

📺 On *Another World,* the role of the Assistant District Attorney was played by Billy Dee Williams (1966–67) and Alex Wipf (1967–68).

The biggest trial of Williams' tenure as *Another World*'s Assistant District Attorney was the first-degree homicide trial of sensitive Missy Palmer (Carol Roux), accused of stabbing small-town crook Danny Fargo (Antony Ponzini). When the real killer was revealed, Missy was set free.

📺 On *The Guiding Light,* the role of Dr. Jim Frazier was enacted by Billy Dee Williams and James Earl Jones during 1966. Jim's wife, Martha, was played by Cicely Tyson in 1966, and Ruby Dee in 1967.

Dr. Jim and his nurse wife Martha both were on the staff of Cedars Hospital in Springfield. This was one of the first portrayals of an integrated workplace on a soap.

JoBeth Williams

I want my children to know that I like what I do.
—JoBeth Williams, 1997

Lovely JoBeth Williams appeared on two soaps: Somerset, as Carrie Wheeler from 1975–76, and Guiding Light, as Brandy Shellooe from 1977–81. Courtesy of Soap Opera Digest.

Born: December 6, 1948, in Houston, Texas, to Roger and Frances Williams

Education: Brown University (Providence, Rhode Island)

Debuts: stage—*Moonchildren* (1973); television—*Somerset* (1975) as Carrie Wheeler; film—*Kramer vs. Kramer* (1979)

Honors: Nominated for Emmy Awards in 1983, 1988, and 1995; nominated for Academy Award in 1995

Marital Status: Married director John Pasquin, 1982; two adopted sons, Will and Nick

Distinctive, understated roles in vital films mark the career of JoBeth Williams, an actress and a woman who has set herself apart not only in a body of excellent work, but a personal life of ultimate triumph.

JoBeth received her bachelor's degree in English from Brown University in 1970. From there, she gravitated towards acting, joining the prestigious Trinity Repertory Theatre in Rhode Island. She made her New York stage debut in the off-Broadway production of *Moonchildren*. Other stage credits include: the Peter Sellers-directed *Idiot's Delight*, costarring Stacy Keach; *Antony and Cleopatra*, costarring Robert Foxworth; *Cat on a Hot Tin Roof*, and *Uncle Vanya*. Such a wide scope of roles in comedy and drama gave JoBeth the experience and confidence she needed to tackle television.

It was in 1975 that she joined the cast of *Somerset*, playing reporter Carrie Wheeler. She remained with the show until its final fadeout, on New Year's

Eve 1976. After spending the next year on the stage, she joined another soap, *Guiding Light*, as another reporter, Brandy Shellooe. Her recurring and pivotal role on that daytime drama ended in 1981. During her tenure on GL, she appeared in her first feature film, the multi-award-winning *Kramer vs. Kramer* (1979), playing Phyllis Bernard, costar Dustin Hoffman's overnight guest. Not a bad film debut.

Williams has made wise choices in her acting career, appearing in widely successful films (1982's *Poltergeist* and its 1986 sequel, *Poltergeist II*, 1983's *The Big Chill*), as well as making a mark in important television vehicles. She was Emmy-nominated for *Adam* (1983) and starred in its 1986 sequel, *Adam: His Song Continues*. The influential Fox series *America's Most Wanted* grew out of this real-life story, and has been hosted since 1988 by John Walsh, the real-life father of murdered youngster Adam Walsh. For playing surrogate mother Marybeth Whitehead in the 1988 TV miniseries *Baby M*, JoBeth earned her second Emmy nomination. In the 1995 series *The Client* (taking as the basis for its plot lines John Grisham's best-selling novel), Williams played Atlanta attorney and child advocate Reggie Love, a recovering alcoholic whose two children were taken from her by the courts because of her drinking. (Of note is the fact the well-received 1994 film of this novel starred another soap opera alumna, **Susan Sarandon**, as Reggie Love.)

For years, JoBeth and her husband, director John Pasquin, whom she married in 1982, had struggled with infertility; JoBeth suffered four miscarriages and unsuccessful in-vitro fertilization. The couple adopted son Will in 1987, and son Nick in 1990; after growing close to Nick's birth mother through several interviews, JoBeth and John were allowed into the delivery room to cut Nick's umbilical cord.

In 1994, JoBeth made her directorial debut with a thirty-minute short film, *On Hope*, for Showtime cable's "Directed By" series. The movie, which stars Mercedes Ruehl, earned Williams and co-producer Michele McGuire a 1995 Academy Award nomination for Best Live Action Short Film. In 1997, she costarred with Tim Allen in the tropical romp *Jungle 2 Jungle*.

In 1995, she was a guest at the Commencement Forum at her alma mater, Brown University. When asked, "Why do so many actors feel it is necessary to get facelifts?" JoBeth responded, "If you saw your face fifty feet high—it's scary!"

JoBeth Williams has done it all—stage, television, and film, both as a performer and as a director. However, in her role as a mother (" . . . being parents didn't only mean passing our genes on"), she finds, perhaps, her greatest joy, and her ultimate satisfaction.

Films: 1979: *Kramer vs. Kramer*. 1980: *The Dogs of War*; *Stir Crazy*. 1982: *Poltergeist*; *Endangered Species*. 1983: *The Big Chill*. 1984: *American Dreamer*; *Teachers*. 1986: *Desert Bloom*; *Poltergeist II: The Other Side*. 1988: *Memories of Me*. 1989: *Welcome Home*. 1991: *Switch*; *Dutch*.

1992: *Stop! Or My Mom Will Shoot*; *Me, Myself and I*. 1994: *Wyatt Earp*; *On Hope* (director/producer only); *Parallel Lives*. 1997: *Jungle 2 Jungle*; *Just Write*; *When Danger Follows You Home*. 1998: *Little City*; *Justice*.

TV movies: 1980: *Fun and Games*. 1981: *The Big Black Pill*. 1983: *The Day After*; *Adam*. 1985: *Kids Don't Tell*. 1986: *Adam: His Song Continues*. 1987: *Murder Ordained*. 1988: *Baby M*. 1989: *My Name Is Bill W*. 1990: *Child in the Night*. 1991: *Victim of Love*. 1992: *Jonathan: The Boy Nobody Wanted*. 1993: *Final Appeal*; *Chantilly Lace*; *Sex, Love and Cold Hard Cash*. 1994: *Voices from Within*. 1995: *A Season of Hope*. 1996: *Breaking Through*; *Ruby Jean and Joe*. 1998: *A Chance of Snow*. Forthcoming: *It Came from the Sky*.

TV miniseries: 1998: *From the Earth to the Moon*.

TV series: 1975–76: *Somerset*. 1977–81: *Guiding Light*. 1992: *Fish Police* (voice only). 1995–96: *The Client*.

Meet Carrie and Brandy

On *Somerset*, the role of Carrie Wheeler was originated, and solely played, by JoBeth Williams (1975–76).

In its final season, *Somerset* offered a story line surrounding Julian Cannell (Joel Crothers) and his newspaper, featuring two bright reporters, Steve Slade (Gene Bua) and Carrie Wheeler, and their continuing attempt to wipe out organized crime. By the soap's finale, Carrie and Steve were engaged (after he survived life-saving surgery).

On *Guiding Light*, the character of Brandy Shellooe was played by Sandy Faison (1977) and JoBeth Williams (1977–81).

Brandy was a reporter, and the catalyst in one of the biggest story lines *Guiding Light* has ever seen. Back when Justin Marler (Tom O'Rourke) was married to Sara McIntyre (Millette Alexander), his flirtations with Brandy caused him many problems. However, that was just a warmup. After Jackie Marler (Cindy Pickett) caught her husband Justin in bed with Brandy while Jackie and Justin were on their honeymoon (!), she took off and later put her and Justin's child up for adoption without even telling Justin she was pregnant. That baby wound up being adopted by Alan Spaulding (Christopher Bernau)—it was Phillip Spaulding.

Robin Wright-Penn

In society, is it the healthiest relationship? No! But, does it breed the most love? I think so. We're pretty sick and crazy but hopefully not that sick. Our love is so deep because it is so complicated.
—Robin Wright-Penn, on her marriage to Sean Penn, 1997

Robin Wright-Penn (seen here with a costar) played unlucky-in-love Kelly Capwell on Santa Barbara *in 1984. Courtesy of Shooting Star.*

Born: April 8, 1966, in Dallas, Texas; birth name, Robin Virginia Wright

Debuts: television—*Santa Barbara* (1985) as Kelly Capwell; film—*Hollywood Vice Squad* (1986)

Award: Won Golden Space Needle Award, as Best Actress, for her role as Hedda in *Loved*, 1997

Honors: Nominated for Daytime Emmy Awards in 1985, 1986, and 1987; named one of Soaps' Most Beautiful Women by *Soap Opera Digest*, 1988; nominated for Golden Globe in 1995; nominated for Screen Actors' Guild Awards in 1995 and 1998; nominated for Independent Spirit Award in 1998

Marital Status: Married actor Dane Witherspoon, 1984, divorced; married actor Sean Penn, April 27, 1996; two children, daughter Dylan and son Hopper

Worked with Her Husband in: films—*State of Grace* (1990), *The Crossing Guard* (1995, he directed her), *She's So Lovely* (1997), and *Hurlyburly* (1998)

She is well known as the wife of Madonna's ex, Sean Penn. She has dated several Hollywood hunks, has turned down roles some actresses would die for, and is a true leading lady who combines fresh looks with real talent.

Robin Virginia Wright spent her early years as an international model, both in Paris and in Japan. After completing high school in La Jolla, California, she decided to become an actress. To begin her career, she created the role of Kelly Capwell on *Santa Barbara*, when the show debuted on NBC-TV on July 30, 1984. While she was on the daytime soap, she appeared in her film debut, in *Hollywood Vice Squad* (1986). She also became involved with her *Santa Barbara* costar, Dane Witherspoon, who played Joe Perkins in 1984, and the two married. In her three seasons on the show, Robin was nominated three times for a Daytime Emmy Award as Outstanding Ingenue. She left the soap in 1987.

She immediately received her first starring role in a feature film. In *The Princess Bride* (1987), directed by Rob Reiner, Robin played Buttercup, the central character in the charming hit. This screen portrayal established a running theme in Wright's characters—the damsel-in-distress on the surface who is achingly human at the core. She radiated in such roles in *Denial* (1991), *Toys* (1992), *The Crossing Guard* (1995), *Moll Flanders* (1996), and *She's So Lovely* (1997). Her most successful turn, and her strongest character to date, was in the multi-award-winning *Forrest Gump* (1994). Robin received a Best Supporting Actress Golden Globe nomination for her role as Forrest's fiercely independent girlfriend Jenny Curran.

Robin's career has been noteworthy, in addition, for the roles that got away. Before her first pregnancy, she had been offered, and accepted, the part of Maid Marian in Kevin Costner's *Robin Hood: Prince of Thieves* (1991), but had to back out due to her pending motherhood. She passed on two meaty roles, as Dr. Chase Meridian (played by Nicole Kidman) in B*atman Forever* (1995) and as the lead (played by Julia Ormand) in *Sabrina* (1995), in order to costar in *The Crossing Guard* (1995), directed by Sean Penn.

When she played Kathleen Flannery in *State of Grace* (1990), which dealt with an Irish mob based in New York, she first met Penn, one of her co-leads. Both were still married, she to Witherspoon, he to Madonna. They began a romance that, ultimately, ended both of their marriages, and resulted in the birth of their first child, daughter Dylan Frances, on April 13, 1991. In 1994, Robin gave birth to their second child, a son named Hopper. The parents, however, endured a fickle on-and-off relationship until their April 27, 1996, marriage. She then changed her name to Robin Wright-Penn, yet used her married name for only one film billing: *She's So Lovely*.

Hollywood marriages are never easy. Despite dizzying negative odds, and a fulsome history of disasters, it appears that Robin Wright-Penn, wife, mother, and movie star, has the formula well under control.

Films: 1986: *Hollywood Vice Squad*. 1987: *The Princess Bride*. 1990: *State of Grace*. 1993: *Toys*; *The Playboys*. 1991: *Denial*. 1994: *Forrest Gump*. 1995: *The Crossing Guard*. 1996: *Moll Flanders*. 1997: *Loved*; *She's So Lovely* (billed as Robin Wright-Penn). 1998: *Hurlyburly*; *Just to Be Together*. 1999: *Message in a Bottle*.

TV series: 1984–88: *Santa Barbara*.

Meet Kelly

On *Santa Barbara*, the role of Kelly Capwell was played by Robin Wright (1984–88), Kimberly McArthur (1988), Carrington Garland (1989–91), and Eileen Davidson (1991–93).

Kelly was the daughter of C. C. (Jed Allan) and Sophia Wayne Capwell (Rosemary Forsyth, then Judith McConnell). She worked in the cosmetics division of a local pharmaceutical firm, and modeled on the side.

During the Wright years on the program, Kelly was married to Joe Perkins (Dane Witherspoon, then Mark Arnold), who was killed in 1985 by a jealous ex-lover of Kelly, Peter Flint (Stephen Meadows). She then fell in love with Nick Hartley (David Haskell). They got engaged. Foolish Kelly spent one night of passion with Nick's brother Dylan (Page Mosely). On the day of her wedding to Nick, she admitted this affair, and the nuptials were off. Eventually, Nick and Kelly reunited, but Dylan remained quite smitten.

One of Kelly's most memorable story lines revolved around Dylan. One night, he came after Kelly. In self-defense, she pushed him out the window of the Presidential Suite of the family's Capwell Hotel. Dylan had brandished a gun—but Kelly confused Dylan with Flint (Joe's murderer), and her confusion sent her to a mental institution. She was sent overseas to recover.

Kelly eventually married Jeffrey Conrad (Ross Kettle) and became pregnant, but lost the baby after surviving a plane crash.

Some Soap "Coulda Beens"

Superstar Julia Roberts tried out for roles on *All My Children* (the Linda Warner character, nabbed by Melissa Leo) and *Santa Barbara* (Kelly Capwell, originated by Robin Wright), but was rejected for both parts.

Rising young star Brendan Fraser auditioned for the role of Brian Bodine on *All My Children*, but lost it to Matt Borlenghi.

Other future superstars who were denied roles in daytime soaps were Penelope Ann Miller (on *As the World Turns*), Kevin Costner (on *Days of Our Lives*), and Sharon Stone (on *General Hospital*).

Cher was *this close* to getting the role of Ruby Ashford on *Search for Tomorrow* in 1983. When she backed out at the last minute, Mamas and the Papas veteran Michelle Phillips stepped in.

Ian Ziering

On Guiding Light, *Ian Ziering (seen here with Paige Turko) played Cameron Stewart, an innocent good guy with a drug-dealing bad dad, from 1986–89. Courtesy of* Soap Opera Digest.

Keep in mind that life does not give you a dress rehearsal. As far as I know we get to do this only once. And I want to capture every goal I set for myself and climb as high as I possibly can. And I want to do and accomplish everything I set my mind to. Do everything right the first time.

—Ian Ziering, 1997

Born: March 30, 1964, in West Orange, New Jersey; birth name Ian Andrew Ziering; two older brothers, Jeffrey and Barry

Education: William Paterson College (Wayne, New Jersey)

Debuts: stage—*Richard III* (1970); television—*The Doctors* (1981) as Erich Aldrich; film—*Endless Love* (1981)

Marital Status: Married model Nikki Schieler, July 4, 1997

He has done stage, television, film, and modeling, has had a private tour of the White House, and is married to a former *Playboy* Miss September. Ian Ziering has already had quite a career. And he has hardly even begun.

While he was in second grade, it was learned that Ian (pronounced "eye-in") suffered from dyslexia. He recalled the discovery of the learning disability: "We had some tests done and it was discovered that I was mixing and flipping numbers and letters." By sixth grade, after intensive training with flash cards, he was able to succeed at math, and read up to standard levels.

His before-the-camera career began in print advertising, modeling, as a youngster, for the Sears department store chain in local New Jersey newspapers. He started acting at age twelve. At fourteen, in 1978, he appeared in a TV commercial for Fruit of the Loom underwear, the first of thirty-five TV spots in which he has appeared.

"I always wanted to be a working actor," Ian recalled. "I was never a very rebellious child. I was very happy growing up. I had nothing to rebel against."

In 1981 he started a seven-month stint on Broadway, as John in the musical *I Remember Mama*, and a national tour as Neil in *Peter Pan*. Ian appreciated the unique nature of the live performance: "The stage is one of the most exhilarating mediums for actors performing. You are in front of a live audience and that is something you don't feel in any other area of the entertainment industry other than the stage."

In 1981, he appeared in his feature film debut, as Sammy, Brooke Shields' younger brother, in *Endless Love*. That same year, too, he began a year-long run on *The Doctors*, cast as Erich Aldrich, younger brother to Billy, played by another up-and-comer, **Alec Baldwin**. Ian left the soap in 1982. What a shame: in a subsequent story line, Erich had a date with none other than guest star Brooke Shields.

While working toward his B.A. in dramatic arts at William Paterson College in Wayne, New Jersey, Ziering won a continuing role on *Guiding Light*, as Cameron Stewart. He was a pivotal supporting player on the soap from 1986, the year of his college graduation, until 1988.

Next, Ian went to California to do local Toyota commercials. He was also in the Cheese Puffs TV ads which featured young men bouncing the cans in basketball fashion.

On October 4, 1990, *Beverly Hills, 90210* debuted, costarring Ian as Steve Sanders, with a cast of talented young actors that included fellow soap alumnus **Luke Perry**. Ian branched out by writing the *90210* episode "Sentenced to Life," which dealt with Steve's community service stint in a nursing home, and his friendship with an old actor (Milton Berle), suffering from Alzheimer's disease. The show, aired in January 1994, was tremendously praised, later earning an honor from the Alzheimer's Association of Los Angeles.

Coincident with this tribute, in June 1995, Ian, together with his parents and *Melrose Place* star Kristin Davis, had a private tour of the White House, and an impromptu visit with President Bill Clinton.

In 1996, Ian provided the voice of Wildwing to the ABC-TV Disney animated series *Mighty Ducks*. "I have a lot in common with Wildwing," Ziering noted. "I'm a bit of a daredevil myself, and we both have a strong sense of adventure." That sense manifested itself in Ian's hobby of restoring old cars and his participation in fast sports. He also bungee jumps, and races cars, especially his Corvette.

On July 4, 1997, Ziering married his long-time girlfriend Nikki Schieler who was *Playboy* magazine's Miss September 1997.

It cannot be forgotten that, along the way of his life and career, Ziering has defeated a challenging learning disorder. "Dyslexia is an overcome-able thorn. You can succeed, and flourish."

Case in point—Ian Ziering himself.

Films: 1981: *Endless Love*. 1994: *Savate*.

TV movies: movies—1995: *The Women of Spring Break*. 1996: *No Way Back*; *Subliminal Seduction*.

TV series: 1981–82: *The Doctors*. 1986–88: *Guiding Light*. 1990–present: *Beverly Hills, 90210*. 1995: *Biker Mice from Mars* (voice only); 1996: *Mighty Ducks* (voice only). 1998: *Godzilla: The Series* (voice only).

Meet Erich and Cameron

◘ On *The Doctors*, the role of Erich Aldrich was played by Keith Blanchard (1973–77), Thor Fields (1977–81), Ian Ziering (1981–82), and Mark Andrews (1982).

Erich was a minor, though long-standing, character on the show, brother to Billy (then Alec Baldwin) and Stephanie Aldrich (Renee Pearl, then Anne Rose Brooks).

◘ On *Guiding Light*, the role of Cameron Stewart was originated, and solely played by, Ian Ziering (1986–88).

Cameron, often called "Cam," was an early love interest for Dinah Marler (then Paige Turco). His abusive father George (Joe Lambie) was a drug addict and dealer: in 1987, Cam was busted for possession of drugs that belonged to George.

Cameron left town, in 1988, after Dinah turned her affections to Alan-Michael Spaulding (then Carl Tye Evans); before he left, however, he made certain that Dear Old Dad was arrested on drug charges.

chapter 2

Look Who Else Began on Daytime!

While the preceding biographies of soap opera graduates is extensive, there are many additional prominent names in this category. It is guaranteed that the following list of daytime television alumni will produce a few more surprises. The names are listed alphabetically with their soap role(s), show(s), and year(s).

F. Murray Abraham (b. 1939) Joshua Browne, *How to Survive a Marriage*, 1974–75

Alan Alda (b. 1936) Gilbert Parker, *The House on High Street*, 1959–60

Ana Alicia (b. 1956) Alicia Nieves, *Ryan's Hope*, 1977–78

Richard Dean Anderson (b. 1950) Dr. Jeff Webber, *General Hospital*, 1976–81

Armand Assante (b. 1949) Johnny McGee, *How to Survive a Marriage*, 1974–75; Dr. Mike Powers, *The Doctors*, 1975–77

Martin Balsam (1919–1996) extra role, *Love of Life*, early 1950s; Harold Matthews, *The Greatest Gift*, 1954–55; Joey Gordon, *Valiant Lady*, 1955

Bonnie Bedelia (b. 1946) Sandy Porter, *Love of Life*, 1961–67

Robby Benson (b. 1956) Bruce Carson, *Search for Tomorrow*, 1971–73

Corbin Bernsen (b. 1954) Kenny Graham, *Ryan's Hope*, 1984–85

David Birney (b. 1939) Mark Elliot, *Love Is a Many Splendored Thing*, 1969–70; Oliver Harrell, *A World Apart*, 1970–71

Linda Blair (b. 1959) Allyn Jaffe, *Hidden Faces*, 1969

Jordana Brewster (b. 1980) Anita Santos, *All My Children*, 1995; Nikki Munson, *As the World Turns*, 1995–98

Ellen Burstyn (b. 1932) Dr. Kate Bartok, *The Doctors*, 1965 (billed as Ellen McRae)

Vanessa Bell Calloway (b. 1957) Yvonne Caldwell, *All My Children*, 1984; Denise Preston, *Days of Our Lives*, 1985; Charlene, *Days of Our Lives*, 1988

Dyan Cannon (b. 1939) young married woman, *For Better Or Worse*, 1960; Lisa Crowder, *Full Circle*, 1960–61

Tia Carrere (b. 1966) Jade Soong, *General Hospital*, 1983–85

Dixie Carter (b. 1939) Brandy Henderson Drake, *The Edge of Night*, 1974–76

Nell Carter (b. 1948) Ethel Green, *Ryan's Hope*, 1979

Shawn Christian (b. 1965) Mike Kasnoff, *As the World Turns*, 1994–97

Eddie Cibrian (b. 1973) Matt Clark, *The Young and the Restless*, 1994–96

Jill Clayburgh (b. 1944) Grace Bolton, *Search for Tomorrow*, 1969–70

Margaret Colin (b. 1957) Paige Madison, *The Edge of Night*, 1979–80; Margo Montgomery Hughes, *As the World Turns*, 1981–83

Tyne Daly (b. 1946) Caroline Beale, *General Hospital*, 1968

Brad Davis (1949–1991) Alexander Kronos, *How to Survive a Marriage*, 1974

Sandy Dennis (1937–1992) Alice Holden, *The Guiding Light*, 1956

Morgan Fairchild (b. 1950) Jennifer Pace, *Search for Tomorrow*, 1973–77; Sydney Chase, *The City*, 1995–96

Debrah Farentino (b. 1961) Sloane Denning Clegg, *Capitol*, 1982–87 (billed as Deborah Mullowney)

Mike Farrell (b. 1939) Scott Banning, *Days of Our Lives*, 1968–70

Constance Ford (1923–1993) Lynn Sherwood, *Woman with a Past*, 1954; *The Way of the World*, 1955; Rose Peabody, *Search for Tomorrow*, 1955–56; Eve Morris, *The Edge of Night*, 1964–65; Ada Davis Downs McGowan Hobson, *Another World*, 1967–93

Faith Ford (b. 1964) Julia Shearer, *Another World*, 1983–84

Steven Ford (b. 1956) Andy Richards, *The Young and the Restless*, 1981–87

Paul Michael Glaser (b. 1943) Dr. Peter Chernak, *Love Is a Many Splendored Thing*, 1969–70; Dr. Joe Corelli, *Love of Life*, 1971–72

Lee Grant (b. 1927) Rose Peabody, *Search for Tomorrow*, 1953–54

Charles Grodin (b. 1935) Matt Crane, *The Young Marrieds*, 1965

Annabelle Gurwitch (b. 1964) Gina Daniels, *Guiding Light*, 1984–85

Wings Hauser (b. 1948) Greg Foster, *The Young and the Restless*, 1977–81

Marg Helgenberger (b. 1958) Siobhan Ryan, *Ryan's Hope*, 1982–85

Lauryn Hill (b. 1975) Kira, *As the World Turns*, 1992

Hal Holbrook (b. 1925) Grayling Dennis, *The Brighter Day*, 1954–59

Kate Jackson (b. 1948) Daphne Harridge Collins, *Dark Shadows*, 1970–71

Raul Julia (1940–1994) Miguel Garcia, *Love of Life*, 1971

Ken Kercheval (b. 1935) Dr. Nick Hunter, *Search for Tomorrow*, 1965–67 and 1972–73; Archie Borman, *The Secret Storm*, 1968; Larry Kirby, *How to Survive a Marriage*, 1974

Jack Klugman (b. 1922) Jim Hanson, *The Greatest Gift*, 1954–55

Don Knotts (b. 1924) Wilbur Peterson, *Search for Tomorrow*, 1953–55

Harley Jane Kozak (b. 1957) Brette Wheeler, *Texas*, 1981–82; Annabelle Sims Reardon, *Guiding Light*, 1983–85; Mary Duvall McCormick, *Santa Barbara*, 1986

Jane Krakowski (b. 1969) Rebecca "T. R." Kendall, *Search for Tomorrow*, 1984–86

Swoosie Kurtz (b. 1944) Ellie Bradley, *As the World Turns*, 1971

Audrey Landers (b. 1959) Heather Lawrence Kane, *Somerset*, 1974–76; Charlotte Hesser, *One Life to Live*, 1990–91

Joe Lando (b. 1961) Jake Harrison, *One Life to Live*, 1990–92; Macauley West, *Guiding Light*, 1993

Louise Lasser (b. 1939) Jackie, *The Doctors*, 1963–64

Melissa Leo (b. 1962) Linda Warner, *All My Children*, 1984–85

Téa Leoni (b. 1966) Lisa Di Napoli, *Santa Barbara*, 1984

Judith Light (b. 1949) Karen Wolek, *One Life to Live*, 1977–83

Hal Linden (b. 1931) Larry Carter, *Search for Tomorrow*, 1969

Audra Lindley (1918–1997) Laura Tompkins, *From These Roots*, 1959–61; Sue Knowles, *Search for Tomorrow*, 1962; Liz Matthews, *Another World*, 1964–69

Tony LoBianco (b. 1936) Nick Capello Turner, *Hidden Faces*, 1968–69; Dr. Joe Corelli, *Love of Life*, 1972–73

Nia Long (b. 1970) Katherine "Kat" Speakes, *Guiding Light*, 1991–93

Dorothy Lyman (b. 1947) Julie Stark, *A World Apart*, 1971; Elly Jo Jamison, *The Edge of Night*, 1972–73; Sister Margaret, *One Life to Live*, 1975; Opal Gardner, *All My Children*, 1981–83; Rebecca Whitmore, *Generations*, 1990–91; Faith, *The Bold and the Beautiful*, 1991–92

Wendie Malick (b. 1950) *Love of Life*, 1980

Vanessa Marcil (b. 1969) Brenda Barrett, *General Hospital*, 1992–98

Andrea Marcovicci (b. 1948) Dr. Betsy Chernak, *Love Is a Many Splendored Thing*, 1970–73

Marsha Mason (b. 1942) Lily, *Dark Shadows*, 1966; Laura Blackburn, *Where the Heart Is*, 1971; Judy Cole, *Love of Life*, 1972

Andrea McArdle (b. 1963) Wendy Wilkins, *Search for Tomorrow*, 1974–77

Glynnis O'Connor (b. 1956) Dee Stewart, *As the World Turns*, 1973; Margo Hughes, *As the World Turns*, 1990

John O'Hurley (b. circa 1956) *The Edge of Night*, 1984; Keith Lane (1984–86) and Jonathan Matalaine (1984–85), *Loving* (dual roles); Steven Slade, *Santa Barbara*, 1986; Jim Grainger, *The Young and the Restless*, 1988; Greg Bennett, *General Hospital*, 1992

Jameson Parker (b. 1947) Dale Robinson, *Somerset*, 1976; Brad Vernon, *One Life to Live*, 1976–78

Ryan Phillippe (b. 1975) Billy Douglas, *One Life to Live*, 1992–93

Parker Posey (b. 1968) Tess Shelby, *As the World Turns*, 1991–92

James Rebhorn (b. 19__) Bradley Raines, *Guiding Light*, 1983–86; Henry Lange, *As the World Turns*, 1988–91

Lisa Rinna (b. 1965) Billie Reed, *Days of Our Lives*, 1993–95

Eric Roberts (b. 1956) Ted Bancroft, *Another World*, 1977

Victoria Rowell (b. 1960) Drucilla Barber Winters, *The Young and the Restless*, 1990–98

Gena Rowlands (b. 1936) Paula Graves, *Way of the World*, 1955

Emma Samms (b. 1960) Holly Sutton Scorpio, *General Hospital*, 1982–93; Paloma, *General Hospital*, early 1990s

Laura San Giacomo (b. 1962) Luisa, *All My Children*, late 1980s

Roy Scheider (b. 1935) Jonas Falk, *Love of Life*, 1965–66; Bob Hill, *The Secret Storm*, 1967

Kyra Sedgwick (b. 1965) Julia Shearer, *Another World*, 1982–83

David Selby (b. 1941) Quentin Collins/Grant Douglas, *Dark Shadows*, 1968–71

Ted Shackelford (b. 1946) Raymond Gordon, *Another World*, 1975–77

John Wesley Shipp (b. 1955) Dr. Kelly Nelson, *Guiding Light*, 1980–84; Doug Cummings, *As the World Turns*, 1988; Martin Ellis, *Santa Barbara*, 1990; Carter Jones, *All My Children*, 1992

Grant Show (b. 1962) Rick Hyde, *Ryan's Hope*, 1984–87

Richard Simmons (b. 1948) Himself, *General Hospital*, 1979–81

Rena Sofer (b. 1968) Amelia "Rocky" McKenzie Domeq, *Loving*, 1988–91; Louis Cerullo Ashton, *General Hospital*, 1993–96

Rick Springfield (b. 1949) Dr. Noah Drake, *General Hospital*, 1981–83

John Stamos (b. 1963) Blackie Parrish, *General Hospital*, 1982–84

Sherry Stringfield (b. 1967) Blake Lindsay, *Guiding Light*, 1989–92

Susan Sullivan (b. 1944) April Morrison, *Best of Everything*, 1970; Nancy Condon, *A World Apart*, 1970–71; Lenore Moore Curtin, *Another World*, 1971–76

Ernest Thompson (b. 1950) Tony Cooper, *Somerset*, 1972–74

Paige Turco (b. 1969) Dinah Morgan Marler, *Guiding Light*, 1987–89; Melanie Cortlandt Rampal, *All My Children*, 1989–91

Blair Underwood (b. 1964) Bobby Blue, *One Life to Live*, 1985–86

Joan Van Ark (b. 1943) Janine Whitney, *Days of Our Lives*, 1970

Trish Van Devere (b. 1945) Patti Barron, *Search for Tomorrow*, 1967; Meredith Lord, *One Life to Live*, 1968

Abe Vigoda (b. 1921) Ezra Braithwaite/Otis Greene, *Dark Shadows*, 1966; Leo Coronal, *One Life to Live*, 1984; Joe Kravitz, *As the World Turns*, 1985; Lyle DeFranco, *Santa Barbara*, 1986

Jessica Walter (b. 1941) Julie Murano, *Love of Life*, 1962–65; Eleanor Armitage, *One Life to Live*, 1996–97

Steven Weber (b. 1961) Kevin Gibson, *As the World Turns*, 1985–86
Michael T. Weiss (b. 1962) Mike Horton, *Days of Our Lives*, 1985–90
Efrem Zimbalist Jr. (b. 1923) Jim Gavin, *Concerning Miss Marlowe*, 1954–55

chapter 3

They Were on Soaps, Too?

Many prominent actors and actresses, late in their careers, moved to daytime television, enjoying substantial soap runs after successes on stage, radio, film, and television. They are listed alphabetically, with their soap role(s), show(s), and dates (where available).

Edie Adams (b. 1929) Rosanne, *As the World Turns*

Robert Alda (1914–1986) Dr. Stuart Whyland, *Days of Our Lives*, 1981

Morey Amsterdam (1908–1996) Morey, *The Young and the Restless*, 1990

Dame Judith Anderson (1897–1992) Minx Lockridge, *Santa Barbara*, 1984–87

Dana Andrews (1912–1992) Thomas Boswell, *Bright Promise*, 1969–72

Pearl Bailey (1918–1990) Corinne, *As the World Turns*, 1982

Freddie Bartholomew (1924–1992) director, *Edge of Night*; executive producer, *As the World Turns* and *Search for Tomorrow*

Joan Bennett (1910–1990) Elizabeth Collins Stoddard (1966–71), Naomi Collins (1967), Judith Collins Trask (1969), Flora Collins (1970–71), *Dark Shadows*

Eric Braeden (b. 1943) Victor Newman, *The Young and the Restless*, 1980–present

Ruth Buzzi (b. 1936) Leticia Bradford, *Days of Our Lives*, 1983

Rory Calhoun (b. 1922) Judge Judson Tyler, *Capitol*, 1982–87

Macdonald Carey (1913–1994) Dr. Tom Horton Sr., *Days of Our Lives*, 1965–94

Shawn Cassidy Dusty Walker, *General Hospital*, 1987

Imogene Coca (b. 1908) Alice Hammond, *As the World Turns*, 1983

Bert Convy (1933–1991) Glenn Hamilton, *Love of Life*, 1963

Courteney Cox (b. 1964) Bunny, *As the World Turns*, 1985

Arlene Dahl (b. 1924) Lucinda Schenk, *One Life to Live*, 1981–84

Ruby Dee (b. 1924) Martha Frazier, *The Guiding Light*, 1967

John deLancie (b. 1948) Eugene Bradford, *Days of Our Lives*, 1982–86, 1989

Phyllis Diller (b. 1917) Fairy Godmother, *As the World Turns*, 1984; Gladys, *The Bold and the Beautiful*, 1995

Troy Donahue (b. 1936) R. B. Keefer, *The Secret Storm*, 1970

Olympia Dukakis (b. 1931) Dr. Barbara Moreno, *Search for Tomorrow*, 1983

Keir Dullea (b. 1936) Dr. Mark Jarrett, *Guiding Light*, 1986

Charles Durning (b. 1923) Gil McGowan, *Another World*, 1972

Joan Fontaine (b. 1925) Page Williams, *Ryan's Hope*, 1980

Mary Frann (1943–1998) D. B. Bentley, *Return to Peyton Place*, 1973–74; Amanda Peters, *Days of Our Lives*, 1974–79

Zsa Zsa Gabor (b. 1919) Lydia Marlowe, *As the World Turns*, 1981

Farley Granger (b. 1925) Dr. Will Vernon, *One Life to Live*, 1976–77; Earl Mitchell, *As the World Turns*, 1986–87

Eileen Heckart (b. 1919) Ruth Perkins, *One Life to Live*, 1987; Wilma Bern, *One Life to Live*, 1992

Tippi Hedren (b. 1935) Helen McClain, *The Bold and the Beautiful*, 1991

Celeste Holm (b. 1919) Clara/Lydia Woodhouse, *Loving*, 1987; Isabelle Alden, *Loving*, 1991–92

Kim Hunter (b. 1922) Nola Madison/Martha Cory, *The Edge of Night*, 1979–80

Anne Jeffreys (b. 1923) Sylvia Bancroft, *Bright Promise*, 1969–72; Amanda Barrington, *General Hospital*, 1984

Carolyn Jones (1929–1983) Myrna Clegg, *Capitol*, 1982–83

Christopher Knight (b. 1957) Leigh Hobson, *Another World*, 1981

Ted Knight (1923–1986) Colonel Tate, *The Clear Horizon*, 1960

Diane Ladd (b. 1932) Kitty Styles, *The Secret Storm*, 1971–72

Lisa Loring (b. 1958) Cricket Montgomery Ross, *As the World Turns*, 1981–83

Hugh Marlowe (1911–1982) Jim Matthews, *Another World*, 1969–82

Anne-Marie Martin (b. 19__) Gwen Davies, *Days of Our Lives*, 1982–85

David McCallum (b. 1933) Maurice Vermeil, *As the World Turns*, 1983

Rue McClanahan (b. 1935) Caroline Johnson, *Another World*, 1970–71; Margaret Jardin, *Where the Heart Is*, 1971–72

Dorothy McGuire (b. 1918) Cora Miller, *The Young and the Restless*, 1984

Dylan Neal (b. 1969) Dylan Shaw, *The Bold and the Beautiful*, 1994–97

Maureen O'Sullivan (1911–1998) Emma Witherspoon, *Guiding Light*, 1984

Betsy Palmer (b. 1929) Suz Becker, *As the World Turns*, 1981

Sydney Penny (b. 1971) B. J. Walker Lockridge, *Santa Barbara*, 1992–93; Julia Santos Keefer, *All My Children*, 1993–97

Mackenzie Phillips (b. 1959) Rachel Sullivan, *Guiding Light*, 1996

Esther Ralston (1902–1994) Helen Lee, *Our Five Daughters*, 1962

Anne Revere (1903–1990) Agnes Lake, *Search for Tomorrow*; Marguerite Beaulac, *Ryan's Hope*, 1976

Howard E. Rollins Jr. (1950–1996) Ed Harding, *Another World*, 1982

Charlotte Ross (b. 1968) Eve Baron Donovan Deveraux, *Days of Our Lives*, 1987–91

Charles Ruggles (1886–1989) Cicero P. Sweeney, *The World of Mr. Sweeney*, 1954–55

Gale Sondergaard (1899–1985) Amanda Key, *Best of Everything*, 1970; Marguerite Beaulac, *Ryan's Hope*, 1976

Beatrice Straight (b. 1918) Vinnie Phillips, *Love of Life*, 1970; Gladys Biddleworth, *Santa Barbara*, mid-1980's

Grady Sutton (1906–1995) Jed Simmons, *The Egg and I*, 1951–52

Daniel J. Travanti (b. 1940) Spence Andrews, *General Hospital*, 1979

Robert Vaughn (b. 1932) Rick Hamlin, *As the World Turns*, 1995

Ruth Warrick (b. 1916) Janet Johnson, R.N., *The Guiding Light*, 1955–56; Edith Hughes, *As the World Turns*, 1956–60; Phoebe English Tyler Wallingford Matthews Wallingford, *All My Children*, 1970–present

Teresa Wright (b. 1918) Grace Cummings, *Guiding Light*, 1986

chapter 4

Your Guest Guess...

Listed are prominent guest stars, grouped by the program on which they appeared. After each name is the character played (if known), and the year in which the performer appeared on the soap (if available).

All My Children

Paul Anka, as owner of Nexus
Russell Baker, as himself
Kathy Bates, as prison inmate *"Belle Bodelle,"* 1984
Peabo Bryson, as himself
Jimmy Buffett, as himself
Warren Buffett, as himself
Carol Burnett, *"Mrs. Johnson,"* 1976; *"Verla Grubbs,"* 1983 and 1995
Timothy Busfield, Pine Valley University campus extra
Barbara Bush, as herself
Dick Cavett, as himself
Dom DeLuise, as a traffic cop
Robert Downey Jr., college football player
Boomer Esiason, as himself, 1988
Betty Ford, as herself
Kathie Lee Gifford, as herself
Leslie Gore, as herself

Virginia Graham, as herself
David Allen Grier, as doctor
Edward Koch, as himself
Melba Moore, as herself
Tom Murphy, as himself (CEO of ABC)
Aaron Neville, as himself
Rosie O'Donnell, "*Naomi*," 1996
Ed O'Neill, as private investigator
Regis Philbin, as himself
Sally Jessy Raphael, as herself
RuPaul, as a *The Cutting Edge* interviewee
Jerry Stiller, as himself, 1983
Elizabeth Taylor, as a charwoman, 1983
Cheryl Tiegs, as herself
Donald Trump, as himself
Robert Urich, day player
Gwen Verdon, "*Judith Sawyer*," 1982
Oprah Winfrey, as a Baltimore news anchor, early 1980s
Stevie Wonder, as himself, 1986

Another World

Theodore Bikel, "*Henry Davenport*," 1982–83
Bill Boggs, as a talk show host, pre-1984
Dick Cavett, as magician "*Oliver Twist*" who hypnotized Felicia Gallant, 1988
Jose Ferrer, "*Reuben Marino*," 1983
Roberta Flack, as herself
Crystal Gayle, as herself, 1987
Virginia Graham, as herself, a guest for the twenty-fifth anniversary, 1989
Liberace, as himself, 1985 and 1986
Marla Maples, as Jason's date, 1988
Ronnie Milsap, as himself, sang at a Chicago blues bar, 1991
Sally Jessy Raphael, as herself, comforted Felicia over Lucas' death, 1992
Ving Rhaimes, as kidnapper "*Czaja Carnek*," 1986
Joan Rivers, "*Meredith Dunston*," public relations wiz, 1997
Ann Sheridan, "*Kathryn Corning*," 1965–66
Betty White, "*Brenda Barlowe*," an old girlfriend of Mac's; appeared as part of "Where's Betty?" an NBC promotion, January 1988

As the World Turns

Patti Austin, as herself, 1991
Tony Bennett, as himself, 1985

Dr. Joyce Brothers, as herself, 1981
Joey Buttafuoco, as a thug, 1995
Rita Coolidge, as herself, 1992
Gloria DeHaven, "*Sara Fuller*," 1966–67
Aretha Franklin, as herself
Lee Greenwood, as himself, 1992
Margaret Hamilton, "*Miss Peterson*," 1971
Whitney Houston, duet with Jermaine Jackson, 1984
Jermaine Jackson, as himself, 1984
Johnny Mathis, as himself, 1991
Nicole Miller, as herself
Melba Moore, as herself, 1986
Eddie Murphy, stunt double
Roy Rogers, as himself
Martin Sheen, "*Jack Davis*," mid-1960s, early 1970s
Bobby Short, as himself, early 1970s

Best of Everything

Geraldine Fitzgerald, "*Violet Jordan*," 1970

The Bold and the Beautiful

Steve Allen, as himself, 1993
Dr. Joyce Brothers, as herself, 1989
Carol Channing, as herself, 1993
Jose Eber, as himself, 1994
Fabio, as himself, 1993
Charlton Heston, as himself, 1993
Jayne Meadows, as herself, 1993
Mike Piazza, as himself, 1994
Tommy Tune, as himself, 1995

The Brighter Day

Jack Lemmon

Capitol

Lana Wood, "*Fran Burke*," 1983

The Clear Horizon

Beau Bridges

Dark Shadows

Harvey Keitel, as bar patron

Days of Our Lives

Pamela Anderson, "*Cindy*," 1992
Christina Applegate, "*Baby Burt Grizzell*," 1972
Cindy Crawford, as a teenager, 1978
Janet Dailey, as herself
Lolita Davidovich, "*Mona*," 1985
Michael Dorn, "*Jimmy*," 1986–87
Bob Eubanks, as himself (host of *The Newlywed Game*), 1986
Farrah Fawcett, 1970
Leeza Gibbons, as woman passerby, 1994; as "*Nurse Barbara*," 1995
Kathie Lee Gifford, as nurse
Mary Hart, as newscaster "*Betty Howard*," 1980
Al Jarreau, as himself, 1984
Gordon Jump, as a waiter, 1966
Marilyn McCoo, "*Tamara Price*," 1986–87
LeAnn Rimes, "*Madison*," 1998
Pat Sajak, "*Kevin Hathaway*," 1983
Betty White, in the police station; appeared as part of "Where's Betty?" an
    NBC promotion, January 1988

The Doctors

Johnny Carson, as himself, 1964
James Coco, as himself
Arlene Francis, as herself, 1964
Van Johnson, as himself, 1964
Melba Moore, as herself
Tony Randall, as himself
Rex Reed, as himself
Mercedes Ruehl, as nurse
Brooke Shields, "*Elizabeth Harrington*," 1982

The Edge of Night

Amanda Blake, "*Dr. Julia Stanhower*," 1984
Dick Cavett, "*Moe Eberhardt*," 1983
Professor Irwin Corey, as a hobo
Jack Gilford, as a nosy taxi driver

Frank Gorshin, "*Smiley Wilson*," 1981–82
Martin Sheen, "*Roy Sanders*"
John Travolta, day player

General Hospital

Eddie Albert, as himself, 1983
Tom Arnold, "*Billy 'Baggs' Boggs*," 1994
The Artist Formerly Known as Prince, as himself
Milton Berle, "*Mickey Miller*," 1984
Sammy Davis Jr., "*Eddie Phillips*," 1982
Julio Iglesias, as himself, 1994
Dr. Irene Kassorla, as herself, 1980
Sally Kirkland, as a prostitute
Melissa Manchester, as herself, 1994
Leonard Nimoy, as drug dealer "*Bennie*," 1963
Roseanne, "*Jennifer Smith*"
Elizabeth Taylor, "*Helena Cassadine*," 1981

Guiding Light

Elizabeth Allen
The B-52s, as themselves
Ed Begley Sr.
Joan Bennett, as herself, 1982
Judy Collins, as herself
Taina Elg
Aretha Franklin, as herself
Rudolph Giuliani, as himself, 1998
Jennifer Holliday, as herself
Robin Leach, as himself
Roy Rogers, as himself
Christopher Walken, occasional fill-ins for brother Glenn Walken as "*Mike Bauer*," 1954–56

Love of Life

Warren Beatty, extra
Sammy Davis Jr., as himself, late 1970s

Loving

Marla Maples, as herself

One Life to Live

The Beach Boys, as themselves, 1988
Kurtis Blow, as himself, 1991
Dr. Joyce Brothers, as herself, 1971
Imogene Coca, as cleaning woman-turned-model
Sammy Davis Jr., "*Chip Warren*," 1980, 1981, 1983
Tammy Grimes, "*Mary Margaret Donahue*"
Robin Leach, as himself (host of "The Daisy Awards," a Daytime Emmy
    parody)
Little Richard, as himself, 1995
Reba McIntyre, as herself, 1992, 1994
Donna Rice, "*Jeannie*," 1985
Walter Slezak, "*Laslo Braedeker*," 1974
Ivana Trump, as herself (on the show's 6,000th episode)
Dr. Ruth Westheimer, as herself, 1992, 1993
Peggy Wood, "*Dr. Kate Nolan*," 1969

The Road of Life

Jack Lemmon, as a surgeon

Ryan's Hope

Ellen Barkin
Van Johnson, as himself
Regis Philbin, "*Malachy Malone*," late 1980s
Otto Preminger, as himself
Christopher Reeve, as himself
Sylvia Sidney, "*Sister Mary Joel*," 1975

Santa Barbara

Charles Barkley, as a bartender, 1991
Dr. Joyce Brothers, as herself, 1989
David Hasselhoff, as himself, 1984
Rich Little, as a sperm donor, 1990
Virginia Mayo, "*Peaches Delight*"
Pat Sajak, as himself, 1988
Rudy Vallee, as convict
Jean-Claude Van Damme, as a male stripper
Ray Walston, "*Mr. Bottoms*"
Vanna White, as herself

Search for Tomorrow

Robert De Niro, day player
Rowdy Gaines, as a drowning victim rescuer
Dustin Hoffman, day player
Hulk Hogan, as himself, 1985
Melissa Manchester, as herself
Michelle Phillips, as "*Ruby Ashford*," 1983
Lilia Skala, "*Magda Leshinsky*,"1969–70
Mel Torme, as himself

The Secret Storm

Joan Crawford, "*Joan Borman Kane*," 1968
John Travolta, day player

Texas

Virginia Graham, "*Stella Stanton*," 1982

The Young and the Restless

Aretha Franklin, as herself
Wayne Gretsky, "*Wayne*," 1983
Rich Little, as himself
Geraldo Rivera, as himself, 1991

Alphabetical List of Daytime Network Television Soaps

Name of Soap	Dates Aired	Network
All My Children	January 5, 1970–present	ABC
Another World	May 4, 1964–present	NBC
As the World Turns	April 2, 1956–present	CBS
Ben Jarrod	April 1, 1963–June 28, 1963	NBC
Bennetts, The	July 6, 1953–January 8, 1954	NBC
Best of Everything	March 30, 1970–September 25, 1970	ABC
Bold and the Beautiful, The	March 23, 1987–present	CBS
Bright Promise	September 29, 1969–March 31, 1972	NBC
Brighter Day, The	January 4, 1954–September 28, 1962	CBS
Capitol	March 29, 1982–March 20, 1987	CBS
City, The	November 13, 1995–March 28, 1997	ABC
Clear Horizon, The	July 11, 1960–March 11, 1961; February 26, 1962–June 11,1962	CBS
Concerning Miss Marlowe	July 5, 1954–July 1, 1955	NBC
Confidential for Women	March 28, 1966–July 8, 1966	ABC
Dark Shadows	June 27, 1966–April 2, 1971	ABC
Date with Life, A	October 10, 1955–June 29, 1956	NBC
Days of Our Lives	November 8, 1965–present	NBC
Dr. Kildare	September 28, 1961–August 30, 1966	NBC
Doctors, The	April 1, 1963–December 31, 1982	NBC
Edge of Night, The	April 2, 1956–December 28, 1984	CBS/ABC
Egg and I, The	September 3, 1951–August 1, 1952	CBS

Name of Soap	Dates Aired	Network
Fairmeadows, U.S.A.	November 4, 1951–April 27, 1952	NBC
First Hundred Years, The	December 4, 1950–June 27, 1952	CBS
First Love	July 5, 1954–December 30, 1955	NBC
Follow Your Heart	August 3, 1953–January 8, 1954	NBC
For Better or Worse	June 29, 1959–June 24, 1960	CBS
For Richer, for Poorer	December 6, 1977–September 29, 1978	NBC
From These Roots	June 30, 1958–December 29, 1961	NBC
Full Circle	June 27, 1960–March 10, 1961	NBC
General Hospital	April 1, 1963–present	ABC
Generations	March 27, 1989–January 25, 1991	NBC
Golden Windows	July 5, 1954–April 8, 1955	NBC
Greatest Gift, The	August 30, 1954–July 1, 1955	NBC
Guiding Light (The)	June 30, 1952–present	CBS
Hawkins Falls	April 2, 1951–July 1, 1955	NBC
Hidden Faces	December 30, 1968–June 27, 1969	NBC
Hotel Cosmopolitan	August 19, 1957–April 11, 1958	CBS
House on High Street, The	September 28, 1959–February 5, 1960	NBC
How to Survive a Marriage	January 7, 1974–April 18, 1975	NBC
Kitty Foyle	January 13, 1958–June 27, 1958	NBC
Love Is a Many Splendored Thing	September 18, 1967–March 23, 1973	CBS
Love of Life	September 24, 1951–February 1, 1980	CBS
Lovers and Friends	January 3, 1977–May 6, 1977	NBC
Loving	June 26, 1983–November 13, 1995	ABC
Miss Susan	March 12, 1951–December 28, 1951	NBC
Modern Romances	October 4, 1954–September 19, 1958	NBC
Moment of Truth	January 4, 1965–November 5, 1965	NBC
Morning Star	September 27, 1965–July 1, 1966	NBC
Never Too Young	September 27, 1965–June 24, 1966	ABC
Nurses, The	September 27, 1965–March 31, 1967	ABC
One Life to Live	July 15, 1968–present	ABC
One Man's Experience	October 6, 1952–April 10, 1953	DuMont
One Man's Family	March 1, 1954–April 1, 1955	NBC
One Woman's Experience	October 6, 1952–April 3, 1953	DuMont
O'Neills, The	September 6, 1949–January 20, 1950	DuMont
Our Five Daughters	January 2, 1962–September 28, 1962	NBC
Our Private World	May 5, 1965–September 10, 1965	CBS
Paradise Bay	September 27, 1965–July 1, 1966	NBC
Port Charles	June 1, 1997–present	ABC
Portia Faces Life	April 5, 1954–July 1, 1955	CBS
Return to Peyton Place	April 3, 1972–January 4, 1974	NBC
Road of Life, The	December 13, 1954–July 1, 1955	CBS
Road to Reality	October 17, 1960–March 31, 1961	ABC

Name of Soap	Dates Aired	Network
Ryan's Hope	July 7, 1975–January 13, 1989	ABC
Santa Barbara	July 30, 1984–January 15, 1993	NBC
Search for Tomorrow	September 3, 1951–December 26, 1986	CBS/NBC
Secret Storm, The	February 1, 1954–February 8, 1974	CBS
Seeking Heart, The	July 5, 1954–December 10, 1954	CBS
Somerset	March 30, 1970–December 31, 1976	NBC
Sunset Beach	January 6, 1997–present	NBC
Texas	August 4, 1980–December 31, 1982	NBC
These Are My Children	January 31, 1949–February 25, 1949	NBC
Three Steps to Heaven	August 3, 1953–December 31, 1954	NBC
Time for Us, A	December 28, 1964–December 16, 1966	ABC
Time to Live, A	July 5, 1954–December 31, 1954	NBC
Today Is Ours	June 30, 1958–December 26, 1958	NBC
Valiant Lady	October 12, 1953–August 16, 1957	CBS
Verdict Is Yours, The	September 2, 1957–September 28, 1962	CBS
Way of the World	January 3, 1955–October 7, 1955	NBC
Where the Heart Is	September 8, 1969–March 23, 1973	CBS
Woman to Remember, A	February 21, 1949–July 15, 1949	DuMont
Woman with a Past	February 1, 1954–July 2, 1954	CBS
World Apart, A	March 30, 1970–June 25, 1971	ABC
World of Mr. Sweeney, The	October 4, 1954–December 31, 1955	NBC
Young and the Restless, The	March 26, 1973–present	CBS
Young Dr. Malone	December 29, 1958–March 29, 1963	NBC
Young Marrieds, The	October 5, 1964–March 25, 1966	ABC

Chronological List of Daytime Network Television Soaps

Name of Soap	Dates Aired	Network
These Are My Children	January 31, 1949–February 25, 1949	NBC
A Woman to Remember	February 21, 1949–July 15, 1949	DuMont
The O'Neills	September 6, 1949–January 20, 1950	DuMont
The First Hundred Years	December 4, 1950–June 27, 1952	CBS
Miss Susan	March 12, 1951–December 28, 1951	NBC
Hawkins Falls	April 2, 1951–July 1, 1955	NBC
The Egg and I	September 3, 1951–August 1, 1952	CBS
Search for Tomorrow	September 3, 1951–December 26, 1986	CBS/NBC
Love of Life	September 24, 1951–February 1, 1980	CBS
Fairmeadows, U.S.A.	November 4, 1951–April 27, 1952	NBC
(The) Guiding Light	June 30, 1952–present	CBS
One Man's Experience	October 6, 1952–April 10, 1953	DuMont
One Woman's Experience	October 6, 1952–April 3, 1953	DuMont
The Bennetts	July 6, 1953–January 8, 1954	NBC
Follow Your Heart	August 3, 1953–January 8, 1954	NBC
Three Steps to Heaven	August 3, 1953–December 31, 1954	NBC
Valiant Lady	October 12, 1953–August 16, 1957	CBS
The Brighter Day	January 4, 1954–September 28, 1962	CBS
The Secret Storm	February 1, 1954–February 8, 1974	CBS
Woman with a Past	February 1, 1954–July 2, 1954	CBS
Portia Faces Life	April 5, 1954–July 1, 1955	CBS
Concerning Miss Marlowe	July 5, 1954–July 1, 1955	NBC

Name of Soap	Dates Aired	Network
One Man's Family	March 1, 1954–April 1, 1955	NBC
First Love	July 5, 1954–December 30, 1955	NBC
Golden Windows	July 5, 1954–April 8, 1955	NBC
The Seeking Heart	July 5, 1954–December 10, 1954	CBS
A Time to Live	July 5, 1954–December 31, 1954	NBC
The Greatest Gift	August 30, 1954–July 1, 1955	NBC
The World of Mr. Sweeney	October 4, 1954–December 31, 1955	NBC
Modern Romances	October 4, 1954–September 19, 1958	NBC
The Road of Life	December 13, 1954-July 1, 1955	CBS
Way of the World	January 3, 1955–October 7, 1955	NBC
A Date with Life	October 10, 1955–June 29, 1956	NBC
The Edge of Night	April 2, 1956–December 28, 1984	CBS/ABC
As the World Turns	April 2, 1956–present	CBS
Hotel Cosmopolitan	August 19, 1957–April 11, 1958	CBS
The Verdict Is Yours	September 2, 1957–September 28, 1962	CBS
Kitty Foyle	January 13, 1958–June 27, 1958	NBC
Today Is Ours	June 30, 1958–December 26, 1958	NBC
From These Roots	June 30, 1958–December 29, 1961	NBC
Young Dr. Malone	December 29, 1958–March 29, 1963	NBC
For Better or Worse	June 29, 1959–June 24, 1960	CBS
The House on High Street	September 28, 1959–February 5, 1960	NBC
Full Circle	June 27, 1960–March 10, 1961	NBC
The Clear Horizon	July 11, 1960–March 11, 1961; February 26, 1962–June 11, 1962	CBS
Road to Reality	October 17, 1960–March 31, 1961	ABC
Dr. Kildare	September 28, 1961–August 30, 1966	NBC
Our Five Daughters	January 2, 1962–September 28, 1962	NBC
Ben Jarrod	April 1, 1963–June 28, 1963	NBC
The Doctors	April 1, 1963–December 31, 1982	NBC
General Hospital	April 1, 1963–present	ABC
Another World	May 4, 1964–present	NBC
The Young Marrieds	October 5, 1964–March 25, 1966	ABC
A Time for Us	December 28, 1964–December 16, 1966	ABC
Moment of Truth	January 4, 1965–November 5, 1965	NBC
Our Private World	May 5, 1965–September 10, 1965	CBS
Morning Star	September 27, 1965–July 1, 1966	NBC
Never Too Young	September 27, 1965–June 24, 1966	ABC
The Nurses	September 27, 1965–March 31, 1967	ABC
Paradise Bay	September 27, 1965–July 1, 1966	NBC
Days of Our Lives	November 8, 1965–present	NBC
Confidential for Women	March 28, 1966–July 8, 1966	ABC
Dark Shadows	June 27, 1966–April 2, 1971	ABC

Name of Soap	Dates Aired	Network
Love Is a Many Splendored Thing	September 18, 1967–March 23, 1973	CBS
One Life to Live	July 15, 1968–present	ABC
Hidden Faces	December 30, 1968–June 27, 1969	NBC
Where the Heart Is	September 8, 1969–March 23, 1973	CBS
Bright Promise	September 29, 1969–March 31, 1972	NBC
All My Children	January 5, 1970–present	ABC
Best of Everything	March 30, 1970–September 25, 1970	ABC
Somerset	March 30, 1970–December 31, 1976	NBC
A World Apart	March 30, 1970–June 25, 1971	ABC
Return to Peyton Place	April 3, 1972–January 4, 1974	NBC
The Young and the Restless	March 26, 1973–present	CBS
How to Survive a Marriage	January 7, 1974–April 18, 1975	NBC
Ryan's Hope	July 7, 1975–January 13, 1989	ABC
Lovers and Friends	January 3, 1977–May 6, 1977	NBC
For Richer, for Poorer	December 6, 1977–September 29, 1978	NBC
Texas	August 4, 1980–December 31, 1982	NBC
Capitol	March 29, 1982–March 20, 1987	CBS
Loving	June 26, 1983–November 13, 1995	ABC
Santa Barbara	July 30, 1984–January 15, 1993	NBC
The Bold and the Beautiful	March 23, 1987–present	CBS
Generations	March 27, 1989–January 25, 1991	NBC
The City	November 13, 1995–March 28, 1997	ABC
Sunset Beach	January 6, 1997–present	NBC
Port Charles	June 1, 1997–present	ABC

Chronological List of Daytime Emmy Acting Awards

At the May 14, 1972, Emmy Awards, the Academy of Television Arts and Sciences inaugurated a new award dedicated to outstanding achievements in daytime TV drama. Previously, only nighttime work was honored. Listed here are the Emmys awarded for acting excellence, victors and nominees, starting in 1973 (as, in 1972, only one Daytime Emmy was awarded, to the outstanding program of the year, *The Doctors*). Winners' names are preceded by a star (★).

1972-73

Presented May 20, 1973

Outstanding Achievement by an Individual in Daytime Drama
Macdonald Carey (Tom Horton Sr., *Days of Our Lives*)
★ Mary Fickett (Ruth Martin, *All My Children*)

1973-74

Presented May 28, 1974

Best Actor
John Beradino (Dr. Steve Hardy, *General Hospital*)
★ Macdonald Carey (Tom Horton Sr., *Days of Our Lives*)
Peter Hansen (Lee Baldwin, *General Hospital*)

Best Actress
Rachel Ames (Audrey Hardy, *General Hospital*)
Mary Fickett (Ruth Martin, *All My Children*)
★ Elizabeth Hubbard (Dr. Althea Davis, *The Doctors*)
Mary Stuart (Joanne Gardner, *Search for Tomorrow*)

1974-75

Presented May 15, 1975

Outstanding Actor
John Beradino (Dr. Steve Hardy, *General Hospital*)
★ Macdonald Carey (Tom Horton Sr., *Days of Our Lives*)
Bill Hayes (Doug Williams, *Days of Our Lives*)

Outstanding Actress
Rachel Ames (Audrey Hardy, *General Hospital*)
★ Susan Flannery (Dr. Laura Horton, *Days of Our Lives*)
Susan Seaforth Hayes (Julie Olson, *Days of Our Lives*)
Ruth Warrick (Phoebe Tyler, *All My Children*)

1975-76

Presented May 11, 1976

Outstanding Actor
John Beradino (Dr. Steve Hardy, *General Hospital*)
Macdonald Carey (Tom Horton Sr., *Days of Our Lives*)
★ Larry Haines (Stu Bergman, *Search for Tomorrow*)
Bill Hayes (Doug Williams, *Days of Our Lives*)
Michael Nouri (Steve Kaslo, *Search for Tomorrow*)
Shepperd Strudwick (Victor Lord, *One Life to Live*)

Outstanding Actress
Denise Alexander (Lesley Williams, *General Hospital*)
★ Helen Gallagher (Maeve Ryan, *Ryan's Hope*)
Susan Seaforth Hayes (Julie Olson, *Days of Our Lives*)
Frances Heflin (Mona Kane, *All My Children*)
Mary Stuart (Joanne Vincente, *Search for Tomorrow*)

1976-77

Presented May 12, 1977

Outstanding Actor
★ Val Dufour (John Wyatt, *Search for Tomorrow*)
Farley Granger (Will Vernon, *One Life to Live*)
Larry Haines (Stu Bergman, *Search for Tomorrow*)

Larry Keith (Nick Davis, *All My Children*)
James Pritchett (Dr. Matt Powers, *The Doctors*)

Outstanding Actress
Nancy Addison (Jillian Coleridge, *Ryan's Hope*)
★ Helen Gallagher (Maeve Ryan, *Ryan's Hope*)
Beverlee McKinsey (Iris Carrington, *Another World*)
Mary Stuart (Joanne Vincente, *Search for Tomorrow*)
Ruth Warrick (Phoebe Tyler, *All My Children*)

1977-78

Presented June 7, 1978

Outstanding Actor
Matthew Cowles (Billy Clyde Tuggle, *All My Children*)
Larry Keith (Nick Davis, *All My Children*)
Michael Levin (Jack Fenelli, *Ryan's Hope*)
★ James Pritchett (Dr. Matt Powers, *The Doctors*)
Andrew Robinson (Frank Ryan, *Ryan's Hope*)
Michael Storm (Dr. Larry Wolek, *One Life to Live*)

Outstanding Actress
Mary Fickett (Ruth Martin, *All My Children*)
Jennifer Harmon (Cathy Craig, *One Life to Live*)
Susan Seaforth Hayes (Julie Williams, *Days of Our Lives*)
★ Laurie Heineman (Sharlene Frame, *Another World*)
Susan Lucci (Erica Kane, *All My Children*)
Beverlee McKinsey (Iris Carrington, *Another World*)
Victoria Wyndham (Rachel Cory, *Another World*)

1978-79

Presented May 17, 1979

Outstanding Actor
Jed Allan (Don Craig, *Days of Our Lives*)
Nicholas Benedict (Phil Brent, *All My Children*)
John Clarke (Mickey Horton, *Days of Our Lives*)
Joel Crothers (Dr. Miles Cavanaugh, *The Edge of Night*)
★ Al Freeman Jr. (Ed Hall, *One Life to Live*)
Michael Levin (Jack Fenelli, *Ryan's Hope*)

Outstanding Actress
Nancy Addison (Jillian Coleridge, *Ryan's Hope*)
★ Irene Dailey (Liz Matthews, *Another World*)
Helen Gallagher (Maeve Ryan, *Ryan's Hope*)

Susan Seaforth Hayes (Julie Williams, *Days of Our Lives*)
Beverlee McKinsey (Iris Bancroft, *Another World*)
Victoria Wyndham (Rachel Cory, *Another World*)

Outstanding Supporting Actor
Lewis Arlt (David Sutton, *Search for Tomorrow*)
Bernard Barrow (Johnny Ryan, *Ryan's Hope*)
Joseph Gallison (Dr. Neil Curtis, *Days of Our Lives*)
Ron Hale (Dr. Roger Coleridge, *Ryan's Hope*)
★ Peter Hansen (Lee Baldwin, *General Hospital*)
Mandel Kramer (Bill Marceau, *The Edge of Night*)

Outstanding Supporting Actress
Rachel Ames (Audrey Hardy, *General Hospital*)
Susan Brown (Dr. Gail Adamson, *General Hospital*)
Lois Kibbee (Geraldine Whitney Saxon, *The Edge of Night*)
Frances Reid (Alice Horton, *Days of Our Lives*)
★ Suzanne Rogers (Maggie Horton, *Days of Our Lives*)

1979-80

Presented June 2 and 4, 1980

Outstanding Actor
John Gabriel (Dr. Seneca Beaulac, *Ryan's Hope*)
Michael Levin (Jack Fenelli, *Ryan's Hope*)
Franc Luz (Dr. John Bennett, *The Doctors*)
James Mitchell (Palmer Cortlandt, *All My Children*)
William Mooney (Paul Martin, *All My Children*)
★ Douglass Watson (Mackenzie Cory, *Another World*)

Outstanding Actress
Julia Barr (Brooke English, *All My Children*)
Leslie Charleson (Monica Quartermaine, *General Hospital*)
Kim Hunter (Nola Madison, *The Edge of Night*)
★ Judith Light (Karen Wolek, *One Life to Live*)
Beverlee McKinsey (Iris Bancroft, *Another World*)
Kathleen Noone (Ellen Shepherd, *All My Children*)

Outstanding Supporting Actor
Vasili Bogazianos (Mickey Dials, *The Edge of Night*)
★ Warren Burton (Eddie Dorrance, *All My Children*)
Larry Haines (Stu Bergman, *Search for Tomorrow*)
Ron Hale (Roger Coleridge, *Ryan's Hope*)
Julius LaRosa (Renaldo, *Another World*)
Shepperd Strudwick (Timothy McCauley, *Love of Life*)

Outstanding Supporting Actress
Deidre Hall (Dr. Marlena Evans, *Days of Our Lives*)
★ Francesca James (Kelly Cole, *All My Children*)
Lois Kibbee (Geraldine Whitney Saxon, *The Edge of Night*)
Elaine Lee (Mildred Trumble, *The Doctors*)
Valerie Mahaffey (Ashley Bennett, *The Doctors*)

Outstanding Cameo Appearance
Sammy Davis Jr. (Chip Warren, *One Life to Live*)
Joan Fontaine (Page Williams, *Ryan's Hope*)
Kathryn Harrow (Pat Reyerson, *The Doctors*)
★ Hugh McPhillips (Hugh Pearson, *Days of Our Lives*)
Eli Mintz (The Locksmith, *All My Children*)

1980-81

Presented May 19 and 21, 1981

Outstanding Actor
Larry Bryggman (Dr. John Dixon, *As the World Turns*)
Henderson Forsythe (Dr. David Stewart, *As the World Turns*)
Tony Geary (Luke Spencer, *General Hospital*)
James Mitchell (Palmer Cortlandt, *All My Children*)
★ Douglass Watson (Mackenzie Cory, *Another World*)

Outstanding Actress
Julia Barr (Brooke English, *All My Children*)
Helen Gallagher (Maeve Ryan, *Ryan's Hope*)
★ Judith Light (Karen Wolek, *One Life to Live*)
Susan Lucci (Erica Kane, *All My Children*)
Robin Strasser (Dorian Lord, *One Life to Live*)

Outstanding Supporting Actor
Richard Backus (Barry Ryan, *Ryan's Hope*)
Matthew Cowles (Billy Clyde Tuggle, *All My Children*)
Justin Deas (Tom Hughes, *As the World Turns*)
★ Larry Haines (Stu Bergman, *Search for Tomorrow*)
William Mooney (Paul Martin, *All My Children*)

Outstanding Supporting Actress
Randall Edwards (Delia Reid, *Ryan's Hope*)
★ Jane Elliot (Tracy Quartermaine, *General Hospital*)
Lois Kibbee (Geraldine Whitney Saxon, *The Edge of Night*)
Elizabeth Lawrence (Myra Murdoch, *All My Children*)
Jacklyn Zeman (Bobbie Spencer, *General Hospital*)

1981-82

Presented June 8, 1982

Outstanding Actor
Larry Bryggman (Dr. John Dixon, *As the World Turns*)
Stuart Damon (Dr. Alan Quartermaine, *General Hospital*)
• Tony Geary (Luke Spencer, *General Hospital*)
James Mitchell (Palmer Cortlandt, *All My Children*)
Richard Shoberg (Tom Cudahy, *All My Children*)

Outstanding Actress
Leslie Charleson (Dr. Monica Quartermaine, *General Hospital*)
Ann Flood (Nancy Karr, *The Edge of Night*)
Sharon Gabet (Raven Alexander Whitney, *The Edge of Night*)
Susan Lucci (Erica Kane, *All My Children*)
★ Robin Strasser (Dorian Lord, *One Life to Live*)

Outstanding Supporting Actor
Gerald Anthony (Marco Dane, *One Life to Live*)
★ David Lewis (Edward Quartermaine, *General Hospital*)
Doug Sheehan (Joe Kelly, *General Hospital*)
Darnell Williams (Jesse Hubbard, *All My Children*)

Outstanding Supporting Actress
Elizabeth Lawrence (Myra Murdoch, *All My Children*)
★ Dorothy Lyman (Opal Gardner, *All My Children*)
Meg Mundy (Mona Aldrich Croft, *The Doctors*)
Louise Shaffer (Rae Woodard, *Ryan's Hope*)

1982-83

Presented June 6, 1983

Outstanding Actor
Peter Bergman (Dr. Cliff Warner, *All My Children*)
Stuart Damon (Dr. Alan Quartermaine, *General Hospital*)
Tony Geary (Luke Spencer, *General Hospital*)
James Mitchell (Palmer Cortlandt, *All My Children*)
★ Robert S. Woods (Bo Buchanan, *One Life to Live*)

Outstanding Actress
Leslie Charleson (Dr. Monica Quartermaine, *General Hospital*)
Susan Lucci (Erica Kane, *All My Children*)
★ Dorothy Lyman (Opal Gardner, *All My Children*)
Erika Slezak (Vicki Buchanan, *One Life to Live*)
Robin Strasser (Dorian Lord, *One Life to Live*)

Outstanding Supporting Actor
Anthony Call (Herb Callison, *One Life to Live*)
Al Freeman Jr. (Ed Hall, *One Life to Live*)
Howard E. Rollins Jr. (Ed Harding, *Another World*)
John Stamos (Blackie Parrish, *General Hospital*)
★ Darnell Williams (Jesse Hubbard, *All My Children*)

Outstanding Supporting Actress
Kim Delaney (Jenny Gardner, *All My Children*)
Eileen Herlie (Myrtle Fargate, *All My Children*)
Robin Mattson (Heather Webber, *General Hospital*)
★ Louise Shaffer (Rae Woodard, *Ryan's Hope*)
Brynn Thayer (Jenny Janssen, *One Life to Live*)
Marcy Walker (Liza Colby, *All My Children*)

1983–84

Presented June 27, 1984

Outstanding Actor
★ Larry Bryggman (Dr. John Dixon, *As the World Turns*)
Joel Crothers (Dr. Miles Cavanaugh, *The Edge of Night*)
Stuart Damon (Dr. Alan Quartermaine, *General Hospital*)
Terry Lester (Jack Abbott, *The Young and the Restless*)
Larkin Malloy (Sky Whitney, *The Edge of Night*)
James Mitchell (Palmer Cortlandt, *All My Children*)

Outstanding Actress
Ann Flood (Nancy Karr, *The Edge of Night*)
Sharon Gabet (Raven Alexander Whitney, *The Edge of Night*)
Deidre Hall (Dr. Marlena Evans Brady, *Days of Our Lives*)
Susan Lucci (Erica Kane, *All My Children*)
★ Erika Slezak (Vicki Buchanan, *One Life to Live*)

Outstanding Supporting Actor
Anthony Call (Herb Callison, *One Life to Live*)
★ Justin Deas (Tom Hughes, *As the World Turns*)
Louis Edmonds (Langley Wallingford, *All My Children*)
David Lewis (Edward Quartermaine, *General Hospital*)
Paul Stevens (Brian Bancroft, *Another World*)

Outstanding Supporting Actress
Loanne Bishop (Rose Kelly, *General Hospital*)
Christine Ebersole (Maxie McDermott, *One Life to Live*)
★ Judi Evans (Beth Raines, *Guiding Light*)
Eileen Herlie (Myrtle Fargate, *All My Children*)

Lois Kibbee (Geraldine Whitney Saxon, *The Edge of Night*)
Marcy Walker (Liza Colby, *All My Children*)

1984-85

Presented August 1, 1985

Outstanding Actor
Larry Bryggman (Dr. John Dixon, *As the World Turns*)
David Canary (Adam/Stuart Chandler, *All My Children*)
Terry Lester (Jack Abbott, *The Young and the Restless*)
James Mitchell (Palmer Cortlandt, *All My Children*)
★ Darnell Williams (Jesse Hubbard, *All My Children*)

Outstanding Actress
Deidre Hall (Dr. Marlena Evans Brady, *Days of Our Lives*)
Susan Lucci (Erica Kane, *All My Children*)
Gillian Spencer (Daisy Cortlandt, *All My Children*)
Robin Strasser (Dorian Lord, *One Life to Live*)
★ Kim Zimmer (Reva Shayne Lewis, *Guiding Light*)

Outstanding Supporting Actor
Anthony Call (Herb Callison, *One Life to Live*)
Louis Edmonds (Langley Wallingford, *All My Children*)
★ Larry Gates (H. B. Lewis, *Guiding Light*)
David Lewis (Edward Quartermaine, *General Hospital*)
Robert Lupone (Zach Grayson, *All My Children*)

Outstanding Supporting Actress
Norma Connolly (Ruby Anderson, *General Hospital*)
Eileen Herlie (Myrtle Fargate, *All My Children*)
Maeve Kinkead (Vanessa Chamberlain, *Guiding Light*)
Elizabeth Lawrence (Myra Murdoch Sloane, *All My Children*)
★ Beth Maitland (Tracy Abbott, *The Young and the Restless*)

Outstanding Juvenile/Young Man
★ Brian Bloom (Dusty Donovan, *As the World Turns*)
Steve Caffrey (Andrew Preston, *All My Children*)
Michael Knight (Tad Martin, *All My Children*)
Michael O'Leary (Rick Bauer, *Guiding Light*)
Jack Wagner (Frisco Jones, *General Hospital*)

Outstanding Ingenue
Kristian Alfonso (Hope Williams Brady, *Days of Our Lives*)
★ Tracey E. Bregman (Lauren Fenmore, *The Young and the Restless*)
Melissa Leo (Linda Warner, *All My Children*)
Lisa Trusel (Melissa Anderson, *Days of Our Lives*)
Tasia Valenza (Dottie Thorton Martin, *All My Children*)

1985-86

Presented July 17, 1986

Outstanding Actor
Scott Bryce (Craig Montgomery, *As the World Turns*)
Larry Bryggman (Dr. John Dixon, *As the World Turns*)
★ David Canary (Adam/Stuart Chandler, *All My Children*)
Nicholas Coster (Lionel Lockridge, *Santa Barbara*)
Terry Lester (Jack Abbott, *The Young and the Restless*)
Robert S. Woods (Bo Buchanan, *One Life to Live*)

Outstanding Actress
Elizabeth Hubbard (Lucinda Walsh, *As the World Turns*)
Susan Lucci (Erica Kane, *All My Children*)
Peggy McKay (Caroline Brady, *Days of Our Lives*)
★ Erica Slezak (Vicki Buchanan, *One Life to Live*)
Kim Zimmer (Reva Shayne Lewis, *Guiding Light*)

Outstanding Supporting Actor
Louis Edmonds (Langley Wallingford, *All My Children*)
Al Freeman Jr. (Ed Hall, *One Life to Live*)
Larry Gates (H. B. Lewis, *Guiding Light*)
Gregg Marx (Tom Hughes, *As the World Turns*)
★ John Wesley Shipp (Doug Cummings, *As the World Turns*)

Outstanding Supporting Actress
Dame Judith Anderson (Minx Lockridge, *Santa Barbara*)
Uta Hagen (Hortense, *One Life to Live*)
Eileen Herlie (Myrtle Fargate, *All My Children*)
★ Leann Hunley (Anna DiMera, *Days of Our Lives*)
Kathleen Widdoes (Emma Snyder, *As the World Turns*)

Outstanding Younger Leading Man
Brian Bloom (Dusty Donovan, *As the World Turns*)
Jon Hensley (Holden Snyder, *As the World Turns*)
Vincent Irizarry (Lujack, *Guiding Light*)
★ Michael Knight (Tad Martin, *All My Children*)
Don Scardino (Dr. Chris Chapin, *Another World*)

Outstanding Ingenue
Martha Byrne (Lily Walsh, *As the World Turns*)
Debbi Morgan (Angie Hubbard, *All My Children*)
Jane Krakowski (T. R. Kendall, *Search for Tomorrow*)
★ Ellen Wheeler (Vicky/Marley Love, *Another World*)
Robin Wright (Kelly Capwell, *Santa Barbara*)

1986-87

Presented June 30, 1987

Outstanding Actor
Eric Braeden (Victor Newman, *The Young and the Restless*)
Scott Bryce (Craig Montgomery, *As the World Turns*)
★ Larry Bryggman (Dr. John Dixon, *As the World Turns*)
Terry Lester (Jack Abbott, *The Young and the Restless*)
★ A Martinez (Cruz Castillo, *Santa Barbara*)

Outstanding Actress
Elizabeth Hubbard (Lucinda Walsh, *As the World Turns*)
Susan Lucci (Erica Kane, *All My Children*)
Frances Reid (Alice Horton, *Days of Our Lives*)
Marcy Walker (Eden Capwell, *Santa Barbara*)
★ Kim Zimmer (Reva Shayne Lewis, *Guiding Light*)

Outstanding Supporting Actor
Anthony Call (Herb Callison, *One Life to Live*)
Justin Deas (Keith Timmons, *Santa Barbara*)
Richard Eden (Brick Wallace, *Santa Barbara*)
Al Freeman Jr. (Ed Hall, *One Life to Live*)
★ Gregg Marx (Tom Hughes, *As the World Turns*)

Outstanding Supporting Actress
Lisa Brown (Iva Snyder, *As the World Turns*)
Robin Mattson (Gina Capwell, *Santa Barbara*)
Peggy McKay (Caroline Brady, *Days of Our Lives*)
★ Kathleen Noone (Ellen Chandler, *All My Children*)
Kathleen Widdoes (Emma Snyder, *As the World Turns*)

Outstanding Younger Leading Man
Brian Bloom (Dusty Donovan, *As the World Turns*)
Jon Hensley (Holden Snyder, *As the World Turns*)
★ Michael Knight (Tad Martin, *All My Children*)
Grant Show (Rick Hyde, *Ryan's Hope*)
Billy Warlock (Frankie Brady, *Days of Our Lives*)

Outstanding Ingenue
Tracey E. Bregman (Lauren Fenmore, *The Young and the Restless*)
★ Martha Byrne (Lily Walsh, *As the World Turns*)
Jane Krakowski (T. R. Kendall, *Search for Tomorrow*)
Krista Tesreau (Mindy Lewis, *Guiding Light*)
Robin Wright (Kelly Capwell, *Santa Barbara*)

Outstanding Guest Performer
Pamela Blair (Ronda, *All My Children*)
Eileen Heckart (Ruth Perkins, *One Life to Live*)
Celeste Holm (Clara/Lydia Woodhouse, *Loving*)
Terrance Mann (Jester, *As the World Turns*)
★ John Wesley Shipp (Martin Ellis, *Santa Barbara*)

1987-88

Presented June 29, 1988

Outstanding Lead Actor
Larry Bryggman (Dr. John Dixon, *As the World Turns*)
★ David Canary (Adam/Stuart Chandler, *All My Children*)
Robert Gentry (Ross Chandler, *All My Children*)
Stephen Nichols (Steve "Patch" Johnson, *Days of Our Lives*)
A Martinez (Cruz Castillo, *Santa Barbara*)

Outstanding Lead Actress
★ Helen Gallagher (Maeve Ryan, *Ryan's Hope*)
Elizabeth Hubbard (Lucinda Walsh, *As the World Turns*)
Susan Lucci (Erica Kane, *All My Children*)
Erica Slezak (Vicki Buchanan, *One Life to Live*)
Marcy Walker (Eden Capwell, *Santa Barbara*)

Outstanding Supporting Actor
Bernie Barrow (Johnny Ryan, *Ryan's Hope*)
Nicholas Coster (Lionel Lockridge, *Santa Barbara*)
★ Justin Deas (Keith Timmons, *Santa Barbara*)
Mark LaMura (Mark Dalton, *All My Children*)
David Lewis (Edward Quartermaine, *General Hospital*)

Outstanding Supporting Actress
Lisa Brown (Iva Snyder, *As the World Turns*)
Eileen Fulton (Lisa Miller, *As the World Turns*)
Maeve Kinkead (Vanessa Chamberlain, *Guiding Light*)
Robin Mattson (Gina Capwell, *Santa Barbara*)
Arleen Sorkin (Calliope Jones, *Days of Our Lives*)
★ Ellen Wheeler (Cindy Parker, *All My Children*)

Outstanding Younger Leading Man
Scott deFreitas (Andy Dixon, *As the World Turns*)
Andrew Kavovit (Paul Stenbeck, *As the World Turns*)
Ross Kettle (Jeffrey Conrad, *Santa Barbara*)
Robert Duncan McNeil (Charlie Brent, *All My Children*)
★ Billy Warlock (Frankie Brady, *Days of Our Lives*)

Outstanding Ingenue
Tichina Arnold (Zena Brown, *Ryan's Hope*)
Andrea Evans (Tina Lord, *One Life to Live*)
Lauren Holly (Julie Chandler, *All My Children*)
★ Julianne Moore (Frannie/Sabrina Hughes, *As the World Turns*)
Robin Wright (Kelly Capwell, *Santa Barbara*)

1988–89

Presented June 29, 1989

Outstanding Lead Actor
Larry Bryggman (Dr. John Dixon, *As the World Turns*)
★ David Canary (Adam/Stuart Chandler, *All My Children*)
A Martinez (Cruz Castillo, *Santa Barbara*)
James Mitchell (Palmer Cortlandt, *All My Children*)
Douglass Watson (Mackenzie Cory, *Another World*)

Outstanding Lead Actress
Jeanne Cooper (Katherine Chancellor, *The Young and the Restless*)
Elizabeth Hubbard (Lucinda Walsh, *As the World Turns*)
Susan Lucci (Erica Kane, *All My Children*)
★ Marcy Walker (Eden Capwell, *Santa Barbara*)

Outstanding Supporting Actor
Joseph Campanella (Harper Deveraux, *Days of Our Lives*)
★ Justin Deas (Keith Timmons, *Santa Barbara*)
David Forsyth (Dr. John Hudson, *Another World*)
Quinn Redeker (Rex Sterling, *The Young and the Restless*)

Outstanding Supporting Actress [a tie]
Jane Elliot (Anjelica Deveraux, *Days of Our Lives*)
★ Nancy Lee Grahn (Julia Wainwright, *Santa Barbara*)
Robin Mattson (Gina Capwell, *Santa Barbara*)
★ Debbi Morgan (Dr. Angie Hubbard, *All My Children*)
Arleen Sorkin (Calliope Jones, *Days of Our Lives*)

Outstanding Juvenile Male
★ Justin Gocke (Brandon Capwell, *Santa Barbara*)
Andrew Kavovit (Paul Stenbeck, *As the World Turns*)
Darryl Utley (Benjy DiMera, *Days of Our Lives*)

Outstanding Juvenile Female
Noelle Beck (Trisha Alden, *Loving*)
Martha Byrne (Lily Walsh, *As the World Turns*)
Anne Heche (Vicky/Marley Love, *Another World*)
★ Kimberly McCullough (Robin Scorpio, *General Hospital*)

1989-90

Presented June 28, 1990

Outstanding Lead Actor
Peter Bergman (Jack Abbott, *The Young and the Restless*)
Eric Braeden (Victor Newman, *The Young and the Restless*)
David Canary (Adam/Stuart Chandler, *All My Children*)
★ A Martinez (Cruz Castillo, *Santa Barbara*)
Stephen Schnetzer (Cass Winthrop, *Another World*)

Outstanding Lead Actress
Jeanne Cooper (Katherine Chancellor, *The Young and the Restless*)
Elizabeth Hubbard (Lucinda Walsh, *As the World Turns*)
Finola Hughes (Anna Devane, *General Hospital*)
Susan Lucci (Erica Kane, *All My Children*)
★ Kim Zimmer (Reva Shayne Lewis, *Guiding Light*)

Outstanding Supporting Actor
Roscoe Born (Robert Barr, *Santa Barbara*)
★ Henry Darrow (Rafael Castillo, *Santa Barbara*)
Robert Gentry (Ross Chandler, *All My Children*)
Quinn Redeker (Rex Sterling, *The Young and the Restless*)
Kristoff St. John (Adam Marshall, *Generations*)
Kin Shriner (Scotty Baldwin, *General Hospital*)
Jerry ver Dorn (Ross Marler, *Guiding Light*)

Outstanding Supporting Actress
★ Julia Barr (Brooke English, *All My Children*)
Mary Jo Catlett (Mary Finnegan, *General Hospital*)
Michelle Forbes (Sonni/Solita Carrera, *Guiding Light*)
Lynn Herring (Lucy Coe, *General Hospital*)
Jess Walton (Jill Abbott, *The Young and the Restless*)

Outstanding Juvenile Male
Bryan Buffington (Little Billy Lewis, *Guiding Light*)
★ Andrew Kavovit (Paul Stenbeck, *As the World Turns*)

Outstanding Juvenile Female
★ Cady McClain (Dixie Cooney, *All My Children*)
Kimberly McCullough (Robin Scorpio, *General Hospital*)
Charlotte Ross (Eve Donovan, *Days of Our Lives*)
Liz Vassey (Emily Ann Sago, *All My Children*)

1990-91

Presented June 27, 1991

Outstanding Lead Actor
★ Peter Bergman (Jack Abbott, *The Young and the Restless*)
David Canary (Adam/Stuart Chandler, *All My Children*)
Nicholas Coster (Lionel Lockridge, *Santa Barbara*)
A Martinez (Cruz Castillo, *Santa Barbara*)
James Reynolds (Henry Marshall, *Generations*)

Outstanding Lead Actress
Julia Barr (Brooke English, *All My Children*)
Jeanne Cooper (Katherine Chancellor, *The Young and the Restless*)
Elizabeth Hubbard (Lucinda Walsh, *As the World Turns*)
★ Finola Hughes (Anna Devane, *General Hospital*)
Susan Lucci (Erica Kane, *All My Children*)

Outstanding Supporting Actor
★ Bernie Barrow (Johnny Ryan, *Ryan's Hope*)
William Christian (Derek Frye, *All My Children*)
Stuart Damon (Dr. Alan Quartermaine, *General Hospital*)
William Roerick (Henry Chamberlain, *Guiding Light*)
Kin Shriner (Scotty Baldwin, *General Hospital*)
Jerry ver Dorn (Ross Marler, *Guiding Light*)

Outstanding Supporting Actress
Darlene Conley (Sally Spectra, *The Bold and the Beautiful*)
Maureen Garrett (Holly Lindsey, *Guiding Light*)
Jill Larson (Opal Gardner, *All My Children*)
★ Jess Walton (Jill Abbott, *The Young and the Restless*)
Kathleen Widdoes (Emma Snyder, *As the World Turns*)

Outstanding Younger Actor
Bryan Buffington (Little Billy Lewis, *Guiding Light*)
Justin Gocke (Brandon Capwell, *Santa Barbara*)
★ Rick Hearst (Alan-Michael Spaulding, *Guiding Light*)
Andrew Kavovit (Paul Stenbeck, *As the World Turns*)
Kristoff St. John (Adam Marshall, *Generations*)

Outstanding Younger Actress
Tricia Cast (Nina Webster, *The Young and the Restless*)
★ Anne Heche (Vicky/Marley Love, *Another World*)
Kimberly McCullough (Robin Scorpio, *General Hospital*)
Ashley Peldon (Marah Shayne, *Guiding Light*)
Charlotte Ross (Eve Donovan, *Days of Our Lives*)

1991-92

Presented June 23, 1992

Outstanding Lead Actor
★ Peter Bergman (Jack Abbott, *The Young and the Restless*)
David Canary (Adam/Stuart Chandler, *All My Children*)
Nicholas Coster (Lionel Lockridge, *Santa Barbara*)
A Martinez (Cruz Castillo, *Santa Barbara*)
Michael Zaslow (Roger Thorpe, *Guiding Light*)

Outstanding Lead Actress
Jeanne Cooper (Katherine Chancellor, *The Young and the Restless*)
Elizabeth Hubbard (Lucinda Walsh, *As the World Turns*)
Susan Lucci (Erica Kane, *All My Children*)
★ Erica Slezak (Vicki Buchanan, *One Life to Live*)
Jessica Tuck (Megan Gordon, *One Life to Live*)

Outstanding Supporting Actor
Bernie Barrow (Louis Slavinsky, *Loving*)
★ Thom Christopher (Carlo Hesser, *One Life to Live*)
Rick Hearst (Alan-Michael Spaulding, *Guiding Light*)
Charles Keating (Carl Hutchins, *Another World*)
Jerry ver Dorn (Ross Marler, *Guiding Light*)

Outstanding Supporting Actress
Darlene Conley (Sally Spectra, *The Bold and the Beautiful*)
Linda Dano (Felicia Gallant, *Another World*)
Maureen Garrett (Holly Lindsey, *Guiding Light*)
Lynn Herring (Lucy Coe, *General Hospital*)
★ Maeve Kinkead (Vanessa Chamberlain, *Guiding Light*)

Outstanding Younger Actor
Scott deFreitas (Andy Dixon, *As the World Turns*)
Jeff Phillips (Hart Jessup, *Guiding Light*)
★ Kristoff St. John (Neil Winters, *The Young and the Restless*)
Patrick Stuart (Will Cortlandt, *All My Children*)
Dondre Whitfield (Terrence Frye, *All My Children*)

Outstanding Younger Actress
★ Tricia Cast (Nina Webster, *The Young and the Restless*)
Beth Ehlers (Harley Davidson Cooper, *Guiding Light*)
Alla Korot (Jenna Norris, *Another World*)
Cady McClain (Dixie Cooney, *All My Children*)
Melissa Reeves (Jennifer Horton, *Days of Our Lives*)

1992-93

Presented May 26, 1993

Outstanding Lead Actor
Peter Bergman (Jack Abbott, *The Young and the Restless*)
★ David Canary (Adam/Stuart Chandler, *All My Children*)
Mark Derwin (A. C. Mallet, *Guiding Light*)
A Martinez (Cruz Castillo, *Santa Barbara*)
Robert S. Woods (Bo Buchanan, *One Life to Live*)
Michael Zaslow (Roger Thorpe, *Guiding Light*)

Outstanding Lead Actress
Julia Barr (Brooke English, *All My Children*)
★ Linda Dano (Felicia Gallant, *Another World*)
Ellen Dolan (Margo Hughes, *As the World Turns*)
Maeve Kinkead (Vanessa Chamberlain, *Guiding Light*)
Susan Lucci (Erica Kane, *All My Children*)

Outstanding Supporting Actor
★ Gerald Anthony (Marco Dane, *General Hospital*)
Thom Christopher (Carlo Hesser, *One Life to Live*)
Rick Hearst (Alan-Michael Spaulding, *Guiding Light*)
Charles Keating (Carl Hutchins, *Another World*)
Kin Shriner (Scotty Baldwin, *General Hospital*)

Outstanding Supporting Actress
Kimberlin Brown (Sheila Carter, *The Young and the Restless*)
Jane Elliot (Tracy Quartermaine, *General Hospital*)
Jill Larson (Opal Gardner, *All My Children*)
★ Ellen Parker (Maureen Bauer, *Guiding Light*)
Tonja Walker (Alex Olanov, *One Life to Live*)

Outstanding Younger Actor
Matt Borlenghi (Brian Bodine, *All My Children*)
Bryan Buffington (Little Billy Lewis, *Guiding Light*)
Kristoff St. John (Neil Winters, *The Young and the Restless*)
★ Monti Sharp (David Grant, *Guiding Light*)
Dondre Whitfield (Terrence Frye, *All My Children*)

Outstanding Younger Actress
Beth Ehlers (Harley Davidson Cooper, *Guiding Light*)
Melissa Hayden (Bridget Reardon, *Guiding Light*)
Sydney Penny (B. J. Walker, *Santa Barbara*)
Kelly Ripa (Hayley Vaugh, *All My Children*)
★ Heather Tom (Victoria Newman, *The Young and the Restless*)

1993-94

Presented May 25, 1994

Outstanding Lead Actor
Peter Bergman (Jack Abbott, *The Young and the Restless*)
Charles Keating (Carl Hutchins, *Another World*)
Peter Simon (Dr. Ed Bauer, *Guiding Light*)
Robert S. Woods (Bo Buchanan, *One Life to Live*)
★ Michael Zaslow (Roger Thorpe, *Guiding Light*)

Outstanding Lead Actress
Julia Barr (Brooke English, *All My Children*)
Linda Dano (Felicia Gallant, *Another World*)
Fiona Hutchison (Jenna Bradshaw, *Guiding Light*)
★ Hillary B. Smith (Nora Gannon, *One Life to Live*)
Kathleen Widdoes (Emma Snyder, *As the World Turns*)

Outstanding Supporting Actor
Ian Buchanan (Dr. James Warwick, *The Bold and the Beautiful*)
Thom Christopher (Dante Partoue, *Loving*)
★ Justin Deas (Buzz Cooper, *Guiding Light*)
Patrick Tovatt (Cal Stricklyn, *As the World Turns*)
Jerry ver Dorn (Ross Marler, *Guiding Light*)

Outstanding Supporting Actress
Signy Coleman (Hope Adams, *The Young and the Restless*)
Hillary Edson (Dr. Eve Guthrie, *Guiding Light*)
Maureen Garrett (Holly Lindsey, *Guiding Light*)
★ Susan Haskell (Marty Saybrooke, *One Life to Live*)
Sharon Wyatt (Tiffany Hill, *General Hospital*)

Outstanding Younger Actor
Scott deFreitas (Andy Dixon, *As the World Turns*)
★ Roger Howarth (Todd Manning, *One Life to Live*)
Monti Sharp (David Grant, *Guiding Light*)
Dondre Whitfield (Terrence Frye, *All My Children*)

Outstanding Younger Actress
Martha Byrne (Lily Walsh, *As the World Turns*)
Sarah Michelle Gellar (Kendall Hart, *All My Children*)
★ Melissa Hayden (Bridget Reardon, *Guiding Light*)
Melina Kanakaredes (Eleni Cooper, *Guiding Light*)
Heather Tom (Victoria Newman, *The Young and the Restless*)

1994-95

Presented May 19, 1995

Outstanding Lead Actor
Peter Bergman (Jack Abbott, *The Young and the Restless*)
David Canary (Adam/Stuart Chandler, *All My Children*)
★ Justin Deas (Buzz Cooper, *Guiding Light*)
Brad Maule (Dr. Tony Jones, *General Hospital*)
Michael Zaslow (Roger Thorpe, *Guiding Light*)

Outstanding Lead Actress
Leslie Charleson (Dr. Monica Quartermaine, *General Hospital*)
Marj Dusay (Alexandra Spaulding, *Guiding Light*)
Maeve Kinkead (Vanessa Chamberlain, *Guiding Light*)
Susan Lucci (Erica Kane, *All My Children*)
★ Erika Slezak (Vicki Buchanan, *One Life to Live*)

Outstanding Supporting Actor
Ian Buchanan (Dr. James Warwick, *The Bold and the Beautiful*)
Keith Hamilton Cobb (Noah Keefer, *All My Children*)
Rick Hearst (Alan-Michael Spaulding, *Guiding Light*)
Roger Howarth (Todd Manning, *One Life to Live*)
★ Jerry ver Dorn (Ross Marler, *Guiding Light*)

Outstanding Supporting Actress
Jean Carol (Nadine Cooper, *Guiding Light*)
Melina Kanakaredes (Eleni Cooper, *Guiding Light*)
Sydney Penny (Julia Santos, *All My Children*)
★ Rena Sofer (Lois Cerullo, *General Hospital*)
Jacklyn Zeman (Bobbie Spencer, *General Hospital*)

Outstanding Younger Actor
Jason Biggs (Pete Wendall, *As the World Turns*)
Bryan Buffington (Little Billy Lewis, *Guiding Light*)
★ Jonathan Jackson (Lucky Spencer, *General Hospital*)
Tommy Michaels (Timmy Dillon, *All My Children*)

Outstanding Younger Actress
★ Sarah Michelle Gellar (Kendall Hart, *All My Children*)
Kimberly McCullough (Robin Scorpio, *General Hospital*)
Rachel Miner (Michelle Bauer, *Guiding Light*)
Heather Tom (Victoria Newman, *The Young and the Restless*)

1995-96

Presented May 22, 1996

Outstanding Lead Actor
Maurice Benard (Sonny Corinthos, *All My Children*)
Peter Bergman (Jack Abbott, *The Young and the Restless*)
Eric Braeden (Victor Newman, *The Young and the Restless*)
David Canary (Adam/Stuart Chandler, *All My Children*)
★ Charles Keating (Carl Hutchins, *Another World*)

Outstanding Lead Actress
Jensen Buchanan (Vicky Hudson, *Another World*)
Linda Dano (Felicia Gallant, *Another World*)
Susan Lucci (Erica Kane, *All My Children*)
★ Erika Slezak (Vicki Carpenter, *One Life to Live*)
Jess Walton (Jill Abbott, *The Young and the Restless*)

Outstanding Supporting Actor
Frank Beaty (Brent Lawrence, *Guiding Light*)
Ian Buchanan (Dr. James Warwick, *The Bold and the Beautiful*)
Stuart Damon (Dr. Alan Quartermaine, *General Hospital*)
David Forsyth (Dr. John Hudson, *Another World*)
Michael Sutton (Stone Cates, *General Hospital*)
★ Jerry ver Dorn (Ross Marler, *Guiding Light*)

Outstanding Supporting Actress
Rosalind Cash (Mary Mae Ward, *General Hospital*)
★ Anna Holbrook (Sharlene Frame Hudson, *Another World*)
Victoria Rowell (Drucilla Winters, *The Young and the Restless*)
Michelle Stafford (Phyllis Romalotti, *The Young and the Restless*)
Tonya Lee Williams (Dr. Olivia Hastings, *The Young and the Restless*)

Outstanding Younger Actor
Nathan Fillion (Joey Buchanan, *One Life to Live*)
Jonathan Jackson (Lucky Spencer, *General Hospital*)
★ Kevin Mambo (Marcus Williams, *Guiding Light*)
Shemar Moore (Malcolm Winters, *The Young and the Restless*)
Joshua Morrow (Nicholas Newman, *The Young and the Restless*)

Outstanding Younger Actress
Kimberly J. Brown (Marah Lewis, *Guiding Light*)
Martha Byrne (Lily Walsh Grimaldi, *As the World Turns*)
Sharon Case (Sharon Collins, *The Young and the Restless*)
★ Kimberly McCullough (Robin Scorpio, *General Hospital*)
Heather Tom (Victoria Newman, *The Young and the Restless*)

1996-97

Presented May 21, 1997

Outstanding Lead Actor
Peter Bergman (Jack Abbott, *The Young and the Restless*)
Eric Braeden (Victor Newman, *The Young and the Restless*)
David Canary (Adam/Stuart Chandler, *All My Children*)
★ Justin Deas (Buzz Cooper, *Guiding Light*)
Tony Geary (Luke Spencer, *General Hospital*)

Outstanding Lead Actress
Jensen Buchanan (Vicky Hudson, *Another World*)
Genie Francis (Laura Spencer, *General Hospital*)
Susan Lucci (Erica Kane, *All My Children*)
★ Jess Walton (Jill Abbott, *The Young and the Restless*)

Outstanding Supporting Actor
Maurice Benard (Sonny Corinthos, *All My Children*)
★ Ian Buchanan (Dr. James Warwick, *The Bold and the Beautiful*)
Stuart Damon (Dr. Alan Quartermaine, *General Hospital*)
Aaron Lustig (Dr. Tim Reid, *The Young and the Restless*)
Brad Maule (Dr. Tony Jones, *General Hospital*)
Scott Reeves (Ryan McNeil, *The Young and the Restless*)

Outstanding Supporting Actress
Eva LaRue Callahan (Dr. Maria Santos, *All My Children*)
Vanessa Marcil (Brenda Barrett, *General Hospital*)
Victoria Rowell (Drucilla Winters, *The Young and the Restless*)
★ Michelle Stafford (Phyllis Romalotti, *The Young and the Restless*)
Jacklyn Zeman (Bobbie Spencer Cassadine, *General Hospital*)

Outstanding Younger Actor
Steve Burton (Jason Quartermaine, *General Hospital*)
Jonathan Jackson (Lucky Spencer, *General Hospital*)
★ Kevin Mambo (Marcus Williams, *Guiding Light*)
Shemar Moore (Malcolm Winters, *The Young and the Restless*)
Joshua Morrow (Nicholas Newman, *The Young and the Restless*)

Outstanding Younger Actress
★ Sarah Brown (Carly Roberts, *General Hospital*)
Sharon Case (Sharon Newman, *The Young and the Restless*)
Christie Clark (Carrie Brady, *Days of Our Lives*)
Kimberly McCullough (Robin Scorpio, *General Hospital*)
Heather Tom (Victoria Newman, *The Young and the Restless*)

1997-98

Presented May 15, 1998

Outstanding Lead Actor
Peter Bergman (Jack Abbott, *The Young and the Restless*)
★ Eric Braeden (Victor Newman, *The Young and the Restless*)
David Canary (Adam/Stuart Chandler, *All My Children*)
Tony Geary (Luke Spencer, *General Hospital*)
Kin Shriner (Scotty Baldwin, *Port Charles*)

Outstanding Lead Actress
Eileen Davidson (Kristen Blake, *Days of Our Lives*)
Susan Lucci (Erica Kane, *All My Children*)
★ Cynthia Watros (Annie Sutton Lewis, *Guiding Light*)
Jacklyn Zeman (Bobbie Spencer Cassadine, *General Hospital*)
Kim Zimmer (Reva Shayne Lewis, *Guiding Light*)

Outstanding Supporting Actor
Grant Aleksander (Phillip Spaulding, *Guiding Light*)
Ian Buchanan (Dr. James Warwick, *The Bold and the Beautiful*)
★ Steve Burton (Jason Quartermaine, *General Hospital*)
Scott Reeves (Ryan McNeil, *The Young and the Restless*)
Michael Knight (Tad Martin, *All My Children*)

Outstanding Supporting Actress
★ Julia Barr (Brooke English, *All My Children*)
Amy Carlson (Josie Watts, *Another World*)
Amy Ecklund (Abigail Blume, *Guiding Light*)
Vanessa Marcil (Brenda Barrett, *General Hospital*)
Victoria Rowell (Drucilla Winters, *The Young and the Restless*)

Outstanding Younger Actor
Jensen Ackles (Eric Brady, *Days of Our Lives*)
Tyler Christopher (Nikolas Cassadine, *General Hospital*)
★ Jonathan Jackson (Lucky Spencer, *General Hospital*)
Bryant Jones (Nate Hastings, *The Young and the Restless*)
Kevin Mambo (Marcus Williams, *Guiding Light*)
Joshua Morrow (Nick Newman, *The Young and the Restless*)

Outstanding Younger Actress
★ Sarah Brown (Carly Roberts, *General Hospital*)
Christie Clark (Carrie Brady, *Days of Our Lives*)
Camryn Grimes (Cassie, *The Young and the Restless*)
Rhonda Ross Kendrick (Toni Burrell, *Another World*)
Heather Tom (Victoria Newman, *The Young and the Restless*)

Bibliography

Numerous Web sites were consulted in the research of facts and biographies of the soaps and the stars. In all likelihood, given the constant change on the Internet, half of the sites that could be listed here would be defunct or have different addresses by press time. However, there are hundreds of marvelously entertaining and factual sites dedicated to issues of interest to soap fans and star followers, and the best of the major sites are listed below. Therefore, it is suggested that searches be done to find sites that can help you find what you are interested in. Two of the best and most succinct search engines are Dogpile (*http://www.dogpile.com*) and Yahoo! (*http://www.yahoo.com*)—simply type in the name of the person or program you want to know more about. Happy hunting!

Annuals, Newspapers, and Periodicals

Afternoon TV

Daily Variety

Day TV

Daylight TV

Daytime TV Magazine

Daytime TV Stars

Entertainment Weekly

Hollywood Reporter

Los Angeles Times

Movieline

New York Times

Newsweek

People

Premiere

Soap Opera Digest

Soap Opera Magazine

Soap Opera Update

Soap Opera Weekly

Time

TV by Day Yearbook

TV Guide

Vanity Fair

Variety

Who's Who in TV

Books

Brooks, Tim. *The Complete Directory to Prime Time TV Stars.* New York: Ballantine Books, 1987

Brooks, Tim, and Earle Marsh. *The Complete Directory to Prime Time Network TV Shows 1946–present* (Sixth Edition). New York: Ballantine, 1995.

Brown, Gene. *Movie Time.* New York: Macmillan, 1995.

Cassata, Mary, and Barbara Irwin. *The Young and the Restless: Most Memorable Moments.* Los Angeles: General Publishing Group, 1996.

Copeland, Mary Ann. *Soap Opera History.* Lincolnwood, IL: Publications International, Ltd., 1991.

Corey, Melinda, and George Ochoa, comps. *A Cast of Thousands: A Compendium of Who Played What in Film.* 3 vols. New York: Facts on File, 1992.

Dunning, John. *The Encyclopedia of Old-Time Radio.* New York: Oxford University Press, 1998.

Groves, Seli. *Soaps: A Pictorial History of America's Daytime Dramas.* Chicago, IL:Contemporary Books, Inc., 1983.

_____. *The Ultimate Soap Opera Guide.* Detroit, MI: Visible Ink Press, 1995.

Hyatt, Wesley. *The Encyclopedia of Daytime Television.* New York: Billboard Books, 1997.

Inman, David. *The TV Encyclopedia.* New York: Perigee Books, 1991.

Katz, Ephraim. *The Film Encyclopedia* (Third Edition, Fred Klein and Ronald Dean Nolan, revs.). New York: HarperPerennial Library, 1998.

LaGuardia, Robert. *Soap World.* New York: Arbor House, 1983.

_____. *The Wonderful World of TV Soap Operas* (Revised Edition). New York: Ballantine Books, 1977.

Leahey, Mimi, ed. *Soaps: The History, Part One.* Englewood Cliffs, NJ: Dynasty Media Publishing Corp., 1984.

McNeil, Alex. *Total Television: A Comprehensive Guide to Programming from 1948 to the Present* (Fourth Edition). New York: Penguin, 1996.

Meyers, Richard. *The Illustrated Soap Opera Companion.* New York: Drake Publishers, 1977.

1998 People Entertainment Almanac. New York: People Books, 1997.

Pallot, James, ed. *The Movie Guide* (Third Edition). New York: Perigee, 1998.

Parish, James Robert. *Today's Black Hollywood.* New York: Pinnacle Books, 1995.

Parish, James Robert, and Don E. Stanke. *Hollywood Baby Boomers.* New York: Garland, 1992.

Poll, Julie. *As the World Turns: The Complete Family Scrapbook.* Los Angeles: General Publishing Group, 1996.

Poll, Julie with Caelie M. Haines. *Guiding Light: The Complete Family Album*. Los Angeles: General Publishing Group, 1997.

Rout, Nancy E., Ellen Buckley and Barney M. Rout, eds. *The Soap Opera Book*. West Nyack, NY: Todd Publications, 1992.

Rowan, Beth, ed. *1998 A&E Entertainment Almanac*. Boston, MA: Information Please, LLC, 1997.

Russell, Maureen. *Days of Our Lives: A Complete History of the Long-Running Soap Opera*. Jefferson, NC and London: McFarland and Company, 1995.

Schemering, Christopher. *Guiding Light: A 50th Celebration*. New York: Ballantine, 1987.

_____. *The Soap Opera Encyclopedia* (Second Edition). New York: Ballantine, 1987.

Scott, Kathryn Leigh. *Dark Shadows Almanac*. Los Angeles: Pomegranate Press, 1995.

_____. *The Dark Shadows Companion: Twenty-Fifth Anniversary Collection*. Los Angeles: Pomegranate Press, 1990.

Steinberg, Cobbett. *Film Facts*. New York: Facts on File, 1980.

Waggett, Gerard J. *The Official General Hospital Trivia Book*. New York: Hyperion, 1997.

_____. *The Soap Opera Book of Lists*. New York: HarperCollins, 1996.

_____. *The Soap Opera Encyclopedia*. New York: HarperCollins, 1997.

Waldron, Robert. *The Bold and the Beautiful: A Tenth Anniversary Celebration*. New York: HarperCollins, 1996.

Walker, John, ed. *Halliwell's Filmgoer's Companion* (Twelfth Edition). New York: HarperCollins, 1997.

Warner, Gary. *All My Children: The Complete Family Scrapbook*. Los Angeles: General Publishing Group, 1994.

_____. *General Hospital: The Complete Scrapbook*. Los Angeles: General Publishing Group, 1995.

_____. *One Life to Live: Thirty Years of Memories*. New York: Hyperion, 1998.

Zenka, Lorraine. *Days of Our Lives: The Complete Family Album*. New York: HarperCollins, 1995.

Recommended Web Sites

All My Children—http://www.abc.com/soaps/allmychildren/index.html
Another World—
http://www.nbc.com/tvcentral/shows/anotherworld/index.html
As the World Turns—http://marketing.cbs.com/daytime/atwt/
The Bold and the Beautiful—http://marketing.cbs.com/daytime/bb/
Days of Our Lives—http://www.nbc.com/tvcentral/shows/daysofourlives/
General Hospital—http://www.abc.com/soaps/generalhospital/index.html

Guiding Light—http://marketing.cbs.com/daytime/gl/
One Life to Live—http://www.abc.com/soaps/onelifetolive/index.html
Port Charles—http://www.abc.com/soaps/portcharles/index.html
Soap Opera Central—http://www.amcpages.com/soapcentral/
Soap Opera Digest—http://www.soapdigest.com/
Sony's Soap City—http://www.spe.sony.com/soapcity/
Sunset Beach—http://www.nbc.com/tvcentral/shows/sunsetbeach/
The Young and the Restless—http://marketing.cbs.com/daytime/yr/

Recommended Usenet Groups

ABC Network Soaps—news:rec.arts.tv.soaps.abc
All My Children—news:alt.tv.all-my-children
Another World—news:alt.fan.another-world
CBS Network Soaps—news:rec.arts.tv.soaps.cbs
Dark Shadows—news:alt.tv.dark_shadows
Days of Our Lives—news:alt.tv.days-of-our-lives
Daytime Soaps—news:rec.arts.tv.soaps.misc *and* news:rec.arts.tv.soaps
General Hospital—news:alt.tv.general-hospital
One Life to Live—news:alt.tv.one-life-to-live
Port Charles—news:alt.tv.port-charles

Index

All names in **bold** are featured in chapter 2.

A

Academy Awards, 65, 67, 69–70, 131, 135, 137, 178, 195

Access Hollywood, 22

Alien film series, 214

"All I Need," 211

All My Children, 19–20, 32, 34, 46–47, 52–55, 70, 93–95, 124–26, 197, 199

Allen, Debbie, 167

Allen, Woody, 142, 214

Alley, Kirstie, 49

Allure, 148

Ally McBeal, 78–79

Amadeus, 111

"Amanda Cousins," 34

Amistad, 90

"Amy Russell," 57

Anastasia, 45, 102, 173

Anderson, Richard Dean, 118

"Angelica Clegg," 119

Annie Hall, 213–14

Another World, 17, 19, 21, 28, 89–90, 97–98, 101–103, 120–23, 139–41, 151, 160–61, 163, 188, 199–200, 215, 220–21

Anspaugh, David, 63

Apocalypse Now, 72

As the World Turns, 12, 17–20, 54, 56–57, 70, 97–98, 121, 128, 130, 151–52, 173–74, 180, 192–93, 195–97, 216–18

Aunt Jenny's True Life Stories, 16

"Austin Reed," 155

Autobiography of Miss Jane Pittman, The, 204–205

"Avis Ryan," 215

B

Baby M, 223

Bacon, Kevin, 26–28, 80

Bailey, Pearl, 89

Baldwin, Alec, 29–31, 229

Ball, Lucille, 76, 80

Bancroft, Anne, 67

Bard College, 104–105

Basinger, Kim, 29, 30

Batman, 220

Batman & Robin, 82

Batman Forever, 60, 132, 226

Bauer, Jaime Lyn, 182

Baum, L. Frank, 166

Baywatch, 39–40, 114–15

Bearse, Amanda, 32–34

Becker, 50

Beetlejuice, 30
Behind the Screen, 199
Bell, William, 182
"Ben Harper," 170–71
Ben Jarrod, 18
Bennetts, The, 18
Berenger, Tom, 35–38, 137
Besch, Bibi, 51, 199
Best of Everything, 70
"Betsy Stewart Montgomery
    Andropolous," 174
Betty and Bob, 15
Betty Ford Clinic, 102
Beverly Hills, 90210, 22, 159–61, 208,
    229
"Bianca Montgomery," 47
Big Chill, The, 36, 137, 223
Big Hit, The, 176
Big Sister, 13, 16
Billingsley, Barbara, 200
"Billy Allison Aldrich," 31
Blair, Linda, 111
Bleeth, Yasmine, 39–41, 158, 160,
    190–91
Body Heat, 201–202
Bold and the Beautiful, The, 21, 208
Boogie Nights, 151
Boston University, 150–51, 195–96
Boyz N the Hood, 72
Braeden, Eric, 61
"Brandy Shellooe," 224
Brat Pack, The, 149
Brian's Song, 220
Brighter Day, The, 18, 66, 68–69
Brighton Art College, 62–63
Broken Arrow, 190
Brown University, 222–23
Buffy the Vampire Slayer, 63, 94, 160
Burgi, Richard, 121
Byrne, Martha, 97

C
Caan, James, 220
Cabaret, 119, 140
Cain, Dean, 118
Calgary Herald, 176
Call Me Anna, 66
Calvin Klein, 154, 176
Camay, 16
Cambridge University, 185–86
"Cameron Stewart," 230

Capitol, 21, 118–19
Capshaw, Kate, 42–44
"Carmen," 83
Carnegie-Mellon University, 48–49,
    216–17
Carrey, Jim, 124–25, 132
"Carrie Wheeler," 224
Cates, Phoebe, 135, 137
Catholic University of America, 178–79
Chabert, Lacey, 45–47
Charleson, Leslie, 143
Cheers, 48–49, 101–102
Chicago Hope, 97
China Beach, 54–56
*Choices of the Heart: The Margaret
    Sanger Story*, 56
"Chris Austen," 194
City, The, 161
City of Angels, 173
Clara, Lu 'n' Em, 14
Cleese, John, 137
Cliffhanger, 199
Colbys, The, 22
Colgate, 14
College of Charleston, 96
College roommates, 134
Columbia University, 192
Conboy, John, 21
Concerning Miss Marlowe, 18–19
Connolly, Norma, 147
Corbett, Michael, 116
Cornell University, 168–69
Cosby, 167
Cosby, Bill, 165–67, 206
Cosby Show, The, 110, 165–67
"Courtney Wright," 167
Cox, Courteney, 125, 183
Crawford, Joan, 145
Curtis, Jamie Lee, 137, 140
Cutter to Houston, 30

D
"D. J. LaSalle," 191
Daily Variety, 72
Dallas, 22, 105–106, 143, 157, 162–63,
    182, 198
Danson, Ted, 48–51, 215
Dark Shadows, 13, 20
Darrow, 79
Davis, Geena, 163
Davis, Miles, 204, 206

Day TV Annual, 157
Days of Our Lives, 12, 19, 68, 81–83, 153–55, 184, 186–88
Daytime TV, 172, 186
De Anza College, 117–18
Dead Man Walking, 178–79, 188
Dean, James, 153, 161, 208–209
"Deborah Saxon," 77
Dee, Ruby, 130, 206, 221
DeGeneres, Ellen, 120–22
Delaney, Kim, 34, 52–54
Delany, Dana, 54–57
De Niro, Robert, 121, 140
Depp, Johnny, 121
"Derek Mason," 98
Dey, Susan, 111
Dharma and Greg, 97
DiCaprio, Leonardo, 58–61, 77
Dillon, Matt, 137, 196
Diner, 27
"Dr. Cunard," 102–103
"Dr. Jerry Turner," 130
"Dr. Jim Frazier," 130, 221
"Dr. Mark Toland," 133
Dr. Strangelove; or How I Learned to Stop Worrying and Love the Bomb, 127–28
Doctors, The, 17–20, 29–31, 70, 85–87, 201–203, 228–30
Downey, Robert, Jr., 137
Downey, Roma, 62–64, 93
Dragon: The Bruce Lee Story, 125
Dreams Come True, 16
Drescher, Fran, 186
Driving Miss Daisy, 89
Dukakis, Olympia, 184, 199
Duke, Patty, 65–69, 118
Dumb and Dumber, 125
Dynasty, 22, 220

E
Earth 2, 176
East Central College, 210
East Side, West Side, 204–205
Eastwood, Clint, 75–76, 143, 202
"Ed Gibson," 107
Eden, Barbara, 105
Edge of Night, The, 17, 20, 42–44, 61, 70, 75–77, 105, 150–52
Egg and I, The, 18
Electric Company, The, 89

Elephant Man, The, 111
"Ellen Dennis," 68–69
Emerald Point, 22
Emmy Awards, 48, 52–53, 55, 65, 71, 87, 92, 100, 120, 127, 131, 150–51, 181, 192, 204, 254–74
Empire, 172, 178, 213
Empire Strikes Back, The, 111, 220
Entertainment Tonight, 22
Eric, 111
"Erich Aldrich," 230
Estevez, Emilio, 148
Eton College, 185–86
Executioner's Song, The, 131–32

F
Falcon Crest, 22
Far and Away, 96–97
Faraway Hill, 16
Fences, 127, 220
Fictional soap locales, 91
Field, Sally, 137
Field of Dreams, 128, 140
Fifty Most Beautiful People in the World (*People* magazine), 29, 39, 55, 58, 62, 78, 81, 92, 120, 146, 153, 162, 172, 175, 178, 181, 216
Filmweb, 89
First Corps Endeavors, 36
First Hundred Years, The, 17–18
First Love, 18
Fish Called Wanda, A, 135, 137
Fishburne, Laurence, 71–74
Fisher, Frances, 61, 75–77
Flame in the Wind, A, see: *A Time for Us*
Flamingo Road, 22
Fleder, Gary, 88
Flockhart, Calista, 78–80
Florida State University, 207–208
Follow Your Heart, 18
Footloose, 27
Ford, Harrison, 30, 43, 121
Ford, Steven, 184
Forosoco, 26
Forrest Gump, 226
Fox, Michael J., 161
Fox, Vivica A., 81–84
Frakes, Jonathan, 85–87
Francis, Genie, 85–86, 199
"Frannie and Sabrina Hughes," 152

Frasier, 100–102
Freeman, Morgan, 88–91
Friends, 39, 183
"Frisco Jones," 212
From Daytime to Nighttime Soaps, 107–109
Fugitive, The, 30, 131–32, 151
Fulton, Eileen, 193

G

Geary, Anthony, 147
Gellar, Sarah Michelle, 47, 63, 92–95, 160
General Hospital, 18–19, 21–22, 70, 86, 110, 112, 147, 149, 175–77, 185–88, 197–200, 210–12
Generations, 20, 82–83, 199
George Washington University, 30
Getting Personal, 83
Gettysburg, 36
Ghost, 147
Gibson, Thomas, 96–98
Gilmore, Gary, 132
Givens, Robin, 124, 132, 163
Glass Menagerie, The, 78–79
Glory! Glory!, 193
Glover, Danny, 140
Goldberg, Whoopi, 50, 140, 202
Golden Globe Awards, 48, 65, 78, 88, 100, 127, 131, 162, 181, 201, 213
Golden West College, 81
Golden Windows, 18
GoodFellas, 140
Gore, Al, 132
Gorillas in the Mist, 214
Grammer, Kelsey, 100–103
Grant, Charles, 53
Great White Hope, The, 127–28
Greatest Gift, The, 18
Guiding Light, 12, 16, 19, 27–28, 61, 70, 76–80, 87, 93–94, 127–28, 130, 138, 197, 205–206, 219–21, 223–24, 229–30
Gypsy, 46

H

Hagman, Larry, 104–107, 111
Hamill, Mark, 110–12
Hamner, Earl, 193
Harvard University, 85, 131–32, 134
Hasselhoff, David, 113–16
Hatcher, Teri, 67, 117–19, 196
Hawkins Falls, 18

Hawkins, Michael, 189, 191
"Hayley Wilson," 57
Heche, Anne, 120–23, 151, 188
Helgenberger, Marg, 56, 190
Hickland, Catherine, 114, 116
Hitchcock, Alfred, 121, 170
Holbrook, Hal, 67
Holly, Lauren, 101, 124–26, 132
Hollywood Walk of Fame, 113, 204
Holmes, Scott, 217
Homecoming, The, 193
Houseman, John, 136, 169
How to Survive a Marriage, 20, 191
Howard University, 165–66
Hulce, Tom, 140
Hunt for Red October, The, 30
Hurt, William, 202

I

I Know What You Did Last Summer, 94
I Dream of Jeannie, 105
Imerg, 218
In & Out, 137, 183
Independence Day, 56, 81–82
Indiana Jones and the Temple of Doom, 43
Indiana University, 135–36
Inge, William, 17
Interview with the Vampire, 60, 162, 164, 190

J

"Jackie Templeton," 149
Jacqueline Bouvier Kennedy Onassis, 20, 63, 93
"Jagger Cates," 177
James Dean: Race with Destiny, 208
"Jed Andrews," 183–84
"Jenny Gardner," 54
"Jinx Avery Mallory," 44
"Joanna Leighton," 64
Joe Franklin Show, The, 189
"Joey Perrini," 141
John's Other Wife, 16
Johnson, Don, 40
Jones, James Earl, 127–30, 206, 220–21
Jones, Tommy Lee, 121, 131–33
"Joshua West Hall," 74
Joy Luck Club, The, 216–18
"Julie Cortlandt," 126
Julliard, 101, 132, 134
Just Plain Bill, 15

K

Kasdan, Lawrence, 137, 202
Kate Loves a Mystery, 157
Katzman, Leonard, 198
Kelley, David E., 79
"Kelly Capwell," 227
"Kendall Hart," 95
"Kent Murray," 112
King, 206
Kline, Kevin, 135–38, 183
Knight, Michael E., 116
Knight Rider, 114
Knots Landing, 22, 30, 105, 142–43, 211
Krakowski, Jane, 79

L

"Laura Donnelly," 144
"Laura Templeton," 200
Leave It to Beaver, 199
Lee, Hannibal "Iowa," Jr., 73
"LeeAnn Demerest," 41
Legends of the Fall, 163
Lever Brothers, 16
"Lien Truong Hughes," 218
Liotta, Ray, 139–41
Logan, Michael, 22
Lois & Clark: The New Adventures of Superman, 118
Long, Nia, 72, 82
Long, Shelley, 49, 101
Los Angeles City College, 88–89, 110
Los Angeles Times, 122
Losing Chase, 26, 27
Lost in Space, 46
Lost World, The, 151
Love Is a Many Splendored Thing, 142–44, 191
Love of Life, 13, 18, 20–21, 54–57, 70, 119, 168–71
Love Story, 131–32
Lovers and Friends, 17, 21
Loving, 20, 159–61
Lucci, Susan, 46, 93
Lucy & Desi: Before the Laughter, 76
Lyman, Frankie, 83

M

Ma Perkins, 13, 15
MacGyver, 118
Magnum, P.I., 181–82
Major League, 36

Malandro, Kristina, 210–11
Marcantel, Christopher, 28
"Marcy Thompson Cushing," 197
"Marley and Vicky Love," 122–23
Married......With Children, 32–33
Marshall, Thurgood, 166
"Martha Frazier," 206
Martin, Mary, 104–105
Martin, Steve, 121, 202
Mary Noble, Backstage Wife, 15
"Mary Ryan Fenelli," 158
"Maya," 83–84
McDonald, Susan, 43
Meet Joe Black, 164
Melrose Place, 22, 154, 211, 229
Men in Black, 132
Midler, Bette, 46
Midwest Productions, 161
Mills, Donna, 105, 142–44
Miracle Worker, The, 65, 67
Mrs. Wiggs of the Cabbage Patch, 16
Mitchum, Carrie, 207–208
Mitchum, Robert, 208
Moore, Demi, 121, 146–49, 198–99
Moore, Julianne, 122, 150–52
Morgan, Shelly Taylor, 22
Morning Star, 18
Morrison, Toni, 166
Movieline, 125
Mozart, Wolfgang Amadeus, 111
Mulan, 218
Muldoon, Patrick, 153–55, 208
Mulgrew, Kate, 41, 156–58
Murphy Brown, 156, 186
My Cousin Vinny, 195–96

N

"Nadia's Theme," 13
Nanny, The, 185–86
Nash Bridges, 40
National Academy of Fine Arts and Design, 219
National Audubon Society, 50
"Ned Bates," 161
Neuwirth, Bebe, 101
Never Too Young, 18
New Day in Eden, A, 22, 210–11
New York University, 156–57, 172–73, 195
Nighttime soap operas, 21–22, 107–109
Nixon, Agnes, 19, 72
"Nola Dancy Aldrich," 203

Norman, Jessye, 166
Northern Exposure, 199
Nurses, The, 18
NYPD Blue, 52, 53

O
O'Donnell, Rosie, 172
Oldest Living Confederate Widow Tells All, The, 206
One Hundred Most Powerful People in Hollywood, 172
One Life to Live, 17, 19–20, 35–37, 40–41, 62–64, 70, 72, 74, 131–33, 138, 151, 165–67, 189–91, 197, 208–209
One Man's Family, 21
Othello, 73, 128
Our Five Daughters, 18
Our Gal Sunday, 15
Our Private World, 17

P
Pacific Palisades, 22
Painted Dreams, 17
Pakula, Alan J., 136
Palin, Michael, 137
Paltrow, Gwyneth, 164
Papp, Joseph, 135
Parade, 136
Paradise Bay, 18
Partridge Family, The, 111
Party of Five, 45–46
"Patrice Kahlman," 180
Patty Duke Show, The, 67
Pease, Patsy, 185
Peggy Sue Got Married, 202
Penn, Sean, 179, 225–26
Pennsylvania State University, 85
People, 163–64, 176, 208
Perry, Luke, 94, 159–61, 229
Peyton Place, 22
Phillips, Irna, 17, 18
Piccolo, Brian, 220
Picket Fences, 124–25
Pirates of Penzance, The, 135–37
Pitt, Brad, 162–64
Platoon, 35–36
Poltergeist, 223
Port Charles, 21
Portia Faces Life, 18
Premiere, 172
Presley, Elvis, 153

Primary Colors, 106
Prince, Hal, 136
Princess Bride, The, 226
Prizzi's Honor, 201–202
Proctor and Gamble, 15, 19
Psycho, 121, 151
Pure Soap, 22

Q
Quaid, Dennis, 172–73

R
Radio soaps, 13–16
Rashad, Ahmad, 166–67
Rashad, Phylicia, 165–67
Rat Pack, The, 141
Rattray, Heather, 97
Rear Window, 170
Redford, Robert, 79, 163
Reese, Della, 64
Reeve, Christopher, 168–71
Reiner, Rob, 173, 226
Return of the Jedi, 111, 220
Rice, Anne, 35, 164
Rinso, 13
Road of Life, The, 18, 70
Road to Reality, The, 17
Robbins, Tim, 178–79
"Rocket," 144
Roddenberry, Gene, 86
Rolling Stone, 93
Romance of Helen Trent, The, 15
Romper Room, 58–60
Ronstadt, Linda, 136
Roosevelt, Theodore, 37
Roots, 206
Roots: The Next Generation, 193
Ross, Diana, 166, 220
Ross, John and Ethel, 66
"Roy Bingham," 90–91
Rutgers University, 78–79
"Ryan Fenelli," 41
Ryan, Meg, 172–74, 180
Ryan's Hope, 20, 39–41, 70, 156–58, 160, 189–91
Ryder, Winona, 190

S
Sabato, Antonio, Jr., 175–77
St. Elmo's Fire, 147
Samms, Emma, 186
San Francisco Bay Guardian, 73

Santa Barbara, 20, 59–61, 70, 211–12, 225–26
"Sarah Fairbanks," 180
Sarah Lawrence College, 124, 132
Sarandon, Susan, 178–180, 188
Savannah, 22
Sayers, Gale, 220
Schumacher, Joel, 147
Search for Tomorrow, 12, 18, 20, 26–28, 70, 130, 135–36, 138, 179–80, 184
Secret Storm, The, 19, 142, 144–45
Sedgwick, Kyra, 26–28
Seeking Heart, The, 18
Seinfeld, 117–18, 196
Selleck, Tom, 49, 137, 181–84
Serial Mom, 203
Se7en, 90, 162, 164
Seven Years in Tibet, 162, 164
"Shane Donovan," 187
Shanendoah, 86
Shaughnessy, Charles, 185–87
Silverman, Fred, 157
Simpsons, The, 102, 160, 203
Sinatra, Frank, 141, 182
Single Guy, The, 217
Singleton, John, 72
Six Days, Seven Nights, 121
Six Degrees of Kevin Bacon, 26
Slater, Christian, 60, 189–91, 195
Slater, Mary Jo, 189
Sleepless in Seattle, 172–73
Smith Family, The, 14
Smith, Stephen, 101
Smith, Will, 82, 132
"Snapper Foster," 115–16
Soap, 22
Soap music, 13
Soap opera, defined, 13
Soap Opera Digest, 43, 176, 225
Soapdish, 118, 137
Somerset, 17–18, 21, 48–49, 51, 70, 213–14, 222, 224
Something About Amelia, 48, 50
Song of the City, 16
Soul Food, 81–82
Southwest Missouri State College, 201–202
Spelling, Aaron, 154, 160
Spielberg, Steven, 42–43, 151, 176
Stallone, Sylvester, 118, 196, 199, 202
Stanford University, 48–49, 213–14

Star Search, 45–46
Star Trek, 85, 87, 190
Star Trek: First Contact, 86, 102
Star Trek: Insurrection, 86
Star Trek: The Next Generation, 86, 102, 118
Star Trek: Voyager, 156–57
Star Wars, 110–11, 128
Starship Troopers, 154, 208
State University of New York, 134
Steel Magnolias, 199
Steenburgen, Mary, 50
"Stephanie Simmons," 84
Stewart, Jimmy, 170
Still Me, 170
Stone, Oliver, 36
Streetcar Named Desire, A, 29–30
Sullivan, Anne, 67
Sunset Beach, 211
Superman, 168–69, 171
"Suzette Saxon," 77
Swanson, Kristy, 94

T
Tales of the City, 97–98
Tandy, Jessica, 89
Tarantino, Quentin, 197
Tartikoff, Brandon, 114
Tarzan and the Lost City, 209
"Teenage Mason Capwell," 60–61
Television soap operas, 16–21
Texas, 17–18, 87
Thelma & Louise, 163, 179
These Are My Children, 17–18
This Boy's Life, 59
Thomas, Richard, 130, 192–94
Three Steps to Heaven, 18–19
Tillman, George, Jr., 82
"Tim Siegel," 37–38
"Tim Werner," 28
Time for Us, A, 193–94
Time to Live, A, 18
Titanic, 60–61, 75–76, 214
"Tod Adamson," 28
Today's Children, 17
"Tom Carroll," 87
"Tom Conway," 51
"Tom Hughes," 194
Tomei, Marisa, 189, 195–97
Tony Awards, 71, 127, 135–37
Total Recall 2, 86
Touched by an Angel, 63, 169

Tour of Duty, 53–54
Travolta, John, 190
Turner, Ike, 73
Turner, Janine, 149, 198–200
Turner, Kathleen, 111, 201–203
Tuskegee Airmen, The, 73, 82
Twelve Monkeys, 162, 164
Two Trains Running, 73
"Ty Moody," 209
Typical week on the soaps, 23
Tyson, Cicely, 130, 204–206, 220–21

U
Unforgiven, 76, 90
Universal Studios, 211
University of Arizona, 210–11
University of Connecticut, 172
University of Illinois, 142
University of Maryland, 201–202
University of Miami, 139–40
University of Michigan, 127–28
University of Missouri, 35–36, 42, 162–63, 210
University of Southern California, 32, 153, 181–82
Untamed Heart, 189, 195–96
Us, 147

V
Van Dien, Casper, 154, 207–209
Van Gogh, Vincent, 62
Vanity Fair, 148
Variety, 161
Vaughn, Vince, 121
Verdict Is Yours, The, 18
Very Bad Things, 191
Viewers for Quality Television Award, 55, 100, 124
Village People, The, 166

W
Wagner, Jack, 210–12
Wait Until Dark, 197
Walker, Tonya, 208
Waltons, The, 86, 192–93
War Bride, 16
"Warren Lockridge," 212
Waters, John, 203
Weaver, Sigourney, 188, 213–15
Wen, Ming-Na, 216–18
Wesleyan University, 55–56

West Side Story, 140, 211
What's Eating Gilbert Grape?, 60
When Harry Met Sally..., 173
Whitehead, Marybeth, 223
Who's Who in Daytime TV, 146
Why Do Fools Fall in Love, 83
William Paterson College, 228–29
Williams, Billy Dee, 130, 206, 219–21
Williams, JoBeth, 137, 215, 222–24
Williams, Robin, 169
Williams, Vanessa, 82
Willis, Bruce, 146, 148, 164
Willis, Victor, 166
Winger, Debra, 202
Wings, 102
Winslet, Kate, 77
Winsor, Roy, 18–19
Wiz, The, 165–66
Woman Called Moses, A, 206
Woman Named Jackie, A, 63, 93
Woman to Remember, A, 199
Women of Brewster Place, The, 206
"Woody Reed," 138
World Apart, A, 70, 178–80
World of Mr. Sweeney, The, 18
Wright-Penn, Robin, 225–27

Y
Yale University, 213–14
Young and the Restless, The, 13–14, 20–21, 61, 82, 84, 113–14, 116, 138, 182–84, 188, 199
Young Doctors in Love, 146, 198–99
You've Got Mail, 173

Z
Zee, Eric Michael, 218
Ziering, Ian, 160, 228–30

About the Author

ANNETTE M. D'AGOSTINO was born on Staten Island, New York, where at an early age she first developed her appreciation for the unique entertainment of soap operas. She received her B.A. in speech communication from St. John's University (Staten Island), her M.A. in communication from William Paterson College (Wayne, New Jersey), and post-graduate accreditation in secondary education from Hofstra University (Hempstead, New York). Amid her studies, she faithfully followed her to-remain-nameless *four* favorite soaps. While in college, she took a sociology course titled "Women, Culture, and Society." As her final paper for the class, she wrote a study entitled "Women's Changing Roles on Soap Operas." That paper remains one of her fondest academic memories. She is a former college professor of speech communication and rhetorical studies at William Paterson College (now called William Paterson University) and Hofstra University, and now devotes her time to freelance film research and writing—all the while regretting the lack of time she has to keep up with her soaps. She is legendary comedian Harold Lloyd's official family biographer, and has written three silent film-oriented reference books, including *Harold Lloyd: A Bio-Bibliography* (Greenwood Press, 1994). She maintains a Web site devoted to Lloyd's life and career, located at http://www.haroldlloyd.com/. She resides in Los Angeles, California.